STATA PROGRAMMING
REFERENCE MANUAL
RELEASE 8

A Stata Press Publication
STATA CORPORATION
College Station, Texas

Stata Press, 4905 Lakeway Drive, College Station, Texas 77845

The suggested citation for this software is

StataCorp. 2003. *Stata Statistical Software: Release 8.0*. College Station, TX: Stata Corporation.

Contents of Programming Reference Manual

intro . . . . Introduction to programming manual

break . . . . Suppress Break key
byable . . . . Make programs byable

capture . . . . Capture return code
char . . . . Characteristics
class . . . . Class programming
class exit . . . . Exit class member program and return result
classutil . . . . Class program utility
comments . . . . Add comments to programs
confirm . . . . Argument verification
continue . . . . Break out of loops
creturn . . . . Return c-class values

#delimit . . . . Change delimiter
dialogs . . . . Dialog programming
discard . . . . Drop automatically loaded programs
display . . . . Display strings and values of scalar expressions

ereturn . . . . Post estimation results
error . . . . Display generic error message and exit
_estimates . . . . Manage estimation results
exit . . . . Exit from a program or do-file

file . . . . Read and write ASCII text and binary files
file formats .dta . . . . Description of .dta file format
findfile . . . . Find file in path
foreach . . . . Loop over items
forvalues . . . . Loop over consecutive values

gettoken . . . . Low-level parsing

hexdump . . . . Display hexadecimal report on file

if . . . . if programming command

macro . . . . Macro definition and manipulation
macro lists . . . . Manipulate lists
mark . . . . Mark observations for inclusion
matrix . . . . Introduction to matrix commands
matrix accum . . . . Form cross-product matrices
matrix constraint . . . . Constrained estimation
matrix define . . . . Matrix definition, operators, and functions
matrix eigenvalues . . . . Eigenvalues of nonsymmetric matrices
matrix get . . . . Access system matrices
matrix mkmat . . . . Convert variables to matrix and vice versa
matrix rowname . . . . Name rows and columns
matrix score . . . . Score data from coefficient vectors
matrix svd . . . . Singular value decomposition
matrix symeigen . . . . Eigenvalues and eigenvectors of symmetric matrices
matrix utility . . . . List, rename, and drop matrices

more . . . . Pause until key is pressed

numlist . . . . Parse numeric lists

pause . . . . Program debugging command
postfile . . . . Save results in Stata dataset
_predict . . . . Obtain predictions, residuals, etc. after estimation programming command
preserve . . . . Preserve and restore data
program . . . . Define and manipulate programs

quietly . . . . Quietly and noisily perform Stata command

_return . . . . Preserve saved results
return . . . . Return saved results
_rmcoll . . . . Remove collinear variables
rmsg . . . . Return messages
_robust . . . . Robust variance estimates

scalar . . . . Scalar variables
serset . . . . Create and manipulate sersets
sleep . . . . Pause for a specified time
smcl . . . . Stata Markup and Control Language
sortpreserve . . . . Sort within programs
syntax . . . . Parse Stata syntax
sysdir . . . . Set system directories

tabdisp . . . . Display tables
tokenize . . . . Divide strings into tokens
trace . . . . Debug Stata programs

unab . . . . Unabbreviate variable list
unabcmd . . . . Unabbreviate command name

version . . . . Version control

while . . . . Looping
window fopen . . . . Display open/save dialog box
window manage . . . . Manage window characteristics
window menu . . . . Create menus
window push . . . . Copy command into Review window
window stopbox . . . . Display message box

Subject Table of Contents

This is the complete contents for this manual. References to inserts from other Stata manuals that we feel would be of interest to programmers are also included.

Data manipulation and management

Functions and expressions

[U]   User's Guide, Chapter 16 .... Functions and expressions
[R]   egen .... Extensions to generate
[R]   functions .... Functions

Utilities

Basic utilities

[U]   User's Guide, Chapter 8 .... Stata's online help and search facilities
[U]   User's Guide, Chapter 18 .... Printing and preserving output
[U]   User's Guide, Chapter 19 .... Do-files
[R]   about .... Display information about my version of Stata
[R]   by .... Repeat Stata command on subsets of the data
[R]   copyright .... Display copyright information
[R]   do .... Execute commands from a file
[R]   doedit .... Edit do-files and other text files
[R]   exit .... Exit Stata
[R]   help .... Obtain online help
[R]   level .... Set default confidence level
[R]   log .... Echo copy of session to file or device
[R]   obs .... Increase the number of observations in dataset
[R]   #review .... Review previous commands
[R]   search .... Search Stata documentation
[R]   translate .... Translate smcl files and logs to other formats
[R]   view .... View files and logs

Error messages

[U]   User's Guide, Chapter 11 .... Error messages and return codes
[R]   error messages .... Error messages and return codes
[P]   error .... Display generic error message and exit
[P]   rmsg .... Return messages

Saved results

[U]   User's Guide, Section 16.6 .... Accessing results from Stata commands
[U]   User's Guide, Section 21.8 .... Accessing results calculated by other programs
[U]   User's Guide, Section 21.9 ..... Accessing results calculated by estimation commands
[U]   User's Guide, Section 21.10 .... Saving results
[P]   creturn .... Return c-class values
[R]   estimates .... Estimation results
[P]   return .... Return saved results
[R]   saved results .... Saved results

Internet

[U]   User's Guide, Chapter 32 .... Using the Internet to keep up to date
[R]   checksum .... Calculate checksum of file
[R]   net .... Install and manage user-written additions from the net
[R]   net search .... Search Internet for installable packages
[R]   netio .... Commands to control Internet connections
[R]   news .... Report Stata news
[R]   sj .... SJ installation instructions
[R]   ssc .... Install and uninstall packages from SSC
[R]   update .... Update Stata

Data types and memory

[U]   User's Guide, Chapter 7 .... Setting the size of memory
[U]   User's Guide, Section 15.2.2 .... Numeric storage types
[U]   User's Guide, Section 15.4.4 .... String storage types
[U]   User's Guide, Section 16.10 .... Precision and problems therein
[U]   User's Guide, Chapter 26 .... Commands for dealing with strings
[R]   compress .... Compress data in memory
[R]   data types .... Quick reference for data types
[R]   limits .... Quick reference for limits
[R]   matsize .... Set the maximum number of variables in a model
[R]   memory .... Memory size considerations
[R]   missing values .... Quick reference for missing values
[R]   recast .... Change storage type of variable

Advanced utilities

[R]   assert .... Verify truth of claim
[R]   cd .... Change directory
[R]   checksum .... Calculate checksum of file
[R]   copy .... Copy file from disk or URL
[R]   db .... Launch dialog
[P]   dialogs .... Dialog programming
[R]   dir .... Display filenames
[P]   discard .... Drop automatically loaded programs
[R]   erase .... Erase a disk file
[P]   hexdump .... Display hexadecimal report on file
[R]   mkdir .... Create directory
[R]   more .... The —more— message
[R]   query .... Display system parameters
[P]   quietly .... Quietly and noisily perform Stata command
[R]   set .... Quick reference for system parameters
[R]   shell .... Temporarily invoke operating system
[P]   smcl .... Stata Markup and Control Language
[P]   sysdir .... Set system directories
[R]   type .... Display contents of files
[R]   which .... Display location and version for an ado-file

Matrix commands

Basics

[U]   User's Guide, Chapter 17 .... Matrix expressions
[P]   matrix .... Introduction to matrix commands
[P]   matrix define .... Matrix definition, operators, and functions
[P]   matrix utility .... List, rename, and drop matrices

Programming

[P]   matrix accum .... Form cross-product matrices
[R]   ml .... Maximum likelihood estimation
[P]   ereturn .... Post estimation results
[P]   matrix rowname .... Name rows and columns
[P]   matrix score .... Score data from coefficient vectors

Other

[P]   matrix constraint .... Constrained estimation
[P]   matrix eigenvalues .... Eigenvalues of nonsymmetric matrices
[P]   matrix get .... Access system matrices
[P]   matrix mkmat .... Convert variables to matrix and vice versa
[P]   matrix svd .... Singular value decomposition
[P]   matrix symeigen .... Eigenvalues and eigenvectors of symmetric matrices

Programming

Basics

[U]   User's Guide, Chapter 21 .... Programming Stata
[U]   User's Guide, Section 21.3 .... Macros
[U]   User's Guide, Section 21.11 .... Ado-files
[P]   comments .... Add comments to programs
[P]   program .... Define and manipulate programs
[P]   macro .... Macro definition and manipulation
[P]   return .... Return saved results

Program control

[U]   User's Guide, Section 21.11.1 .... Version
[P]   version .... Version control
[P]   continue .... Break out of loops
[P]   foreach .... Loop over items
[P]   forvalues .... Loop over consecutive values
[P]   if .... if programming command
[P]   while .... Looping
[P]   error .... Display generic error message and exit
[P]   capture .... Capture return code

Parsing and program arguments

[U]   User's Guide, Section 21.4 .... Program arguments
[P]   syntax .... Parse Stata syntax
[P]   confirm .... Argument verification
[P]   gettoken .... Low-level parsing

[P]   numlist .... Parse numeric lists
[P]   tokenize .... Divide strings into tokens

Console output

[P]   display .... Display strings and values of scalar expressions
[P]   tabdisp .... Display tables

Commonly used programming commands

[P]   byable .... Make programs byable
[P]   #delimit .... Change delimiter
[P]   exit .... Exit from a program or do-file
[P]   quietly .... Quietly and noisily perform Stata command
[P]   mark .... Mark observations for inclusion
[P]   more .... Pause until key is pressed
[P]   preserve .... Preserve and restore data
[P]   matrix .... Introduction to matrix commands
[P]   scalar .... Scalar variables
[P]   smcl .... Stata Markup and Control Language
[P]   sortpreserve .... Sort with programs
[TS] tsrevar .... Time-series operator programming command

Debugging

[P]   pause .... Program debugging command
[P]   trace .... Debug Stata programs

Advanced programming commands

[P]   break .... Suppress Break key
[P]   char .... Characteristics
[P]   class .... Class programming
[P]   class exit .... Exit class member program and return result
[P]   classutil .... Class programming utility
[P]   _estimates .... Manage estimation results
[P]   file .... Read and write ASCII text and binary files
[P]   findfile .... Find file in path
[P]   macro .... Macro definition and manipulation
[P]   macro lists .... Manipulate lists
[R]   ml .... Maximum likelihood estimation
[P]   postfile .... Save results in Stata dataset
[P]   _predict   ...   Obtain predictions, residuals, etc. after estimation programming command
[P]   _return .... Preserve saved results
[P]   _rmcoll .... Remove collinear variables
[P]   _robust .... Robust variance estimates
[P]   serset .... Create and manipulate sersets
[P]   unab .... Unabbreviate variable list
[P]   unabcmd .... Unabbreviate command name
[P]   window fopen .... Display open/save dialog box
[P]   window menu .... Create menus
[P]   window stopbox .... Display message box

Special interest programming commands

[CL] cluster programming subroutines . . . . Add cluster analysis routines
[CL] cluster programming utilities . . . . Cluster analysis programming utilities
[ST] st_is . . . . Survival analysis subroutines for programmers
[TS] tsrevar . . . . Time-series operator programming command

File formats

[P] file formats .dta . . . . Description of .dta file format

Interface features

[P] dialogs . . . . Dialog programming
[R] doedit . . . . Edit do-files and other text files
[R] edit . . . . Edit and list data using data editor
[P] sleep . . . . Pause for a specified time
[P] smcl . . . . Stata Markup and Control Language
[P] window fopen . . . . Display open/save dialog box
[P] window manage . . . . Manage window characteristics
[P] window menu . . . . Create menus
[P] window push . . . . Copy command into Review window
[P] window stopbox . . . . Display message box

Cross-Referencing the Documentation

When reading this manual, you will find references to other Stata manuals. For example,

[U] **29 Overview of Stata estimation commands**

[R] **regress**

[CL] **cluster programming subroutines**

The first is a reference to Chapter 29, *Overview of Stata estimation commands* in the *Stata User's Guide*, the second is a reference to the `regress` entry in the *Stata Base Reference Manual*, and the third is a reference to the `cluster programming subroutines` entry in the *Stata Cluster Analysis Reference Manual*.

All of the manuals in the Stata Documentation have a shorthand notation, such as [U] for the *User's Guide* and [R] for the *Base Reference Manual*.

The complete list of shorthand notations and manuals is as follows:

[GSM]	*Getting Started with Stata for Macintosh*
[GSU]	*Getting Started with Stata for Unix*
[GSW]	*Getting Started with Stata for Windows*
[U]	*Stata User's Guide*
[R]	*Stata Base Reference Manual*
[G]	*Stata Graphics Reference Manual*
[P]	*Stata Programming Reference Manual*
[CL]	*Stata Cluster Analysis Reference Manual*
[XT]	*Stata Cross-Sectional Time-Series Reference Manual*
[SVY]	*Stata Survey Data Reference Manual*
[ST]	*Stata Survival Analysis & Epidemiological Tables Reference Manual*
[TS]	*Stata Time-Series Reference Manual*

Detailed information about each of these manuals may be found online at

`http://www.stata-press.com/manuals/`

Title

intro — Introduction to programming manual

Description

This entry describes the *Stata Programming Reference Manual*.

Remarks

In this manual, you will find

1. Stata's matrix-manipulation commands,

2. commands for programming Stata,

3. commands and discussions of interest to programmers, and

4. commands that are of such a technical nature that you would nearly have to be a programmer to use them, even if they have nothing to do with programming (e.g., `hexdump`).

This manual is referred to as [P] in cross-references, and is organized alphabetically.

If you are new to Stata's programming commands, we recommend that you first read the chapter on programming Stata in the *User's Guide*; see [U] **21 Programming Stata**. After reading this chapter, we recommend that you read the following sections from this manual:

[P] **program**	Define and manipulate programs
[P] **sortpreserve**	Sorting within programs
[P] **byable**	Making programs byable
[P] **macro**	Macro definition and manipulation

You may also find the Subject Table of Contents, which immediately follows the Table of Contents, helpful.

We also recommend the Stata NetCourses^{TM}. At the time that this introduction was written, our current offerings of Stata programming NetCourses included

NC-151 An introduction to Stata programming
NC-152 Advanced Stata programming

To learn more about NetCourses and to view the current offerings of NetCourses, visit http://www.stata.com/info/products/netcourse.

To learn about writing your own maximum-likelihood estimation commands, we recommend the book *Maximum-likelihood Estimation with Stata*.

What's new, programming-wise

1. Stata now supports multiple missing values: ., .a, .b, ..., .z. The new ones (.a, .b, ..., .z) are called extended missing values. The ordering is

$$\text{all numbers} < . < .a < .b < \cdots < .z$$

1

So, instead of coding

```
    ... if myvyar !=.
```

and

```
    ... if myvyar ==.
```

you should code

```
    ... if myvar <.
```

and

```
    ... if myvar >=.
```

When `version` is set less than 8, all missing values are treated as being the same, so that old code continues to work. See [U] **15.2.1 Missing values** for details.

2. `version` has a new option, `missing`, which can be used to request the modern treatment of missing values by old programs without updating them in other ways; see [P] **version**.

3. You may no longer code open-brace–*command*–close-brace on the same line, as in "if 'n'==0 { exit }". You may, however, omit the braces: "if 'n'==0 exit" or "if ('n'==0) exit". The brace–*command*–brace syntax continues to be allowed under version control; see [P] **if**.

4. Matrices may now contain missing values. If `version` < 8, in some cases, missing values may not be assigned to matrices.

   Matrix commands, such as `matrix symeigen` and `matrix svd`, that require matrices to not have missing values have been modified to verify that there are no missing values before proceeding.

5. A new way of posting and redisplaying estimation results has been added. Replacing the previous `estimates` command, which may still be accessed under version control, are the new commands `ereturn`, `_estimates`, and a new `estimates` command.

   `estimates` is a new user command that provides a method for storing and restoring estimation results; see [R] **estimates**.

   `ereturn` is a programmer's command to post estimation results; see [P] **ereturn**.

   `_estimates` is a programmer's utility to hold and to restore estimation results; see [P] **_estimates**.

   The mapping between the old `estimates` command and the new commands is as follows:

estimates local	ereturn local
estimates scalar	ereturn scalar
estimates matrix	ereturn matrix
estimates clear	ereturn clear
estimates list	ereturn list
estimates post	ereturn post
estimates repost	ereturn repost
estimates display	ereturn display
estimates hold	_estimates hold
estimates unhold	_estimates unhold
estimates dir	_estimates dir
estimates drop	_estimates drop
_estimates clear	(new)

6. Many new functions have been added to Stata, and the existing functions have been reorganized. There are 15 new programming functions, 5 new matrix functions, 4 new string functions, 8 new math functions, and 16 new probability and density functions. Modifications were made to three existing functions: `cond()`, `recode()`, and `round()`. All of Stata's probability distribution and density functions will now return values over the entire real number line.

   a. The modified `cond(x,a,b,[d])` function now has an optional fourth argument that is returned in case x evaluates to missing. If the fourth argument is not specified, then $x =$ missing returns b.

      The modified `recode(x,x_1,x_2,..., x_n)` function now returns missing if the sequence is not weakly increasing. $x_i = .$ is interpreted as $+\infty$.

      In the modified `round(x[.y])` function, the second argument y, which specifies the unit of rounding, is now optional, and defaults to 1.

      See the *Programming functions* section in [R] **functions**.

   b. The new programming functions `maxbyte()`, `maxdouble()`, `maxfloat()`, `maxint()`, `maxlong()`, `minbyte()`, `mindouble()`, `minfloat()`, `minint()`, and `minlong()` find the largest and smallest number of each numerical data type. `epsdouble()` and `epsfloat()` give the smallest step size for floating point and double precision numbers. The function `byteorder()` gives the byte order for writers of binary files, and `irecode()` is another flavor of the `recode()` function.

      The new programming functions `chop()` and `clip()` return x rounded to an integer and x within a range.

      See the *Programming functions* section in [R] **functions** for details.

   c. The new matrix functions are `issym()` to determine if a matrix is symmetric, `matuniform()` to make a matrix filled with uniformly distributed random numbers, `matmissing()` to indicate if elements of a matrix are missing, `hadamard()` to compute the Hadamard product of two matrices, and `vec()` which turns a matrix into a column vector. See the sections *Matrix functions returning matrices* and *Matrix functions returning scalars* in [P] **matrix define** for details.

   d. The new string functions are `plural()` for making plurals, `proper()` for getting the correct capitalization, `word()` to find a specific word of a string, and `wordcount()` to count the number of words in a string. See the *String functions* section in [R] **functions** for details.

   e. The new math functions include `tanh()`, the hyperbolic tangent, and its inverse, `atanh()`; `logit()` and `invlogit()`; and `cloglog()`, the complimentary log-log function, and its inverse, `invcloglog()`. New functions `ceil()` and `floor()` find the least integer greater than x and the greatest integer less than x, respectively. See the *Mathematical functions* section in [R] **functions** for details.

   f. The new probability distribution and density functions include the first and second derivatives for the gamma distribution, `dgammapda()`, `dgammapdada()`, `dgammapdadx()`, `dgammapdx()`, and `dgammapdxdx()`. A variety of density functions have been added: `betaden()`, `gammaden()`, `nbetaden()`, `tden()`, `Fden()`, and `nFden()` for calculating both central and noncentral distributions. New distribution functions and inverses are `nibeta()`, `invnibeta()`, `nFtail()`, and `invnFtail()`. See the *Probability distribution and density functions* section in [R] **functions** for details.

7. The new c-class contains constants such as the value of pi and current values of system parameters and settings. Typing `creturn list` displays the current settings. See [P] **creturn**.

8. The `define` in `program define` *myprog* is now optional. You may type simply `program` *myprog*; see [P] **program**.

9. Several new `set trace` ... features have been added to assist in debugging programs.

   a. `set traceexpand` specifies whether a line in a program is to be shown both before and after macro expansion.

   b. `set tracedepth` specifies the level of nesting that should be included in the trace.

   c. `set tracesep` specifies whether a horizontal separator line that displays the name of the subroutine should be displayed in the trace whenever a subroutine is called or exits.

   d. `set traceindent` specifies whether the displayed lines of code should be indented according to their nesting level.

   e. `set tracenumber` specifies whether the nesting level should be displayed at the front of the program lines.

   In addition to these new commands, the original value of `set trace` will be restored when the program or file ends.

   See [P] **trace** for details about the new features.

10. The new comment indicators `//` and `///` allow new ways of specifying comments and joining lines in do-files and ado-files. See [P] **comments**.

11. The `postfile` command now allows for the posting of string variables! `postfile` now accepts a *newvarlist* rather than a *varlist*, so storage types may be specified, including strings. See [P] **postfile**.

12. The new macro assignment commands `local ++`*lclname* and `local --`*lclname* may be used to increment and decrement *lclname*. See the section *Macro assignment* in [P] **macro**.

13. Macro expansion now allows `++` and `--` prefix and suffix operators. '`++`*a*' means increment *a* by 1 and substitute the resulting value. '*a*`++`' means substitute the current value of *a* and then increment it by 1. '`--`*a*' and '*a*`--`' do the same, except that they decrement. See [U] **21.3.7 Macro expansion operators**.

14. Macro expansion now allows evaluation of expressions, such as '`=2*(`'`i`''`+1)`', and it allows the use of macro extended functions, such as '`: var label `'`myvar`''. See [U] **21.3.7 Macro expansion operators**.

15. A new macro expansion function `macval(`*lclname*`)` gives the contents of *lclname* as is, without recursive expansion. See [P] **macro**.

16. Five new macro extended functions have been added, which we mention below. (Another nine new macro extended functions have been added to support the use of the new `serset` command; see below.)

   a. The new macro extended function `list` allows manipulations of lists (think list of variable names, list of filenames, etc.). For instance, *a*|*b* forms the union of *a* and *b* without repeating in the results the elements that are in both *a* and *b*. *a&b* returns the intersection, elements in both *a* and *b*. There is more; see [P] **macro lists**.

   b. The new macro extended function `constraint` gives information on constraints. See the section *Macro extended functions for extracting data attributes* in [P] **macro**.

   c. The new macro extended function `permname` assists in naming variables. See the section *Macro extended function for naming variables* in [P] **macro**.

   d. The new macro extended function `dir` obtains file and directory names. See the section *Macro extended functions for accessing filenames and paths* in [P] **macro**.

   e. The new macro extended function `length` returns the length in characters of a macro. See the section *Macro extended functions for parsing* in [P] **macro**.

17. Many macro extended functions have disappeared. That is, they have disappeared from the documentation, even though they still work. For instance, to find out whether more was on or off, there was :set more. Now, it is gone. c(more) returns the more setting, and lots more. This is not only more logical, it is now easier to find these settings; just type creturn list. See [P] **creturn**.

18. The syntax command has two new descriptors:

    a. The new namelist descriptor provides an alternative to the varlist descriptor. namelist relaxes the restriction that the names that the user types be variable names. namelist can be specified in place of varlist at the front of a command, and namelist can be specified inside option arguments.

    b. The new anything descriptor makes it easier for programmers to parse almost-standard syntax; that is, nonstandard syntax up to if, in, weight, or options, and standard thereafter.

    See [P] **syntax**.

19. gettoken has two new options: bind and qed(*lmacname*). bind specifies that expressions within parentheses or brackets are to be bound together even when not parsing on () and []. qed() specifies a local macroname that is to be filled in with 1 or 0 according to whether the returned token was enclosed in quotes in the original string. See [P] **gettoken**.

20. assert has a new option null that forces a return code of 8 on null assertions; see [R] **assert**.

21. confirm has two new subcommands: confirm matrix and confirm scalar; see [P] **confirm**.

22. SMCL has three additions. The new {ccl} directive outputs the value contained in a constant and current-value class (c()) object. {center:*text*} now also allows {center #:*text*}, which specifies that text is to be centered within a width of # columns. {dialog *dialogname*:*text*} launches a dialog box. See [P] **smcl**.

23. matrix list has a new nodotz option that specifies .z missing values should be listed as blanks. See [P] **matrix utility**.

24. matrix score has a new forcezero option that specifies that missing variables are to be ignored when summing. See [P] **matrix score**.

25. The new findfile command looks for a file along a specified path and returns the name in r(fn). See [P] **findfile**.

26. The new file command allows programmers to read and write both ASCII text and binary files. See [P] **file**.

27. The new matrix opaccum command forms a new matrix based on the outer product, within a specified group, of a specified variable. See [P] **matrix accum**.

28. The new matrix eigenvalues command calculates eigenvalues of nonsymmetric matrices. See [P] **matrix eigenvalues**.

29. The new unabcmd command returns a Stata command in unabbreviated form. See [P] **unabcmd**.

30. Object-oriented programming has been added to Stata. Classes are defined by the new class command in .class files. Among other features, classes provide inheritance, encapsulation of data structures and programs, and program name overloading. Stata's new graphics and new GUI are implemented via classes. See [P] **class**.

31. Stata has a new GUI and that GUI is programmable. Dialog boxes are created in .dlg files; see [P] **dialogs**.

32. Stata has new graphics and that graphics is programmable; see the *Stata Graphics Reference Manual*.

33. The new `serset` command is another part of Stata's new graphics. At least, that is why it was implemented. In fact, its use is not limited to that. A serset is a collection of variables from a dataset that coexists in memory along with the current dataset, and whose values can be accessed quickly. The new `serset` command creates and manipulates sersets. See [P] **serset**.

34. The new `markin` command—for use after `marksample`, `mark`, and `markout`—creates a macro containing the smallest in *range* that contains the if *exp*. See [P] **mark**.

35. The `matrix dispCns` command has a new option, `r`, that specifies that the output of `matrix dispCns` should be suppressed, and that the macros `r(cns#)` and `r(k)` should be filled in, instead. See [P] **matrix constraint**.

36. The `clear` command now closes all open files created by `file` and `postfile`, clears all sersets, clears are classes, closes all open graphs, and clears all the other things that you would expect given the new additions to Stata. See [R] **drop**.

37. `save` has a new `emptyok` option that allows saving zero-variable—zero-observation datasets, and `merge` and `append` have been certified to work with empty datasets. Thus, in loops that build datasets, you no longer have to treat the first addition specially. You can create an empty result at the outset, and then just `append` or `merge` to the previous result. See [R] **save**.

38. `describe using` has a new `varlist` option that specifies that the saved results `r(varlist)` and `r(sortlist)` are to be saved along with the other saved results. `r(varlist)` will contain the names of the variables in the dataset, and `r(sortlist)` will contain the names of the variables by which the data are sorted. Thus, you no longer have to use a dataset to find out about it. See [R] **describe**.

39. The maximum number of nested do-files has been increased from 32 to 64.

40. The maximum number of held estimates has been increased from 10 to 20.

41. Stata has always understood both `~=` and `!=`, and `~` and `!` to mean not. We have always documented `~=` and `~`, and relegated `!=` and `!` to technical notes, thinking that `~` would be more natural to mathematically trained professionals. Since nearly everyone these days associates the symbol `!` with not, we have updated our documentation. In your programs, use whichever. Neither is better than the other.

There are other new additions to Stata that will be of interest to programmers, but, because they are of interest to others, too, they are documented in [U] **1.3 What's new**. For instance, you can now obtain the random-number seed at one point in a program and reset it in another:

```
...
. local seed = "`c(seed)'"
...
. set seed `seed'
...
```

`ml` has lots of new features, and the list goes on. Do see [U] **1.3 What's new**.

Also See

Complementary:	[U] **21 Programming Stata**,
	Maximum Likelihood Estimation with Stata
Background:	[R] **intro**

Title

> **break** — Suppress Break key

Syntax

> nobreak *stata_command*
>
> break   *stata_command*

Typical usage is

```
nobreak {
        ...
        capture noisily break ...
        ...
}
```

Description

nobreak temporarily turns off recognition of the *Break* key. It is seldom used. break temporarily re-establishes recognition of the *Break* key within a nobreak block. It is even more seldom used.

Remarks

Stata commands honor the *Break* key. This honoring is automatic and, for the most part, requires no special code as long as you follow these guidelines:

1. Obtain names for new variables from tempvar; see [U] **21.7.1 Temporary variables**.

2. Obtain names for other memory aggregates such as scalars and matrices from tempname; see [U] **21.7.2 Temporary scalars and matrices**.

3. If you need to temporarily change the user's data, use preserve to save it first; see [U] **21.6 Temporarily destroying the data in memory**.

4. Obtain names for temporary files from tempfile; see [U] **21.7.3 Temporary files**.

If you follow these guidelines, your program will be robust to the user pressing *Break* because Stata itself will be able to put things back as they were.

Still, there are instances when a program must commit to executing a group of commands that, were *Break* honored in the midst of the group, would leave the user's data in an intermediate, undefined state. nobreak is for those instances.

▷ Example

You are writing a program and following all the guidelines listed above. In particular, you are using temporary variables. There is a point in your program, however, where you wish to list the first five values of the temporary variable. You would like, temporarily, to give the variable a pretty name, so you temporarily rename it. If the user were to press *Break* during the period the variable is renamed, however, Stata would not know to drop it, and it would be left behind in the user's data. You wish to avoid this. In the code fragment below, 'myv' is the temporary variable:

7

```
nobreak {
        rename 'myv' Result
        list Result in 1/5
        rename Result 'myv'
}
```

It would not be appropriate to code the fragment as

```
nobreak rename 'myv' Result
nobreak list Result in 1/5
nobreak rename Result 'myv'
```

because the user might press *Break* during the periods between the commands.

◁

Also See

Complementary: [P] **capture**

Background: [U] **12 The Break key**

Title

byable — Make programs byable

Description

This entry discusses the writing of programs so that they will allow the use of Stata's by *varlist*: prefix. If you take no special actions and write the program myprog, then by *varlist*: cannot be used with it:

```
. by foreign:  myprog
myprog may not be combined with by
r(190);
```

By reading this section, you will learn how to modify your program so that by does work with it:

```
. by foreign:  myprog
```

```
-> foreign = Domestic
```
   (*output for first by-group appears*)

```
-> foreign = Foreign
```
   (*output for first by-group appears*)

```
. _
```

Remarks

Remarks are presented under the headings

> *byable(recall) programs*
> *The use of sort in byable(recall) programs*
> *Byable estimation commands*
> *byable(onecall) programs*
> *The use of sort by byable(onecall) programs*
> *Combining byable(onecall) with byable(recall)*
> *The by-group header*

If you have not read [P] **sortpreserve**, please do so soon; it is relevant.

Programs that are written to be used with by *varlist*: are said to be "byable". Byable programs do not require the use of by *varlist*:; they merely allow it. There are two ways that programs can be made to be byable, known as byable(recall) and byable(onecall).

byable(recall) is easy to use, and is sufficient for programs that report the results of calculation (class-1 programs as defined in [P] **sortpreserve**). byable(recall) is the method most commonly used to make programs byable.

byable(onecall) is more work to program, and is intended for use in all other cases (class-2 and class-3 programs as defined in [P] **sortpreserve**).

byable(recall) programs

Pretend that you already have written a program (ado-file) and that it works; it merely does not allow by. If your program reports the results of calculations (think summarize, regress, and most of the other statistical commands), then probably all you have to do to make your program byable is add the option byable(recall) to its program statement. For instance, if your program statement currently reads

```
program myprog, rclass sortpreserve
        . . .
end
```

change it to read

```
program myprog, rclass sortpreserve byable(recall)
        . . .
end
```

The only change you should need to make is to add byable(recall) to the program statement. Adding byable(recall) will be the only change required if

1. Your program leaves behind no newly created variables. Your program might create temporary variables in the midst of calculation, but it must not leave behind new variables for the user. If your program has a generate() option, for instance, some extra effort will be required.

2. Your program uses marksample or mark to restrict itself to the relevant subsample of the data. If your program does not use marksample or mark, some extra effort will be required.

Here is how byable(recall) works: If your program is invoked with a by *varlist*: prefix, your program will be executed K times, where K is the number of by-groups formed by the by-variables. Each time your program is executed, marksample will know to mark out the observations that are not being used in the current by-group.

Therein is the reason for the two guidelines on when you only need to include byable(recall) to make by *varlist*: work:

1. If your program creates permanent, new variables, then it will create those variables when it is executed for the first by-group, meaning that those variables will already exist when it is executed for the second by-group, causing your program to issue an error message.

2. If your program does not use marksample to identify the relevant subsample of the data, then each time it is executed, it will use too many observations—it will not honor the by-group—and so will produce what are incorrect results.

There are ways around both problems, and here is more than you need:

(Continued on next page)

function _by()	takes no arguments
	returns 0 when program is not being by'd
	returns 1 when program is being by'd
function _bylastcall()	takes no arguments
	returns 1 when program is not being by'd
	returns 1 when program is being by'd and is
	being called with the last by-group
	returns 0 otherwise
function _byindex()	takes no arguments
	returns 1 when program is not being by'd
	returns 1, 2, . . . when by'd and 1st call, 2nd call, . . .
macro '_byindex'	contains nothing when program is not being by'd
	contains name of temporary variable when program is being by'd
	variable contains 1, 2, . . . for each observation in data
	recorded value indicates to which by-group
	each observation belongs
macro '_byvars'	contains nothing when program is not being by'd
	contains names of the actual by-variables otherwise

So let's consider the problems one at a time, beginning with the second problem. Your program does not use `marksample`, and we will assume that your program has good reason for not doing so, because the easy fix would be to use `marksample`. Still, your program must somehow be determining which observations to use, and we will assume that you are creating a 'touse' temporary variable containing 0 if the observation is to be omitted from the analysis and 1 if it is to be used. Somewhere, early in your program, you are setting the 'touse' variable. Right after that, make the following addition (shown in bold):

```
program ..., ... byable(recall)
        ...
        if _by() {
                quietly replace 'touse' = 0 if '_byindex' != _byindex()
        }
        ...
end
```

The fix is easy: you ask if you are being by'd and, if so, you set 'touse' to 0 in all observations for which the value of 'byindex' is not equal to the by-group you are currently considering, namely, _byindex().

The first problem is also easy to fix. Pretend that your program has a generate(*newvar*) option. Ergo, your code must contain

```
program ..., ...
        ...
        if "'generate'" != "" {
                ...
        }
        ...
end
```

Change the program to read

```
program ..., ... byable(recall)
      ...
      if "`generate'" != "" & _bylastcall() {
            ...
      }
      ...
end
```

Note that _bylastcall() will be 1 (meaning true) whenever your program is not being by'd and, when it is being by'd, when the program is being executed for the last by-group. The result is that the new variable will be created containing only the values for the last by-group, but, with a few exceptions, that is how all of Stata works. Alternatives are discussed under byable(onecall).

All the other macros and functions that are available are for creating special effects and are rarely used in byable(recall) programs.

The use of sort in byable(recall) programs

You may use sort freely within byable(recall) programs and, in fact, you can use any other Stata command you wish; there are simply no issues. You may even use sortpreserve to restore the sort order at the conclusion of your program; see [P] **sortpreserve**.

We will discuss the issue of sort in depth just to convince you that there is nothing with which you must be concerned.

When a byable(recall) program receives control and is being by'd, the data are guaranteed to be sorted by '_byvars' only when _byindex() = 1—only on the first call. If the program re-sorts the data, the data will remain re-sorted on the second and subsequent calls, even if sortpreserve is specified. This may sound like a problem, but it is not. sortpreserve is not being ignored; the data will be restored to their original order after the final call to your program. Let's go through the two cases: either your program uses sort or it does not.

1. If your program finds it necessary to use sort, it will probably need a different sort order for each by-group. For instance, a typical program that uses sort will include lines such as

   ```
   sort `touse' `id' ...
   ```

   and so move the relevant sample to the top of the dataset. Note that this byable(recall) program makes no reference to the '_byvars' themselves, nor does it do anything differently when the by prefix is specified and when it is not. That is typical; it is a rare byable(recall) program that finds it necessary to refer to the '_byvars' directly.

   In any case, since this program is sorting the data explicitly every time it is called (and we know it must be because byable(recall) programs are executed once for each by-group), there is no reason for Stata to waste its time restoring a sort order that will just be undone anyway. The original sort order only needs to be re-established after the final call.

2. The other alternative is that the program does not use sort. In that case, it is free to exploit that the data are sorted on '_byvars'. Because the data will be sorted on the first call, the program does no sorts, so the data will be sorted on the second call, and so on. It is a rare byable(recall) program that would exploit the sort order, but the program is free to do so.

Byable estimation commands

Estimation commands are natural candidates for the byable(recall) approach. There is, however, one issue that requires special attention. Estimation commands really have two syntaxes: One at the time of estimation

[by *varlist*:] *estcmd varlist* . . . [, *estimation_options replay_options*]

and another for redisplaying results:

estcmd [, *replay_options*]

With estimation commands, by is not allowed when results are redisplayed. This is what we must arrange for in our program, and that is easy enough. The general outline for an estimation command is

```
program estcmd, ...
        if replay() {
                if "`e(cmd)'"!="estcmd"  error 301
                syntax [, replay_options ]
        }
        else {
                syntax ... [, estimation_options replay_options ]
                ...estimation logic...
        }
        ...display logic...
```

and to this, we make the changes shown in bold:

```
program estcmd, ... byable(recall)
        if replay() {
                if "`e(cmd)'"!="estcmd" error 301
                if _by() error 190
                syntax [, replay_options ]
        }
        else {
                syntax ... [, estimation_options replay_options ]
                ...estimation logic...
        }
        ...display logic...
```

In addition to adding byable(recall), we add the line

```
                if _by() error 190
```

in the case where we have been asked to redisplay results. If we are being by'd (if _by() is true), then we issue error 190 (request may not be combined with by).

byable(onecall) programs

byable(onecall) is more work to use. We strongly recommend using byable(recall) whenever possible.

The main use of byable(onecall) is to create programs such as generate and egen, which allow the by prefix, but which operate on all the data and create a new variable containing results for all the different by-groups.

byable(onecall) programs are, as the name implies, executed only once. The byable(onecall) program is responsible for handling all the issues concerning the by, and it is expected to do that by using

function _by()	takes no arguments
	returns 0 when program is not being by'd
	returns 1 when program is being by'd
macro '_byvars'	contains nothing when program is not being by'd
	contains names of the actual by-variables otherwise
macro '_byrc0'	contains nothing or "rc0"
	contains "rc0" if by's rc0 option was specified

In byable(onecall) programs, you are responsible for everything, including the output of by-group headers, if you want them.

The typical candidates for byable(onecall) are programs that do something special and odd with the by-variables. We offer the following guidelines:

1. Ignore that you are going to make your program byable when you first write it. Instead, include a by() option on your program. Since your program cannot be coded using byable(recall), you already know that the by-variables are entangled with the logic of your routine. Make your program work.

2. Now go back and modify your program. Include byable(onecall) on the program statement line. Remove the by(varlist) from your syntax statement and, immediately after the syntax statement, add the line

   ```
   local by "'_byvars'"
   ```

3. Test your program. If it worked before, it will still work now. To use what was the by() option, you put the by *varlist*: prefix out front.

4. Ignore the macro '_byrc0'. It is a rare byable program that does anything different when the user specifies by's rc0 option.

The use of sort by byable(onecall) programs

You may use sort freely within byable(onecall) programs. You may even use sortpreserve to restore the sort order at the conclusion of your program.

When a byable(onecall) program receives control and is being by'd, the data are guaranteed to be sorted by '_byvars'.

Combining byable(onecall) with byable(recall)

One use of byable(onecall) is as an interface to other byable programs. Let's pretend that you are writing a command—we will call it switcher—that calls one of two other commands based perhaps on some aspect of what the user typed or, perhaps, based on what was previously estimated. The rule by which switcher decides to call one or the other does not matter for this discussion; what is important is that switcher switches between what we will call prog1 and prog2. prog1 and prog2 might be actual Stata commands, or Stata commands that you have written, or even subroutines of switcher.

We will further imagine that prog1 and prog2 have been implemented using the byable(recall) method, and we now want switcher to allow the by prefix, too. The easy way to do that is

```
program switcher, byable(onecall)
        if _by() {
                local by "by '_byvars', '_byrc0':"
        }
        if (whatever makes us decide in favor of prog1) {
                'by' prog1 '0'
        }
        else    'by' prog2 '0'
end
```

switcher works by recreating the by *varlist*: prefix in front of prog1 or prog2 if by was specified. switcher will be executed only once even if by was specified. prog1 and prog2 will be executed repeatedly.

In the above outline, it is not important that prog1 and prog2 were implemented using the byable(recall) method. They could just as well be implemented using byable(onecall), and switcher would change not at all.

The by-group header

Usually, when you use a command with by, a header is produced above each by-group:

```
. by foreign:  summarize mpg weight
```

```
-> foreign = Domestic
   (output for first by-group appears )
```

```
-> foreign = Foreign
   (output for first by-group appears )
. _
```

The by-group header does not always appear:

```
. by foreign:  generate new = sum(mpg)
. _
```

When you write your own programs, the header will appear by default if you use byable(recall), and will not appear if you use byable(onecall).

If you want the header and use byable(onecall), you will have to write the code to output it.

If you do not want the header and use byable(recall), you can specify byable(recall, noheader):

```
program ..., ... byable(recall, noheader)
        ...
end
```

Also See

Complementary: [P] **program**, [P] **sortpreserve**

Background: [R] **by**

Title

capture — Capture return code

Syntax

capture *command*

Description

capture executes *command*, suppressing all its output (including error messages, if any) and issuing a return code of zero. The actual return code generated by *command* is stored in the built-in scalar _rc.

Remarks

capture is useful in do-files and programs since their execution terminates when a command issues a nonzero return code. Preceding sensitive commands with the word capture allows the do-file or program to continue in spite of errors. In addition, do-files and programs can be made to respond appropriately to any situation by conditioning their remaining actions on the contents of the scalar _rc.

▷ Example

You will never have cause to use capture interactively, but a few interactive experiments will demonstrate what capture does:

```
. drop _all
. list myvar
no variables defined
r(111);
. capture list myvar
. display _rc
111
```

When we said list myvar, we were told that we had no variables defined and got a return code of 111. When we said capture list myvar, we got no output and a zero return code. First, you should wonder what happened to the message "no variables defined". capture suppressed that message. It suppresses (eats) all output produced by the command it is capturing. Next, we see no return code message, so the return code was zero. We already know that typing list myvar generates a return code of 111, so capture ate that, too.

capture places the return code in the built-in scalar _rc. When we display the value of this scalar, we see that it is 111.

◁

▷ Example

Now that we know what `capture` does, let's put it to use. `capture` is used in programs and do-files. In some cases, you will write programs that do not care about the outcome of a Stata command. You may want to ensure, for instance, that some variable does not exist in the dataset. You could do so by including `capture drop result`.

If `result` exists, it is now gone. If it did not exist, `drop` did nothing and its nonzero return code and the error message have been intercepted. The program (or do-file) continues in any case. If you have written a program that creates a variable named `result`, it would be good practice to begin such a program with `capture drop result`. This way, you could use the program repeatedly without having to worry whether the variable `result` already exists.

◁

❑ Technical Note

When combining `capture` and `drop`, never say something like `capture drop var1 var2 var3`. Remember that Stata commands do either exactly what you say or nothing at all. We might think that our command would be guaranteed to eliminate `var1`, `var2`, and `var3` from the data if they exist. It is not. Imagine that `var3` did not exist in the data. `drop` would then do nothing. It would *not* drop `var1` and `var2`. To achieve the desired result, we must give three commands:

```
capture drop var1
capture drop var2
capture drop var3
```

❑

▷ Example

Here is another example of using `capture` to dispose of nonzero return codes: When using do-files to define programs, it is quite common to begin the definition with `capture program drop` *progname* and then put `program` *progname*. This way, you can rerun the do-file to load or reload the program.

◁

▷ Example

Let's consider programs whose behavior is contingent upon the outcome of some command. You write a program and want to ensure that the first argument (the macro '`1`') has the interpretation of a new variable. If it does not, you want to issue an error message:

```
capture confirm new variable `1'
if _rc!=0 {
        display "`1' already exists"
        exit _rc
}
( program continues. . . )
```

You use the `confirm` command to determine if the variable already exists, and then condition your error message on whether `confirm` thinks '`1`' can be a new variable. We did not have to go to the trouble in this case. `confirm` would have automatically issued the appropriate error message, and its nonzero return code would have stopped the program anyway.

◁

▷ Example

As before, you write a program and want to ensure that the first argument has the interpretation of a new variable. This time, however, if it does not, you want to use the name _answer in place of the name specified by the user:

```
capture confirm new variable '1'
if _rc!=0 {
        local 1 _answer
        confirm new variable '1'
}
( program continues... )
```

◁

▷ Example

There may be instances where you want to capture the return code but not the output. You do that by combining `capture` with `noisily`. For instance, we might change our program to read

```
capture noisily confirm new variable '1'
if _rc!=0 {
        local 1 _answer
        display "I'll use _answer"
}
( program continues... )
```

`confirm` will generate some message such as "...already exists", and then we will follow that message with "I'll use _answer".

◁

❑ Technical Note

`capture` can be combined with {} to produce *capture blocks.* Consider the following:

```
capture {
        confirm var '1'
        confirm integer number '2'
        confirm number '3'
}
if _rc!=0 {
        display "Syntax is variable integer number"
        exit 198
}
( program continues... )
```

If any of the commands in the capture block fail, the subsequent commands in the block are aborted, but the program continues with the `if` statement.

Capture blocks can be used to intercept the *Break* key, as in

```
capture {
        stata_commands
}
if _rc==1 {
        Break key cleanup code
        exit 1
}
( program continues... )
```

Remember that *Break* always generates a return code of 1. There is no reason, however, to restrict the execution of the cleanup code to *Break* only. Our program might fail for some other reason, such as insufficient room to add a new variable, and we would still want to engage in the cleanup operations. A better version would read

```
capture {
        stata_commands
}
if _rc!=0 {
        local oldrc = _rc
        Break key and error cleanup code
        exit 'oldrc'
}
( program continues... )
```

❏

❏ Technical Note

The treatment of `exit` inside capture blocks is also worth noting. If, in our program above, the *stata_commands* included an `exit` or an `exit 0`, the program would terminate and return 0. Neither the *cleanup* nor the *program continues* code would be executed. If *stata_commands* included an `exit 198`, or any other `exit` that sets a nonzero return code, however, the program would not exit. `capture` would catch the nonzero return code, and execution would continue with the *cleanup code*.

❏

Also See

Complementary: [P] **break**, [P] **confirm**

Background: [U] **21.2 Relationship between a program and a do-file**

Title

Syntax

char [define] *evarname*[*charname*] [["]*text*["]]

char <u>lis</u>t   [*evarname*[[*charname*]]]

char <u>ren</u>ame   *varname*₁ *varname*₂

where *evarname* is a variable name or _dta and *charname* is a characteristic name. In the syntax diagrams, distinguish carefully between [ ], which you type, and [ ], which indicates that the element is optional.

Description

See [U] **15.8 Characteristics** for a description of characteristics. These commands allow manipulating characteristics.

Remarks

We begin by showing how the commands work mechanically, and then continue to demonstrate the commands in more realistic situations.

char define sets and clears characteristics, although there is no reason to type the define:

```
. char _dta[one] this is char named one of _dta
. char _dta[two] this is char named two of _dta
. char mpg[one]  this is char named   one   of mpg
. char mpg[two] "this is char named   two   of mpg"
. char mpg[three] "this is char named three of mpg"
```

Whether we include the double quotes does not matter. You clear a characteristic by defining it to be nothing:

```
. char mpg[three]
```

char list is used to list existing characteristics; it is typically used for debugging purposes:

```
. char list
    _dta[two]      :  this is char named two of _dta
    _dta[one]      :  this is char named one of _dta
    mpg[two]       :  this is char named   two    of mpg
    mpg[one]       :  this is char named   one    of mpg
. char list _dta[]
    _dta[two]      :  this is char named two of _dta
    _dta[one]      :  this is char named one of _dta
. char list mpg[]
    mpg[two]       :  this is char named   two    of mpg
    mpg[one]       :  this is char named   one    of mpg
. char list mpg[one]
    mpg[one]       :  this is char named   one    of mpg
```

20

The order may surprise you—it is the way it is because of how Stata's memory-management routines work—but it does not matter.

char rename moves all the characteristics associated with *varname*$_1$ to *varname*$_2$:

```
. char rename mpg weight
. char list
      _dta[two]      :  this is char named two of _dta
      _dta[one]      :  this is char named one of _dta
   weight[two]      :  this is char named   two     of mpg
   weight[one]      :  this is char named   one     of mpg
. char rename weight mpg                 // put it back
```

The contents of specific characteristics may be obtained in the same way as local macros by referencing the characteristic name between left and right single quotes; see [U] **15.8 Characteristics**.

```
. display "`mpg[one]'"
this is char named   one     of mpg
. display "`_dta[]'"
two one
```

Referring to a nonexisting characteristic returns null string:

```
. display "the value is |`mpg[three]'|"
the value is ||
```

How to program with characteristics

▷ Example

You are writing a program that needs the value of the variable recording "instance" (first time, second time, etc.). You want your command to have an option ins(*varname*), but, after the user has specified the variable once, you want your program to remember it in the future, even across sessions. An outline of your program is

```
program ...
        version 8.0
        syntax ... [, ... ins(varname) ... ]
        ...
        if "`ins'"=="" {
                local ins "`_dta[Instance]'"
        }
        confirm variable `ins'
        char _dta[Instance] : `ins'
        ...
end
```

◁

▷ Example

You write a program and, among other things, it changes the contents of one of the variables in the user's data. You worry about the user pressing *Break* while the program is in the midst of the change, and so you properly decide to construct the replaced values in a temporary variable and, only at the conclusion, drop the user's original variable and replace it with the new one. In this example, macro `uservar` contains the name of the user's original variable. Macro `newvar` contains the name of the temporary variable that will ultimately replace it.

There are the following issues in duplicating the original variable: You want the new variable to have the same variable label, the same value label, the same format, and the same characteristics.

```
program ...
        version 8.0
        ...
        tempvar newvar
        ...
        ( code creating 'newvar')
        ...
        local varlab : variable label 'uservar'
        local vallab : value label 'uservar'
        local format : format 'uservar'
        label var 'newvar' "'varlab'"
        label values 'newvar' 'vallab'
        format 'newvar' 'format'
        char rename 'uservar' 'newvar'
        drop 'uservar'
        rename 'newvar' 'uservar'
end
```

You are supposed to notice the char rename to move the characteristics originally attached to 'uservar' to 'newvar'. See [P] **macro**, [R] **label**, and [R] **format** for information on the commands preceding the char rename command.

This code is almost perfect, but if you are really concerned about the user pressing *Break*, there is a potential problem. What happens if the user presses *Break* between the char rename and the final rename? The last three lines would be better written as

```
nobreak {
        char rename 'uservar' 'newvar'
        drop 'uservar'
        rename 'newvar' 'uservar'
}
```

Now, even if the user presses *Break* during these last three lines, it will be ignored; see [P] **break**.
◁

Also See

Background: [U] **15.8 Characteristics**,
                    [U] **21.3.6 Extended macro functions**,
                    [U] **21.3.12 Referencing characteristics**

Title

class — Class programming

Description

Classes are a programming feature of Stata that are especially useful for dealing with graphics and GUI problems, although their use need not be restricted to those topics. Class programming is an advanced programming topic, and will not be useful to most programmers.

Remarks

Remarks are presented under the headings

1. Introduction
2. Definitions
    2.1 Class definition
    2.2 Class instance
    2.3 Class context
3. Version control
4. Member variables
    4.1 Types
    4.2 Default initialization
    4.3 Specifying initialization
    4.4 Specifying initialization 2, .new
    4.5 Alternate way of declaring
    4.6 Scope
    4.7 Adding dynamically
5. Inheritance
6. Member programs' return values
7. Assignment
    7.1 Type matching
    7.2 Arrays and array elements
    7.3 lvalues and rvalues
    7.4 Assignment of reference
8. Built-ins
    8.1 Built-in functions
    8.2 Built-in modifiers
9. Prefix operators
10. Using object values
11. Object destruction
12. Advanced topics
    12.1 Keys
    12.2 Unames
    12.3 Arrays of member variables
Appendix A. The finding, loading, and clearing of class definitions
Appendix B. Jargon
Appendix C. Syntax diagrams
    Appendix C.1 Class declaration
    Appendix C.2 Assignment
    Appendix C.3 Macro substitution
    Appendix C.4 Quick summary of built-ins

23

1. Introduction

A *class* is collection of (1) member variables and (2) member programs. The member programs of a class manipulate or make calculations based on the member variables. Classes are defined in .class files. For instance, we might define the class coordinate in the file coordinate.class:

```
                                    ——— coordinate.class ———
version 8
class coordinate {
            double   x
            double   y
}
program .set
            args x y
            .x = 'x'
            .y = 'y'
end
                                    ——— coordinate.class ———
```

The above file does not create anything. It merely defines the concept of a "coordinate". Now that the file exists, however, you could create a "scalar" variable of type coordinate by typing

```
.coord = .coordinate.new
```

.coord is called an *instance of* coordinate; it contains .coord.x (a particular x coordinate) and .coord.y (a particular y coordinate). Since we did not specify otherwise, .coord.x and .coord.y contain missing values, but we could reset .coord to contain (1,2) by typing

```
.coord.x = 1
.coord.y = 2
```

In this case, we can do that more conveniently by typing

```
.coord.set 1 2
```

because coordinate.class provides a member program called .set that allows us to set the member variables. There is nothing especially useful about .set; we wrote it mainly to emphasize that classes could, in fact, contain member programs. Our coordinate.class definition would be nearly as good if we deleted the .set program. Classes are not required to have member programs, but they may.

If we typed

```
.coord2 = .coordinate.new
.coord2.set 2 4
```

we would now have a second instance of a coordinate, this one named .coord2, and it would contain (2,4).

Now consider another class, line.class:

(Continued on next page)

```
──────────────────────── line.class ────────────────────────
version 8
class line {
            coordinate c0
            coordinate c1
}
program .set
            args x0 y0 x1 y1
            .c0.set 'x0' 'y0'
            .c1.set 'x1' 'y1'
end
program .length
            class exit sqrt(('.c0.y'-'.c1.y')^2 + ('.c0.x'-'.c1.x')^2)
end
program .midpoint
            local cx = ('.c0.x' + '.c1.x')/2
            local cy = ('.c0.y' + '.c1.y')/2
            tempname b
            .'b'=.coordinate.new
            .'b'.set 'cx' 'cy'
            class exit .'b'
end
──────────────────────── line.class ────────────────────────
```

Like `coordinate.class`, `line.class` has two member variables—they are named `.c0` and `.c1`—but rather than being numbers, `.c0` and `.c1` are `coordinates` as we have previously defined the term. Thus, the full list of the member variables for `line.class` are

`.c0`	first `coordinate`
`.c0.x`	x value (a double)
`.c0.y`	y value (a double)
`.c1`	second `coordinate`
`.c1.x`	x value (a double)
`.c1.y`	y value (a double)

If we typed

```
.li = .line.new
```

then we would have a `line` named `.li` in which

`.li.c0`	first coordinate of `line` `.li`
`.li.c0.x`	x value (a double)
`.li.c0.y`	y value (a double)
`.li.c1`	second `coordinate` of `line` `.li`
`.li.c1.x`	x value (a double)
`.li.c1.y`	y value (a double)

What are the values of these variables? Since we did not specify otherwise, `.li.c0` and `.li.c1` will receive default values for their type, `coordinate`. That default is (.,.), because we did not specify otherwise when we defined `lines` or `coordinates`. Ergo, the default values are (.,.) and (.,.), and we have a missing line.

As with `coordinate`, we included the member function `.set` to make setting the line easier. We can type

```
.li.set 1 2 2 4
```

and we will have a line going from (1,2) to (2,4).

`line.class` contains the following member programs:

`.set`	program to set `.c0` and `.c1`
`.c0.set`	program to set `.c0`
`.c1.set`	program to set `.c1`
`.length`	program to return length of line
`.midpoint`	program to return coordinate of midpoint of line

`.set`, `.length`, and `.midpoint` came from `line.class`. `.c0.set` and `.c1.set` came from `coordinate.class`.

Member program `.length` returns the length of the line.

```
.len = .li.length
```

would create `.len` containing the result of `.li.length`. The result of running the program `.length` on the object `.li`. `.length` returns a double, and therefore, `.len` will be double.

`.midpoint` returns the midpoint of a line.

```
.mid = .li.midpoint
```

would create `.mid` containing the result of `.li.midpoint`. The result of running the program `.midpoint` on the object `.li`. `.midpoint` returns a coordinate, and therefore, `.mid` will be a coordinate.

2. Definitions

2.1 Class definition

Class *classname* is defined in file *classname*`.class`. The definition does not create any instances of the class.

The *classname*`.class` file has three parts:

```
———————————————————————————— classname.class ——————————————
version ...             // Part 1: version statement
class   classname {     // Part 2: declaration of member variables
            . . .
}
program ...             // Part 3: code for member programs
          . . .
end
program ...
          . . .
end
. . .
———————————————————————————— classname.class ——————————————
```

2.2 Class instance

To create a "variable" *name* of type *classname*, you type

```
.name = .classname.new
```

After that, *.name* is variously called an identifier, class variable, class instance, object, object instance, or sometimes just an instance. Call it what you will, the above creates new thing *.name*—or replaces existing thing *.name*—to contain the result of an application of the definition of *classname*. And, just as with any variable, you can have many different variables with many different names all of the same type.

.name is called a first-level or top-level identifier. *.name1.name2* is called a second-level identifier, and so on. Assignment into top-level identifiers is allowed (1) if the identifier does not already exist or (2) if the identifier exists and is of type *classname*. If the top-level identifier already exists and is of a different type, you must drop the identifier first and then recreate it; see *Object destruction*.

Consider the assignment

> *.name1.name2* = *.classname*.new

The above statement is allowed if *.name1* already exists and if *.name2* is declared, in *.name1*'s class definition, to be of type *classname*. In that case, *.name1.name2* previously contained a *classname* instance and now contains a *classname* instance, the difference being that the old contents were discarded and replaced with the new ones. The same rule applies to third-level and higher identifiers.

Classes, and class instances, may also contain member programs. Member programs are identified in the same way as class variables. *.name1.name2* might refer to a member variable or to a member program.

2.3 Class context

When a class program executes, it executes in the context of the current instance. For example, consider the instance creation

> .mycoord = .coordinate.new

and recall that coordinate.class provides member program .set, which reads

```
program .set
                args x y
                .x = 'x'
                .y = 'y'
end
```

Assume that we type ".mycoord.set 2 4". When .set executes, it executes in the *context* of .mycoord. In the program, the references to .x and .y are assumed to be to .mycoord.x and .mycoord.y. If we typed ".other.set", the references would be to .other.x and .other.y.

Look at the statement ".x = 'x'" in .set. Pretend 'x' is 2 so that, after macro substitution, the statement reads ".x = 2". Is this a statement that the first-level identifier .x is to be set to 2? No, it is a statement that *.impliedcontext*.x is to be set to 2. The same would be true whether .x appeared to the right of the equal sign or anywhere else in the program.

The rules for resolving things like .x and .y are actually more complicated. They are resolved to the implied context if they exist in the implied context, and otherwise they are interpreted to be in the global context. Hence, in the above examples, .x and .y were interpreted as being references to *.impliedcontext*.x and *.impliedcontext*.y because .x and .y existed in *.impliedcontext*. If, however, our program made a reference to .c, that would be assumed to be in the global context (i.e., to be just .c), because there is no .c in the implied context. This is discussed at length in *Prefix operators*.

If a member program calls a regular program—a regular ado-file—that program will also run in the same class context; for example, if .set included the lines

```
move_to_right
.x = r(x)
.y = r(y)
```

and program `move_to_right.ado` had lines in it referring to `.x` and `.y`, they would be interpreted as *.impliedcontext*`.x` and *.impliedcontext*`.y`.

In all programs—member programs or ado-files—we can explicitly control whether we want identifiers in the implied context or globally with the `.Local` and `.Global` prefixes; see *Prefix operators*.

3. Version control

The first thing that should appear in a `.class` file is a `version` statement; see [P] **version**. For example, `coordinate.class` reads

───────────────────────────── coordinate.class ─────────────────
```
version 8
[ class statement defining member variables omitted ]
program .set
                args x y
                .x = 'x'
                .y = 'y'
end
```
───────────────────────────── coordinate.class ─────────────────

The `version 8` at the top of the file specifies not only that, when the class definition is read, it should be interpreted according to version 8 syntax, but it also specifies that when each of the member programs run, they should be interpreted according to version 8. Thus, you do not need to include a `version` statement inside the definition of each member program, although you may if you want that one program to run according to the syntax of a different version of Stata.

Including the `version` statement at the top, however, is of vital importance. Stata is under continual development and so is the class subsystem. Syntax and features can change. Including the `version` command is how you ensure that your class continues to work as you intended.

4. Member variables

4.1 Types

The second thing that appears in a `.class` file is the definition of the member variables. We have seen two examples,

───────────────────────────── coordinate.class ─────────────────
```
version 8
class coordinate {
                double  x
                double  y
}
[ member programs omitted ]
```
───────────────────────────── coordinate.class ─────────────────

and

─────────────── line.class ───────────────
```
version 8
class line {
          coordinate c0
          coordinate c1
}
```
[*member programs omitted*]
─────────────── line.class ───────────────

In the first example, the member variables are .x and .y, and in the second, .c0 and .c1. In the first example, the member variables are of type double, and in the second, of type coordinate, another class.

The member variables may be of *type*

double	double precision scalar numeric value, which includes missing values ., .a, . . . , and .z
string	scalar string value, with minimum length 0 ("") and maximum length the same as for macros, which is to say, long
classname	other classes, excluding the class being defined
array	array containing any of the *types*, including other arrays

A class definition might read

─────────────── todolist.class ───────────────
```
version 8
class todolist {
          double   n        // number of elements in list
          string   name     // who the list is for
          array    list     // the list itself
          actions  x        // things that have been done
}
```
─────────────── todolist.class ───────────────

In the above, note that actions is a class, not a primitive type. Somewhere else, we have written actions.class, which defines what we mean by actions.

Note that arrays are not typed when they are declared. An array is not an array of doubles or an array of strings or an array of coordinates; rather, each array element is separately typed at run time, so an array may turn out to be an array of doubles or an array of strings or an array of coordinates, or it may turn out that its first element is a double, its second element a string, its third element a coordinate, its fourth element something else, and so on.

Similarly, arrays are not declared to be of a predetermined size. The size is automatically determined at run time according to how the array is used. In addition, arrays can be sparse. The first element of an array might be a double, its fourth element a coordinate, and its second and third elements left undefined. There is no inefficiency associated with this. Later, a value might be assigned to the fifth element of the array, thus extending it, or a value might be assigned to the second and third elements, thus filling in the gaps.

4.2 Default initialization

When an instance of a class is created, the member variables are filled in as follows:

`double`	. (missing value)
`string`	`" "`
classname	as specified by class definition
`array`	empty, an array with no elements yet defined

4.3 Specifying initialization

You may specify in *classname*`.class` the initial values for member variables. To do this, you type an equal sign after the identifier, and then you type the initial value. For example,

```
───────────────────── todolist.class ─────────────
version 8
class todolist {
          double  n   = 0
          string  name = "nobody"
          array   list = {"show second syntax", "mark as done"}
          actions x   = .actions.new arguments
}
───────────────────── todolist.class ─────────────
```

The initialization rules are

`double` *membervarname* = ...

> After the equal sign, you may type any number or expression. If you wish to initialize the member variable with a missing value (., .a, .b, ..., .z), you must enclose the missing value in parentheses. Examples include
>
> ```
> double n = 0
> double a = (.)
> double b = (.b)
> double z = (2+3)/sqrt(5)
> ```
>
> Alternatively, after the equal sign, you may specify the identifier of a member variable to be copied or a member program to be run as long as the member variable is a `double` or the program returns a `double`. If a member program is specified and it requires arguments, they must be specified following the identifier. Examples include
>
> ```
> double n = .clearcount
> double a = .gammavalue 4 5 2
> double b = .color.cvalue, color(green)
> ```
>
> The identifiers are interpreted in terms of the global context, not the class context being defined. Thus, `.clearcount`, `.gammavalue`, and `.color.cvalue` must exist in the global context.

`string` *membervarname* = ...

> After the equal sign, you type the initial value for the member variable enclosed in quotes, which may either be simple (`"` and `"`) or be compound (`` `" `` and `"'`). Examples include
>
> ```
> string name = "nobody"
> string s = `"quotes "inside" strings"'
> string a = ""
> ```

Alternatively, you may specify a string expression, but you must enclose it in parentheses.

```
string name = ("no" + "body")
string b    = (char(11))
```

Alternatively, you may specify the identifier of a member variable to be copied or a member program to be run as long as the member variable is a `string` or the program returns a `string`. If a member program is specified and it requires arguments, they must be specified following the identifier. Examples include

```
string n = .defaultname
string a = .recapitalize "john smith"
string b = .names.defaults, category(null)
```

The identifiers are interpreted in terms of the global context, not the class context being defined. Thus, `.defaultname`, `.recapitalize`, and `.names.defaults` must exist in the global context.

array *membervarname* = {...}
> After the equal sign, you type the set of elements in braces ({ and }), with each element separated from the next by a comma.
>
> If an element is enclosed in quotes (simple or compound), the corresponding array element is defined to be `string` with the contents specified.
>
> If an element is a literal number excluding `.`, `.a`, ..., and `.z`, the corresponding array element is defined to be `double` and filled in with the number specified.
>
> If an element is enclosed in parentheses, what appears inside the parentheses is evaluated as an expression. If the expression evaluates to a string, the corresponding array element is defined to be `string` and the result filled in. If the expression evaluates to a number, the corresponding array element is defined to be `double` and the result filled in. Missing values may be assigned to array elements by being enclosed in parentheses.
>
> If the element begins with a period, it is interpreted as an object identifier in the global context. That object may be a member variable or a member program. The corresponding array element is defined to be of the same type as the specified member variable or of the same type as the member program returns. If a member program is specified and it requires arguments, the arguments must be specified following the identifier, but the entire syntactical elements must be enclosed in square brackets ([and]).
>
> If the element is nothing, the corresponding array element is left undefined.
>
> Examples include

```
array mixed = {1, 2, "three", 4}
array els   = {.box.new, , .table.new}
array rad   = {[.box.new 2 3], , .table.new}
```

Note the double commas in the last two initializations. The second element is left undefined. Some programmers would code

```
array els   = {.box.new, /*nothing*/, .table.new}
array rad   = {[.box.new 2 3], /*nothing*/, .table.new}
```

to emphasize the null initialization.

classname membervarname = . . .

> After the equal sign, you specify the identifier of a member variable to be copied or a member program to be run as long as the member variable is of type *classname* or the member program returns something of type *classname*. If a member program is specified and it requires arguments, they must be specified following the identifier. In either case, the identifier will be interpreted in the global context. Examples include

```
box mybox1 = .box.new
box mybox2 = .box.new 2 4 7 8, tilted
```

Note that all the types can be initialized by copying other member variables or by running other member programs. These other member variables and member programs must be defined in the global context and not the class context. In such cases, each initialization value or program is, in fact, copied or run only once—at the time the class definition is read—and the values are recorded for future use. This makes initialization fast. This also means, however,

1. If, in class definition called, say, `border.class`, you were to define a member variable that was initialized by `.box.new`, and if `.box.new` counted how many times it is run, even if you were to create 1,000 instances of `border`, you would discover that `.box.new` was run only once! If `.box.new` changed what it returned over time (perhaps due to a change in some state of the system being implemented), the initial values would not change when a new border object was created.

2. If, in `border.class`, you were to define a member variable that is initialized as `.system.curvals.no_of_widgets`, which we will assume is another member variable, even as `.system.curvals.no_of_widgets` changed, you would discover the new instances of `border.class` would have the same value over and over—the value of `.system.curvals.no_of_widgets` current at the time `border.class` was read.

In both of the above examples, the method just described—the prerecorded assignment method of specifying initial values—would be inadequate. The method just described is suitable for specifying constant initial values only.

4.4 Specifying initialization 2, .new

An alternate way to specify how member variables are to be initialized is to define a `.new` program within the class.

To create a new instance of a class, you know that you type

> `. name =. classname.new`

`.new` is, in fact, a member program of *classname*; it is just one that is built-in, and you do not have to define it in order to use it. The built-in `.new` allocates the memory for the instance and fills in the default or specified initial values for the member variables. If you define a `.new`, your `.new` will be run after the built-in `.new` finishes its work.

For example, our example `coordinate.class` could be improved by adding a `.new` member program:

(Continued on next page)

```
———————————————————— coordinate.class ————————————
version 8
class coordinate {
            double  x
            double  y
}
program .new
            if "'0'" != "" {
                    .set '0'
            }
end
program .set
            args x y
            .x = 'x'
            .y = 'y'
end  ——————————————————————— coordinate.class ——————————————
```

With this addition, we could type

```
.coord = .coordinate.new
.coord.set 2 4
```

or we could type

```
.coord = .coordinate.new 2 4
```

We have arranged that .new take arguments—optional ones in this case—that specify where the new point is to be located. We wrote the code so that .new calls .set, although we could just as well have written the code so that the lines in .set appeared in .new and then deleted the .set program. In fact, the two-part construction can be desirable because then we have a function that will reset the contents of an existing class as well.

In any case, by defining your own .new, you can arrange for any sort of complicated initialization of the class, and that initialization can be a function of arguments specified if that is necessary.

The .new program need not return anything; see *Member programs' return values*.

.new programs are not restricted just to filling in initial values. They are programs that you can code however you wish. .new is run every time a new instance of a class is created with one exception: when an instance is created as a member of another instance (in which case, the results are prerecorded).

4.5 Alternate way of declaring

In addition to the syntax,

    type *name* $\left[\ =\ initialization\right]$

where *type* is one of double, string, *classname*, or array, there is an alternate syntax that reads

    name = *initialization*

That is, you may omit specifying *type* when you specify how the member variable is to be initialized because, in that case, the type of the member variable can be inferred from the initialization.

4.6 Scope

In the examples we have seen so far, the member variables are unique to the instance. For example, if we have

```
.coord1 = .coordinate.new
.coord2 = .coordinate.new
```

the member variables of .coord1 have nothing to do with the member variables of .coord2. If we were to change .coord1.x, .coord2.x would remain unchanged.

Classes can also have variables that are shared across all instances of the class. Consider

```
——————————————————————— coordinate2.class ———————————————
version 8
class coordinate2 {
                classwide:
                        double x_origin = 0
                        double y_origin = 0
                instancespecific:
                        double x = 0
                        double y = 0
}
——————————————————————— coordinate2.class ———————————————
```

In this class definition, .x and .y are as they were in coordinate.class—they are unique to the instance. .x_origin and .y_origin, however, are shared across all instances of the class. That is, if we were to type

```
.ac = .coordinate2.new
.bc = .coordinate2.new
```

there would be only one copy of .x_origin and of .y_origin. If we changed .x_origin in .ac,

```
.ac.x_origin = 2
```

we would find that .bc.x_origin had similarly been changed. That is because .ac.x_origin and .bc.x_origin are, in fact, the same variable.

The effects of initialization are a little different in the case of classwide variables. In coordinate2.class, we specified that .origin_x and .origin_y should both be initialized as 0, and so they were when we typed ".ac = .coordinate2.new", creating the first instance of the class. After that, however, .origin_x and .origin_y will never be reinitialized because they need not be recreated, being shared. (That is not exactly accurate, because, once the last instance of a coordinate2 has been destroyed, the variables will need to be reinitialized the next time a new first instance of coordinate2 is created.)

Classwide variables, just as with instance-specific variables, can be of any type. We can define

```
——————————————————————— supercoordinate.class ———————————————
version 8
class supercoordinate {
                classwide:
                        coordinate   origin
                instancespecific:
                        coordinate   pt
}
——————————————————————— supercoordinate.class ———————————————
```

The qualifiers classwide: and instancespecific: are used to designate the scope of the member variables that follow. When neither is specified, instancespecific: is assumed.

4.7 Adding dynamically

Once an instance of a class exists, you can add new (instance-specific) member variables to it. The syntax for doing this is

> *name* .Declare *attribute_declaration*

where *name* is the identifier of an instance and *attribute_declaration* is any valid attribute declaration such as

double	*varname*
string	*varname*
array	*varname*
classname	*varname*

and, on top of that, we can include = and initializer information as defined in *Specifying initialization* above.

For example, we might start with

    .coord = .coordinate.new

and discover that there is some extra information that we would like to carry around with the particular instance .coord. In this case, we want to carry around some color information that we will use later, and we have at our fingertips color.class, which defines what we mean by color. We can type

    .coord.Declare color mycolor

or even

    .coord.Declare color mycolor = .color.new, color(default)

to cause the new class instance to be initialized the way we want. After that command, .coord now contains coord.color and whatever third-or-higher level identifiers color provides. We can still invoke the member programs of coordinate on .coord and, to them, .coord will look just like a coordinate because they will know nothing about the extra information (although if they were to make a copy of .coord, the copy would include the extra information). We can use the extra information in our main program and even in subroutines that we write.

❑ Technical Note

Just as with declaration of member variables inside the class {} statement, you can omit specifying the *type* when you specify the initialization. In the above, also allowed would be

    .coord.Declare mycolor = .color.new, color(default)

❑

5. Inheritance

One class definition can inherit from other class definitions. This is done by including the `inherit`(*classnamelist*) option:

```
——————————————————— newclassname.class ———————————————
version 8
class newclassname {
                 . . .
}, inherit(classnamelist)
program . . .
            . . .
end
. . .
——————————————————— newclassname.class ———————————————
```

newclassname inherits the member variables and member programs from *classnamelist*. In general, *classnamelist* contains one class name. When *classnamelist* contains more than one class name, that is called multiple inheritance.

To be precise, *newclassname* inherits all of the member variables from the classes specified except those that are explicitly defined in *newclassname*, in which case the definition provided in *newclassname*.`class` takes precedence. It is considered bad style to name member variables that conflict.

In the case of multiple inheritance, it is possible that, while a member variable is not defined in *newclassname*, it is defined in more than one of the "parents" (*classnamelist*). In that case, it will be the definition in the rightmost parent that is operative. This too is to be avoided, because it almost always results in programs breaking.

newclassname also inherits all the member programs from the classes specified. Here name conflicts are not considered bad style, and, in fact, redefinition of member programs is one of the primary reasons to use inheritance.

newclassname inherits all the programs from *classnamelist*—even those with names in common— and a way is provided to specify which of the programs that you wish to execute. In the case of single inheritance, if member program `.zifl` is defined in both classes, `.zifl` is taken as the instruction to run `.zifl` as defined in *newclassname*, and `.Super.zifl` is taken as the instruction to run `.zifl` as defined in the parent.

In the case of multiple inheritance, `.zifl` is taken as the instruction to run `.zifl` as defined in *newclassname*, and `.Super`(*classname*)`.zifl` is taken as the instruction to run `.zifl` as defined in the parent *classname*.

A good reason to use inheritance is to "steal" a class and to modify it to suit your purposes. Pretend that you have `alreadyexists.class` and from that you want to make `alternative.class`, something that is very much like `alreadyexists.class`—so much like it that it could be used wherever `alreadyexists.class` is used—but it does one thing a little differently. Perhaps you are writing a graphics system and `alreadyexists.class` defines everything about the little circles used to mark points on a graph, and now you want to create `alternate.class` that does the same, but this time for solid circles. Hence, there is only one member program of `alreadyexists.class` that you want to change: how to draw the symbol.

In any case, we will assume that `alternative.class` is to be identical to `alreadyexists.class`, except that it has changed or improved member function `.zifl`. In such a circumstance, it would not be uncommon to create

```
——————————————————— alternative.class ———————————————
version 8
class alternative {
}, inherit(alreadyexists)
program .zifl
                . . .
end
——————————————————— alternative.class ———————————————
```

Moreover, in writing .zifl, you might very well call .Super.zifl so that the old .zifl performed its tasks, and all you had to do was code what was extra (filling in the circles, say). In the example above, we added no member variables to the class.

Perhaps the new .zifl needs a new member variable—a double—and let us call it .sizeofre-sult. In that case, we might code

```
——————————————————— alternative.class ———————————————
version 8
class alternative {
                double    sizeofresult
}, inherit(alreadyexists)
program .zifl
                . . .
end
——————————————————— alternative.class ———————————————
```

Now let's consider initialization of the new variable .sizeofresult. Perhaps having it initialized as missing is adequate. In that case, our code above is adequate. Suppose that we want to initialize it to 5. In that case, we could include an initializer statement. Perhaps, we need something more complicated that must be handled in a .new. In this final case, it is our responsibility to call the inherited classes' .new programs using the .Super modifier:

```
——————————————————— alternative.class ———————————————
version 8
class alternative {
                double    sizeofresult
}, inherit(alreadyexists)
program .new
                . . .
                .Super.new
                . . .
end
program .zifl
                . . .
end
——————————————————— alternative.class ———————————————
```

6. Member programs' return values

Member programs may optionally return "values", and those can be doubles, strings, arrays, or class instances. These return values can be used in assignment, and thus you can code

```
.len    = .li.length
.coord3 = .li.midpoint
```

Just because a member program returns something does not mean it has to be consumed. The programs .li.length and .li.midpoint can still be executed directly,

```
.li.length
.li.midpoint
```

and, in that case, the return value is ignored. (`.midpoint` and `.length` are member programs that we included in `line.class`. `.length` returns a `double` and `.midpoint` returns a `coordinate`.)

You cause member programs to return values using the `class exit` command; see [P] **class exit**.

Do not confuse returned values with return codes, which all Stata programs set, even member programs. Member programs exit when they execute:

Condition	returned value	return code
`class exit` with arguments	as specified	0
`class exit` without arguments	nothing	0
`exit` without arguments	nothing	0
`exit` with arguments	nothing	as specified
error	nothing	as specified
command having error	nothing	as appropriate

Any of the preceding are valid ways of exiting a member program, although the last is perhaps best avoided. `class exit` without arguments has the same effect as `exit` without arguments; it does not matter which you code.

If a member program returns nothing, the result is as if it returned `string` containing `""` (nothing).

Member programs may, in addition, return values in `r()`, `e()`, and `s()`, just like regular programs. Using `class exit` to return a class result does not prevent member programs from also being r-class, e-class, or s-class.

7. Assignment

Consider `.coord` defined

```
.coord = .coordinate.new
```

That is an example of assignment. A new instance of class `coordinate` is created and assigned to `.coord`. In the same way,

```
.coord2 = .coord
```

is another example of assignment. A copy of `.coord` is made and assigned to `.coord2`.

Assignment is not just allowed with top-level names. The following are also valid examples of assignment:

```
.coord.x = 2
.li.c0 = .coord
.li.c0.x = 2+2
.todo.name = "Jane Smith"
.todo.n = 2
.todo.list[1] = "Turn in report"
.todo.list[2] = .li.c0
```

In each case, what appears on the right is evaluated, and a copy is put into the specified place. Assignment based on the returned value of a program is also allowed, so the following are also valid:

```
.coord.x = .li.length
.li.c0 = .li.midpoint
```

.length and .midpoint are member programs of line.class, and .li is an instance of line. In the first example, .li.length returns a double, and that double is assigned to .coord.x. In the second example, .li.midpoint returns a coordinate, and that coordinate is assigned to li.c0.

Also allowed would be

```
.todo.list[3] = .color.cvalue, color(green)
.todo.list = {"Turn in report", .li.c0, [.color.cvalue, color(green)]}
```

In both examples, the result of running .color.cvalue, color(green) is assigned to the third array element of .todo.list.

7.1 Type matching

All of the examples above are valid because either (1) a new identifier is being created, or (2) the identifier previously existed and was of the same type as the identifier being assigned.

For example, the following would be invalid:

```
.newthing = 2        // valid so far ...
.newthing = "new"    // ... invalid
```

The first line is valid because .newthing did not previously exist. After the first assignment, however, .newthing did exist and was of type double. That caused the second assignment to be invalid, the error being "type mismatch"; r(109).

The following are also invalid:

```
.coord.x = .li.midpoint
.li.c0 = .li.length
```

They are invalid because .li.midpoint returns a coordinate and .coord.x is a double, and because .li.length returns a double and .li.c0 is a coordinate.

7.2 Arrays and array elements

The statements

```
.todo.list[1] = "Turn in report"
.todo.list[2] = .li.c0
.todo.list[3] = .color.cvalue, color(green)
```

and

```
.todo.list = {"Turn in report", .li.c0, [.color.cvalue, color(green)]}
```

do not have the same effect. The first reassigns elements 1, 2, 3, and leaves any other defined elements unchanged. The second replaces the entire array with an array that has only elements 1, 2, and 3 defined.

After an element has been assigned, it may be unassigned (cleared) using .Arrdropel. For example, to unassign .todo.list[1], you type

```
.todo.list[1].Arrdropel
```

Clearing an element does not affect the other elements of the array. In the above example, .todo.list[2] and .todo.list[3] continue to exist.

New and existing elements may be assigned and reassigned freely, except that if an array element already exists, it may only be reassigned to something of the same type.

```
.todo.list[2] = .coordinate[2]
```

would be allowed, but

```
.todo.list[2] = "Clear the coordinate"
```

would not be allowed because `.todo.list[2]` is a `coordinate` and `"Clear the coordinate"` is a `string`. If you wish to reassign an array element to a different type, you first drop the existing array element and then assign it.

```
.todo.list[2].Arrdropel
.todo.list[2] = "Clear the coordinate"
```

7.3 lvalues and rvalues

Not withstanding everything that has been said, the syntax for assignment is, in fact,

lvalue = *rvalue*

lvalue stands for what may appear to the left of the equal sign, and *rvalue* stands for what may appear to the right.

The syntax for specifying an *lvalue* is

$.id\big[.id[\dots]\big]$

where *id* is either a *name* or *name*[*exp*], the latter being the syntax for specifying an array element, and *exp* must evaluate to a number; if *exp* evaluates to a noninteger number, it is truncated.

In addition, an *lvalue* must be assignable, meaning *lvalue* cannot refer to a member program, which is to say, an *id* element of *lvalue* cannot be a program name. (In an *rvalue*, if a program name is specified, it must be in the last *id*.)

The syntax for specifying an *rvalue* is any of the following:

$"\big[string\big]"$

$`"\big[string\big]"\mathrm{'}$

#

exp

(*exp*)

$.id\big[.id[\dots]\big]\ \big[program\_arguments\big]$

{}

$\{el\big[,el[,\dots]\big]\}$

The last two syntaxes concern assignment to arrays and *el* may be

> *nothing*
>
> $"[string]"$
>
> $'"[string]"'$
>
> #
>
> (*exp*)
>
> $.id[.id[\ldots]]$
>
> $[.id[.id[\ldots]]][program\_arguments]]$

Let us consider each of the syntaxes for an *rvalue* in turn:

$"[string]"$ and $'"[string]"'$

    If the *rvalue* begins with a double quote (simple or compound), returned will be a `string` containing *string*. *string* may be very long—up to the length of a macro.

#

    If the *rvalue* is a number excluding missing values `.`, `.a`, ..., and `.z`, returned will be a `double` equal to the number specified.

exp and (*exp*)

    If the *rvalue* is an expression, the expression will be evaluated and the result returned. Returned will be a `double` if the expression returns a numeric result and a `string` if expression returns a string. Expressions returning matrices are not allowed.

    The expression need not be enclosed in parentheses if the expression does not begin with simple- or compound-double quotes and does not begin with a period followed by nothing or a letter. In the cases just mentioned, the expression must be enclosed in parentheses. All expressions may be enclosed in parentheses.

    Note that an implication of the above is that missing value literals must be enclosed in parentheses: *lvalue* = (`.`).

$.id[.id[\ldots]][program\_arguments]$

    If the *rvalue* begins with a period, it is interpreted as an object reference. The object is evaluated and returned. $.id[.id[\ldots]]$ may refer to a member variable or a member program.

    If $.id[.id[\ldots]]$ refers to a member variable, the value of the variable is returned.

    If $.id[.id[\ldots]]$ refers to a member program, then the program will be executed and the result returned. If the member program returns nothing, a `string` containing "" (nothing) is returned.

    If $.id[.id[\ldots]]$ refers to a member program, arguments may be specified following the program name.

`{}` and $\{el[,el[,\ldots]]\}$

    If the *rvalue* begins with an open brace, an `array` is returned.

    If the *rvalue* is `{}`, an empty array is returned.

    If the *rvalue* is $\{el[,el[,\ldots]]\}$, an array containing the specified elements is returned.

    If an *el* is nothing, the corresponding array element is left undefined.

    If an *el* is $"[string]"$ or $'"[string]"'$, the corresponding array element is defined as a `string` containing *string*.

If an *el* is # excluding missing values ., .a, ..., .z, the corresponding array element is defined as a `double` containing the number specified.

If an *el* is (*exp*), the expression is evaluated, and the corresponding array element is defined as a `double` if the expression returns a numeric result and as a `string` if the expression returns a string. Expressions returning matrices are not allowed.

If an *el* is .*id*[.*id*[...]] or [.*id*[.*id*[...]] [*program_arguments*]], the object is evaluated, and the corresponding array element is defined according to what was returned. Note that if the object is a member program and arguments need to be specified, the *el* must be enclosed in square brackets.

Recursive array definitions are not allowed.

Finally, note that in *Specifying initialization*—where we discussed member variable initialization—what actually appears to the right of the equal sign is an *rvalue*, and everything just said applies. The previous discussion was incomplete.

7.4 Assignment of reference

Consider two different identifiers, .*a*.*b*.*c* and .*d*.*e*, that are of the same type. For example, perhaps both are `doubles` or both are `coordinates`. When you type

.*a*.*b*.*c* = .*d*.*e*

the result is to copy the values of .*d*.*e* into .*a*.*b*.*c*. If you type

.*a*.*b*.*c*.`ref` = .*d*.*e*.`ref`

the result is to make .*a*.*b*.*c* and .*d*.*e* be the same object. That is, if you were subsequently to change some element of .*d*.*e*, the corresponding element of .*a*.*b*.*c* would change, and vice versa.

To understand this, think of member values as each being written on an index card. Each instance of a class has its own collection of cards (assuming no classwide variables). When you type

.*a*.*b*.*c*.`ref` = .*d*.*e*.`ref`

the card for .*a*.*b*.*c* is removed and substituted is a note that says to use the card for .*d*.*e*. Thus, both .*a*.*b*.*c* and .*d*.*e* become literally the same object.

More than one object can share references. If we were now to code

.*i*.`ref` = .*a*.*b*.*c*.`ref`

or

.*i*.`ref` = .*d*.*e*.`ref`

the result would be the same: .*i* would also share the already-shared object.

We now have .*a*.*b*.*c*, .*d*.*e*, and .*i* all being the same object. Say we want to make .*d*.*e* back into being its own unique object. We type

.*d*.*e*.`ref` = *anything evaluating to the right type not ending in* `.ref`

We could, for instance, type any of the following:

.*d*.*e*.`ref` = .*classname*.`new`
.*d*.*e*.`ref` = .*j*.*k*
.*d*.*e*.`ref` = .*d*.*e*

All of the above will make *.d.e* unique because what is returned on the right is a copy. The last of the three examples is intriguing because it results in *.d.e* not changing its values but becoming once again unique.

8. Built-ins

.new and .ref are examples of built-in member programs that are included in every class. There are other built-ins as well.

Built-ins may be used on any object except programs and other built-ins. Let *.B* refer to a built-in. Then,

1. if *.a.b.myprog* refers to a program, *.a.b.myprog.B* is an error (and, in fact, *.a.b.myprog.anything* is also an error).

2. *.a.b.B.anything* is an error.

Built-ins come in two flavors, built-in functions and built-in modifiers. Built-in functions return information about the class or class instance on which they operate, but do not modify the class or class instance. Modifiers might return something—in general they do not—but they modify (change) the class or class instance.

With the exception of .new (and that was covered in *Specifying initialization 2, .new*), built-ins may not be redefined.

8.1 Built-in functions

In the documentation below, *object* refers to the context of the built-in function. For example, if *.a.b.F* is how the built-in function *.F* was invoked, then *.a.b* is the object on which it operates.

The built-in functions are

.new
> returns a new instance of *object*. .new may be used whether the *object* is a class name or an instance, although it is most usually used with a class name. For example, if coordinate is a class, .coordinate.new returns a new instance of coordinate.
>
> If .new is used with an instance, a new instance of the class of the object is returned; the current instance is not modified. For example, if *.a.b* is an instance of coordinate, then *.a.b*.new does exactly what .coordinate.new would do; *.a.b* is not modified in any way.
>
> If you define your own .new program, it is run after the built-in .new is run.

.copy
> returns a new instance—a copy—of *object*, which must be an instance. .copy returns a new object that is an exact copy of the original.

.ref
> returns a reference to the object. See *Assignment of reference*.

.objtype
> returns a string indicating the type of *object*. Returned is one of "double", "string", "array", or "*classname*".

.isa
> returns a string indicating the category of *object*. Returned is one of "double", "string", "array", "class", or "classtype". "classtype" is returned when *object* is a class definition; "class" is returned when the object is an instance of a class *(sic)*.

.classname

> returns a string indicating the name of the class. Returned is "*classname*" or, if *object* is of type double, string, or array, returned is "".

.isofclass *classname*

> returns a double. Returns 1 if *object* is of class type *classname* and 0 otherwise. To be of a class type, *object* must be an instance of *classname*, inherited from the class *classname*, or inherited from a class that inherits anywhere along its inheritance path from *classname*.

.objkey

> returns a string that can be used to reference an *object* outside the implied context. See *Keys*.

.uname

> returns a string that can be used as a *name* throughout Stata that corresponds to the object. See *Unames*.

.ref_n

> returns a double. Returned is the total number of identifiers sharing *object*. Returned is 1 if the object is unshared. See *Assignment of reference*.

.arrnels

> returns a double. .arrnels is for use with arrays; it returns the largest index of the array that has been assigned data. If *object* is not an array, it returns an error.

.arrindexof "*string*"

> returns a double. .arrindexof is for use with arrays; it searches the array for the first element equal to *string* and returns the index of that element. If *string* is not found, .arrindexof returns 0. If *object* is not an array, it returns an error.

.classmv

> returns an array containing the .refs of each classwide member variable in *object*. See *Arrays of member variables*.

.instancemv

> returns an array containing the .refs of each instance-specific member variable in *object*. See *Arrays of member variables*.

.dynamicmv

> returns an array containing the .refs of each dynamically allocated member variable in *object*. See *Arrays of member variables*.

.superclass

> returns an array containing the .refs of each of the classes from which the specified object inherited. See *Arrays of member variables*.

8.2 Built-in modifiers

Modifiers are built-ins that change the object to which they are applied. All built-in modifiers have names beginning with a capital letter. The built-in modifiers are

.Declare *declarator*

> returns nothing. .Declare may only be used when *object* is a class instance. .Declare adds the specified new member variable to the class instance. See *Adding dynamically*.

.Arrdropel *#*

> returns nothing. .Arrdropel may only be used with array elements. .Arrdropel drops the specified array element, making it as if it was never defined. .arrnels is, of course, updated.

`.Arrpop`

> returns nothing. `.Arrpop` may only be used with `arrays`. `.Arrpop` finds the top element of an array (largest index), and removes it from the array. To access the top element before popping, use `.`*arrayname*`['.`*arrayname*`.arrnels']`. If *object* is not an array, `.Arrpop` returns an error.

`.Arrpush "`*string*`"`

> returns nothing. `.Arrpush` may only be used with `arrays`. `.Arrpush` pushes *string* onto the end of the array, where end is defined as `.arrnels+1`. If *object* is not an array, `.Arrpush` returns an error.

9. Prefix operators

There are three prefix operators:

```
.Global
.Local
.Super
```

Prefix operators determine how object names such as `.`*a*, `.`*a*`.`*b*, `.`*a*`.`*b*`.`*c*, ... are resolved.

Consider a program invoked by typing `.alpha.myprog`. In program `.myprog`, any lines such as

```
.a = .b
```

are interpreted according to the implied context, if that is possible. To wit, `.a` is interpreted to mean `.alpha.a` if `.a` exists in `.alpha`; otherwise, it is taken to mean `.a` in the global context, which is to say, taken to mean just `.a`. Similarly, `.b` is taken to mean `.alpha.b` if `.b` exists in `.alpha`; otherwise, it is taken to mean `.b`.

What if `.myprog` wants `.a` to be interpreted in the global context even if `.a` exists in `.alpha`? In that case, the code would read

```
.Global.a = .b
```

If instead `.myprog` wanted `.b` to be interpreted in the global context (and `.a` to be interpreted in the implied context), the code would read

```
.a = .Global.b
```

Obviously, if the program wanted both to be interpreted in the global context, the code would read

```
.Global.a = .Global.b
```

`.Local` is the reverse of `.Global`: it ensures that the object reference is interpreted in the implied context. `.Local` is rarely specified because the local context is searched first, but if there is a circumstance where you wish to be certain that the object is not found in the global context, you may specify its reference preceded by `.Local`. Understand, however, that if the object is not found, what must result is an error, so you would need to precede commands containing such references with `capture`; see [P] **capture**.

In fact, if it is used at all, `.Local` is nearly always used in a macro-substitution context—something discussed in the next session—where errors are suppressed and where nothing is substituted when errors occur. Thus, in advanced code, if you were trying to determine whether member variable `.addedvar` exists in the local context, you could code

```
if "'Local.addedvar.objtype'" == "" {
                /* it does not exist */
}
else {
                /* it does */
}
```

The .Super prefix is used only in front of program names and concerns inheritance when one program occults another. This was discussed in *Inheritance*.

10. Using object values

We have discussed definition and assignment of objects, but we have not yet discussed how you might use class objects in a program. How do you refer to their values in a program? How do you find out what a value is, skip some code if the value is one thing, loop if it is another?

The most common way to refer to objects (and the returned results of member programs) is through macro substitution; for example,

```
local x = '.li.c0.x'
local clr "'.color.cvalue, color(green)'"
scalar len = '.coord.length'
forvalues i=1(1)'.todo.n' {
                Mysub "'todo.list['i']'"
}
```

When a class object is quoted, its printable form is substituted. This is defined as

Object type	printable form
string	contents of the string
double	number printed using %18.0g, spaces stripped
array	nothing
classname	nothing or, if member program .macroexpand is defined, then string or double returned

Any object may be quoted, including programs. If the program takes arguments, they are included inside the quotes:

```
scalar len = '.coord.length'
local clr "'.color.cvalue, color(green)'"
```

If the quoted reference results in an error, the error message is suppressed and nothing is substituted.

Similarly, if a class instance is quoted—or a program returning a class instance is quoted—nothing is substituted. That is, nothing is substituted assuming the member program .macroexpand has not been defined for the class, as is usually the case. If .macroexpand has been defined, however, it is executed, and what macroexpand returns—which may be a string or a double—is substituted.

For example, say we wanted to make all objects of type coordinate substitute (#,#) when they were quoted. In the class definition for coordinate, we could define .macroexpand,

```
—————————————————————— coordinate.class ——————————————
version 8
class coordinate {
                [ declaration of member variables omitted ]
        }
[ definitions of class programs omitted ]
program .macroexpand
                local tosub : display "(" '.x' "," '.y' ")"
                class exit "'tosub'"
end
—————————————————————— coordinate.class ——————————————
```

and now coordinates will be substituted. Say .mycoord is a coordinate currently set to (2,3). Understand, if we did not include .macroexpand in the coordinate.class file, typing

   ...'mycoord'...

would not be an error, it would merely result in

   ......

Having defined .macroexpand, it will result in

   ...(2,3)...

Moreover, pretend that .mygraph.myaxis.coord_of is a program requiring an argument that returns a coordinate, and pretend that typing .mygraph.myaxis.coord_of.origin would return where the x- and y-axes meet. If we type

   ...'.mygraph.myaxis.coord_of .origin'...

the result would be

   ...(0,0)...

11. Object destruction

To create an instance of a class, you type

   .name = *.classname*.new $\left[\textit{arguments}\right]$

To destroy the resulting object and thus release the memory associated with it, you type

   classutil drop *.name*

(See [P] **classutil** for more information on the classutil command.) You can only drop top-level instances. Objects deeper than that are dropped when the higher level object containing them are dropped, and classes are automatically dropped when the last instance of the class is dropped.

In addition, any top-level object named with a name obtained from tempname—see [P] **macro**—is automatically dropped when the program concludes. Even so, tempname objects may be returned by class exit. The following is valid:

```
program .tension
                ...
                tempname a b
                .'a' = .bubble.new
                .'b' = .bubble.new
                ...
                class exit .'a'
end
```

The program creates two new class instances of `bubbles` in the global context, both with temporary names. We can be assured that `.‘a’` and `.‘b’` are global because the names ‘a’ and ‘b’ were obtained from `tempname` and, therefore, cannot already exist in whatever context in which `.tension` runs. Therefore, when the program ends, `.‘a’` and `.‘b’` will be automatically dropped. Even so, `.tension` can return `.‘a’`. It can do that because, at the time `class exit` is executed, the program has not yet concluded, and `.‘a’` still exists. You can even code

```
program .tension
                ...
                tempname a b
                .‘a’ = .bubble.new
                .‘b’ = .bubble.new
                ...
                class exit .‘a’.ref
        end
```

and that also will return `.a` and, in fact, will be faster because no extra copy will be made. This form is recommended when returning an object stored in a temporary name. Do not, however, add `refs` on the end of "real" (nontemporary) objects being returned, because then you would be returning not just the same values as in the real object, but the object itself.

You can clear the entire class system by typing `discard`; see [P] **discard**. There is no `classutil` drop _all command. That is because Stata's graphics system also uses the class system, and dropping all the class definitions and instances would cause `graph` difficulty. `discard` also clears all open graphs, so the disappearance of class definitions and instances causes `graph` no difficulty.

During the development of class-based systems, it is recommended that you type `discard` whenever you make a change to any part of the system, no matter how minor or how certain you are that no instances of the definition modified yet exist.

12. Advanced topics

12.1 Keys

The `.objkey` built-in function returns a `string` called a key that can be used to reference the object as an *rvalue* but not as an *lvalue*. This would typically be used in

```
local k = ‘.a.b.objkey’
```

or

```
.c.k = .a.b.objkey
```

where `.c.k` is a `string`. Thus, the keys stored could be subsequently used as follows:

`.d = .‘k’.x`	meaning to assign `.a.b.x` to `.d`
`.d = .‘.c.k’.x`	(same)
`local z = ‘.‘k’.x’`	meaning to put value of `.a.b.x` in ‘z’
`local z = ‘.‘.c.k’.x’`	(same)

The point of the above is that it does not matter if the key is stored in a macro or a string member variable—it can be used equally well—and in all cases, you use the key by macro quoting.

A key is a special string that stands for the object. Why not, you wonder, simply type `.a.b` rather than `.‘.c.k’` or `.‘k’`? The answer has to do with implied context.

Pretend that .myvar.bin.myprogram runs .myprogram. Obviously, it runs .myprogram in the context .myvar.bin. Thus, .myprogram can include lines such as

```
.x = 5
```

and that is understood to mean that .myvar.bin.x is to be set to 5. .myprogram, however, might also include a line that reads

```
.Global.utility.setup '.x.objkey'
```

In this case, .myprogram is calling a utility that runs in a different context (namely, .utility), but myprogram needs to pass .x—of whatever type it might be—to the utility as an argument. Perhaps .x is a coordinate, and .utility.setup expects to receive the identifier of a coordinate as its argument. .myprogram, however, does not know that .myvar.bin.x is the full name of .x, which is what .utility.setup will need, so .myprogram passes '.x.objkey'. Program .utility.setup can use what it receives as its argument just as if it contained .myvar.bin.x, except that .utility.setup cannot use that received reference on the left-hand side of an assignment.

If myprogram needed to pass to .utility.setup a reference to the entire implied context (.myvar.bin), the line would read

```
.Global.utility.setup '.objkey'
```

because .objkey by itself means to return the key of the implied context.

12.2 Unames

The built-in function .uname returns a *name* that can be used throughout Stata that uniquely corresponds to the object. The mapping is one-way. Unames can be obtained for objects, but the original object's name cannot be obtained from the uname.

Pretend that you have object .a.b.c, and you wish to obtain a name you can associate with that object because you want to create a variable in the current dataset, or a value label, or whatever else, to go along with the object. Later, you want to be able to re-obtain that name from the object's name. .a.b.c.uname will provide that name. The name will be ugly, but it will be unique. The name is not temporary: it will be your responsibility to drop whatever you create with the name later.

Unames are, in fact, based on the object's .ref. That is to say, consider two objects .a.b.c and .d.e and pretend that they refer to the same data; that is, you have previously executed

```
.a.b.c.ref = .d.e.ref
```

or

```
.d.e.ref = .a.b.c.ref
```

In that case, .a.b.c.uname will equal .d.e.uname. The names returned are unique to the data being recorded, not the identifiers used to arrive to the data.

As an example of use, within Stata's graphics system sersets are used to hold the data behind a graph; see [P] **serset**. An overall graph might consist of a number of graphs. In the object nesting for a graph, each individual graph has its own object holding a serset for its use. The individual objects, however, are shared when the same serset will work for two or more graphs, so that the same data are not recorded again and again. That is accomplished by simply setting their .refs equal. Much later in the graphics code, when that code is writing a graph out to disk for saving, it needs to figure out which sersets need to be saved, and it does not wish to write shared sersets out multiple times. Stata finds out what sersets are shared by looking at their unames and, in fact, also uses the unames to help it keep track of which sersets go with which graph.

12.3 Arrays of member variables

Note: The following functions are of little use in class programming. They are of use to those writing utilities to describe the contents of the class system, such as the features documented in [P] **classutil**.

The built-in functions .classmv, .instancemv, and .dynamicmv each return an array containing the .refs of each classwide, instance-specific, and dynamically declared member variables. These array elements may be used as either *lvalues* or *rvalues*.

.superclass also returns an array containing .refs, these being to the classes from which the current object inherited. These array elements may be used as *rvalues* but should not be used as lvalues, since they refer to underlying class definitions themselves.

.classmv, .instancemv, .dynamicmv, and .superclass, although documented as built-in functions, are not really functions but instead are built-in member variables. This means that, unlike built-in functions, their references may be followed by other built-in functions, and it is not an error to type, for instance,

        ... .li.instancemv.arrnels ...

and it would be odd (but allowed) to type

        .myarray = .li.instancemv

It would be odd simply because there is no reason to copy them given you can use them in place.

Each of the above member functions are a little sloppy in that they return nothing (produce an error) if there are no classwide, instance-specific, and dynamically declared member variables, or no inherited classes. This sloppiness has to do with system efficiency, and the proper way to work around the sloppiness is to obtain the number of elements in each array as 0'.classmv.arrnels', 0'.instancemv.arrnels', 0'.dynamicmv.arrnels', and 0'.superclass.arrnels'. If an array does not exist, then nothing will be substituted, and you will still be left with the result 0.

For example, assume .my.c is of type coordinate2, defined as

```
───────────────────────────── coordinate2.class ─────────────────────
version 8
class coordinate2 {
                classwide:
                        double x_origin = 0
                        double y_origin = 0
                instancespecific:
                        double x = 0
                        double y = 0
    }
    ───────────────────────────── coordinate2.class ─────────────────────
```

Then,

referring to	is equivalent to referring to
.my.c.classmv[1]	.my.c.c.x_origin
.my.c.classmv[2]	.my.c.c.y_origin
.my.c.instancemv[1]	.my.c.c.x
.my.c.instancemv[2]	.my.c.c.y

If any member variables were added dynamically using .Dynamic, they could equally well be accessed via .my.c.dynamicmv[] or their names. Either of the above could be used on the left or right of an assignment.

If `coordinate2.class` inherited from another class (it does not), referring to `.coordinate2.superclass[1]` would be equivalent to referring to the inherited class; `.coordinate2.superclass[1].new`, for instance, would be allowed.

These "functions" are mainly of interest to those writing utilities to act on class instances as a general structure.

Appendix A. The finding, loading, and clearing of class definitions

As mentioned, the definition for class *xyz* is located in file *xyz*.`class`.

Stata looks for *xyz*.`class` along the ado-path in the same way it looks for ado-files; see [U] **20.5 Where does Stata look for ado-files?** and see [P] **sysdir**.

Class definitions are loaded automatically, as they are needed, and are cleared from memory as they fall into disuse.

When you type `discard`, all class definitions and all existing instances of classes are dropped; see [P] **discard**.

Appendix B. Jargon

built-in: a member program which is automatically defined, such as `.new`. A **built-in function** is a member program that returns a result without changing the object on which it was run. A **built-in modifier** is a member program that changes the object on which it was run and might return a result as well.

class: a name for which there is a class definition. If we say that `coordinate` is a class, then *coordinate*.`class` is the name of the file that contains its definition.

class instance: a "variable"; a specific, named copy (instance) of a class with its member values filled in; an identifier that is defined to be of *type classname*.

classwide variable: A member variable that is shared by all instances of a class. Its alternative is an instance-specific variable.

inheritance: the ability to define a class in terms of one (single inheritance) or more (multiple inheritance) existing classes. The existing class is typically called the base or super class, and by default, the new class inherits all of the member variables and member programs of the base class.

identifier: the name by which an object is identified, such as `.mybox`, `.mybox.x`, etc.

implied context: the instance on which a member program is run. For example, in `.`*a*`.`*b*`.myprog`, `.`*a*`.`*b* is the implied context, and any references to, say, `.`*x* within the program, are first assumed to, in fact, be references to `.`*a*`.`*b*`.`*x*.

instance: a class instance.

instance-specific variable: a member variable which is unique to each instance of a class; each instance has its own copy of the member variable. Its alternative is a classwide variable.

lvalue: an identifier that may appear to the left of the `=` assignment operator.

member program: a program that is a member of a class or of an instance.

member variable: a variable that is a member of a class or of an instance.

object: a class or an instance; most commonly this is a synonym for an instance, but in formal syntax definitions, if something is said to be allowed to be used with an object, that means it may be used with a class or with an instance.

polymorphism: when a system allows the same program name to invoke different programs according to the class of the object. For example, `.draw` might invoke one program when used on a star object `.mystar.draw` and a different program when used on a box object `.mybox.draw`.

reference: most often the word is used according to its English-language definition, but a `.ref` reference can be used to obtain the data associated with an object. If two identifiers have the same reference, then they are the same object.

return value: what an object returns, which might be of type `double`, `string`, `array`, or *class*. Generally, return value is used in discussions of member programs, but all objects have a return value; they typically return a copy of themselves.

rvalue: an identifier that may appear to the right of the = assignment operator.

scope: how it is determined to what object an identifier references. `.a.b` might be interpreted in the global context and literally mean `.a.b`, or it might be interpreted in an implied context to mean `.impliedcontext.a.b`.

shared object: An object to which two or more different identifiers refer.

type: the type of a member variable, or of a return value, which is either `double`, `string`, `array`, or *class*.

Appendix C. Syntax diagrams

Appendix C.1 Class declaration

class $\left[newclassname\right]$ {

$\quad$ $\left[\underline{\text{class}}\text{wide:}\right]$

$\qquad$ $\left[type\ \ mvname\ \left[=\ rvalue\right]\right]$

$\qquad$ $\left[mvname\ =\ rvalue\right]$

$\qquad$ $\left[\dots\right]$

$\quad$ $\left[\underline{\text{instance}}\text{specific:}\right]$

$\qquad$ $\left[type\ \ mvname\ \left[=\ rvalue\right]\right]$

$\qquad$ $\left[mvname\ =\ rvalue\ \right]$

$\qquad$ $\left[\dots\right]$

$\quad$ } $\left[,\ \text{inherit}(classnamelist)\right]$

where

$\quad$ *mvname* stands for member variable name;

$\quad$ *rvalue* is defined in *Appendix C.2 Assignment*; and

$\quad$ *type* is $\left\{classname\ \mid\ \textbf{double}\ \mid\ \textbf{string}\ \mid\ \textbf{array}\right\}$.

The .Declare built-in may be used to add a member variable to an existing class instance,

> .*id*[.*id*[...]] .Declare *type newmvname* [= *rvalue*]
>
> .*id*[.*id*[...]] .Declare *newmvname* = *rvalue*

where *id* is {*name* | *name*[*exp*] }, the latter being how you refer to an array element; *exp* must evaluate to a number. If *exp* evaluates to a noninteger number, it is truncated.

Appendix C.2 Assignment

> *lvalue* = *rvalue*
>
> *lvalue*.ref = *lvalue*.ref   *(sic)*
>
> *lvalue*.ref = *rvalue*

where

> *lvalue* is .*id*[.*id*[...]]
>
> *rvalue* is

>> " [*string*] "
>>
>> ' " [*string*] " '
>>
>> #
>>
>> *exp*
>>
>> (*exp*)
>>
>> .*id*[.*id*[...]]
>>
>> [.*id*[.*id*[...]]].*pgmname* [*pgm_arguments*]
>>
>> [.*id*[.*id*[...]]].Super[(*classname*)].*pgmname* [*pgm_arguments*]
>>
>> {}
>>
>> {*el* [,*el* [,...]]}

The last two syntaxes concern assignment to arrays; *el* may be

>> *nothing*
>>
>> " [*string*] "
>>
>> ' " [*string*] " '
>>
>> #
>>
>> (*exp*)
>>
>> .*id*[.*id*[...]]
>>
>> [.*id*[.*id*[...]]].*pgmname*
>>
>> [[.*id*[.*id*[...]]].*pgmname* [*pgm_arguments*]]
>>
>> [[.*id*[.*id*[...]]].Super[(*classname*)].*pgmname* [*pgm_arguments*]]

id is {*name* | *name*[*exp*] }, the latter being how you refer to an array element; *exp* must evaluate to a number. If *exp* evaluates to a noninteger number, it is truncated.

Appendix C.3 Macro substitution

Values of member variables or values returned by member programs can be substituted in any Stata command line in any context using macro quoting. The syntax is

... ` .*id* [.*id* [...]] ' ...

... ` [.*id* [.*id* [...]]] .*pgmname* ' ...

... ` [.*id* [.*id* [...]]] .*pgmname* *pgm_arguments* ' ...

... ` [.*id* [.*id* [...]]] .Super [(*classname*)] .*pgmname* ' ...

... ` [.*id* [.*id* [...]]] .Super [(*classname*)] .*pgmname* *pgm_arguments* ' ...

Nested substitutions are allowed. For example,

... ` . ` tmpname ' .x ' ...

... ` ` ref ' ' ...

In the above, perhaps local `tmpname` was obtained from `tempname`, and perhaps local `ref` contains ".myobj.cvalue".

When a class object is quoted, its printable form is substituted. This is defined as

Object type	printable form
string	contents of the string
double	number printed using %18.0g, spaces stripped
array	nothing
classname	nothing or, if member program .macroexpand is defined, the string or double returned

If the quoted reference results in an error, the error message is suppressed and nothing is substituted.

Appendix C.4 Quick summary of built-ins

Built-ins come in two flavors: (1) built-in functions—built-ins that return a result, but do not change the object on which they are run, and (2) built-in modifiers—built-ins that might return a result but more importantly modify, the object on which they are run.

(Continued on next page)

Built-in functions (may be used as *rvalues***)**

.*object*.id	creates new instance of .*object*
.*instance*.copy	makes a copy of .*instance*
.*instance*.ref	for using in assignment by reference
.*object*.objtype	returns "double", "string", "array", or "*classname*"
.*object*.isa	returns "double", "string", "array", "class", or "classtype"
.*object*.classname	returns "*classname*" or " "
.*object*.isofclass *classname*	returns 1 if .*object* is of class type *classname*
.*object*.objkey	returns a string that can be used to reference object outside the implied context
.*object*.uname	returns a string that can be used as name throughout Stata; name corresponds to .*object*'s .ref.
.*object*.ref_n	returns number (double) of total number of identifiers sharing object
.*array*.arrnels	returns number (double) corresponding to largest index of the array assigned
.*array*.arrindexof "*string*"	searches array for first element equal to *string* and returns the index (double) of element or returns 0
.*object*.classmv	returns array containing the .refs of each classwide member of .*object*
.*object*.instancemv	returns array containing the .refs of each instance-specific member of .*object*
.*object*.dynamicmv	returns array containing the .refs of each dynamically added member of .*object*
.*object*.superclass	returns array containing the .refs of each of the classes from which .*object* inherited

Built-in modifiers

.*instance*.Declare *declarator*	returns nothing; adds member variable to instance; see *Class declaration*
.*array*[*exp*].Arrdropel #	returns nothing; drops the specified array element
.*array*.Arrpop	returns nothing; finds the top element and removes it
.*array*.Arrpush "*string*"	returns nothing; adds string to end of array

Also See

Complementary:	[P] **class exit**, [P] **classutil**, [P] **sysdir**
Background:	[U] **20.5 Where does Stata look for ado-files?**

Title

---
class exit — Exit class member program and return result

Syntax

> `class exit` $\big[\textit{rvalue}\big]$

where *rvalue* is

$$" \big[\textit{string}\big]"$$
$$` " \big[\textit{string}\big]" \,'$$
$$\#$$
$$exp$$
$$(exp)$$
$$.id\big[.id\big[\ldots\big]\big] \quad \big[\textit{program\_arguments}\big]$$
$$\{\}$$
$$\{el\big[,el\big[,\ldots\big]\big]\}$$

See [P] **class** for more information on *rvalues*.

Description

`class exit` exits a class member program, and optionally returns the specified result.

`class exit` may be used only from class member programs; see [P] **class**.

Remarks

Do not confuse returned values with return codes, which all Stata programs set, including member programs. Member programs exit when they execute.

Condition	returned value	return code
`class exit` with arguments	as specified	0
`class exit` without arguments	nothing	0
`exit` without arguments	nothing	0
`exit` with arguments	nothing	as specified
`error`	nothing	as specified
command having error	nothing	as appropriate

Any of the preceding are valid ways of exiting a member program, although the last is perhaps best avoided. `class exit` without arguments has the same effect as `exit` without arguments; it does not matter which you use.

Examples

```
class exit sqrt(('.c0.y1'-'.c1.y0')^2 + ('.c0.y1'-'.c1.y0')^2)
class exit "'myresult'"
class exit (.)
class exit "true"
class exit { 'one', 'two'}
class exit .coord
class exit .coord.x
tempname a
...
class exit .'a'
```

Warning: Distinguish carefully between "`class exit .a`" and "`class exit (.a)`". The first returns a copy of the instance `.a`. The second returns a double equal to the extended missing value `.a`.

Also See

Complementary: [P] **class**, [P] **exit**

Title

classutil — Class programming utility

Syntax

classutil drop *instance* [*instance* [...]]

classutil describe *object* [, recurse newok]

classutil dir [*pattern*] [, all detail]

classutil cdir [*pattern*]

classutil which *classname* [, all]

where

object, *instance*, and *classname* may be specified with or without a leading period.

instance and *object* are as defined in [P] **class**: *object* is an *instance* or a *classname*.

pattern is as allowed with the match() function: * means 0 or more characters go here, and ? means exactly one character goes here.

Command cutil is a synonym for classutil.

Description

If you have not yet read [P] **class**, please do so. classutil stands outside the class system, and provides utilities for examining and manipulating what it contains.

classutil drop drops the specified top-level class instances from memory. To drop all class objects, type discard; see [P] **discard**.

classutil describe displays a description of an object.

classutil dir displays a list of all defined objects.

classutil cdir displays a directory of all classes available.

classutil which lists which .class file will correspond to the class specified.

(Continued on next page)

Options

Options for classutil describe

recurse specifies that classutil describe should be repeated on any class instances or definitions that occur within the specified object. Consider the case where you type classutil describe .myobj, and myobj contains myobj.c0, which is a coordinate. Without the recurse option, you will be informed that myobj.c0 is a coordinate, and classutil describe will stop right there.

With the recurse option, you will be informed that myobj.c0 is a coordinate, and then classutil describe will proceed to describe .myobj.c0, just as if you had typed 'classutil describe .myobj.c'. If .myobj.c0 itself includes classes or class instances, they too will be described.

newok is relevant only when describing a class, although it is allowed, and ignored, at other times. newok allows classes to be described even when no instances of the class exist.

When asked to describe a class, Stata needs to access information about that class, and Stata only knows the details about a class when one or more instances of the class exist. If there are no instances, Stata is stuck—it does not know that anything other than a class of that name exists. newok specifies that, in such a circumstance, Stata may temporarily create an instance of the class using .new. If Stata is not allowed to do this, then Stata cannot describe the class. The only reason you are being asked to specify newok is because in some complicated systems, running .new can have side effects, although in most complicated and well-written systems, that will not be the case.

Options for classutil dir

all specifies that class definitions (classes) are to be listed, as well as top-level instances.

detail specifies that a more detailed description of each of the top-level objects should be provided. The default is simply to list the names of the objects in tabular form.

Options for classutil which

all specifies that classutil which list all files along the search path with the specified name, not just the first one (the one Stata will use).

Remarks

Remarks are presented under the headings

classutil drop
classutil describe
classutil dir
classutil cdir
classutil which

classutil drop

`classutil drop` may only be used with top-level instances, top-level meaning that the name has no dots in it other than the leading dot, and instances meaning objects other than classes. If `.mycoord` is of type `coordinate` (or of type `double`), it would be allowed to drop `.mycoord` but not `coordinate` (or `double`). Thus, each of the following would be valid, assuming each is not a class definition:

```
. classutil drop .this
. classutil drop .mycolor
. classutil drop .this .mycolor
```

The following would be invalid, assuming `coordinate` is a class:

```
. classutil drop coordinate
```

There is no need to drop classes, because they are automatically dropped when the last instance of them is dropped.

The following would not be allowed, because they are not top-level objects:

```
. classutil drop .this.that
. classutil drop .mycolor.color.rgb[1]
```

Second, third, and higher level objects are dropped when the top-level objects containing them are dropped.

In all of the examples above, we have shown objects identified with leading periods, as is typical. The period may, however, be omitted.

```
. classutil drop this mycolor
```

❏ Technical Note

Stata's graphics are implemented using classes. If you have a graph displayed, be careful not to drop objects that are not yours. If you drop a system object, Stata will not crash, but `graph` may produce some strange error messages. If you are starting a development project, it is best to [P] **discard** before starting—that will eliminate all objects and clear any graphs. This way, the only objects defined will be the objects you have created.

❏

classutil describe

`classutil describe` presents a description of the object specified. The object may be a class or an instance, and may be of any depth. The following are all valid:

```
. classutil describe coordinate
. classutil describe .this
. classutil describe .color.rgb
. classutil describe .color.rgb[1]
```

The object may be specified with or without a leading period; it makes no difference.

Also see above the descriptions of the `recurse` and `newok` options. The following would also be allowed:

```
. classutil describe coordinate, newok
. classutil describe line, recurse
. classutil describe line, recurse newok
```

classutil dir

classutil dir lists all top-level instances currently defined. Note the emphasis on instances: class definitions (*classes*) are not listed. classutil dir, all will list all objects, including the class definitions.

If option detail is specified, a more detailed description is presented, but it is still less detailed than that provided by classutil describe.

pattern, if specified, is as defined for Stata's match() function: * means 0 or more characters go here, and ? means exactly one character goes here. If *pattern* is specified, only top-level instances or objects matching the pattern will be listed. Examples include

```
. classutil dir
. classutil dir, detail
. classutil dir, detail all
. classutil dir c*
. classutil dir *_g, detail
```

classutil cdir

classutil cdir lists the available classes. Without arguments, all classes are listed. If *pattern* is specified, only classes matching the pattern are listed:

```
. classutil cdir
. classutil cdir c*
. classutil cdir coord*
. classutil cdir *_g
. classutil cdir color_?_?_*
```

pattern is as defined for Stata's match() function: * means 0 or more characters go here, and ? means exactly one character goes here.

classutil cdir obtains the list by searching for *.class files along the ado-path; see [P] **sysdir**.

classutil which

classutil which identifies the .class file associated with class *classname* and displays lines from the file that begin with *!. For example,

```
. classutil which mycolortype
C:\ado\personal\mycolortype.class
*! version 1.0.1
. classutil which badclass
file "badclass.class" not found
r(611);
```

classutil which searches in the standard way for the .class files, which is to say, by looking for it along the ado-path; see [P] **sysdir**.

(Continued on next page)

With the `all` option, `classutil which` lists all files along the search path with the specified name, not just the first one found (the one Stata would use):

```
. classutil which mycolortype
C:\ado\personal\mycolortype.class
*! version 1.0.1
C:\ado\plus\m\mycolortype.class
*! version 1.0.0
```

`*!` lines have to do with versioning. `*` is one of Stata's comment markers, and so `*!` lines are comment lines. `*!` is a convention that some programmers use to record version or author information. If there are no `*!` lines, then only the filename is listed.

Saved Results

`classutil drop` returns nothing.

`classutil describe` returns macro `r(type)` containing `double`, `string`, *classname*, or `array` and in `r(bitype)` the same, except that, if `r(type)=="`*classname*`"`, `r(bitype)` contains `class` or `instance` depending on whether the object is the definition or an instance of the class.

`classutil cdir` returns in macro `r(list)` the names of the available classes matching the pattern specified. The names will not be preceded by a period.

`classutil dir` returns in macro `r(list)` the names of the top-level instances matching the pattern specified as currently defined in memory. The names will be preceded by a period if the corresponding object is an instance, and will be unadorned if the corresponding object is a class definition.

`classutil which` without the `all` option returns in `r(fn)` the name of the file found; the name is not enclosed in quotes. With the `all` option, `classutil which` returns in `r(fn)` the names of all the files found, listed one after the other, and each enclosed in quotes.

Also See

Complementary: [P] **class**

Title

comments — Add comments to programs

Description

This entry provides a quick reference for how to specify comments in programs. See [U] **19.1.2 Comments and blank lines in do-files** for additional details.

Remarks

Comments may be added to programs in three ways:

- begin the line with *;
- begin the comment with //; or
- place the comment between /* and */ delimiters.

Here are examples of each:

```
* a sample analysis job
version 8
use census
/* obtain the summary statistics */
tabulate region  // there are 4 regions in this dataset
summarize marriage

* a sample analysis job
version 8
use /* obtain the summary statistics */ census
tabulate region
//  there are 4 regions in this dataset
summarize marriage
```

Note that the comment indicator * may only be used at the beginning of a line, but it does have the advantage that it can be used interactively. * indicates that the line is to be ignored.

The // comment indicator may be used at the beginning or at the end of a line. Note, however, that if the // indicator is at the end of a line, it must be preceded by one or more blanks. That is, you cannot type the following:

```
tabulate region// there are 4 regions in this dataset
```

// indicates that the rest of the line is to be ignored.

The /* and */ comment delimiter has the advantage that it may be used in the middle of a line, but it is more cumbersome to type than the other two comment indicators. What appears inside /* */ is ignored.

(Continued on next page)

❑ Technical Note

There is a fourth comment indicator /// that instructs Stata to view from /// to the end of a line as a comment, and to join the next line with the current line. For example,

```
args a              /// input parameter for a
     b              /// input parameter for b
     c              //  input parameter for c
```

is equivalent to

```
args a b c
```

/// is one way to make long lines more readable:

```
replace final_result =                      ///
        sqrt(first_side^2 + second_side^2)  ///
        if type == "rectangle"
```

Although another popular method is

```
replace final_result =                      /*
*/ sqrt(first_side^2 + second_side^2)  /*
*/ if type == "rectangle"
```

Like the // comment indicator, the /// indicator must be preceded by one or more blanks.

❑

Also See

Related: [P] **#delimit**

Background: [U] **19.1.2 Comments and blank lines in do-files**,
[U] **21.11.2 Comments and long lines in ado-files**

Title

> **confirm** — Argument verification

Syntax

<u>con</u>firm <u>e</u>xistence $\left[string \right]$

<u>con</u>firm $\left[new \right]$ <u>f</u>ile *filename*

<u>con</u>firm <u>name</u>s *names*

<u>con</u>firm $\left[integer \right]$ <u>n</u>umber $\left[string \right]$

<u>con</u>firm <u>matrix</u> $\left[string \right]$

<u>con</u>firm <u>sca</u>lar $\left[string \right]$

<u>con</u>firm $\left[new \mid numeric \mid \underline{str}ing \mid type \right]$ <u>v</u>ariable $\left[varlist \right]$

where *type is* $\left\{ byte \mid int \mid long \mid float \mid double \mid str\# \right\}$

Description

confirm verifies that the arguments following confirm ... are of the claimed type and issues the appropriate error message and nonzero return code if they are not.

Remarks

confirm is useful in *do-files* and *programs* when you do not want to bother issuing your own error message. confirm can also be combined with capture to detect and handle error conditions before they arise; also see [P] **capture**.

confirm existence

confirm existence displays the message " '' found where something expected", and returns 6 if *string* does not exist.

confirm file

confirm file verifies that *filename* exists and is readable, and issues the appropriate error message and return code if not.

confirm new file verifies that *filename* does not exist and that *filename* could be opened for writing, and issues the appropriate error message and return code if not.

The possible error messages and return codes are

Message	Return Code
'' found where filename expected	7
file ____ not found	601
file ____ already exists	602
file ____ could not be opened	603

Messages 7 and 603 are possible for both confirm file and confirm new file. In the case of confirm new file, message 603 indicates that the filename is invalid or that the specified directory does not exist. For instance, confirm new file *newdir\newfile* generates an error because, while the file would be new, it could not be opened because *newdir* does not exist and so is not a valid file for writing.

confirm names

confirm names verifies that the argument or arguments are valid names according to Stata's naming conventions. It produces the message

$$\text{\textit{text} invalid name}$$

with return code 7 if the name(s) are not valid.

confirm number

confirm number verifies that the argument can be interpreted as a number, such as 1, 5.2, -5.2, or 2.5e+10. It produces the message

$$\{\textit{text} \mid \text{nothing}\} \text{ found where number expected}$$

with return code 7 if not.

confirm integer number adds the restriction that the argument must be an integer, such as 1 or 2.5e+10, but not 5.2 or −5.2. If not, it produces a return code of 7 and a slight variation on the message above:

$$\{\textit{text} \mid \text{nothing}\} \text{ found where integer expected}$$

confirm matrix

confirm matrix verifies that *string* is a matrix. It produces the message

$$\text{matrix \textit{text} not found}$$

with return code 111 if *string* is not a matrix.

confirm scalar

confirm scalar verifies that *string* is a scalar. It produces the message

scalar *text* not found

with return code 111 if *string* is not a scalar.

confirm variable

confirm variable verifies that the *varlist* can be interpreted as an existing *varlist* of any types of variables. If not, the appropriate error message and nonzero return code are returned:

Message	Return Code
'' found where numeric variable expected	7
'' found where string variable expected	7
no variables defined	111
____ not found	111
____ invalid name	198

confirm numeric variable adds the restriction that all the variables are numeric. If the variable exists but is not numeric, the message " '' found where numeric variable expected" is displayed, and return code 7 is issued.

confirm string variable adds the restriction that all the variables are strings. If the variable exists but is not a string variable, then the message " '' found where string variable expected" is displayed, and return code 7 is issued.

confirm *type* variable verifies that all variables are of the indicated storage type. For instance, confirm int variable myvar or confirm float variable myvar thatvar. As with confirm string variable, the additional appropriate message and return code 7 are possible.

confirm new variable verifies that the *varlist* can be interpreted as a new *varlist*. The possible messages and return codes are

Message	Return Code
'' found where varname expected	7
____ already defined	110
____ invalid name	198

▷ Example

confirm is a cheap way to include minimal syntax checking in your programs. For instance, you have written a program that is supposed to take a single, integer argument. Although you do not have to include any syntax checking at all—the program will probably blow up with some error if the argument is incorrect—it is safer to add one line at the top of the program:

```
confirm integer number '1'
```

Now if the first argument is not an integer, you will get a reasonable error message and the program will stop automatically.

◁

▷ Example

More sophisticated programs often combine the `confirm` and `capture` commands. For instance, `ttest` has a complex syntax: If the user types `ttest var=5`, it tests that the mean of `var` is 5 using one set of formulas, and if the user types `ttest var=var2`, it tests equality of means using another set of formulas. Which it does is determined by whether there is a number or a variable to the right of the equal sign. This was done by

```
capture confirm number 'exp'
if _rc==0 {
        (code for test against a constant)
        exit
}
(code for test of two variables)
```

◁

Also See

Complementary: [P] **capture**

Title

> **continue** — Break out of loops

Syntax

continue $\left[\,,\ \underline{\text{break}}\right]$

Description

The continue command within a foreach, forvalues, or while loop breaks execution of the current loop iteration and skips the remaining commands within the loop. Execution resumes at the top of the loop unless the break option is specified, in which case, execution resumes with the command following the looping command. See [P] **foreach**, [P] **forvalues**, and [P] **while** for a discussion of the looping commands.

Options

break indicates that the loop is to be exited. The default is to skip the remaining steps of the current iteration and to resume loop execution again at the top of the loop.

Remarks

We illustrate continue with the forvalues command, but it can be used in the same way with the foreach and while commands.

▷ Example

The following forvalues loop lists the odd and even numbers from one to four.

```
. forvalues x = 1(1)4 {
  2.          if mod(`x',2) {
  3.                  display "`x' is odd"
  4.          }
  5.          else {
  6.                  display "`x' is even"
  7.          }
  8. }
1 is odd
2 is even
3 is odd
4 is even
```

It could be coded using the continue command instead of else.

```
. forvalues x = 1(1)4 {
  2.          if mod(`x',2) {
  3.                  display "`x' is odd"
  4.                  continue
  5.          }
  6.          display "`x' is even"
  7. }
1 is odd
2 is even
3 is odd
4 is even
```

When continue is executed, any remaining statements that exist in the loop are ignored. Execution continues at the top of the loop where, in this case, forvalues sets the next value of 'x', compares that with 4, and then perhaps begins the loop again.

◁

▷ Example

continue, break causes execution of the loop to stop; it prematurely exits the loop.

```
. forvalues x = 6/1000 {
  2.          if mod(`x',2)==0 & mod(`x',3)==0 & mod(`x',5)==0 {
  3.                  display "The least common multiple of 2, 3, and 5 is `x'"
  4.                  continue, break
  5.          }
  6. }
The least common multiple of 2, 3, and 5 is 30
```

Although the forvalues loop was scheduled to go over the values 6 to 1,000, the continue, break statement forced it to stop after 30.

◁

Also See

Complementary:	[P] **foreach**, [P] **forvalues**, [P] **while**
Related:	[P] **if**
Background:	[U] **21 Programming Stata**

Title

creturn — Return c-class values

Syntax

<u>creturn</u> <u>list</u>

Description

Stata's c-class, c(), contains the values of system parameters and settings, along with certain constants such as the value of pi. c() values may be referenced, but may not be assigned.

Remarks

The c-class values are presented under the headings

> *System values*
> *Directories and paths*
> *System limits*
> *Numerical and string limits*
> *Memory settings*
> *Current dataset*
> *Output settings*
> *Graphics settings*
> *Efficiency settings*
> *Network settings*
> *Trace (program debugging) settings*
> *Other settings*
> *Other*

Note that there may be other c-class values that have been added since the printing of this manual. Type `help creturn` for up-to-date information.

System values

c(current_date) returns the current date as a string in the format "*dd Mon yyyy*", where *dd* is the day of the month; *Mon* is one of Jan, Feb, Mar, Apr, May, Jun, Jul, Aug, Sep, Oct, Nov, Dec; and *yyyy* is the year.

Examples:
01 Jan 2003
26 Mar 2003
02 Dec 2002

c(current_time) returns the current time as a string in the format "*hh:mm:ss*", where *hh* is the hour 00 through 23, *mm* is the minute 00 through 59, and *ss* is the second 00 through 59.

Examples:
09:42:55
13:02:01
09:06:46

c(rmsg_time) returns a numeric scalar equal to the elapsed time last reported as a result of set rmsg on.

c(stata_version) returns a numeric scalar equal to the version of Stata that you are running. In Stata 8, this number is 8; in Stata 8.1, 8.1; and in Stata 9, 9. Note that this is the version of Stata that you are running, and not the version being mimicked by the version command.

c(version) returns a numeric scalar equal to the version currently set by the version command; see [P] **version**.

c(born_date) returns a string in the same format as c(current_date) containing the date of the Stata executable that you are running; see [R] **update**.

c(flavor) returns a string containing "Small" or "Intercooled" according to the version of Stata that you are running. Note that c(flavor) == "Intercooled" for both Stata/SE and Intercooled Stata.

c(SE) returns a numeric scalar equal to 1 if you are running Stata/SE and 0 otherwise.

c(mode) returns a string containing "" or "batch", depending on whether Stata was invoked in interactive mode (the usual case) or batch mode (using, perhaps, the -b option of Stata for Unix).

c(console) returns a string containing "" or "console", depending on whether you are running a windowed version of Stata or Stata(console).

c(os) returns a string containing "Windows", "Unix", or "MacOSX", depending on the operating system that you are using. Note that the list of alternatives, while complete as of the date of this writing, may not be complete.

c(osdtl) returns an additional string, depending on the operating system, providing the release number or other details about the operating system. c(osdtl) is often "".

c(machine_type) returns a string attempting to describe the hardware platform, such as "PC", "Macintosh", "Sun SPARC", etc.

c(byteorder) returns a string containing "lohi" or "hilo", depending on the byteorder of the hardware. Consider a two-byte integer. On some computers, the most significant byte is written first, and so x'0001' (meaning the byte 00 followed by 01) would mean the number 1. Such computers are designated "hilo". Other computers write the least-significant byte first, so x'0001' would be 256 and 1 would be x'0100'. Such computers are designated "lohi".

Directories and paths

Note: the directory paths returned below usually end in a directory separator, so if you wish to construct the full path name of file abc.def in directory c(...), you code

        ...'c(...)'abc.def...

and not

        ...'c(...)'/abc.def...

If c(...) returns a directory name, and that directory name does not end in a directory separator, a special note of the fact is made.

(*Continued on next page*)

c(sysdir_stata) returns a string containing the name of the directory (folder) in which Stata is installed. More technically, c(sysdir_stata) returns the STATA directory as defined by sysdir; see [P] **sysdir**.

Example: C:\STATA/

The above example contains no typographical errors. Under Windows, the directory name will end in forward slash. That is so you can code things such as 'c(sysdir_stata)''filename'. If c(sysdir_stata) ended in backslash, Stata's macro expander would interpret the backslash as an escape character, and so not expand 'filename'.

c(sysdir_updates) returns a string containing the name of the directory (folder) in which Stata is to find the official ado-file updates. More technically, c(sysdir_updates) returns the UPDATES directory as defined by sysdir; see [P] **sysdir**.

Example: C:\STATA\ado\updates/

c(sysdir_base) returns a string containing the name of the directory (folder) in which the original official ado-files that were shipped with Stata were installed.

c(sysdir_site) returns a string containing the name of the directory (folder) in which user-written additions may be installed for site-wide use. More technically, c(sysdir_site) returns the SITE directory as defined by sysdir; see [P] **sysdir**.

Example: C:\STATA\ado\site/

c(sysdir_plus) returns a string containing the name of the directory (folder) in which additions written by others may be installed for personal use. More technically, c(sysdir_plus) returns the PLUS directory as defined by sysdir; see [P] **sysdir**.

Example: C:\ado\plus/

c(sysdir_personal) returns a string containing the name of the directory (folder) in which additions written by you may be installed. More technically, c(sysdir_personal) returns the PERSONAL directory as defined by sysdir; see [P] **sysdir**.

Example: C:\ado\personal/

c(sysdir_oldplace) identifies another directory in which personally written ado-files might be installed. c(sysdir_oldplace) has to do with compatibility with very ancient versions of Stata.

c(adopath) returns a string containing the directories that are to be searched whenever Stata is attempting to locate an ado-file. The path elements are separated by a semicolon (;), and the elements themselves may be directory names, "." to indicate the current directory, or sysdir references.

Example: UPDATES;BASE;SITE;.;PERSONAL;PLUS;OLDPLACE

c(pwd) returns a string containing the current (working) directory.

Example: C:\data

Note that c(pwd) does not end in a directory separator, so, in a program, if you wished to save the name of the file abc.def prefixed by the current directory (say, because you were about to change directories and still wanted to refer to the file), you would code

```
local file "'c(pwd)'/abc.def"
```

or

```
local file "'c(pwd)''c(dirsep)'abc.def"
```

The second form is to be slightly preferred if your interest is in constructing "pretty" filenames, but the first form is acceptable because all Statas understand forward slash (/) as a directory separator.

`c(dirsep)` returns a string containing "/" for Macintosh, Unix, and Windows operating systems.

Example: /

Note that for Windows operating systems, forward slash (/) is returned rather than backslash (\). Stata for Windows understands both, but, in programs, use of forward slash is recommended because backslash can interfere with Stata's interpretation of macro expansion characters. Do not be concerned if the result of your code is a mix of backslash and forward slash characters, such as \a\b/myfile.dta; Stata will understand it just as it would understand /a/b/myfile.dta or \a\b\myfile.dta.

System limits

`c(max_N_theory)` and `c(max_N_current)` each return a numeric scalar reporting the maximum number of observations allowed. `c(mac_N_theory)` and `c(max_N_current)` are seldom equal.

`c(max_N_theory)` reports the maximum number of observations that Stata can process if it has enough memory. This is usually 2,147,483,647.

`c(max_N_current)` reports the maximum number of observations that Stata can process given the current amount of memory allocated to Stata. You can change the amount of memory, and hence this number, using the set memory command; see [R] **memory**.

`c(max_k_theory)` and `c(max_k_current)` each return a numeric scalar reporting the maximum number of variables allowed. `c(max_k_theory)` returns the theoretical maximum number of variables allowed. `c(max_k_current)` returns the current maximum possible due to the number of observations you currently have in memory, and may be the same as or less than, but never more than, `c(max_k_theory)`. In the case of Stata/SE, `c(max_k_theory)` is determined by the set maxvar command.

`c(max_width_theory)` and `c(max_width_current)` each return a numeric scalar equal to the maximum width of an observation. The width of an observation is defined as the sum of the byte lengths of its individual variables. If you had a dataset with 2 int variables, 3 floats, 1 double, and a str20 variable, the width of the dataset would be $2*2 + 3*4 + 8 + 20 = 44$ bytes.

`c(max_width_theory)` returns the theoretical maximum width allowed.
`c(max_width_current)` returns the current maximum possible due to the number of observations you currently have in memory, and may be the same as or less than, but never more than, `c(max_width_theory)`. In the case of Stata/SE, `c(max_width_theory)` is affected by the set maxvar command.

`c(min_matsize)` and `c(max_matsize)` each return a numeric scalar reporting the minimum and maximum values to which matsize may be set. If the version of Stata you are running does not allow the setting of matsize, the two values will be equal. `c(matsize)`, documented under *Memory settings* below, returns the current value of matsize.

`c(max_macrolen)` and `c(macrolen)` each return a numeric scalar reporting the maximum length of macros. `c(max_macrolen)` and `c(macrolen)` may not be equal under Stata/SE, and will be equal otherwise. For Stata/SE, macrolen is set according to maxvar: the length is long enough to hold a macro referring to every variable in the dataset.

`c(max_cmdlen)` and `c(cmdlen)` each return a numeric scalar reporting the maximum length of a Stata command. `c(max_cmdlen)` and `c(cmdlen)` may not be equal under Stata/SE, and will be equal otherwise. For Stata/SE, cmdlen is set according to maxvar: the length is long enough to hold a command referring to every variable in the dataset.

c(namelen) returns a numeric scalar equal to 32, which is the current maximum length of names in Stata.

Numerical and string limits

c(mindouble), c(maxdouble), and c(epsdouble) each return a numeric scalar. c(mindouble) is the largest negative number that can be stored in the 8-byte double storage type. c(maxdouble) is the largest positive number that can be stored in a double. c(epsdouble) is the smallest nonzero, positive number (epsilon) that when added to 1 and stored as a double does not equal 1.

c(minfloat), c(maxfloat), and c(epsfloat) each return a numeric scalar that reports for the 4-byte float storage type what c(mindouble), c(maxdouble), and c(epsdouble) report for double.

c(minlong) and c(maxlong) return scalars reporting the largest negative number and the largest positive number that can be stored in the 4-byte, integer long storage type. Note that there is no c(epslong) but, if there were, it would return 1.

c(minint) and c(maxint) return scalars reporting the largest negative number and the largest positive number that can be stored in the 2-byte, integer int storage type.

c(minbyte) and c(maxbyte) return scalars reporting the largest negative number and the largest positive number that can be stored in the 1-byte, integer byte storage type.

c(maxstrvarlen) returns the longest str# string storage type allowed, which will be 244 in the case of Stata/SE and 80 otherwise. Do not confuse c(maxstrvarlen) with c(macrolen). c(maxstrvarlen) corresponds to string variables stored in the data.

Memory settings

c(memory) returns a numeric scalar reporting the amount of memory allocated to Stata's data area, as set by set memory. The number is returned in bytes.

c(maxvar) returns a numeric scalar reporting the maximum number of variables currently allowed in a dataset, as set by set maxvar if you are running Stata/SE. Otherwise, c(maxvar) is a constant.

c(matsize) returns a numeric scalar reporting the current value of matsize, as set by set matsize.

Current dataset

c(N) returns a numeric scalar equal to _N, the number of observations in the dataset in memory. In an expression context, it makes no difference whether you refer to _N or c(N). The advantage of c(N) is in nonexpression contexts. Say you are calling a subroutine mysub that takes as an argument the number of observations in the dataset. In that case, you could code

```
        local nobs = _N
        mysub 'nobs'
```

   or

```
        mysub 'c(N)'
```

The second requires less typing.

c(k) returns a numeric scalar equal to the number of variables in the dataset in memory. c(k) is equal to r(k) returned by describe.

c(width) returns a numeric scalar equal to the width, in bytes, of the dataset in memory. If you had a dataset with 2 int variables, 3 floats, 1 double, and a str20 variable, the width of the dataset would be $2*2 + 3*4 + 8 + 20 = 44$ bytes. c(width) is equal to r(width), which is returned by describe.

c(changed) returns a numeric scalar equal to 0 if the dataset in memory has not changed since it was last saved and 1 otherwise. c(changed) is equal to r(changed) returned by describe.

c(filename) returns a string containing the filename last specified with a use or save, such as "http://www.stata-press.com/data/r8/auto.dta". c(filename) is equal to $S_FN.

c(filedate) returns a string containing the date and time the file in c(filename) was last saved, such as "7 Jul 2002 13:51". c(filedate) is equal to $S_FNDATE.

Output settings

c(more) returns a string containing "on" or "off" according to the current set more setting.

c(rmsg) returns a string containing "on" or "off" according to the current set rmsg setting.

c(dp) returns a string containing "period" or "comma" according to the current set dp setting.

c(linesize) returns a numeric scalar equal to the current set linesize setting.

c(pagesize) returns a numeric scalar equal to the current set pagesize setting.

c(logtype) returns a string containing "smcl" or "text" according to the current set logtype setting.

c(linegap) returns a numeric scalar equal to the current set linegap setting. If set linegap is irrelevant under the version of Stata that you are running, c(linegap) returns a system missing value.

c(scrollbufsize) returns a numeric scalar equal to the current set scrollbufsize setting. If set scrollbufsize is irrelevant under the version of Stata that you are running, c(scrollbufsize) returns a system missing value.

c(varlabelpos) returns a numeric scalar equal to the current set varlabelpos setting. If set varlabelpos is irrelevant under the version of Stata that you are running, c(varlabelpos) returns a system missing value.

c(reventries) (Windows only) returns a numeric scalar containing the maximum number of commands stored by the Review window.

Graphics settings

c(graphics) returns a string containing "on" or "off" according to the current set graphics setting.

c(scheme) returns the name of the current set scheme.

c(printcolor) returns "automatic", "asis", or "grayscale" according to the current set printcolor setting.

Efficiency settings

c(adosize) returns a numeric scalar equal to the current set adosize setting.

c(maxdb) returns a numeric scalar containing the maximum number of dialog boxes whose contents are remembered from one invocation to the next during a session.

c(virtual) returns a string containing "on" or "off" according to the current set virtual setting.

Network settings

c(checksum) returns a string containing "on" or "off" according to the current set checksum setting.

c(timeout1) returns a numeric scalar equal to the current set timeout1 setting.

c(timeout2) returns a numeric scalar equal to the current set timeout2 setting.

c(httpproxy) returns a string containing "on" or "off" according to the current set httpproxy setting.

c(httpproxyhost) returns a string containing the name of the proxy host or "" if no proxy host is set. c(httpproxyhost) is only relevant if c(httpproxy) = "on".

c(httpproxyport) returns a numeric scalar equal to the proxy port number. c(httpproxyport) is only relevant if c(httpproxy) = "on".

c(httpproxyauth) returns a string containing "on" or "off" according to the current set httpproxyauth setting. c(httpproxyauth) is only relevant if c(httpproxy) = "on".

c(httpproxyuser) returns a string containing the name of the proxy user, if one is set, or "" otherwise. c(httpproxyuser) is only relevant if c(httpproxy) = "on" and c(httpproxyauth) = "on".

c(httpproxypw) returns a string containing "*" if a password is set or "" otherwise. c(httpproxypw) is only relevant if c(httpproxy) = "on" and c(httpproxyauth) = "on".

Trace (program debugging) settings

c(trace) returns a string containing "on" or "off" according to the current set trace setting.

c(tracedepth) returns a numeric scalar reporting the current set tracedepth setting.

c(tracesep) returns a string containing "on" or "off" according to the current set tracesep setting.

c(traceindent) returns a string containing "on" or "off" according to the current set traceindent setting.

c(traceexpand) returns a string containing "on" or "off" according to the current set traceexpand setting.

c(tracenumber) returns a string containing "on" or "off" according to the current set tracenumber setting.

Other settings

c(type) returns a string containing "float" or "double" according to the current set type setting.

c(level) returns a numeric scalar equal to the current set level setting.

c(seed) returns a string containing the current set seed setting. This records the current state of the random number generator uniform().

c(searchdefault) returns a string containing "local", "net", or "all" according to the current search default setting.

Other

c(pi) returns a numerical scalar equal to _pi, the value of the ratio of the circumference to the diameter of a circle. In an expression context, it makes no difference whether you use c(pi) or _pi. c(pi), however, may be used (enclosed in single quotes) in other contexts.

c(rc) returns a numerical scalar equal to _rc, the value set by the capture command. In an expression context, it makes no difference whether you use c(rc) or _rc. c(rc), however, may be used (enclosed in single quotes) in other contexts. This is less important than it sounds because you could just as easily type '=_rc'.

Also See

Related: [P] **return**,

[R] **query**, [R] **set**

Title

#delimit — Change delimiter

Syntax

#delimit { cr | ; }

Description

The #delimit command resets the character that marks the end of a command. It may be used only in do-files or ado-files.

Remarks

#delimit (pronounced *pound-delimit*) is a Stata preprocessor command. *#commands* do not generate a return code, nor do they generate ordinary Stata errors. The only error message associated with *#commands* is "unrecognized #command".

Commands given from the console are always executed when you press carriage return, also called the *Enter* key. #delimit cannot be used interactively, so you cannot change Stata's interactive behavior.

Commands in a do-file, however, may be delimited with a carriage return or a semicolon. When a do-file begins, the delimiter is carriage return. The command '#delimit ;' changes the delimiter to a semicolon. To restore the carriage return delimiter inside a file, use #delimit cr.

When a do-file begins execution, the delimiter is automatically set to carriage return even if it was called from another do-file that set the delimiter to semicolon. Also, the current do-file need not worry about restoring the delimiter to what it was because Stata will do that automatically.

▷ Example

```
/*
     When the do-file begins, the delimiter is carriage return:
*/
use basedata, clear
/*
     The last command loaded our data.
     Let's now change the delimiter:
*/
```

```
#delimit ;
summarize sex
           salary ;
/*
    Since the delimiter is semicolon, it doesn't matter that our
    command took two lines.
    We can change the delimiter back:
*/
#delimit cr
summarize sex salary
/*
    Now our lines once again end on return.  The semicolon delimiter
    is often used when loading programs:
*/
capture program drop fix
program fix
    confirm var '1'
    #delimit ;
    replace '1' = .  if salary>=. | salary==0 |
                      hours>=.  | hours==0 ;
    #delimit cr
end
fix var1
fix var2
```
◁

❑ Technical Note

Just because you have long lines does not mean you must change the delimiter to semicolon. Stata does not care that the line is long. Also, there are other ways to indicate that more than one physical line is one logical line. One popular choice is ///:

```
replace '1' = .  if salary>=. | salary==0 | ///
                  hours>=.  | hours==0
```

See [P] comments.

❑

Also See

Background: [U] **19.1.3 Long lines in do-files**,

[U] **21.11.2 Comments and long lines in ado-files**,

[P] **comments**

Title

dialogs — Dialog programming

Description

Dialog-box programs—also called dialog resource files—allow you to define the appearance of a dialog box, to specify how the controls of the dialog box interact with how the user fills them in (such as the hiding or disabling of specific areas), and to specify the ultimate action that is to be taken (such as running a Stata command) when the user presses **OK** or **Submit**.

Remarks

Remarks are presented under the headings

1. Introduction
2. Concepts
   2.1 Organization of the .dlg file
   2.2 Position, sizes, and the DEFINE command
   2.3 Default values
   2.4 Memory (recollection)
   2.5 I-actions and member functions
   2.6 U-actions and communication options
   2.7 The distinction between i-actions and u-actions
   2.8 Error and consistency checking
3. Commands
   3.1 VERSION
   3.2 INCLUDE
   3.3 DEFINE
   3.4 POSITION
   3.5 LIST
   3.6 DIALOG
       3.6.1 CHECKBOX on/off input control
       3.6.2 RADIO on/off input control
       3.6.3 SPINNER numeric input control
       3.6.4 EDIT string input control
       3.6.5 VARLIST and VARNAME string input controls
       3.6.6 FILE string input control
       3.6.7 LISTBOX list input control
       3.6.8 COMBOBOX list input control
       3.6.9 BUTTON special input control
       3.6.10 TEXT static control
       3.6.11 GROUPBOX static control
       3.6.12 FRAME static control
   3.7 OK, SUBMIT, and CANCEL u-action buttons
   3.8 HELP and RESET helper buttons
4. SCRIPT

(Continued on next page)

5. PROGRAM
  5.1 Concepts
    5.1.1 Vnames
    5.1.2 Enames
    5.1.3 rstrings: cmdstring and optstring
    5.1.4 Adding to an rstring
  5.2 Flow control commands
    5.2.1 if
    5.2.2 call
    5.2.3 exit
  5.3 Error checking and presentation commands
    5.3.1 require
    5.3.2 stopbox
  5.4 Command-construction commands
    5.4.1 by
    5.4.2 bysort
    5.4.3 put
    5.4.4 varlist
    5.4.5 weight
    5.4.6 ifexp
    5.4.7 inrange
    5.4.8 beginoptions and endoptions
      5.4.8.1 option
      5.4.8.2 optionarg
    5.4.9 allowxi and xi
  5.5 Command-execution commands
    5.5.1 stata
    5.5.2 clear
6. Example
Appendix A: Jargon
Appendix B: Class definition of dialog boxes
Appendix C: Interface guidelines for dialog boxes

1. Introduction

At a programming level, the purpose of a dialog box is to produce a Stata command to be executed. Along the way, it is to be hoped that it provides the user with an intuitive and consistent experience—that is your job as a dialog-box programmer—but the ultimate output is to be

    `list mpg weight` or `regress mpg weight if foreign` or `append using myfile`

or whatever other Stata command is appropriate. Dialog boxes are limited to executing a single Stata command, but that does not limit what can be done, because that Stata command can be an ado-file that you also write. (Actually, there is another way around the one-command limit, which we will discuss in *5.1.3 rstring: cmdstring and optstring.*)

This ultimate result is called the dialog box's *u-action*.

The u-action of the dialog box is determined by the code you write, called dialog code, which you store in a `.dlg` file. The name of the `.dlg` file is important, because it determines the name of the dialog box. When a user types

    `. db regress`

it is `regress.dlg` that is executed. The file is found in the same way as Stata looks for ado-files—by looking along the ado-path; see [P] **sysdir**. The fact that `regress.dlg` happens to run `regress` commands is due to the dialog code that appears inside the `regress.dlg` file. `regress.dlg` could just as well execute `probit` commands or even `merge` commands if the code were written differently.

.dlg files have three purposes:

1. to describe how the dialogs are to look;

2. to describe how the input controls of the dialogs are to interact with each other; and

3. to describe how the u-action is to be constructed from the user's input.

Items (1) and (2) determine how intuitive and consistent the user finds the experience. Item (3) determines what the dialog box does. Item (2) refers to how some fields are disabled or hidden and so cannot be mistakenly filled in until the user clicks something, checks something, or fills in a certain result.

2. Concepts

A dialog box is composed of *controls*. "Controls" is the technical jargon for the things such as edit fields, checkboxes, etc. that the user fills in. Actually, those are called *input controls*, because there are other types of "controls" that the user does not fill in, called *static controls*. Static controls are the fixed text and lines that appear in the dialog. Calling them controls is admittedly confusing, but that is what they are called and dialog programming is loaded with other jargon as well. See *Appendix A* below for the definitions of the jargon we will use.

In the jargon we use, a *dialog box* is comprised of *dialogs*, and *dialogs* are comprised of *controls*. When a dialog box contains multiple dialogs, only one dialog is shown at a time. In this case, access to the dialogs is made possible through small tabs. Clicking on the tab associated with a dialog makes that dialog active.

The dialog box may contain the *helper buttons* Help (shown as a small button with a question mark on it) and Reset (shown as a small button with an **R** on it). These buttons appear in the dialog box—not the individual dialogs—and so in a multiple-dialog dialog box, they appear regardless of the dialog (tab) selected.

The Help helper button displays a help file associated with the dialog box.

The Reset helper button resets the dialog box to its initial state. Each time a user invokes a particular dialog box, it will remember the values last set for its controls. The reset button allows the user to restore the default values for all controls on the dialog box.

The dialog box may also include the *u-action buttons* OK, Submit, and Cancel. Like the helper buttons, u-action buttons appear in the dialog box—not the individual dialogs—and so in a multiple-dialog dialog box, they appear regardless of the dialog (tab) selected.

The OK u-action button means to construct the u-action and send it off to Stata for execution and, in addition, to close the dialog box.

The Submit u-action button means to construct the u-action and send it off to Stata for execution but to leave up the dialog box.

The Cancel u-action button means to forget it; construct no u-action and close the dialog box.

A dialog box does not have to have all these u-action buttons, but it will need at least one.

(Continued on next page)

Thus, the nesting is

> Dialog box, *which contains*
>> Dialog 1, *which contains*
>>> input controls *and* static controls
>>
>> Dialog 2, *which is optional and which, if defined, contains*
>>> input controls *and* static controls
>>
>> [. . .]
>> Helper buttons, *which are optional and which, if defined, contain*
>>> [Help *button*]
>>> [Reset *button*]
>>
>> U-action buttons, *which contain*
>>> [OK *button*]
>>> [Submit *button*]
>>> [Cancel *button*]

or, said differently,

1. a dialog box must have at least one dialog, must have one set of u-action buttons, and may have helper buttons;

2. a dialog must have at least one control, and it may have many controls; and

3. the u-action buttons may include any of OK, Submit, and Cancel, and must include at least one of them.

Here is a simple .dlg file that will execute the kappa command, although it does not allow if *exp* and in *range*:

```
———————————————— mykappa.dlg ————————
// ----------------- set version number and define size of box ---------
VERSION 8
POSITION . . 290 200

// ---------------------------------------- define a dialog ---------
DIALOG main, label("kappa - Interrater agreement")
BEGIN
        TEXT    tx_var 10  10 270 ., label("frequency variables:")
        VARLIST vl_var  @ +20   @ ., label("frequencies")
END

// -------------------- define the u-action and helper buttons ---------
OK     ok1, label("OK")
CANCEL can1, label("Cancel")
SUBMIT sub1, label("Submit")
HELP   hlp1, view("help kappa")
RESET  res1

// ------------------------- define how to assemble u-action ---------
PROGRAM command
BEGIN
        put "kappa "
        varlist main.vl_var
END
———————————————— mykappa.dlg ————————
```

(Continued on next page)

2.1 Organization of the .dlg file

A `.dlg` file consists of seven parts, although some of them are optional:

```
─────────────────── dialogboxname.dlg ───────────────────
VERSION 8                Part 1: version number
POSITION ...             Part 2: set size of dialog box
DEFINE ...               Part 3, optional: common definitions
LIST ...
DIALOG ...               Part 4: dialog definitions
    BEGIN
        FILE ...              ... which contain input controls
        BUTTON ...
        CHECKBOX ...
        COMBOBOX ...
        EDIT ...
        LISTBOX ...
        RADIO ...
        SPINNER ...
        VARLIST ...
        VARNAME ...
        FRAME ...             ... and static controls
        GROUPBOX ...
        TEXT ...
    END
        repeat DIALOG... BEGIN... END  as necessary
SCRIPT ...               Part 5, optional: i-action definitions
    BEGIN                     ... usually done as scripts
        ...
    END
PROGRAM ...                   ... but sometimes as programs
    BEGIN
        ...
    END
OK ...                   Part 6: u-action and helper button definitions
CANCEL ...
SUBMIT ...
HELP ...
RESET ...
PROGRAM command          Part 7: u-action definition
    BEGIN
        ...
    END
─────────────────── dialogboxname.dlg ───────────────────
```

The VERSION statement must appear at the top; the other parts may appear in any order.

I-actions, mentioned in *Part 5*, are intermediate actions such as hiding or showing, disabling or enabling a control, or the opening of the Viewer to display something, etc., while leaving the dialog up and still waiting for the user to fill in more or press a u-action button.

2.2 Positions, sizes, and the DEFINE command

Part of specifying how a dialog is to appear is defining where things go and how big they are.

Positions are indicated by a pair of numbers, *x* and *y*. They are measured in pixels, and are interpreted as being measured from the top-left corner: *x* is how far to the right and *y* is how far down.

Sizes are similarly indicated by a pair of numbers, *xsize* and *ysize*. They, too, are measured in pixels, and indicate the size starting at the top-left corner of the object.

Any command that needs a position or a size always takes all four numbers—position and size—and you must specify all four. In addition to each element being allowed to be a number, some extra codes are allowed. A position or size element is defined as

> **#**   any unsigned integer number, such as 0, 1, 10, 200, . . .
>
> **.**   (period) meaning the context-specific default value for whatever is this position/size element. . is allowed only with heights of controls (remember, heights are measured down) and for the initial position of a dialog box.
>
> **@**   means the previous value for this position/size element. If @ is used for an *x* or a *y*, then the *x* or *y* from the preceding command will be used. If @ is used for a *xsize* or a *ysize*, then the previous *xsize* or *ysize* will be used.
>
> **+#**   means a positive offset from the last value (meaning to the right or down or bigger). If +10 is used for *x*, the result will be 10 pixels to the right of the previous. If +10 were used for a *ysize*, it would mean 10 pixels taller.
>
> **-#**   means a negative offset from the last value (meaning to the left or up or smaller). If -10 is used for *y*, the result will be 10 pixels above the previous. If -10 were used for a *xsize*, it would mean 10 pixels narrower.
>
> *name*   means the value last recorded for *name* by the DEFINE command.

The DEFINE command has syntax

DEFINE *name* $\left\{ . \mid \# \mid +\# \mid -\# \mid @x \mid @y \mid \underline{@xsize} \mid \underline{@ysize} \right\}$

and may appear anywhere in our dialog code, even inside the BEGIN/END of DIALOG. Anywhere you need to specify a position or size element, you can use a *name* defined by DEFINE.

The first four possibilities for how *name* is defined have the obvious meaning: . means default, # means number specified, +# means positive offset, and -# means negative offset. The other four possibilities, @x, @y, @xsize, and @ysize, refer to the previous *x*, *y*, *xsize*, and *ysize* values, with previous meaning previous at the time the DEFINE command was issued.

(Continued on next page)

2.3 Default values

Another issue concerning the programming of input controls is loading them with their initial, or default, values. For instance, perhaps we want one checkbox checked and another unchecked, and we want an edit field filled in with "Default title".

The syntax of the CHECKBOX command, which creates checkboxes, is

CHECKBOX ... $\left[\right.$, ...default(*defnumval*) ...$\left.\right]$

In checkboxes, the default() option specifies how the box is to initially be filled in and 1 corresponds to checked and 0 to unchecked.

In the syntax of EDIT, which creates edit fields, is

EDIT ... $\left[\right.$, ...default(*defstrval*) ...$\left.\right]$

In edit fields, default() specifies what the box is initially to contain.

Wherever *defnumval* appears in a syntax diagram, you may type

defnumval	meaning
#	meaning the number specified
literal #	same as #
c(*name*)	value of c(*name*), see [P] **creturn**
r(*name*)	value of r(*name*), see [P] **return**
e(*name*)	value of e(*name*), see [P] **ereturn**
s(*name*)	value of s(*name*), see [P] **return**
global *name*	value of global macro $*name*

Wherever *defstrval* appears in a syntax diagram, you may type

defstrval	meaning
string	meaning the string specified
literal *string*	same as *string*
c(*name*)	contents of c(*name*), see [P] **creturn**
r(*name*)	contents of r(*name*), see [P] **return**
e(*name*)	contents of e(*name*), see [P] **ereturn**
s(*name*)	contents of s(*name*), see [P] **return**
char *varname*[*charname*]	value of characteristic, see [P] **char**
global *name*	contents of global macro $*name*

Note: If *string* is enclosed in double quotes (simple or compound), the first set of such quotes are stripped.

(Continued on next page)

List and combo boxes present the user with a list of things from which they may choose. In the jargon, rather than specifying their initial or default values, the boxes are said to be populated. The syntax for creating a list-box input control is

> LISTBOX ... [, ... contents(*conspec*) ...]

Wherever a *conspec* appears in a syntax diagram, you may type

list *listname*

> populates the box with the specified list, which you create separately using the LIST command. LIST has the following syntax:
>
>   LIST
>   BEGIN
>   *item to appear*
>   *item to appear*
>   ...
>   END

matrix

> populates the box with the names of all matrices currently defined in Stata.

vector

> populates the box with the names of all $1 \times k$ and $k \times 1$ matrices currently defined in Stata.

row

> populates the box with the names of all $1 \times k$ matrices currently defined in Stata.

column

> populates the box with the names of all $k \times 1$ matrices currently defined in Stata.

square

> populates the box with the names of all $k \times k$ matrices currently defined in Stata.

scalar

> populates the box with the names of all scalars currently defined in Stata.

constraint

> populates the box with the names of all constraints currently defined in Stata.

estimates

> populates the box with the names of all saved estimates currently defined in Stata.

char *varname*[*charname*]

> populates the box with the elements of the characteristic *varname*[*charname*], parsed on spaces.

e(*name*)

> populates the box with the elements of e(*name*), parsed on spaces.

global

> populates the box with the names of all global macros currently defined in Stata.

valuelabels

> populates the box with the names of all values labels currently defined in Stata.

(Continued on next page)

2.4 Memory (recollection)

All the input control commands have a `default()` or `contents()` option that specifies how the control is to be filled in; for example,

CHECKBOX ... $\Big[$, ... default(*defnumval*) ... $\Big]$

In this command, if *defnumval* evaluates to 0, the checkbox starts by being unchecked. Otherwise, it is checked. If `default()` is not specified, the box starts as being unchecked.

The emphasis is on starts: dialogs remember how they were last filled in during a session, so the next time the user invokes the dialog box that contains this CHECKBOX command, the `default()` option will be ignored in favor of how the user last left it. That is, the setting will be remembered unless you, the dialog-box programmer, specify the input control's `nomemory` option:

CHECKBOX ... $\Big[$, ... default(*defnumval*) nomemory ... $\Big]$

`nomemory` specifies that the dialog-box manager is not to remember between invocations how the control is filled in; it is always to reset it according to the default, whether than default is explicitly specified or implied.

Whether or not you specify `nomemory`, explicit or implicit defaults are also restored when the user presses the Reset helper button.

The contents of dialog boxes are only remembered during a session, not between them. Within a session, the [P] **discard** command causes Stata to forget the contents of all dialog boxes.

The issue of initialization and memory is in fact more complicated than it first appears. Consider a list box. A list box is populated, and might be populated with the currently saved estimates. If the dialog box containing this list box is closed and reopened, the available estimates may have changed. Therefore, list boxes are always repopulated according to the instructions given. Even so, list boxes do remember the choice that was made. If that choice is still among the possibilities, that choice will be the one chosen unless `nomemory` is specified; otherwise, the choice goes back to being the default—the first choice in the list of alternatives.

The same issues arise with combo boxes, and that is why some controls have the option `default()` and others `contents()`. `default()` is used once, and, after that, memory is substituted (unless `nomemory` is specified). `contents()` is always used—`nomemory` or not—but the choice made is remembered (unless `nomemory` is specified).

(Continued on next page)

2.5 I-actions and member functions

I-actions—intermediate actions—refer to all actions taken along the way to producing the u-action. An i-action might disable or hide controls when another control is checked or unchecked, although there are lots of other possibilities. I-actions are always optional.

I-actions are invoked by on*() options—options that begin with the letters "on". For instance, the syntax for the CHECKBOX command—the command for defining a checkbox control—is

CHECKBOX *controlname* ... $\Big[$, ...onclickon(*iaction*) onclickoff(*iaction*) ... $\Big]$

onclickon() is the i-action to be taken when the checkbox is checked, and onclickoff() is the i-action for when the checkbox is unchecked. You do not have to fill in the onclickon() and onclickoff() options—the checkbox will work fine taking no i-actions—but you may fill them in if you want, say, to disable or to enable other controls when this control is checked. For instance, you might code

CHECKBOX sw2 ... , onclickon(d2.sw3.show) onclickoff(d2.sw3.hide) ...

d2.sw3 is how you refer to the control named sw3 in the dialog d2 (for instance, the control we just defined is named sw2). hide and show are called member functions. hide is the member function that hides a control and show is its inverse. Controls have other member functions as well; what member functions are available is documented with the command that creates the specific control.

Lots of commands have on*() options that allow the specification of i-actions. When *iaction* appears in a syntax diagram, what is allowed is

. (period)
   Do nothing; take no action. This is the default if you do not specify the on*() option.

gaction *dialogname*.*controlname*.*memberfunction* $\big[$*arguments*$\big]$
   Execute the specified *memberfunction* on the specified control, where *memberfunction* may be

   $\big\{$hide$\,|\,$show$\,|\,$disable$\,|\,$enable$\,|\,$*something_else* $\big[$*arguments*$\big]\big\}$

   All controls provide the *memberfunctions* hide, show, disable, and enable, and some controls make other, special *memberfunctions* available, too.

   hide specifies that the control is to disappear from view (if it has not already done so). show specifies that it is to reappear (if it is not already visible).

   disable specifies that the control is to be disabled (if is it not already). enable specifies that it is to be enabled (if it is not already).

   arguments are allowed in case the *memberfunction* needs them. For instance, CHECKBOX provides a special *memberfunction*

   setlabel *string*

   which sets the text shown next to the checkbox, and so you might specify onclickon(`"gaction main.robust.setlabel "Robust VCE""`). Anytime a *string* is required, you must place quotes around it if *string* contains a space. When specifying an *iaction* inside the parentheses of an option, it is easier to leave them off unless they are required due to a space. That is because, if you do specify them, you must enclose the entire contents of the option in compound double quotes as in the example above.

dialogname.*controlname*.*memberfunction* $\big[$*arguments*$\big]$
   Same as gaction; the gaction is optional.

action *memberfunction* [*arguments*]
   Same as gaction *currentdialog.currentcontrol.memberfunction*; executes the specified *member-function* on the current control.

view *topic*
   Display *topic* in viewer; see [R] **view**.

script *scriptname*
   Execute the specified script. A script is a set of lines, each specifying an *iaction*. So, if you wanted to disable three things, gaction would be insufficient. You would instead define a script containing the three gaction lines.

program *programname*
   Execute the specified dialog-box program. Programs can do more than scripts because they provide if-statement flow of control (among other things), but they are more difficult to write, and rarely are the extra capabilities needed when specifying i-actions.

2.6 U-actions and communication options

Remember that the ultimate goal of a dialog box is to construct a u-action—a Stata command to be executed. What that command should be depends on how the user fills in the dialog box.

You, the dialog-box programmer, construct that command by writing a dialog-box program, also known as a PROGRAM. You arrange that the program be invoked by specifying the uaction() option allowed with OK, SUBMIT, and CANCEL u-action buttons. For instance, the syntax of OK is

   OK ... [, ...uaction(*pgmname*) target(*target*) ...]

pgmname is the name of the dialog program you write and target() specifies how the command constructed by *pgmname* is to be executed. In most cases, you will simply want Stata to execute the command, which could be coded target(stata), but since that is the default, most programmers omit the target() option altogether.

The dialog-box program you write accesses the information the user has filled in and outputs the Stata command to be executed. Without going into details, the program might say to construct the command by first outputting the word regress, and to follow that by the *varlist* the user specified in the varlist field of the first dialog and follow that by if *exp*, getting the expression from what the user filled in in such-and-such edit field of the second dialog, but do that only if the user filled in an expression. Otherwise, omit the if *exp* in its entirety, and then follow that by ....

Dialogs and input controls are named, and in your dialog-box program, when you want to refer to what a user has filled in, you refer to *dialogname.inputcontrolname*. *dialogname* was determined when you coded the DIALOG command to create the dialog,

   DIALOG *dialogname* ...

and *inputcontrolname* was determined when you coded the input-control command to create the input control; for instance,

   CHECKBOX *inputcontrolname* ...

The details are discussed in Section *5 PROGRAM*, but do not get lost in the details. Worry first about coding how the dialogs look, and worry second about how to translate what the user specifies into the u-action.

Nevertheless, on the various commands that specify how dialogs look, there is an option you can specify that will make writing the u-action program easier. The communication option option(), so called because it communicates something about the control to the u-action program, is allowed with every control. For instance, on the CHECKBOX command, you could code

        CHECKBOX ... , ... option(robust) ...

and doing that, when you got to writing your dialog-box PROGRAM, you would find it easier to associate the robust option in the command you are constructing with whether this box was checked. Communication options never alter how a control looks or works, they just make extra information available to the PROGRAM that makes writing the u-action routine easier.

Do not worry much about communication options when writing your dialog. Wait until you are writing the corresponding u-action program. Then, it will be obvious what communication options you should have specified, and you can go back and specify them.

2.7 The distinction between i-actions and u-actions

In this documentation, we distinguish between i-actions and u-actions, but, if you read carefully, you will realize that the distinction is more syntactical than real. One way we have distinguished i-actions from u-actions is to note that only u-actions can run Stata commands. In fact, i-actions can also run Stata commands, it is just that you code them differently. In addition, in the vast majority of dialog boxes, you never do this.

Nevertheless, if you were writing a dialog box to edit a Stata graph, you might very well construct your dialog box so that it contained no u-actions and only i-actions! Some of those i-actions might invoke Stata commands, and so would more resemble u-actions than i-actions, but they would nevertheless still be i-actions because, syntactically, you would specify them that way.

As you already know, i-actions can invoke PROGRAMs, and PROGRAMs serve two purposes: the coding of i-actions and the coding of u-actions. PROGRAMs themselves, however, have the ability to submit commands to Stata, and therein lies the key. I-actions can invoke PROGRAMs, and PROGRAMs can invoke Stata commands. How this is done is discussed in *Section 5.1.3* and *5.5.*

Now that you know that i-actions and u-actions can be programmed to be virtually indistinguishable, our advice to you is not to do that except in rare, special circumstances. Users expect to fill in a dialog box and to be given the opportunity to press OK or Submit before anything too severe happens.

2.8 Error and consistency checking

In filling in the dialogs you construct, the user might make errors. One alternative is simply to ignore that possibility and let Stata complain when it executes the u-action command you construct. Even in well-written dialog boxes, you will let many errors be handled in this way, because discovering all the problems would require rewriting the entire logic of the Stata command.

Nevertheless, you will want to catch easy-to-detect errors while the dialog is still up, and the user can easily fix them. Errors come in two forms: outright errors and consistency errors. An example of an outright error would be typing a number in an edit field that is supposed to contain a variable name. An example of a consistency error would be checking two checkboxes that are, logically speaking, mutually exclusive.

Most consistency errors you will want to handle at the dialog level, either by design (if two checkboxes are mutually exclusive, perhaps the information should be collected as radio buttons) or by i-actions (the disabling or even hiding of some fields depending on what has been filled in). The latter was discussed in *Section 2.5.*

Outright errors can be detected and handled in dialog-box programs, and are usually detected and handled in the u-action program. For instance, in your dialog-box program, you can assert that *dialogname.inputcontrolname* must be filled in and pop up a custom error if it is not. Or, the program code can be written so that an automatically generated error message is presented. You will find that all input-control commands have an error() option; for example,

> VARLIST ... $\big[$, ... error(*string*) ... $\big]$

The error() string provides the text to describe the control when the dialog-box manager presents an error. For instance, if we specified

> VARLIST ... $\big[$, ... error(dependent variable) ... $\big]$

the dialog-box manager might use that information to later construct the error message "dependent variable must be specified".

If you do not specify the error() option, the dialog-box manager will use what was specified in the label(), and otherwise, "" is used. The label() option specifies the text that usually appears near the control describing it to the user, but label() will do double duty so that you only need to specify error() when the two strings need to differ.

3. Commands

3.1 VERSION

Syntax

> VERSION #$\big[$.##$\big]$

Description

VERSION specifies how the commands that follow are to be interpreted.

Remarks

VERSION must appear first in the .dlg file (it may be preceded by comments). In the current version of Stata, it should read VERSION 8 or VERSION 8.0 or VERSION 8.00. It makes no difference; all three mean the same thing.

Including VERSION at the top is of vital importance. Stata is under continual development. Syntax and features can change. Including VERSION is how you ensure that your dialog box continues to work as you intended.

3.2 INCLUDE

Syntax

> INCLUDE *includefilename*

where *includefilename* refers to *includefilename*.idlg, and must be specified without the suffix and without a path.

Description

INCLUDE reads and processes the lines from *includefilename*.idlg just as if they were part of the current file being read. INCLUDE may appear in both .dlg and idlg files.

Remarks

The name of the file is specified without a file suffix and without a path. `.idlg` files are searched for along the ado-path, as are `.dlg` files.

`INCLUDE` may appear anywhere in the dialog code, and may appear in both `.dlg` and `.idlg` files; include files may `INCLUDE` other include files. Files may contain multiple `INCLUDE`s. The maximum nesting depth is 10.

3.3 DEFINE

Syntax

DEFINE *name* $\{$ `.` $|$ `#` $|$ `+#` $|$ `-#` $|$ `@x` $|$ `@y` $|$ `@xsize` $|$ `@ysize` $\}$

Description

`DEFINE` creates *name*, which may be used in other commands wherever a position or size element is required.

Remarks

The first four possibilities for how *name* is defined—`.`, `#`, `+#`, and `-#`—specify default, number specified, positive offset, and negative offset.

The other four possibilities—`@x`, `@y`, `@xsize`, and `@ysize`—refer to the previous *x*, *y*, *xsize*, and *ysize* values, with previous meaning previous at the time the `DEFINE` command is issued, not at the time *name* is used.

3.4 POSITION

Syntax

POSITION *x y xsize ysize*

Description

`POSITION` sets the position *x* and *y* for the dialog box relative to Stata's main window, and defines the overall size *xsize* and *ysize* of the dialog box.

Remarks

The position *x* and *y* may each be specified as `.`, and Stata will determine where the dialog box will be displayed; this is recommended.

xsize and *ysize* may not be specified as `.`, because they specify the overall size of the dialog box. One discovers the size by experimentation. If you specify a size that is too small, some elements will flow off the dialog box. If you specify a size that is too large, there were will large amounts of white space on the right and bottom of the dialog box. Good initial guesses for *xsize* and *ysize* are 400 and 300.

`POSITION` may be specified anyplace in the dialog code outside of `BEGIN...END` blocks. It does not matter where it is specified because the entire `.dlg` file is processed before the dialog box is displayed.

3.5 LIST

Syntax

> LIST *newlistname*
>   BEGIN
>   *item*
>   *item*
>   . . .
>   END

Description

LIST creates a named list for use in populating list and combo boxes.

Example

```
LIST choices
    BEGIN
        Statistics
        Graphics
        Data management
    END
...
DIALOG ...
    BEGIN
        ...
        LISTBOX ..., ... contents(choices) ...
        ...
    END
```

3.6 DIALOG

Syntax

> DIALOG *newdialogname* $\left[\, , \, \underline{\text{title}}(\text{"}string\text{"}) \, \underline{\text{tab}}\text{title}(\text{"}string\text{"}) \, \right]$
>   BEGIN
> $\left\{ control\ definition\ statements \, | \, \text{INCLUDE} \, | \, \text{DEFINE} \right\}$
>   . . .
>   END

Description

DIALOG defines a dialog. Every .dlg file must define at least one dialog. Only control definition statements, INCLUDE, and DEFINE are allowed between the BEGIN and END.

Options

title("*string*") defines the text to be displayed in the dialog's title bar.

tabtitle("*string*") defines the text to be displayed on the dialog's tab. Dialogs are tabbed if more than one dialog is defined. When a user clicks on the tab, the dialog becomes visible and active. If only one dialog is specified, the contents of tabtitle() are irrelevant.

3.6.1 CHECKBOX on/off input control

Syntax

CHECKBOX *newcontrolname* *x* *y* *xsize* *ysize* $\Big[$, l̲abel("*string*") e̲rror("*string*")

    default(*defnumval*) n̲omemory groupbox onclickon(*iaction*) onclickoff(*iaction*)

    op̲tion(*optionname*) $\Big]$

Member functions

setlabel *string*	sets text to string
setoff	unchecks checkbox
seton	checks checkbox

The standard member functions hide, show, disable, and enable are also provided.

Returned values for use in PROGRAM

Returns numeric, 0 or 1, depending on whether box is checked.

Description

CHECKBOX defines a checkbox control. A checkbox control is used to indicate an option that is either on or off.

Options

label("*string*") specifies the text to be displayed next to the control. You should specify text that clearly implies two opposite states, so that it's obvious what happens when the checkbox is checked or unchecked.

error("*string*") specifies the text to be displayed in describing this field to the user in automatically generated error boxes.

default(*defnumval*) specifies whether the box is to start as checked or unchecked; it will be unchecked if *defnumval* evaluates to 0, and will be checked otherwise. If default() is not specified, default(0) is assumed.

nomemory specifies that the checkbox is not to remember how it was filled in between invocations.

groupbox makes this checkbox control also a group box into which other controls can be placed to emphasize that they are related. For instance, if this control were such that, if it were checked, three other related checkboxes ought to be enabled so that they could be checked or not, it is considered good style to have a group box around them. The group box is just an outline; it does not cause the controls "inside" to be disabled or hidden or in any other way act differently from if they were outside the group box. On some platforms, radio buttons have precedence over checkbox group boxes. You may place radio buttons within a checkbox group box but do not place a checkbox group box within a group of radio buttons. If you do, you may not be able to click on the checkbox control on some platforms.

onclickon(*iaction*) and onclickoff(*iaction*) specify the i-actions to be invoked when the checkbox is clicked on or clicked off. This could be used, for instance, to hide, show, disable, or enable other input controls. The default i-action is to do nothing. Note that the onclickon() or onclickoff() i-action will be invoked the first time the checkbox is displayed.

option(*optionname*) is a communication option. It associates *optionname* with the value of the checkbox.

Example

```
CHECKBOX robust 10 10 100 ., label(Robust VCE)
```

3.6.2 RADIO on/off input control

Syntax

RADIO *newcontrolname* *x* *y* *xsize* *ysize* $\left[\, , \,\left[\underline{\text{f}}\text{irst} \,|\, \underline{\text{m}}\text{iddle} \,|\, \underline{\text{l}}\text{ast}\right] \, \underline{\text{l}}\text{abel}(\text{"}string\text{"})\right.$

$\underline{\text{e}}\text{rror}(\text{"}string\text{"})$ default(*defnumval*) $\underline{\text{nomem}}$ory onclickon(*iaction*)

onclickoff(*iaction*) $\underline{\text{op}}\text{tion}(optionname)$ $\Big]$

Member functions

setlabel *string*	sets text to string
seton	checks the radio button and unchecks any other buttons in the group

The standard member functions `hide`, `show`, `disable`, and `enable` are also provided.

Returned values for use in PROGRAM

Returns numeric, 0 or 1, depending on whether the button is checked.

Description

RADIO defines a radio button control in a radio button group. Radio buttons are used in groups of two or more to select mutually exclusive, but related, choices when the number of choices is small. Selecting one radio button automatically unselects the others in its group.

Options

first, middle, and last specify whether this radio button is the first, a middle, or the last member of a group. There must be one first and one last. There can be zero, one, or more middle members. middle is the default if no option is specified.

label("*string*") specifies the text to be displayed next to the control.

error("*string*") specifies the text to be displayed in describing this field to the user in automatically generated error boxes.

default(*defnumval*) specifies whether the radio button is to start as selected or unselected; it will be unselected if *defnumval* evaluates to 0, and will be selected otherwise. If default() is not specified, default(0) is assumed unless first is also specified, in which case, default(1) is assumed. It is considered bad style to have anything other than the first button be the default, so this option is rarely specified.

nomemory specifies that the radio button is not to remember how it was filled in between invocations.

onclickon(*iaction*) and onclickoff(*iaction*) specify that i-action be invoked when the radio button is clicked on or clicked off. This could be used, for instance, to hide, show, disable, or enable other input controls. The default i-action is to do nothing. Note that the onclickon() i-action will be invoked the first time the radio button is displayed if it is selected.

option(*optionname*) is a communication option. It associates *optionname* with the value of the radio button.

Example

```
RADIO r1 10  10 100 ., first  label("First choice")
RADIO r2 @ +20   @ ., middle label("Second choice")
RADIO r3 @ +20   @ ., middle label("Third choice")
RADIO r4 @ +20   @ ., last   label("Last choice")
```

3.6.3 SPINNER numeric input control

Syntax

SPINNER *newcontrolname* *x* *y* *xsize* *ysize* $\big[$, <u>l</u>abel("*string*") <u>e</u>rror("*string*")

    default(*defnumval*) <u>nome</u>mory min(*defnumval*) max(*defnumval*) onchange(*iaction*)

    <u>op</u>tion(*optionname*) $\big]$

Member functions

                        setvalue *#*   sets the spinner to *#*

The standard member functions hide, show, disable, and enable are also provided.

Returned values for use in PROGRAM

Returns numeric, the value of the spinner.

Description

SPINNER defines a spinner. A spinner displays an edit field that accepts an integer number, which the user may either increment or decrement by clicking up/down arrows.

Options

label("*string*") specifies a description for the control, but it does not display the label next to the spinner. If you want to label the spinner, you must use a TEXT static control.

error("*string*") specifies the text to be displayed in describing this field to the user in automatically generated error boxes.

default(*defnumval*) specifies the initial integer value of the spinner. If not specified, min() is assumed, and, if that is not specified, 0 is assumed.

nomemory specifies that the spinner is not to remember how it was filled in between invocations.

min(*defnumval*) and max(*defnumval*) set the minimum and maximum integer values of the spinner. min(0) and max(100) are the defaults.

onchange(*iaction*) specifies the i-action to be invoked when the spinner is changed. The default i-action is to do nothing. Note that the onchange() i-action will be invoked the first time the spinner is displayed.

option(*optionname*) is a communication option. It associates *optionname* with the value of the spinner.

Example

```
SPINNER level 10 10 60 ., label(Sig. level) min(5) max(100) ///
   default(c(level)) option(level)
```

3.6.4 EDIT string input control

Syntax

EDIT *newcontrolname* *x* *y* *xsize* *ysize* $\Big[$, <u>l</u>abel(*"string"*) <u>e</u>rror(*"string"*)

default(*defstrval*) <u>nomem</u>ory max(*#*) numonly password onchange(*iaction*)

onclick(*iaction*) <u>op</u>tion(*optionname*) $\Big]$

Member functions

setlabel	*string*	sets the label for the edit field
setvalue	*string*	sets the value shown in the edit field
append	*string*	appends *string* to the value in the edit field
prepend	*string*	prepends *string* to the value of the edit field
insert	*string*	inserts *string* at the current cursor position of the edit field
smartinsert	*string*	smartly inserts *string* at the current cursor position in the edit field. A smartinsert ensures that the inserted text will have leading and trailing spaces around it.

The standard member functions hide, show, disable, and enable are also provided.

Returned values for use in PROGRAM

Returns string, the contents of the edit field.

Description

EDIT defines an edit field. An edit field is a box into which the user may enter and edit text; the width of the box does not limit how much text can be entered.

Options

label(*"string"*) specifies a description for the control, but it does not display the label next to the edit field. If you want to label the edit field, you must use a TEXT static control.

error(*"string"*) specifies the text to be displayed in describing this field to the user in automatically generated error boxes.

default(*defstrval*) specifies the default contents of the edit field. If not specified, default("") is assumed. When there is default text, the current cursor position will be at the end of the text.

nomemory specifies that the edit field is not to remember how it was filled in between invocations.

max(*#*) specifies the maximum number of characters that may be entered into the edit field.

numonly specifies the edit field as only being able to contain period, numeric characters 0 through 9, and − (minus).

password specifies that the characters entered into the edit field be shown on the screen as asterisks or bullets, depending on the operating system.

onchange(*iaction*) specifies the i-action to be invoked when the contents of the edit field are changed. The default i-action is to do nothing. Note that the onchange() i-action will be invoked the first time the spinner is displayed.

onclick(*iaction*) specifies the i-action to be invoked when the user clicks in the edit field.

option(*optionname*) is a communication option. It associates *optionname* with the contents of the edit field.

Example

```
TEXT tlab   10  10 200    ., label("Title")
EDIT title  @ +20   @    ., label("title")
```

3.6.5 VARLIST and VARNAME string input controls

Syntax

$\{$VARLIST $|$ VARNAME$\}$ *newcontrolname* x y *xsize* *ysize* $\Big[$, $\underline{\text{label}}$("*string*") $\underline{\text{error}}$("*string*")

$\underline{\text{default}}$(*defstrval*) $\underline{\text{nomem}}$ory allowcat allowts $\underline{\text{opt}}$ion(*optionname*) $\Big]$

Member functions

setlabel	*string*	sets the label for the varlist edit field
setvalue	*string*	sets the value shown in the varlist edit field
append	*string*	appends *string* to the value in the varlist edit field
prepend	*string*	prepends *string* to the value of the varlist edit field
insert	*string*	inserts *string* at the current cursor position of the varlist edit field
smartinsert	*string*	smartly inserts *string* at the current cursor position in the varlist edit field. A smartinsert ensures that the inserted text will have leading and trailing spaces around it.

The standard member functions hide, show, disable, and enable are also provided.

Returned values for use in PROGRAM

Returns string, the contents of the varlist edit field.

Description

VARLIST and VARNAME are a special case of an edit field. VARLIST provides an edit field into which one or more Stata variable names may be entered (along with standard Stata varlist abbreviation), and VARNAME provides an edit field into which one Stata variable name may be entered (with standard Stata varname abbreviations allowed).

Options

label("*string*") specifies a description for the control, but does not display the label next to the varlist edit field. If you want to label the control, you must use a TEXT static control.

In addition, when the VARNAME or VARLIST input control receives the focus, the label() is displayed at the top of the Variables window to indicate that clicking on variables will result in them being copied to the VARNAME or VARLIST control.

error("*string*") specifies the text to be displayed in describing this field to the user in automatically generated error boxes.

default(*defstrval*) specifies the default contents of the edit field. If not specified, default("") is assumed.

nomemory specifies that the edit field is not to remember how it was filled in between invocations.

allowcat specifies that the control allows xi-style categorical/interaction terms; see [R] **xi**.

allowts specifies that the control allows time-series operators; see [U] **14.4.3 Time-series varlists**.

option(*optionname*) is a communication option. It associates *optionname* with the contents of the edit field.

Example

```
TEXT      dvlab      10  10 200    ., label("Dependent variable")
VARNAME   depvar     @ +20   @     ., label("dep. var")
TEXT      ivlab      @ +30   @     ., label("Independent variables")
VARLIST   idepvars   @ +20   @     ., label("ind. vars.")
```

3.6.6 FILE string input control

Syntax

FILE *newcontrolname x y xsize ysize* [, label("*string*") error("*string*")

    default(*defstrval*) nomemory buttonwidth(#) dialogtitle(*string*) save

    filter(*string*) onchange(*iaction*) option(*optionname*)]

Member functions

setlabel	*string*	sets the label shown on the edit button
setvalue	*string*	sets the value shown in the edit field
append	*string*	appends *string* to the value in the edit field
prepend	*string*	prepends *string* to the value of the edit field
insert	*string*	inserts *string* at the current cursor position of the edit field
smartinsert	*string*	smartly inserts *string* at the current cursor position in the edit field. A smartinsert ensures that the inserted text will have leading and trailing spaces around it.

The standard member functions hide, show, disable, and enable are also provided.

Returned values for use in PROGRAM

Returns string, the contents of the edit field (the file chosen).

Description

FILE is a special edit field with a button on the right for selecting a filename. When the user clicks on the button, a file dialog is displayed. If the user selects a filename and clicks OK, that filename is put into the edit field. The user may alternatively type a filename into the edit field.

Options

label("*string*") specifies the text to appear on the button. The default is label("Browse...").

error("*string*") specifies the text to be displayed in describing this field to the user in automatically generated error boxes.

default(*defstrval*) specifies the default contents of the edit field. If not specified, default("") is assumed.

nomemory specifies that the edit field is not to remember how it was filled in between invocations.

buttonwidth(*#*) specifies the width in pixels of the button. The default is buttonwidth(80). The overall size specified in *xsize* includes the button.

dialogtitle(*string*) is the title to show on the file dialog when you click on the file button.

save specifies that the file dialog allows the user to choose a filename for saving rather then one for opening.

filter consists of pairs of descriptions and wildcard file selection strings separated by "|", such as

     filter("Stata Graphs|*.gph|All Files|*.*")

onchange(*iaction*) specifies an i-action to be invoked when the user changes the chosen file. The default i-action is to do nothing. Note that the onchange() i-action will be invoked the first time the file chooser is displayed.

option(*optionname*) is a communication option. It associates *optionname* with the contents of the edit field.

Example

     FILE fname 10 10 300 ., error("Filename to open") label("Browse...")

3.6.7 LISTBOX list input control

Syntax

     LISTBOX *newcontrolname x y xsize ysize* [, label("*string*") error("*string*") nomemory

         contents(*conspec*) values(*listname*) ondblclick(*iaction*)

         [onselchange(*iaction*) | onselchangelist(*listname*)] option(*optionname*)]

Member functions

setlabel	*string*	sets the label for the list box
setvalue	*string*	sets the currently selected item

The standard member functions hide, show, disable, and enable are also provided.

Returned values for use in PROGRAM

Returns string, the text of the item chosen, or, if values(*listname*) is specified, the text from the corresponding element of *listname*.

Description

LISTBOX defines a list box control. Like radio buttons, a list box allows the user to make a selection from a number of mutually exclusive, but related, choices, yet is more appropriate when the number of choices is large.

Options

label("*string*") specifies a description for the control but it does not display the label next to the control. If you want to label the list box, you must use a TEXT static control.

error("*string*") specifies the text to be displayed in describing this field to the user in automatically generated error boxes.

nomemory specifies that the list box is not to remember the item selected between invocations. Note that there is no default() for a list box, but even so, list boxes remember previous selections by default.

contents(*conspec*) specifies the items to be shown in the list box from which the user may choose. If contents() is not specified, the list box will be empty.

values(*listname*) specifies the list (see *Section 3.5*) for which the values of contents() should match one-to-one. When the user chooses the *k*th element from contents(), the *k*th element of *listname* will be returned. If the lists do not match one-to-one, extra elements of *listname* are ignored, and extra elements of contents() return themselves.

ondblclick(*iaction*) specifies the i-action to be invoked when an item in the list is double clicked. Note that the double-clicked item is selected before the *iaction* is invoked.

onselchange(*iaction*) and onselchangelist(*listname*) are alternatives. They specify the i-action to be invoked when a selection in the list changes.

onselchange(*iaction*) performs the same i-action regardless of which element of the list was chosen.

onselchangelist(*listname*) specifies a vector of *iactions* that should match one-to-one with contents(). If the user selects the *k*th element of contents(), the *k*th i-action from *listname* is invoked. See *Section 3.5* for information on creating *listname*. If the elements of *listname* do not match one-to-one with the elements of contents(), extra elements are ignored, and, if there are too few elements, the last element will be invoked for the extra elements of contents().

option(*optionname*) is a communication option. It associates *optionname* with the element chosen from the list.

Example

```
LIST ourlist
    BEGIN
        Good
        Common or average
        Poor
    END
...
DIALOG ...
    BEGIN
        ...
        TEXT ourlab    10  10 200    ., label("Pick a rating")
        LISTBOX rating  @ +20 150 200, contents(ourlist)
        ...
    END
```

3.6.8 COMBOBOX list input control

Syntax

COMBOBOX *newcontrolname x y xsize ysize* [, label("*string*") error("*string*")

[regular | dropdown | dropdownlist] default(*defstrval*) nomemory

contents(*conspec*) values(*listname*) append

[onselchange(*iaction*) | onselchangelist(*listname*)] option(*optionname*)]

Member functions

`setlabel` *string*	sets the label for the combo box
`setvalue` *string*	in the case of the regular and dropdown combo boxes, sets the value of the edit field. In the case of a dropdown-list, sets the currently selected item.

In addition, except in the case of dropdown lists (option `dropdownlist` specified), the following member functions are also available:

`append` *string*	appends *string* to the value in the edit field
`prepend` *string*	prepends *string* to the value of the edit field
`insert` *string*	inserts *string* at the current cursor position of the edit field
`smartinsert` *string*	smartly inserts *string* at the current cursor position in the edit field. A `smartinsert` ensures that the inserted text will have leading and trailing spaces around it.

The standard member functions `hide`, `show`, `disable`, and `enable` are also provided in all cases.

Returned values for use in PROGRAM

Returns string, the contents of the edit field.

Description

`COMBOBOX` defines regular combo boxes, dropdown combo boxes, and dropdown-list combo boxes. By default, `COMBOBOX` creates a regular combo box; it creates a dropdown combo box if option `dropdown` is specified, and it creates a dropdown-list combo box if option `dropdownlist` is specified.

A regular combo box contains an edit field and a visible list box. The user may make a selection from the list box, which is entered in the edit field, or they may type in the edit field. Multiple selections are allowed by using the `append` option. Regular combo boxes are useful for allowing multiple selections from the list, as well as allowing the user to type in an item not in the list.

A dropdown combo box contains an edit field and a list box that appears when the control is clicked. The user may make a selection from the list box, which is entered into the edit field, or they may type into the edit field. The control has the same functionality and options as a regular combo box, but requires less space. Multiple selections are allowed by using the `append` option. In Windows, the *ysize* determines the height of both the edit field and list box when the list box is displayed. Dropdown combo boxes may be cumbersome to use if the number of choices is large, so their usage should be limited to when the number of choices is small or when space is limited.

A dropdown-list combo box contains a list box that displays only the current selection. Clicking on the control exposes the entire list box allowing the user to make a selection, but the user may not type in the "edit field". The user is forced to choose among the given alternatives. Like a list box, the dropdown-list combo box allows the user to make a selection from a number of mutually exclusive, but related, choices. Dropdown-list combo boxes may be cumbersome to use if the number of choices is large, so their usage should be limited to when the number of choices is small or when space is limited.

Options

label("*string*") specifies a description for the control, but it does not display the label next to the combo box. If you want to label a combo box, you must use a TEXT static control.

error("*string*") specifies the text to be displayed in describing this field to the user in automatically generated error boxes.

regular, dropdown, and dropdownlist specify the type of combo box to be created.

If regular is specified, a regular combo box is created. regular is the default.

If dropdown is specified, a dropdown combo box is created.

If dropdownlist is specified, a dropdown-list combo box is created.

default(*defstrval*) specifies the default contents of the edit field. If not specified, default("") is assumed. default() is not allowed if dropdownlist is specified.

nomemory specifies that the combo box is not to remember the item selected between invocations. Note that even in the case of dropdown lists—where there is no default()—combo boxes remember previous selections by default.

contents(*conspec*) specifies the items to be shown in the list box from which the user may choose. If contents() is not specified, the list box will be empty.

values(*listname*) specifies the list (see *Section 3.5*) for which the values of contents() should match one-to-one. When the user chooses the kth element from contents(), it is the kth element of *listname* that is copied into the edit field. If the lists do not match one-to-one, extra elements of *listname* are ignored, and extra elements of contents() return themselves.

append specifies that selections made from the combo box's list box are to be appended to the contents of the combo box's edit field. By default, selections replace the contents of the edit field. append is not allowed if dropdownlist is also specified.

onselchange(*iaction*) and onselchangelist(*listname*) are alternatives. They specify the i-action to be invoked when a selection in the list changes.

onselchange(*iaction*) performs the same i-action regardless of which element of the list was chosen.

onselchangelist(*listname*) specifies a vector of *iactions* that should match one-to-one with contents(). If the user selects the kth element of contents(), the kth i-action from *listname* is invoked. See *Section 3.5* for information on creating *listname*. If the elements of *listname* do not match one-to-one with the elements of contents(), extra elements are ignored, and, if there are too few elements, the last element will be invoked for the extra elements of contents().

option(*optionname*) is a communication option. It associates *optionname* with the element chosen from the list.

(Continued on next page)

Example

```
LIST namelist
    BEGIN
        John
        Sue
        Frank
    END
...
DIALOG ...
    BEGIN
        ...
        TEXT ourlab    10  10 200   ., label("Pick one or more names")
        COMBOBOX names  @ +20 150 200, contents(namelist) append
        ...
    END
```

3.6.9 BUTTON special input control

Syntax

BUTTON *newcontrolname* *x* *y* *xsize* *ysize* $\Big[$, label("*string*") error("*string*")

onpush(*iaction*) $\Big]$

Member functions

setlabel *string*   sets the label for the button

The standard member functions hide, show, disable, and enable are also provided.

Returned values for use in PROGRAM

None.

Description

BUTTON creates a push button. Push buttons perform instantaneous actions. They do not indicate a state such as on or off, and do not return anything for use by the u-action PROGRAM. Buttons are used to invoke i-actions.

Options

label("*string*") specifies the text to display on the button. You should specify text that contains verbs that describe the action to perform.

error("*string*") specifies the text to be displayed in describing this field to the user in automatically generated error boxes.

onpush(*iaction*) specifies the i-action to be invoked when the button is clicked. If onpush() is not specified, the button does nothing.

Example

```
BUTTON help 10 10 80 ., label("Help") onpush("view help example")
```

3.6.10 TEXT static control

Syntax

> TEXT *newcontrolname* *x* *y* *xsize* *ysize* $\Big[$, <u>l</u>abel("*string*") $\big[$left | center | right$\big]$ $\Big]$

Member functions

> setlabel *string*   sets the text shown

The standard member functions hide, show, disable, and enable are also provided.

Returned values for use in PROGRAM

> None.

Description

> TEXT displays text.

Options

label("*string*") specifies the text to be shown.

left, center, and right are alternatives; they specify the horizontal alignment of the text with respect to *x*. left is the default.

Example

> TEXT dvlab 10 10 200 ., label("Dependent variable")

3.6.11 GROUPBOX static control

Syntax

> GROUPBOX *newcontrolname* *x* *y* *xsize* *ysize* $\Big[$, <u>l</u>abel("*string*") $\Big]$

Member functions

> setlabel *string*   sets the text shown above the group box

The standard member functions hide, show, disable, and enable are also provided.

Returned values for use in PROGRAM

> None.

Description

> GROUPBOX displays a frame (an outline) with text displayed above it. Group boxes are used for grouping related controls together. The grouped controls are sometimes said to be inside the group box, but there is no meaning to that other than the visual effect.

Options

label("*string*") specifies the text to be shown at the top of the group box.

Example

```
GROUPBOX weights 10 10 300 200, label("Weight type")
    RADIO w1 ... , ... label(fweight) first ...
    RADIO w2 ... , ... label(aweight) ...
    RADIO w3 ... , ... label(pweight) ...
    RADIO w4 ... , ... label(iweight) last ...
```

3.6.12 FRAME static control

Syntax

FRAME *newcontrolname* *x* *y* *xsize* *ysize* $\left[\, , \, \underline{l}abel("string") \,\right]$

Member functions

There are no special member functions provided.

The standard member functions hide, show, disable, and enable are provided.

Returned values for use in PROGRAM

None.

Description

FRAME displays a frame (an outline).

Options

label("*string*") specifies the label for the frame, which is not used in any way, but some programmers use to record comments documenting the purpose of the frame.

Remarks

The distinction between a frame and a group box with no label is that a frame draws its outline using the entire dimensions of the control. A group box draws its outline a few pixels offset from the top of the control regardless of whether there is a label or not. A frame is useful for horizontal alignment with other controls.

Example

```
FRAME box 10 10 300 200
    RADIO w1 ... , ... label(fweight) first ...
    RADIO w2 ... , ... label(aweight) ...
    RADIO w3 ... , ... label(pweight) ...
    RADIO w4 ... , ... label(iweight) last ...
```

3.7 OK, SUBMIT, and CANCEL u-action buttons

Syntax

$\{$OK $|$ SUBMIT$\}$ *newbuttonname* $\left[\, , \, \underline{l}abel("string") \; \underline{uact}ion(programname) \right.$

$\left. \underline{tar}get(target) \,\right]$

CANCEL *newbuttonname* $\left[\, , \, \underline{l}abel("string") \,\right]$

Description

OK, CANCEL, and SUBMIT define buttons that, when clicked, invoke a u-action. At least one of the buttons should be defined (or else the dialog will have no associated u-action), only one of each button may be defined, and in most cases, good style dictates defining all three.

OK executes *programname*, removes the dialog box from the screen, and submits the resulting command produced by *programname* to *target*. If no other buttons are defined, clicking on the close icon of the dialog box does the same thing.

SUBMIT executes *programname*, leaves the dialog box on the screen, and submits the resulting command produced by *programname* to *target*.

CANCEL removes the dialog from the screen and does nothing. If this button is defined, clicking on the close icon of the dialog box does the same thing.

Note that you do not specify the location or size of these controls. They will be placed on the dialog box where the user would expect to see them.

Options

label("*string*") defines the text to appear on the button. The default label() is "OK", "Submit", and "Cancel" for the individual buttons.

uaction(*programname*) specifies the PROGRAM to be executed. uaction(command) is the default.

target(*target*) defines what is to be done with the resulting string (command) produced by *programname*. The alternatives are

target(stata): the command is to be executed by Stata. This is the default.

target(stata hidden): the command is to be executed by Stata, but the command itself is not to appear in the Results window. The output from the command will appear normally.

target(cmdwin): the command is to be placed in the Command window so that the user can edit it and then press Enter to submit it.

Example

```
OK ok1
CANCEL can1
SUBMIT sub2
```

3.8 HELP and RESET helper buttons

Syntax

HELP *newbuttonname* [, view("*viewertopic*")]

RESET *newbuttonname*

Description

HELP defines a button that, when clicked, presents *viewertopic* in the Viewer. *viewertopic* is typically specified as "view *helpfile*".

RESET defines a button that, when clicked, resets the values of the controls in the dialog box to their initial state, just as if the dialog box were invoked for the first time. Each time a user invokes a dialog box, its controls will be filled in with the values the user last entered. RESET restores the control values to their defaults.

Note that you do not specify the location, size, or appearance of these controls. They will be placed in the lower-left corner of the dialog box. The HELP button will have a question mark on it. The RESET button will have an **R** on it.

Options

view("*viewertopic*") specifies the topic to appear in the Viewer when the user clicks the button. The default is view("help contents").

Example

```
HELP hlp1, view("help mycommand")
RESET res1
```

4. SCRIPT

Syntax

```
        SCRIPT newscriptname
            BEGIN
                iaction
                 . . .
            END
```

where *iaction* is

    .

    action *memberfunction*

    gaction *dialogname.controlname.memberfunction*

    dialogname.controlname.memberfunction

    script *scriptname*

    view *topic*

    program *programname*

See *Section 2.5* for more information on *iactions*.

Description

SCRIPT defines the *newscriptname*, which in turn defines a compound i-action. I-actions are invoked by the on*() options of the input controls. When a script is invoked, the lines are executed sequentially, and errors, if any, are ignored.

Remarks

CHECKBOX provides onclickon(*iaction*) and onclickoff(*iaction*) options. Let's focus on the onclickon(*iaction*) option. If we wanted to take just one action when the box was checked—say, disabling d1.sw2—we could code

```
CHECKBOX ... , ... onclickon(d1.s2.disable) ...
```

If we wanted to take two actions, say, disabling d1.s3 as well, we would have to use a SCRIPT. On the CHECKBOX command, we would code

```
CHECKBOX ... , ...  onclickon(script buttonsoff) ...
```

and then somewhere else in the .dlg file (it does not matter where), we would code

```
SCRIPT buttonsoff
    BEGIN
        d1.s2.disable
        d1.s3.disable
    END
```

5. PROGRAM

Syntax

```
PROGRAM programname
    BEGIN
        [ program_line | INCLUDE ]
        [...]
    END
```

Description

PROGRAM defines a dialog program. Dialog programs are used (1) to describe complicated i-actions, and (2) to implement u-actions.

Remarks

Dialog programs are used to describe complicated i-actions when flow control (if/then) is necessary, or when you wish to create heavyweight i-actions that invoke Stata commands and so are more like u-actions; otherwise, you should use a SCRIPT. Used this way, programs are invoked when the specified *iaction* is program *programname* in an on*() option of an input control command; for instance,

```
CHECKBOX ... , ... onclickon(program complicated) ...
```

or in a SCRIPT; for instance,

```
CHECKBOX ... , ...  onclickon(script multi) ...
...
SCRIPT multi
    BEGIN
        ...
        program complicated
        ...
    END
```

The primary use of dialog programs, however, is to implement u-actions. The program is to construct and return string, which the dialog-box manager will then interpret as a Stata command. This use of a program is invoked by the uaction() options of OK and SUBMIT; for instance,

```
OK ... , ... uaction(program command) ...
```

The u-action program is nearly always named `command` because, if the `uaction()` option is not specified, `command` is assumed. The u-action program may, however, be named as you please.

Here is an example of a dialog program being used to implement an i-action with if/then flow control:

```
PROGRAM testprog
    BEGIN
        if sample.cb1 & sample.cb2 {
            call sample.txt1.disable
        }
        if !(sample.cb1 & sample.cb2) {
            call sample.txt1.enable
         }
    END
```

Here is an example of a dialog program being used to implement the u-action:

```
PROGRAM command
    BEGIN
        put "mycmd "
        varlist main.vars     //  varlist [main.vars]  would make optional
        ifexp main.if
        inrange main.obs1 main.obs2
        beginoptions
            option options.detail
            optionarg options.title
        endoptions
    END
```

Using scripts to implement heavyweight i-actions is much like implementing u-actions, except (1) the script might not be a function of the input controls, and (2) you must explicitly code the `stata` command to execute what is constructed. Here is an example of a dialog program being used to implement a heavyweight i-action:

```
PROGRAM heavyweight
    BEGIN
        put "myeditcmd, resume"
        stata
    END
```

5.1 Concepts

5.1.1 Vnames

Vname stands for value name and refers to the "value" of a control. Vnames are of the form *dialogname.controlname*; for example, `d2.s2` and `d2.list` would be vnames if input controls `s2` and `list` were defined in `DIALOG d2`:

```
DIALOG d2 ...
    BEGIN
        ...
        CHECKBOX s2 ...
        EDIT list ...
        ...
    END
```

A vname can be numeric or string depending on the control to which it corresponds. In the case of CHECKBOX, it was documented under "Returned value for use in PROGRAM" that CHECKBOX "returns numeric, 0 or 1, depending on whether box is checked.", so d2.s2 is a numeric. For the EDIT input control, it was documented that EDIT returns a string, which is the contents of the edit field, so d2.list is a string.

Different words are sometimes used to describe whether *vname* is numeric or string, including

> *vname* is numeric
> *vname* is string
>
> *vname* is a numeric control
> *vname* is a string control
>
> *vname* returns a numeric result
> *vname* returns a string result

In a program, you may not assign values to vnames; you may only examine their values, and, in the case of u-action (and heavyweight i-action) programs, output them. Thus, dialog programs are pretty relaxed about types. You can ask whether d2.s2 is true or d2.list is true, even though d2.list is a string. In the case of a string, it is true if it is not "". Numeric vnames are true if the numeric result is not 0.

5.1.2 Enames

Enames are an extension of vnames. An *ename* is defined as being

> *vname*
> or(*vname vname ... vname*)
> radio(*dialogname controlname ... controlname*)

or() returns the *vname* of the first in the list that is true (filled in). For instance, the varlist u-action dialog-programming command "outputs" a varlist (see *Section 5.1.3*). If you knew that the varlist was in either control d1.field1 or d1.field2, and knew that both could not be filled in, you might code

```
varlist or(d1.field1 d1.field2)
```

which would have the same effect as

```
if d1.field1 {
    varlist d1.field1
}
if (!d1.field1) & d2.field2 {
    varlist d2.field2
}
```

`radio()` is for dealing with radio buttons. Remember that each radio button is a separate control, and yet, in the set, one knows exactly one is clicked. `radio` finds the clicked one. Typing

```
option radio(d1 b1 b2 b3 b4)
```

would be equivalent to typing

```
option or(d1.b1 d1.b2 d1.b3 d1.b4)
```

which would be equivalent to typing

```
option d1.b2
```

assuming that the second radio button is selected. (The `option` command outputs the option corresponding to a control.)

5.1.3 rstrings: cmdstring and optstring

Rstrings, `cmdstring` and `optstring`, are relevant only in u-action and heavyweight i-action programs.

The purpose of a u-action program is to build and return a string, which Stata will ultimately execute. To do that, dialog programs have an *rstring* to which the dialog-programming commands implicitly contribute. For example,

```
put "kappa"
```

would add "kappa" (without the quotes) to the end of the rstring currently under construction, known as the current rstring. Usually, the current rstring is `cmdstring`, but, within a `beginoptions`/`endoptions` block, the current rstring is switched to `optstring`:

```
beginoptions
    put "kappa"
endoptions
```

The above would add "kappa" (without the quotes) to `optstring`.

When the program concludes, the `cmdstring` and the `optstring` are put together—separated by a comma—and that is the command Stata will execute. In any case, any command that can be used outside of `beginoptions`/`endoptions` can be used inside, and the only difference is the rstring to which the output is directed. Thus, if our entire u-action program read

```
PROGRAM command
    BEGIN
        put "kappa"
        beginoptions
            put "kappa"
        endoptions
    END
```

the result would be to execute the command "`kappa, kappa`".

The difference between a u-action program and a heavyweight i-action program is that you must, in your program, specify that the constructed command be executed. You do this with the `stata` command. The `stata` command can also be used in u-action programs if you wish to execute more than one Stata command:

```
PROGRAM command
    BEGIN
        put , etc.              //  construct first command
        stata                   //  execute first command
        clear                   //  clear cmdstring and optstring
        if _rc {                //  if first command failed . . .
            stopbox stop "First command failed"
        }
        put , etc.              //  construct second command
                                //  execution will be automatic
    END
```

5.1.4 Adding to an rstring

The term *adding to an rstring* has a special definition due to how spaces are treated. Call *A* the rstring and *B* the string being added (say "kappa"). The following rules apply:

1. If *A* does not end in a space and *B* does not begin with a space, the two strings are joined to form "*AB*". If *A* is "this" and *B* is "that", the result is "thisthat".

2. If *A* ends in one or more spaces and *B* does not begin with a space, the spaces at the end of *A* are removed, one space is added, and *B* is joined to form "rightstrip(*A*) B". If A is "this " and *B* is "that", the result is "this that".

3. If *A* does not end in a space and *B* begins with one or more spaces, the spaces at the beginning of *B* are ignored and treated as if there is one space, and the two strings are joined to form "*A* leftstrip(*B*)". If *A* is "this" and *B* is " that", the result is "this that".

4. If *A* ends in one or more spaces and *B* begins with one or more spaces, the spaces at the end of *A* are removed, the spaces at the beginning of *B* are ignored, and the two strings are joined with one space in between to form "rightstrip(*A*) leftstrip(*B*)". If A is "this " and *B* is " that", the result is "this that".

The purpose of these rules is to ensure that multiple spaces do not end up in the resulting string and so that the string will look prettier, and more like a user might have typed it.

When string literals are put, they are nearly always put with a trailing space,

```
put "kappa "
```

so as to ensure that they do not join up with whatever next is put. Note that if what is put next has a leading space, that will be ignored.

5.2 Flow control commands

5.2.1 if

Syntax

```
if ifexp {
    ...
}
```

where *ifexp* may be

ifexp	meaning
(*ifexp*)	order of evaluation
!*ifexp*	logical not
ifexp | *ifexp*	logical or
ifexp & *ifexp*	logical and
H(*vname*)	true if *vname* is hidden or disabled
default(*vname*)	true if *vname* is its default value
vname	true if *vname* is not 0 and not ""
_rc	see *Section 5.5*

Note the recursive definition: An *ifexp* may be substituted into itself to produce more complicated expressions such as ((!d1.s1)&d1.s2)|default(d1.s3).

Also note that the order of evaluation is LEFT-TO-RIGHT; use parentheses.

Description

if executes the code inside the braces if *ifexp* evaluates to true, and skips it otherwise. if commands may be nested.

Example

```
if !H(d1.v1) {
    put "thing=" d1.v1
}
```

5.2.2 call

Syntax

call *iaction*

where *iaction* is

.

action *memberfunction*

gaction *dialogname.controlname.memberfunction*

dialogname.controlname.memberfunction

script *scriptname*

view *topic*

program *programname*

Note that *iaction* "action *memberfunctionname*" is invalid in u-action programs because there is no concept of a current control.

Description

call executes the specified *iaction*.

Example

```
PROGRAM testprog
    BEGIN
        if sample.cb1 & sample.cb2 {
                call gaction sample.txt1.disable
        }
        if !(sample.cb1 & sample.cb2) {
                call gaction sample.txt1.enable
        }
    END
```

5.2.3 exit

Syntax

exit [#]

where $\# >= 0$. The following exit codes have special meaning:

# meaning	
0	exit without error
>0	exit with error
101	program exited due to a missing required object

Description

exit causes the program to exit, and, optionally, to return #.

exit without an argument is equivalent to "exit 0". In u-action programs, the cmdstring, optstring will be sent to Stata for execution.

exit #, $\# > 0$, indicates an error. In u-action programs, the cmdstring, optstring will not be executed. exit 101 has special meaning. When a u-action program exits, Stata will check the exit code for that program, and, if it is 101, will present an error box stating that the user forgot to fill in a required element of the dialog box.

Example

```
if !sample.var1 {
    exit 101
}
```

5.3 Error checking and presentation commands

5.3.1 require

Syntax

require *ename* [*ename* [...]]

where each *ename* is required to be string.

Description

require does nothing on each *ename* that is disabled or hidden.

For the others, require requires the control(s) specified not be empty (""), and produces a stop-box error message such as "dependent variable must be defined" for any that are empty. The "dependent variable" part of the message will be obtained from the control's error() option, or, if that was not specified, the control's label() option or, if that was not specified, will be blank.

Example

```
require main.grpvar
```

5.3.2 stopbox

Syntax

stopbox {stop|note|rusure} ["*line1*" ["*line2*" ["*line3*" ["*line4*"]]]]

Description

stopbox displays a message box containing up to four lines of text. Three types are available:

stop: Displays a message box in which there is only one button, OK, which means the user must accept that he or she made an error and fix it. The program will exit after stopbox stop.

note: Displays a message box in which there is only one button, OK, which means that the user has read the message and now he or she knows. The program will continue after stopbox note.

rusure: Displays a message box in which there are two buttons, OK and Cancel. OK means the user has read the message and still wishes to continue. Cancel means the user does not wish to continue. The program will continue or exit depending on the button pressed by the user.

Also see [P] **window stopbox** for more information.

Example

```
stopbox stop "Nothing has been selected"
```

5.4 Command-construction commands

The command-construction commands are

by,
bysort,
put,
varlist,
weight,
ifexp,
inrange,
beginoptions/option/optionarg/endoptions,
allowxi/xi, and
clear.

Most correspond to the piece of Stata syntax for which they are named:

by *varlist*:*cmd varlist* [*weight*] [if *exp*] [in *range*] , *options*

put corresponds to *cmd* (although it is useful for other things as well) and `allowxi/xi` corresponds to putting `xi:` in front of the entire command; see [R] **xi**.

The command-construction commands (with the exception of `xi`) build `cmdstring` and `optstring` in the order the commands are executed (see *Section 5.1.3*), so you should issue them in the same order as followed by Stata syntax.

Added to the syntax diagrams that follow is a new header,

> Use of `option()` communication.

This refers to the `option()` option on the input control definition, such as CHECKBOX, EDIT, etc.; see *Section 2.6*.

5.4.1 by

Syntax

> by *ename*

where *ename* must contain a string and should probably refer to a VARNAME, VARLIST, or EDIT control.

> Use of `option()` communication: None.

Description

by adds to the current rstring (outputs) nothing if *ename* is hidden, disabled, or empty. Otherwise, *by* outputs "by *varlist*:", followed by a blank, obtaining varlist from *ename*.

Example

> by d2.by

5.4.2 bysort

Syntax

> bysort *ename*

where *ename* must contain a string and should probably refer to a VARNAME, VARLIST, or EDIT control.

> Use of `option()` communication: None.

Description

bysort adds to the current rstring (outputs) nothing if *ename* is hidden, disabled, or empty. Otherwise, *bysort* outputs "bysort *varlist*:", followed by a blank, obtaining varlist from *ename*.

Example

> bysort d2.by

5.4.3 put

Syntax

> put $[\%fmt]$ *putel* $\big[$ $[\%fmt]$ *putel* $[\dots]$ $\big]$

where *putel* may be

> ""
>
> "*string*"
>
> *vname*
>
> /hidden *vname*
>
> /on *vname*
>
> /program *programname*

and *%fmt* is as described in [R] **format**.

The word "output" is hereby defined to mean "add to the current result" in what follows. The put directives are defined as

"" and "*string*"
> Outputs the fixed text specified.

vname
> Outputs the value of the control.

/hidden *vname*
> Outputs the value of the control even if it is hidden or disabled.

/on *vname*
> Outputs nothing if *vname*==0. *vname* must be numeric, and should be the result of a CHECKBOX or RADIO control. /on outputs the text from the control's option() option. Also see *Section 5.4.8.1* for an alternative using the option command.

/program *programname*
> Outputs the cmdstring, optstring returned by *programname*.

If any *vname* is disabled or hidden and not preceded by /hidden, put outputs nothing.

In all cases, if the directive is preceded by *%fmt*, the specified *%fmt* is used to format the result. Otherwise, string results are output as is, and numeric results are output after being formatted with %10.0g format and being stripped of resulting leading and trailing blanks.

Use of option() communication: See /on above.

Description

> put adds to the current rstring (outputs) what is specified.

Remarks

> put "*string*" is often used to add the Stata command to the current rstring. When used in that way, the right way to code is

> put "*commandname* "

Note the trailing blank on *commandname*; see *Section 5.1.4*.

It is also worth emphasizing that put outputs nothing if ANY element specified is hidden or disabled. For instance,

> put "thing=" d1.v1

will output nothing (not even the "thing=") if d1.v1 is hidden or disabled. This is a feature that saves you from having to code

```
if !H(d1.v1) {
    put "thing=" d1.v1
}
```

5.4.4 varlist

Syntax

  varlist *el* $\left[\; el\; \left[\ldots\right]\; \right]$

where an *el* is *ename* or [*ename*] (brackets significant).

Each *ename* must be string, and probably should be the result from a VARLIST, VARNAME, or EDIT control.

If *ename* is not enclosed in brackets, it must not be hidden or disabled.

Use of option() communication: None.

Description

  varlist considers it to be an error if

  1. any of the specified *enames* that are not enclosed in brackets are hidden or disabled

  2. any of the specified *enames* that are not enclosed in brackets are empty (contain "")

In either of those cases, *varlist* displays a stop message box indicating that the varlist must be filled in and exits the program.

  varlist adds to the current rstring (outputs) nothing if

  3. any of the specified *enames* that are enclosed in brackets are hidden or disabled

Otherwise, varlist outputs with leading and trailing blanks the contents of each ename that is not hidden, not disabled, and does not contain "".

Remarks

  varlist is most often used to output the varlist of a Stata command, such as

```
varlist main.depvar [main.indepvars]
```

  varlist can also be used for other purposes as well. You might code

```
if d1.vl {
    put " exog("
    varlist d2.vl
    put ") "
}
```

although coding

```
optionarg d2.vl
```

would be easier to code to achieve the same effect.

5.4.5 weight

Syntax

```
weight ename_t ename_e
```

where *ename_t* may be a string or numeric control, but must have had `option()` filled in with a weight type (one of `weight`, `fweight`, `aweight`, `pweight`, or `iweight`), and *ename_e* must be a string evaluating to the weight expression or variable name.

Use of `option()` communication: *ename_t* must have `option()` filled in the weight type.

Description

`weight` adds nothing to the current rstring if *ename_t* or *ename_e* are hidden, disabled, or contain nothing. Otherwise, output is "[*weighttype=exp*]" with leading and trailing blanks.

Remarks

`weight` is typically used as

```
weight radio(d1 w1 w2 ... wk) d1.wexp
```

where d1.w1, d1.w2, ..., d1.wk are radio buttons, which could be defined as

```
DIALOG d1 ...
    BEGIN
    ...
        RADIO w1 ... , ... label(fweight) first ...
        RADIO w2 ... , ... label(aweight) ...
        RADIO w3 ... , ... label(pweight) ...
        RADIO w4 ... , ... label(iweight) last ...
        ...
    END
```

Not all weight types need to be offered. If a command offers only one kind of weights, you do not need to use radio buttons. You could code

```
weight d1.wt d1.wexp
```

where d1.wt was defined as

```
CHECKBOX wt ... , ... label(fweight) ...
```

5.4.6 ifexp

Syntax

```
ifexp ename
```

where *ename* must be a string control.

Use of `option()` communication: None.

Description

`ifexp` adds to the current rstring (outputs) nothing if *ename* is hidden, disabled, or empty. Otherwise, output is "`if` *exp*", with spaces added in front and behind.

Example

```
if d2.if
```

5.4.7 inrange

Syntax

```
inrange ename_1 ename_2
```

where *ename_1* and *ename_2* must be numeric controls.

Use of option() communication: None.

Description

If *ename_1* is hidden or disabled, results are as if *ename_1* were not hidden and contained 1. If *ename_2* is hidden or disabled, results are as if *ename_1* were not hidden and contained _N, the number of observations in the dataset.

If *ename_1*==1 and *ename_2*==_N, nothing is output (added to the current rstring).

Otherwise, "in *range*" is output with spaces added in front and behind, with the range obtained from *ename_1* and *ename_2*.

Example

```
inrange d2.in1 d2.in2
```

5.4.8 beginoptions and endoptions

Syntax

```
beginoptions
    any dialog-programming command except beginoptions
    ...
endoptions
```

Use of option() communication: None.

Description

beginoptions/endoptions is how you indicate that you wish what is enclosed to be treated as Stata options in the construction of cmdstring, optstring.

The current rstring is, by default, cmdstring. beginoptions changes the current rstring to optstring. endoptions changes it back to being cmdstring. Thus, there are in fact two strings being built. When the dialog program exits normally, if there is anything in optstring, trailing spaces are removed from cmdstring, a comma and a space are added, the contents of optstring are added, and that is what is returned. Thus, a dialog program can have many beginoptions/endoptions blocks, and yet still all the options will appear at the end of the cmdstring.

The command-construction commands option and optionarg are documented below because they usually appear inside a beginoptions/endoptions block, but they can be used outside of beginoptions/endoptions blocks, too. In addition, all the other command-construction commands can be used inside a beginoptions/endoptions block, and the use of put is particularly common.

5.4.8.1 option

Syntax

> option *ename* $\big[$ *ename* $[\dots]$ $\big]$ $\big]$

where *ename* must be a numeric control with 0 indicating that the option is not desired.

Use of option() communication: option() specifies the name of the option.

Description

option adds to the current rstring (outputs) nothing if any of the *enames* specified are hidden or disabled. Otherwise, for each *ename* specified, if *ename* is not equal to 0, the contents of its option() are output.

Remarks

option is an easy way to output switch options such as noconstant, detail, etc. One simply codes

```
option d1.sw
```

where one has previously defined

```
CHECKBOX sw ... , option(detail) ...
```

In this case, detail will be output if the user checked the box.

5.4.8.2 optionarg

Syntax

> optionarg $\big[$*style*$\big]$ *ename* $\big[$ $\big[$*style*$\big]$ *ename* $[\dots]$ $\big]$

where each *ename* may be a numeric or string control and *style* is

style	meaning
/asis	do not quote
/quoted	do quote
/oquoted	quote if necessary
%*fmt*	for use with numeric

Use of option() communication: option() specifies the name of the option.

Description

optionarg adds to the current rstring (outputs) nothing if any of the *enames* specified are hidden or disabled. Otherwise, for each *ename* specified, if *ename* is not equal to "", the *ename*'s option() is output, followed by "(", followed by the *ename*'s contents, followed by ")", with blanks added in front and behind.

Remarks

optionarg is an easy way to output single-argument options such as title() or level(); for instance,

```
optionarg /oquoted d1.ttl
if !default(d1.level) {
    optionarg d1.level
}
```

where one has previously defined

```
EDIT    ttl   ... , ... label(title) ...
SPINNER level ... , ... label(level) ...
```

5.4.9 allowxi and xi

Syntax

```
allowxi
```

```
xi
```

Use of option() communication: None.

Description

allowxi should be coded at the top of the command-construction commands, if it is coded at all. allowxi specifies that i. notation in variables and varlists is to be understood as xi's notation (see [R] **xi**), and that if any i. prefixes appear, the entire cmdstring, optstring is to be prefixed by xi:. allowxi tells varlist (see *Section 5.4.4*) to watch for this.

xi simply states that cmdstring, optstring is to be prefixed by xi:. xi may be specified even if allowxi is not specified, and vice versa. xi may be coded anywhere among the command-construction commands, and is typically coded within an if.

Remarks

allowxi is commonly used. xi is seldom used.

Example

```
allowxi
```

5.5 Command-execution commands

Command execution is automatic when a program is invoked by an input control's uaction() option. Programs so invoked are called u-action programs. No command is executed when a program is invoked by an input control's iaction() option. Programs so invoked are called i-action programs.

The two commands stata and clear are for use in cases when

1. you want to write a u-action program that executes more than one Stata command, or

2. you want to write an i-action program that executes one or more Stata commands (also known as heavyweight i-action programs).

5.5.1 stata

Syntax

```
stata [hidden]
```

Use of option() communication: None.

Description

stata executes the current cmdstring, optstring, waits until the command has finished, and sets _rc to contain the return code from the command.

stata without arguments displays the command in the Results window before execution, just as if the user had typed it. stata hidden does not display the command. In either case, the command's output will appear in the Results window.

5.5.2 clear

Syntax

```
clear [curstring | cmdstring | optstring]
```

Use of option() communication: None.

Description

clear is seldom used, and, when used, is typically specified without arguments. clear clears (resets to "") the specified return string or, specified without arguments, clears cmdstring and optstring. If curstring is specified, clear clears the current return string, which is cmdstring by default or optstring within a beginoptions/endoptions block. In addition, clear (with or without arguments) resets allowxi and xi.

Remarks

clear is used when you wish to execute more than one Stata command. In that case, the procedure is to construct the first Stata command, use stata to execute it, use clear to clear it, construct the second, and so on.

6. Example

The following example will execute the summarize command. In addition to the copy below, a copy can be found among the Stata distribution materials. You can type

```
. which sumexample.dlg
```

to find out where it is.

```
────────────────────sumexample.dlg────────────────────
// sumexample
// version 1.0.0
VERSION 8.0
POSITION . . 320 200
DIALOG main, title("Example simple summarize dialog") tabtitle("Main")
BEGIN
  TEXT    lab    10   10  300    ., label("Variables to summarize:")
  VARLIST vars    @  +20    @    ., label("Variables to sum")
END
```

```
DIALOG options, tabtitle("Options")
BEGIN
  CHECKBOX detail   10   10   300    ., label("Show detailed statistics")  ///
        option("detail")                                                   ///
        onclickon('"gaction options.status.setlabel "(detail is on)"""')   ///
        onclickoff('"options.status.setlabel "(detail is off)"""')
  TEXT     status   @  +20   @    ., label("This label won't be seen")
  BUTTON   btnhide  @  +30  200   ., label("Hide other controls")          ///
        push("script hidethem")
  BUTTON   btnshow  @  +30   @    ., label("Show other controls")          ///
        push("script showthem")
  BUTTON   btngrey  @  +30   @    ., label("Disable other controls")       ///
        push("script disablethem")
  BUTTON   btnnorm  @  +30   @    ., label("Enable other controls")        ///
        push("script enablethem")
END
SCRIPT hidethem
BEGIN
  gaction main.lab.hide
  main.vars.hide
  options.detail.hide
  options.status.hide
END
SCRIPT showthem
BEGIN
  main.lab.show
  main.vars.show
  options.detail.show
  options.status.show
END

SCRIPT disablethem
BEGIN
  main.lab.disable
  main.vars.disable
  options.detail.disable
  options.status.disable
END
SCRIPT enablethem
BEGIN
  main.lab.enable
  main.vars.enable
  options.detail.enable
  options.status.enable
END

OK      ok1, label("Ok")
CANCEL  can1
SUBMIT  sub1
HELP    hlp1, view("help summarize")
RESET   res1

PROGRAM command
BEGIN
  put "summarize"
  varlist main.vars        /* varlist [main.vars] to make it optional */
  beginoptions
    option options.detail
  endoptions
END
```

—————————————————————sumexample.dlg—————————————————————

Appendix A: Jargon

action: An i-action or a u-action.

browser: see **file chooser**.

button: A type of input control; a button causes an i-action to occur when it is clicked. In addition, see u-action buttons, helper buttons, and radio buttons.

checkbox: A type of numeric input control; the user may either check or uncheck what is presented; suitable for obtaining yes/no responses. A checkbox has value 0 or 1 depending on whether the item is checked.

combo box: A type of string input control that has an edit field at the top and a list box underneath. Combo boxes come in three flavors:

A regular combo box has an edit field and a list below it. The user may choose from the list or type into the edit field.

A dropdown combo box also has an edit field and a list, but only the edit field shows. The user can click to expose the list. The user may choose from the list or type into the edit field.

A dropdown-list combo box is more like a list box. An "edit field" shows, the list is hidden, the user can click to expose the list, but the user can only choose elements from the list; he or she cannot type in the "edit field".

control: An **input control** or a **static control**.

control status: Whether a control (input or static) is disabled or enabled; hidden or shown.

dialog(s): The main component(s) of a dialog box in that the dialogs contain all of the controls except for the u-action buttons.

dialog box: Something that pops up onto the screen that the user fills in, and, when the user clicks an action button, causes something to happen (namely, Stata to execute a command).

A dialog box is made up of one or more dialogs, u-action buttons, and a title bar.

If the dialog box contains more than one dialog, only one of the dialogs show at any one time, which being determined by the tab selected.

dialog program: See PROGRAM.

disabled and enabled: A control that is disabled is visually greyed out; otherwise, it is enabled. The user cannot modify disabled input controls. Also see **hidden and exposed**.

.dlg file: The file in which the code defining a dialog box and its actions are stored. If the file is named *xyz*.dlg, the dialog box is said to be named *xyz*.

dlg-program: The entire contents of a .dlg file; the code defining a dialog box and its actions.

edit field: A type of string input control; a box in which the user may type text.

enabled and disabled: see **disabled and enabled**.

exposed and hidden: see **hidden and exposed**.

file browser: see **file chooser**.

file chooser: A type of string input control; presents a list of files from which the user may choose one or type a filename.

frame: A type of static control; a rectangle drawn around a group of controls.

group box: A type of static control; a rectangle drawn around a group of controls with description text at the top.

helper buttons: The buttons Help and Reset. When Help is clicked, the help topic for the dialog box is displayed. When Reset is clicked, the control values of the dialog box are reset to their defaults.

hidden and exposed: A control that is removed from the screen is said to be hidden; otherwise, it is exposed. Hidden input controls cannot be manipulated by the user. A control would also be not shown when it is contained in a dialog that does not have its tab selected in a multi-dialog dialog box; in this case, it may be invisible but whether it is hidden or exposed is another matter. Also see **disabled and enabled**.

i-action: An intermediate action, usually caused by the interaction of a user with an input control, such as the hiding/showing and disabling/enabling of other controls; the opening of the Viewer to display something; or the execution of a SCRIPT or a PROGRAM.

input control: A screen element which the user fills in or sets. Controls include check boxes, buttons, radio buttons, edit fields, spinners, file choosers, etc. Input controls have (set) values, which can be string, numeric, or special. These values reflect how the user has "filled-in" the control. Input controls are said to be string or numeric depending on the type of result they obtain (and how they store it).

Also see **static control**.

label or title: See **title or label**.

list: A programming concept; a vector of elements.

list box A type of string input control; presents a list of things from which the user may choose. A list box has (sets) a string value.

numeric input control An input control that returns (has) a numeric value associated with it.

position: Where something is located, measured from the top-left by how far to the right it is (x) and how far down it is (y).

PROGRAM: A programming concept dealing with the implementation of dialogs. PROGRAMs may be used to implement i-actions or u-actions. Also see **SCRIPT**.

radio buttons: A set of numeric input controls, each a button, of which only one may be selected at a time; suitable for obtaining categorical responses. Each ratio button in the set has (sets) a numeric value, 0 or 1, depending on which button is selected. Only one in the set will be 1.

SCRIPT: A programming concept dealing with the implementation of dialogs. An array of i-actions to be executed one after the other; errors that occur do not stop subsequent actions from being attempted. Also see **PROGRAM**.

size: How large something is, measured from it's top-left corner, as a width (*xsize*) and height (*ysize*). Note that height is measured from the top down.

spinner: A type of numeric input control; presents a numeric value that the user may increment or decrement over a range. A spinner has (sets) a numeric value.

static control: A screen element is much like an input control except that it cannot be interacted with by the end user. Static controls include static text and lines drawn around controls visually to group them together (group boxes and frames). Also see **control** and **input control**.

static text: A static control specifying text to be placed on a dialog.

string input control An input control that returns (has) a string value associated with it.

tabs: The small labels that stick up at the top of each dialog (when there is more than one dialog associated with the dialog box) and on which the user clicks to select the dialog to be filled in.

title or label: The fixed text that appears above or on objects such as dialog boxes, buttons, etc. Controls are usually said to be labeled, whereas dialog boxes are said to be titled.

u-action: What a dialog box causes to happen after the user has filled it in and clicked a u-action button. U stands for ultimate. The point of a dialog box is to result in a u-action.

u-action buttons: The buttons OK, Submit, and Cancel; when one is clicked, causes the ultimate action associated with the dialog box to occur and, perhaps, for the dialog box to close.

varlist or varname control: A type of string input control; an edit field that will also accept input from the Variables window. A varlist or varname control has (sets) a string value.

Appendix B. Class definition of dialog boxes

Dialog boxes are implemented in terms of class programming; see [P] **class**.

The top-level class instance of a dialog box defined in *dialogbox*.dlg is *.dialogbox_*dlg. Dialogs and controls are nested within that, so *.dialogbox_*dlg.*dialogname* would refer to a dialog and *.dialogbox_*dlg.*dialogname.controlname* would refer to a control in the dialog.

*.dialogbox_*dlg.*dialogname.controlname*.value is the current value of the control, which will either be a string or double. You must not change this value.

The member functions of the controls are implemented as member functions of *.dialogbox_*dlg.*dialogname.controlname*, and so may be called in the standard way.

Appendix C. Interface guidelines for dialog boxes

One of Stata's strengths is its strong support for cross-platform use—datasets and programs are completely compatible across platforms. This includes dialogs written in the dialog programming language. Although Windows, Macintosh, and X-Windows share many common graphical user interface elements and concepts, they all vary slightly in their appearance and implementation. This variation makes it difficult to design dialogs that look and behave the same across all platforms. Dialogs should look pleasant on screen to enhance their usability, and achieving this goal often means being platform specific when laying out controls. This often leads to undesirable results on other platforms.

The dialog programming language was written with this in mind, and dialogs that appear and behave the same across multiple operating systems as well as appear pleasant can be created by following some simple guidelines.

Use default heights where applicable: Variations in vertical size requirements of controls across different operating systems can cause a dialog that appears properly on one platform to display controls that overlap each other on another. Using the default *ysize* of . will take these variations into account, and will allow for much easier placement and alignment of controls. Some controls (list boxes, regular combo boxes, group boxes, and frames) still require their *ysize* be specified because their vertical size determines how much information they can reveal.

Use all horizontal space available: There are also variations in the type of fonts that are used to display text labels and control values. These variations can cause some control labels to be truncated (or even word wrapped) if their *xsize* is not large enough for a platform's system font. To prevent this from happening, specify an *xsize* that's as large as possible. For each column of controls, specify the entire column width for each control's *xsize*, even for controls where it is obviously unnecessary. This reduces the chances of a control's label being truncated on another platform, and also allows making changes to the label without having to constantly adjust the *xsize*. If your control barely fits into the space allocated to it, consider making your dialog slightly larger.

Use the appropriate alignment for static text controls: The variations in system fonts also make it difficult to horizontally align static text controls with other controls. Placing a static text control next to an edit field may look good on one platform and show up with too much space between the controls on another, or even may show up truncated.

One solution is to place static text controls above controls that have an edit field and make the static text control as wide as possible. This gives more room for the static text control, and makes it easier to left-justify it with other controls.

For situations where placing a static text control to the left of a control is more appropriate (such as From: and To: edit fields), use right alignment rather than the default left alignment. The two controls will then be equally spaced apart on all platforms. Again, be sure to make the static text control slightly wider than necessary— do not try to left-justify a right-aligned static text control with controls above and below it, because it may not appear left-justified on other platforms, or may even be truncated.

Do not crowd controls: Without making your dialog box unnecessarily large, use all the space that is available. Organize related controls close together, and put some distance between unrelated ones. Do not overload users with lots of controls in a single dialog. If necessary, group controls in separate dialogs. Most importantly, be consistent in how you layout controls.

All vertical size and spacing of controls involves multiples of 10 pixels: The default *ysize* for most controls is 20 pixels. Related controls are typically spaced 10 pixels apart, and unrelated ones are at least 20 pixels apart.

Use the appropriate control for the job: Checkboxes have two states: on or off. A radio button group consisting of two radio buttons similarly has two states. A checkbox is appropriate when what happens when it is either on or off is easy to infer (for example, **Use constant**). A two-radio-button group is appropriate when the opposite state cannot be inferred (for example, **Display graph** and **Display table**).

Radio button groups should contain at least two radio buttons and up to about seven. If you need more choices, consider using a dropdown-list combo box, or if the number of choices is greater than about twelve, a list box. If you require a control that allows multiple selections, consider a regular combo box or dropdown combo box. Dropdown combo boxes can be cumbersome to use if the number of choices is great, so use a regular combo box unless space is limited.

Avoid hiding controls: When attempting to limit the number of choices a user can make, avoid hiding controls when disabling the controls is more suited for that purpose.

Understand control precedence for mouse clicks: Due to the limited size of dialogs, it is often useful to place several controls within the same area and hide and show them as necessary. It is also useful to place controls within other controls such as group boxes and frames for organizational and presentation purposes. However, the order of creation and placement and size of controls can have an effect on which controls receive mouse clicks first or whether they receive them at all.

The control where this can be problematic is the radio button. On some platforms, the space occupied by a group of radio buttons is not the space occupied by the individual radio buttons. It actually is inclusive to the space occupied by the radio button that is closest to the top left corner of the dialog, the widest radio button, and the bottom-most radio button. To prevent a group of radio buttons from preventing mouse clicks from being received by other controls, Stata gives precedence to all other controls except for group boxes and frames. The order of precedence for controls that can receive mouse clicks is first all controls other than radio buttons and checkbox group boxes, then radio buttons, then checkbox group boxes.

If you intend to place two or more groups of radio buttons in the same area and show and hide them as necessary, be sure that when you hide the radio buttons from a group, you hide all radio buttons from a group. The radio button group with precedence over other groups will continue to have precedence as long as any of its radio buttons are visible. Mouse clicks in the space occupied by nonvisible radio buttons in a group with precedence will not pass through to any other groups occupying the same space.

It is always safe to place controls within frames, groupboxes, and checkbox group boxes because all other controls take precedence over those controls.

In practice you should never hide a radio button from a group without hiding the rest of the radio buttons from the group. Consider simply disabling the radio button or buttons instead. It is also not a good idea to hide or show radio buttons from different groups to give them the appearance that they are from the same group. That simply will not work on some platforms and is generally a bad idea anyway.

Radio buttons have precedence over checkbox group boxes. You may place radio buttons within a checkbox group box but do not place a checkbox group box within the space occupied by a group of radio buttons. If you do, you may not be able to click on the checkbox control on some platforms.

Also See

Complementary:	[P] **window menu**,
	[R] **db**

Title

discard — Drop automatically loaded programs

Syntax

```
discard
```

Description

discard drops all automatically loaded programs (see [U] **20.2 What is an ado-file?**); clears e(), r(), and s() saved results (see [P] **return**); eliminates information stored by the most recent estimation command and any other saved estimation results (see [P] **ereturn**); closes any open graphs and drops all sersets (see [P] **serset**); clears all class definitions and instances (see [P] **classutil**); and closes all dialogs and clears their remembered contents (see [P] **dialogs**).

In short, discard causes Stata to forget everything current without forgetting anything important such as the data in memory.

discard may not be abbreviated.

Remarks

Use discard to debug ado-files. Making a change to an ado-file will not cause Stata to update its internal copy of the changed program. discard clears all automatically loaded programs from memory, forcing Stata to refresh its internal copies with the versions residing on disk.

In addition, all of Stata's estimation commands have the ability to reshow their previous output when the command is typed without arguments. They achieve this by storing information on the problem in memory. predict calculates various statistics (predictions, residuals, influence statistics, etc.), vce shows the covariance matrix, lincom calculates linear combinations of estimated coefficients, and test and testnl perform hypotheses tests, all using that stored information. discard eliminates that information, making it appear as if you never estimated the model.

Also See

Complementary:	[P] **class**, [P] **classutil**, [P] **dialogs**
Background:	[U] **20 Ado-files**

Title

> **display** — Display strings and values of scalar expressions

Syntax

$\underline{\text{di}}$splay $\left[\textit{subcommand}\ \left[\textit{subcommand}\ \left[\ldots\right]\right]\right]$

where *subcommand* is

"*double quoted string*"

' "*compound double quoted string*" '

$\left[\%\textit{fmt}\right]\ \left[=\right]\textit{exp}$

as $\left\{\text{text}\,|\,\text{txt}\,|\,\underline{\text{res}}\text{ult}\,|\,\underline{\text{error}}\,|\,\underline{\text{input}}\right\}$

in smcl

$\underline{\ \ }$asis

$\underline{\ \ }\underline{\text{s}}$kip(#)

$\underline{\ \ }\underline{\text{col}}$umn(#)

$\underline{\ \ }\underline{\text{n}}$ewline$\left[(\#)\right]$

$\underline{\ \ }\underline{\text{c}}$ontinue

$\underline{\ \ }\underline{\text{d}}$up(#)

$\underline{\ \ }\underline{\text{r}}$equest(*macname*)

$\underline{\ \ }$char(#)

'

' '

Description

display displays strings and values of scalar expressions. display is the way you produce output from the programs that you write.

Remarks

Interactively, display can be used as a substitute for a hand calculator; see [R] **display**. You can type things such as 'display 2+2'.

display's *subcommands* are used in do-files and programs to produce formatted output. The subcommands are

"*double quoted string*"	displays the string without the quotes
'"*compound double quoted string*"'	displays the string without the outer quotes; allows embedded quotes
$\left[\text{\%}\,fmt\right]\,\left[=\right]\text{exp}$	allows results to be formatted; see [U] **15.5 Formats: controlling how data are displayed**
as *style*	sets the style ("color") for the subcommands that follow; there may be more than one as *style* per display
in smcl	switches from _asis mode to smcl mode; in smcl is the default mode if version is ≥ 7
_asis	switches from smcl mode to _asis mode; _asis is the default mode if version is < 7
_skip(#)	skips # columns
_column(#)	skips to the #th column
_newline	goes to a new line
_newline(#)	skips # lines
_continue	suppresses automatic newline at end of display command
_dup(#)	repeats the next subcommand # times
_request(*macname*)	accepts input from the console and places it into the macro *macname*
_char(#)	displays the character for ASCII code #
,	displays a single blank between two subcommands
, ,	places no blanks between two subcommands

▷ Example

Here is a nonsense program called silly that illustrates the subcommands:

```
. program list silly
silly:
  1.        set obs 10
  2.        gen myvar=uniform()
  3.        di as text _dup(59) "-"
  4.        di "hello, world"
  5.        di %~59s "This is centered"
  6.        di "myvar[1] = " as result myvar[1]
  7.        di _col(10) "myvar[1] = " myvar[1] _skip(10) "myvar[2] = " myvar[2]
  8.        di "myvar[1]/myvar[2] = " %5.4f myvar[1]/myvar[2]
  9.        di "This" _newline _col(5) "That" _newline _col(10) "What"
 10.        di '"She said, "Hello""'
 11.        di substr("abcI can do string expressionsXYZ",4,27)
 12.        di _char(65) _char(83) _char(67) _char(73) _char(73)
 13.        di _dup(59) "-" " (good-bye)"
```

Here is the result of running it:

```
. silly
obs was 0, now 10
------------------------------------------------------------
hello, world
                      This is centered
myvar[1] = .13698408
        myvar[1] = .13698408              myvar[2] = .64322066
myvar[1]/myvar[2] = 0.2130
This
    That
        What
She said, "Hello"
I can do string expressions
ASCII
----------------------------------------------------- (good-bye)
```
◁

Styles

Stata has four styles, called text, result, error, and input. Typically these styles are rendered in terms of color,

$$\text{text} = \text{green}$$

$$\text{result} = \text{yellow}$$

$$\text{error} = \text{red}$$

$$\text{input} = \text{white}$$

or, at least, that is the default in the Results window when the window has a black background. On a white background, the defaults are

$$\text{text} = \text{black}$$

$$\text{result} = \text{black and bold}$$

$$\text{error} = \text{red and bold}$$

$$\text{input} = \text{black}$$

and, in any case, users can reset the styles to be whatever they want them to be by pulling down **Prefs** and choosing **General Preferences**.

The display directives as text, as result, as error, and as input allow you the programmer to specify in which rendition subsequent items in the display statement are to be displayed, so if a piece of your program reads

```
quietly summarize mpg
display as text "mean of mpg = " as result r(mean)
```

what might be displayed is

```
mean of mpg = 21.432432
```

where, above, our use of boldface for the 21.432432 is to emphasize that it would be displayed differently than the "mean of mpg =" part. In the Results window, if we had a black background, the "mean of mpg =" part would be in green and the 21.432432 would be in yellow.

You can switch back and forth among styles within a `display` statement and between `display` statements. Here is how we recommend using the styles:

as `result` should be used to display things that depend on the data being used. For statistical output, think of what would happen if the names of the dataset remained the same but all the data changed. Clearly, calculated results would change. That is what should be displayed as `result`.

as `text` should be used to display the text around the results. Again, think of the experiment where you change the data but not the names. Anything that would not change should be displayed as `text`. This will include not just the names, but table lines and borders, variable labels, etc.

as `error` should be reserved for displaying error messages. as `error` is special in that it not only displays the message as an error (probably meaning that the message is displayed in red), but in that it also forces the message to display even if output is being suppressed. (There are two commands for suppressing output: `quietly` and `capture`. `quietly` will not suppress as `error` messages but `capture` will, the idea being that `capture`, since it captures the return code, is anticipating errors and will take the appropriate action.)

as `input` should never be used unless you are creating a special effect. as `input` (white on a black background) is reserved for what the user types, and the output your program is producing is by definition not being typed by the user. Stata uses as `input` when it displays what the user types.

❑ Technical Note

Prior to Stata 7, `display` had a syntax that allowed the directives in green, in yellow, in blue, in red, and in white. Stata still allows this so that old programs continue to work. The mapping is

$$\text{in green} = \text{as text}$$
$$\text{in yellow} = \text{as result}$$
$$\text{in blue} = \text{as text } (sic)$$
$$\text{in red} = \text{as error}$$
$$\text{in white} = \text{as input}$$

You can use the old or the new syntax in both old and new programs; it does not matter. Notice that the color blue has disappeared; you can specify in blue, but it means as text, which is to say, in green. Blue is no longer available as a color because blue is now reserved for displaying links.

❑

display used with quietly and noisily

`display`'s output will be suppressed by `quietly` at the appropriate times. Consider the following:

```
. program list example1
example1:
  1. di "hello there"
. example1
hello there
. quietly example1
. _
```

The output was suppressed because the program was run `quietly`. Messages displayed as error, however, are considered error messages and are always displayed:

```
. program list example2
example2:
    1.      di as error "hello there"
. example2
hello there
. quietly example2
hello there
```

Even though the program was run `quietly`, the message as error was displayed. Error messages should always be displayed as error so that they will always be displayed at the terminal.

Programs often have parts of their code buried in `capture` or `quietly` blocks. `display`s inside such blocks produce no output:

```
. program list example3
example3:
    1. quietly {
    2.      display "hello there"
    3. }
. example3

.  _
```

Had the `display` included as error, the text would have been displayed, but only error output should be displayed that way. For regular output, the solution is to precede the `display` with `noisily`:

```
. program list example4
example4:
    1. quietly {
    2.      noisily display "hello there"
    3. }
. example4
hello there
```

This method also allows Stata to correctly treat a `quietly` specified by the caller:

```
. quietly example4

.  _
```

Despite its name, `noisily` does not really guarantee that the output will be shown—it restores the output only if output would have been allowed at the instant the program was called.

For more information on `noisily` and `quietly`, see [P] **quietly**.

Columns

   `display` can only move forward and downward. The subcommands that take a numeric argument allow only nonnegative integer arguments. It is not possible to back up to make an insertion in the output.

```
. program list cont
cont:
  1.        di "Stuff" _column(9) "More Stuff"
  2.        di "Stuff" _continue
  3.        di _column(9) "More Stuff"
. cont
Stuff    More Stuff
Stuff    More Stuff
```

display and SMCL

SMCL is Stata's output formatter, and all Stata output passes through SMCL. See [P] **smcl** for a complete description. Here, we just want to emphasize that all the features of SMCL are available to display and so motivate you to turn to the SMCL section of this manual.

In our opening silly example, we included the line

```
di as text _dup(59) "-"
```

That line would have better read

```
di as text "{hline 59}"
```

The first display produces this:

```
-----------------------------------------------------------
```

and the second produces this:

```
_____
```

It was not display that produced that solid line—display just displayed the characters {hline 59}. Output of Stata, however, passes through something called SMCL, and SMCL interprets what it hears. When SMCL heard {hline 59}, SMCL drew a horizontal line 59 characters wide.

SMCL has lots of other capabilities, including the ability to create clickable links in your output that, when you click on them, can even cause other Stata commands to execute.

If you carefully review the SMCL documentation, you will discover lots of overlap in the capabilities of SMCL and display that will lead you to wonder whether you should use display's capabilities or SMCL's. For instance, in the section above, we demonstrated the use of display's _column() feature to skip forward to a column. If you read the SMCL documentation, you will discover that SMCL has a similar feature, {col}. You can type

```
display "Stuff" _column(9) "More Stuff"
```

or you can type

```
display "Stuff{col 9}More Stuff"
```

So, which should you type? The answer is that it makes no difference, and that when you use display's _column() directive, display just outputs the corresponding SMCL {col} directive for you. This rule generalizes beyond _column(). For instance,

```
display as text "hello"
```

and

```
display "{text}hello"
```

are equivalent. There is, however, one important place where display and SMCL are different:

```
display as error "error message"
```

is not quite the same as

```
display "{error}error message"
```

Use `display as error`. The SMCL `{error}` directive sets the rendition to that of errors, but it does not tell Stata that the message is to be displayed even if output is otherwise being suppressed. `display`'s `as error` both sets the rendition and tells Stata to override output suppression if that is relevant.

❑ Technical Note

All Stata output passes through SMCL, and one side effect of that is that open and close brace characters { and } are treated oddly by `display`. Try the following:

```
display as text "{1, 2, 3}"
{1, 2, 3}
```

The result is just as you expect. Now try

```
display as text "{result}"
```

The result will be to display nothing because `{result}` is a SMCL directive. The first displayed something even though it contained braces because `{1, 2, 3}` is not a SMCL directive.

You want to be careful when displaying something that might itself contain braces. You can do that by using `display`'s `_asis` directive. Once you specify `_asis`, whatever follows in the display will be displayed exactly as it is, without SMCL interpretation:

```
display as text _asis "{result}"
{result}
```

You can switch back to allowing SMCL interpretation within the line using the `in smcl` directive:

```
display as text _asis "{result}" in smcl "is a {bf:smcl} directive"
{result} is a smcl directive
```

Each and every `display` command in your program starts off in SMCL mode unless the program is running with `version` set to 6 or before, in which case each and every `display` starts off in `_asis` mode. If you want to use SMCL in old programs without otherwise updating them, you can include `display`'s `in smcl` directive.

❑

Displaying variable names

Let us assume that a program we are writing is to produce a table that looks like this:

Variable	Obs	Mean	Std. Dev.	Min	Max
mpg	74	21.2973	5.785503	12	41
weight	74	3019.459	777.1936	1760	4840
displ	74	197.2973	91.83722	79	425

Putting out the header in our program is easy enough:

```
di in text "    Variable {c |}      Obs" /*
       */ _col(37) "Mean    Std. Dev.      Min      Max"
di in text "{hline 13}{c +}{hline 53}"
```

We use the SMCL directive {hline} to draw the horizontal line, and we use the SMCL characters {c |} and {c +} to output the vertical bar and the "plus" sign where the lines cross.

Now let's turn to putting out the rest of the table. Let us remember that variable names can be of unequal length and can even be very long. If we are not careful, we might end up putting out something that looks like this:

```
     Variable |     Obs      Mean   Std. Dev.      Min      Max
--------------+---------------------------------------------------
miles_per_gallon |      74   21.2973   5.785503           12            41
weight |      74  3019.459   777.1936      1760     4840
displacement |      74   197.2973   91.83722      79      425
```

If it were not for the too-long variable name, we could avoid the problem by displaying our lines with something like this:

```
display in text %12s "'vname'" " {c |}" /*
       */ as result /*
       */ %8.0g 'n' "     " /*
       */ %9.0g 'mean' "  " %9.0g 'sd'    "  " /*
       */ %9.0g 'min'    "  " %9.0g 'max'
```

What we are imagining here is that we write a subroutine to display a line of output and that the display line above appears in that subroutine:

```
program output_line
       args n mean sd min max
       display in text %12s "'vname'" " {c |}" /*
              */ as result /*
              */ %8.0g 'n' "     " /*
              */ %9.0g 'mean' "  " %9.0g 'sd'    "  " /*
              */ %9.0g 'min'    "  " %9.0g 'max'
end
```

In our main routine, we would calculate results and then just call output_line with the variable name and results to be displayed. This subroutine would be sufficient to produce the following output:

```
     Variable |     Obs      Mean   Std. Dev.      Min      Max
--------------+---------------------------------------------------
miles_per_gallon |      74   21.2973   5.785503           12            41
      weight |      74  3019.459   777.1936      1760     4840
displacement |      74   197.2973   91.83722      79      425
```

The short variable name weight would be spaced over because we specified the %12s format. The right way to handle the miles_per_gallon variable is to display its abbreviation using Stata's abbrev() function:

```
program output_line
       args n mean sd min max
       display in text %12s abbrev("'vname'",12) " {c |}" /*
              */ as result /*
              */ %8.0g 'n' "     " /*
              */ %9.0g 'mean' "  " %9.0g 'sd'    "  " /*
              */ %9.0g 'min'    "  " %9.0g 'max'
end
```

With this improved subroutine, we would get the following output:

Variable	Obs	Mean	Std. Dev.	Min	Max
miles_per_~n	74	21.2973	5.785503	12	41
weight	74	3019.459	777.1936	1760	4840
displacement	74	197.2973	91.83722	79	425

The point of this is to convince you to learn about and use Stata's `abbrev()` function. `abbrev("'vname'",12)` returns `'vname'` abbreviated to 12 characters.

If we now wanted to modify our program to produce the following output,

Variable	Obs	Mean	Std. Dev.	Min	Max
miles_per_~n	74	21.2973	5.785503	12	41
weight	74	3019.459	777.1936	1760	4840
displacement	74	197.2973	91.83722	79	425

all we would need do is add a `display` at the end of the main routine that reads

```
di in text "{hline 13}{c BT}{hline 53}"
```

Note the use of `{c BT}`. The characters that we use to draw lines in and around tables are summarized in [P] **smcl**.

❑ Technical Note

Let us now consider outputting the table in the form,

Variable	Obs	Mean	Std. Dev.	Min	Max
miles_per_~n	74	21.2973	5.785503	12	41
weight	74	3019.459	777.1936	1760	4840
displacement	74	197.2973	91.83722	79	425

where the boldfaced entries are clickable, and, if you click on them, the result is to execute `summarize` followed by the variable name. We assume that you have already read [P] **smcl** and so know that the relevant SMCL directive to create the link is `{stata}`, but continue reading even if you have not read [P] **smcl**.

The obvious fix to our subroutine would be simply to add the `{stata}` directive, although to do that we will have to store `abbrev("'vname'",12)` in a macro so that we can refer to it:

```
program output_line
        args n mean sd min max
        local abname = abbrev("'vname'",12)
        display in text %12s "{stata summarize 'vname':'abname'}" /*
            */ " {c |}" /*
            */ as result /*
            */ %8.0g 'n' "   " /*
            */ %9.0g 'mean' "  " %9.0g 'sd'    "  " /*
            */ %9.0g 'min'   "  " %9.0g 'max'
end
```

The SMCL directive `{stata summarize 'vname':'abname'}` says to display `'abname'` as clickable, and, if the user clicks on it, to execute `summarize 'vname'`. Notice that we used the abbreviated name to display and the unabbreviated name in the command.

The single problem with this fix is that our table will not align correctly because display does not know that "{stata summarize `vname':`abname'}" displays only `abname`. To display, the string looks very long and is not going to fit into a %12s field. The solution to that problem is

```
program output_line
        args n mean sd min max
        local abname = abbrev("`vname'",12)
        display in text "{ralign 12:{stata summarize `vname':`abname'}}" /*
                */ " {c |}" /*
                */ as result /*
                */ %8.0g `n' "    " /*
                */ %9.0g `mean' "  " %9.0g `sd'    "  " /*
                */ %9.0g `min' "  " %9.0g `max'
end
```

The SMCL {ralign #:*text*} macro right aligns *text* in a field 12 wide, and so is equivalent to %12s. The *text* that we are asking be aligned is "{stata summarize `vname':`abname'}", but SMCL understands that the only displayable part of the string is `abname', and so will align it correctly.

If we wanted to duplicate the effect of a %-12s format using SMCL, we would use {lalign 12:*text*}.

❏

Obtaining input from the terminal

display's _request(*macname*) option accepts input from the console and places it into the macro *macname*. For example,

```
. display "What is Y? " _request(yval)
What is Y? i don't know
. display "$yval"
i don't know
```

If yval had to be a number, the code fragment to obtain it might be

```
global yval "junk"
capture confirm number $yval
while _rc!=0 {
    display "What is Y? " _request(yval)
    capture confirm number $yval
}
```

One will typically want to store such input into a local macro. Remember that local macros have names that really begin with a '_':

```
local yval "junk"
capture confirm number `yval'
while _rc!=0 {
    display "What is Y? " _request(_yval)
    capture confirm number `yval'
}
```

Also See

Complementary:	[P] **capture**, [P] **quietly**
Related:	[P] **smcl**; [P] **return**,
	[R] **list**, [R] **outfile**
Background:	[U] **15.5 Formats: controlling how data are displayed**,
	[U] **21 Programming Stata**

Title

ereturn — Post estimation results

Syntax

> **ereturn** <u>loc</u>al *name* ...   (see [P] **macro**)
>
> **ereturn** <u>sca</u>lar *name* = *exp*
>
> **ereturn** <u>mat</u>rix *name* $\big[$ = $\big]$ *matname* $\big[$, copy $\big]$
>
> **ereturn** clear
>
> **ereturn** <u>l</u>ist
>
> **ereturn** post **b V** $\big[$**C**$\big]$ $\big[$, <u>dep</u>name(*string*) <u>o</u>bs(*#*) <u>d</u>of(*#*) <u>e</u>sample(*varname*) $\big]$
>
> **ereturn** <u>rep</u>ost $\big[$**b** = **b**$\big]$ $\big[$**V** = **V**$\big]$ $\big[$, <u>e</u>sample(*varname*) <u>ren</u>ame $\big]$
>
> **ereturn** <u>di</u>splay $\big[$, <u>ef</u>orm(*string*) <u>f</u>irst neq(*#*) <u>p</u>lus <u>l</u>evel(*#*) $\big]$

where *name* is the name of the macro, scalar, or matrix that will be returned in e(*name*) by the estimation program, *matname* is the name of an existing matrix, **b** is a $1 \times p$ coefficient vector (matrix), **V** is a $p \times p$ covariance matrix, and **C** is a $c \times (p+1)$ constraint matrix.

Description

ereturn local, **ereturn** scalar, and **ereturn** matrix set the e() macros, scalars, and matrices returned by estimation commands. See [P] **return** for more discussion on returning results.

ereturn clear clears the e() saved results.

ereturn list lists the names and values of the e() returned macros and scalars and the names and sizes of the e() returned matrices from the last estimation command.

ereturn post saves the coefficient vector (b) and variance–covariance (V) matrices in Stata's system areas, making all the post-estimation features described in [U] **23 Estimation and post-estimation commands** available. **ereturn** repost changes the b or V matrix (allowed only after estimation commands that posted their results using **ereturn** post) or changes the declared estimation sample. The specified matrices cease to exist after post or repost; they are literally moved into Stata's system areas. The resulting b and V matrices in Stata's system areas can be reobtained by reference to e(b) and e(V). **ereturn** post and repost deal with only the coefficient and variance–covariance matrices, while **ereturn** matrix is used to save other matrices associated with the estimation command.

ereturn display displays or redisplays the coefficient table corresponding to results that have been previously posted using **ereturn** post or repost.

For a discussion of posting results with constraint matrices (**C** in the syntax diagram above), see [P] **matrix constraint**, but only after reading this entry.

Options

copy specified with ereturn matrix indicates that the matrix is to be copied; that is, the original matrix should be left in place.

depname(*string*) specified with ereturn post supplies a name that should be that of the dependent variable, but can be anything; that name is saved and added to the appropriate place on the output whenever ereturn display is executed.

obs(#) specified with ereturn post supplies the number of observations on which the estimation was performed; that number is saved and stored in e(N).

dof(#) specified with ereturn post supplies the number of (denominator) degrees of freedom that is to be used with t and F statistics, and is saved and stored in e(df_r). This number is used in calculating significance levels and confidence intervals by ereturn display and by subsequent test commands performed on the posted results. If the option is not specified, normal (Z) and χ^2 statistics are used.

esample(*varname*) specified with ereturn post or ereturn repost gives the name of the 0/1 variable indicating the observations involved in the estimation. The variable is removed from the dataset, but is available for use as e(sample); see [U] **23.5 Specifying the estimation subsample**. If the esample() option is not specified with ereturn post, it is set to all zeros (meaning no estimation sample). See [P] **mark** for details of the marksample command that can help create *varname*.

rename is allowed only with the b = b syntax of ereturn repost, and tells Stata to use the names obtained from the specified **b** matrix as the labels for both the **b** and **V** estimation matrices. These labels are subsequently used in the output produced by ereturn display.

eform(*string*) specified with ereturn display indicates that the exponentiated form of the coefficients is to be output, and that reporting of the constant is to be suppressed. *string* is used to label the exponentiated coefficients; see [R] **maximize**.

first requests that Stata display only the first equation and make it appear as if only one equation were estimated.

neq(#) requests that Stata display only the first # equations and make it appear as if only # equations were estimated.

plus changes the bottom separation line produced by ereturn display to have a + symbol at the position of the dividing line between variable names and results. This is useful if you plan on adding more output to the table.

level(#), an option of ereturn display, supplies the significance level for the confidence intervals of the coefficients; see [U] **23 Estimation and post-estimation commands**.

Remarks

Remarks are presented under the headings

> *Estimation class programs*
> *Setting individual estimation results*
> *Posting estimation coefficient and variance–covariance matrices*
> > *Single-equation models*
> > *Multiple-equation models*
> > *Single-equation models masquerading as multiple-equation models*
> > *Setting the estimation sample*
> > *Reposting results*
> > *Minor details: the depname() and dof() options*

For a quick summary of the ereturn command, see [P] **return**.

Estimation class programs

An important feature of Stata is that, after any estimation command, you can obtain individual coefficients and standard errors using _b[] and _se[] (see [U] **16.5 Accessing coefficients and standard errors**); list the coefficients using matrix list e(b); list the variance–covariance matrix of the estimators using matrix list e(V) or in a table using vce (see [R] **vce**); obtain the linear prediction and its standard error using predict (see [R] **predict**); and test linear hypotheses about the coefficients using test (see [R] **test**). Other important information from an estimation command can be obtained from the returned e() results. (For example, the estimation command name is returned in e(cmd). The dependent variable name is returned in e(depvar).) The e() results from an estimation command can be listed using the ereturn list command. All these features are summarized in [U] **23 Estimation and post-estimation commands**.

If you decide to write your own estimation command, your command can share all these features as well. This is accomplished by posting the results you calculate to Stata. The basic outline of an estimation command is

```
program myest, eclass
        version 8.0
        if !replay() {
                syntax whatever [, whatever Level(integer 'c(level)')]
                marksample touse    // see [P] mark
                perform any other parsing of the user's estimation request;
                local depn "dependent variable name"
                local nobs = number of observations in estimation
                tempname b V
                produce coefficient vector 'b' and variance–covariance matrix 'V'
                ereturn post 'b' 'V', obs('nobs') depname('depn') esample('touse')
                ereturn local depvar "'depn'"
                store whatever else you want in e()
                ereturn local cmd "myest"     // set e(cmd) last
        }
        else {    // replay
                if "'e(cmd)'"!="myest" error 301
                syntax [, Level(integer 'c(level)')]
        }
        if 'level'<10 | 'level'>99 {
                di as err "level() must be between 10 and 99 inclusive"
                exit 198
        }
        output any header above the coefficient table;
        ereturn display, level('level')
end
```

We will not discuss here how the estimates are formed, but see [P] **matrix** for an example of programming linear regression and see [R] **ml** for examples of programming maximum likelihood estimators. However the estimates are formed, our interest is in the posting of those results to Stata.

When programming estimation commands, remember to declare them as estimation commands. This is accomplished with the eclass option to program; see [U] **21 Programming Stata**. If you do not specify your program to be eclass, Stata will produce an error if you use ereturn local, ereturn scalar, or ereturn matrix in your program. For more information on the general topic of saving program results, see [P] **return**.

❏ Technical Note

Notice the use of the `replay()` function in our estimation program example. This function is not like other Stata functions; see [R] **functions**. `replay()` simply returns 1 if the command line is empty or begins with a comma, and 0 otherwise. Said more simply, `replay()` indicates whether the command is an initial call to the estimation program (`replay()` returns 0) or a call to redisplay past estimation results (`replay()` returns 1).

In fact,

```
if !replay() {
```

is equivalent to

```
if trim(`"`0'"') == "" | substr((trim(`"`0'"')),1,1) == "," {
```

but is easier to read.

❏

The `ereturn local`, `ereturn scalar`, `ereturn matrix`, `ereturn clear`, and `ereturn list` commands are discussed in the *Setting individual estimation results* section. The `ereturn post`, `ereturn repost`, and `ereturn display` commands are discussed in the *Posting estimation coefficient and variance–covariance matrices* section.

Setting individual estimation results

Stata's estimation commands save the command name in the returned macro `e(cmd)` and the name of the dependent variable in `e(depvar)`. Other macros and scalars are also saved. For example, the estimation sample size is saved in the returned scalar `e(N)`. The model and residual degrees of freedom are saved in `e(df_m)` and `e(df_r)`.

These `e()` macro and scalar results are saved using the `ereturn local` and `ereturn scalar` commands. Matrices may be saved using the `ereturn matrix` command. The coefficient vector `e(b)` and variance–covariance matrix `e(V)`, however, are handled differently, and are only saved using the `ereturn post` and `ereturn repost` commands, which are discussed in the next section.

▷ Example

Assume that we are programming an estimation command called `xyz`, and that we have the dependent variable in `depname`, the estimation sample size in `nobs`, and other important information stored in other local macros and scalars. Additionally, we wish to save an auxiliary estimation matrix that our program has created called `lam` into the saved matrix `e(lambda)`. We would save these results using commands such as the following in our estimation program:

```
...
ereturn local depvar "`depname'"
ereturn scalar N = `nobs'
ereturn matrix lambda lam
...
ereturn local cmd "xyz"
```

◁

The matrix given to the `ereturn matrix` command is removed, and the new `e()` matrix is then made available. For instance, in this example, we have the line

```
ereturn matrix lambda lam
```

After this line has executed, the matrix `lam` is no longer available for use, but you can instead refer to the newly created `e(lambda)` matrix.

The `e()` results from an estimation command can be viewed using the `ereturn list` command.

▷ Example

We regress automobile weight on length and engine displacement using the auto dataset.

```
. use http://www.stata-press.com/data/r8/auto
(1978 Automobile Data)
. regress weight length displ
```

Source	SS	df	MS
Model	41063449.8	2	20531724.9
Residual	3030728.55	71	42686.3176
Total	44094178.4	73	604029.841

Number of obs =	74
F(2, 71) =	480.99
Prob > F =	0.0000
R-squared =	0.9313
Adj R-squared =	0.9293
Root MSE =	206.61

weight	Coef.	Std. Err.	t	P>|t|	[95% Conf. Interval]	
length	22.91788	1.974431	11.61	0.000	18.98097	26.85478
displacement	2.932772	.4787094	6.13	0.000	1.978252	3.887291
_cons	-1866.181	297.7349	-6.27	0.000	-2459.847	-1272.514

```
. ereturn list
scalars:
                 e(N) =  74
              e(df_m) =  2
              e(df_r) =  71
                 e(F) =  480.9907735088096
                e(r2) =  .9312669232040125
              e(rmse) =  206.6066736285298
               e(mss) =  41063449.82964133
               e(rss) =  3030728.548737053
              e(r2_a) =  .9293307801956748
                e(ll) =  -497.9506459758983
              e(ll_0) =  -597.0190609278627
macros:
            e(depvar) :  "weight"
               e(cmd) :  "regress"
           e(predict) :  "regres_p"
             e(model) :  "ols"
matrices:
                 e(b) :  1 x 3
                 e(V) :  3 x 3
functions:
            e(sample)
```

In addition to listing all the `e()` results after an estimation command, you can access individual `e()` results.

```
. display "The command is: `e(cmd)'"
The command is: regress

. display "The adjusted R-squared is: `e(r2_a)'"
The adjusted R-squared is: .9293307801956748

. display "The residual sums-of-squares is: `e(rss)'"
The residual sums-of-squares is: 3030728.548737053

. matrix list e(V)

symmetric e(V)[3,3]
                         length   displacement         _cons
       length         3.8983761
 displacement        -.78935643      .22916272
        _cons        -576.89342      103.13249      88646.064

. matrix list e(b)

e(b)[1,3]
            length   displacement         _cons
    y1    22.917876      2.9327718     -1866.1807
```

For more information on referencing e() results, see [P] **return**.   ◁

The *Reference* manuals' entries for Stata's estimation commands have a *Saved Results* section describing the e() results that are returned by the command. If you are writing an estimation command, we recommend that you save the same kind of estimation results using the same naming convention as Stata's estimation commands. This is important if you want post-estimation commands to work after your estimation command. See [U] **23 Estimation and post-estimation commands** and [P] **return** for details.

When programming your estimation command, you will want to issue either an ereturn clear command or an ereturn post command before you save any estimation results. The ereturn clear command clears all e() results. The ereturn post command, which is discussed in the next section, first clears all previous e() results and then performs the post.

We recommend that the clearing of past estimation results and the setting of new e() results be postponed until late in your program. If an error occurs early in your program, the last successful estimation results will remain intact. The best place in your estimation program to set the e() results is after all other calculations have been completed and before estimation results are displayed.

We also recommend that you save the command name in e(cmd) as your very last act of saving results. This ensures that if e(cmd) is present, then all the other estimation results were successfully saved. Post-estimation commands assume that if e(cmd) is present, then the estimation command completed successfully and all expected results were saved. If you saved e(cmd) early in your estimation command and the user presses *Break* before the remaining e() results are saved, then post-estimation commands operating on the partial results would likely produce an error.

Posting estimation coefficient and variance–covariance matrices

The most important estimation results are the coefficient vector b and the variance–covariance matrix V. Since these two matrices are at the heart of an estimation command, for increased command execution speed, Stata handles these matrices in a special way. The ereturn post, ereturn repost, and ereturn display commands work on these matrices. The ereturn matrix command discussed in the last section cannot be used to save or to post the b and V matrices.

Single-equation models

Before posting, the coefficient vector is stored as a $1 \times p$ matrix and the corresponding variance–covariance matrix as a $p \times p$ matrix. The names bordering the coefficient matrix and those bordering the variance–covariance matrix play an important role. First, they must be the same. Second, it is these names that tell Stata how the results link to Stata's other features.

User estimation results come in two flavors: those for single-equation models and those for multiple-equation models. The absence or presence of equation names in the names bordering the matrix (see [P] **matrix rowname**) tells Stata which it is.

▷ Example

For instance, consider

```
. matrix list b

b[1,3]
         weight         mpg       _cons
y1    1.7465592   -49.512221   1946.0687

. matrix list V

symmetric V[3,3]
            weight         mpg       _cons
weight    .41133468
   mpg    44.601659    7422.863
 _cons   -2191.9032   -292759.82   12938766
```

If these were your estimation results, they would correspond to a single-equation model because the names bordering the matrices have no equation names. Here we post these results:

```
. ereturn post b V

. ereturn display
```

	Coef.	Std. Err.	z	P>|z|	[95% Conf. Interval]	
weight	1.746559	.6413538	2.72	0.006	.4895288	3.003589
mpg	-49.51222	86.15604	-0.57	0.566	-218.375	119.3505
_cons	1946.069	3597.05	0.54	0.588	-5104.019	8996.156

Once the results have been posted, anytime the `ereturn display` command is executed, Stata will redisplay the coefficient table. Moreover, all of Stata's other post-estimation features work. For instance,

```
. correlate, _coef
           weight       mpg      _cons
weight     1.0000
   mpg     0.8072    1.0000
 _cons    -0.9501   -0.9447    1.0000

. test weight

 ( 1)  weight = 0.0

        chi2(  1) =      7.42
      Prob > chi2 =    0.0065

. test weight=mpg/50

 ( 1)  weight - .02 mpg = 0.0

        chi2(  1) =      4.69
      Prob > chi2 =    0.0303
```

If the user were to type `predict pred`, then `predict` would create a new variable based on

$$1.746559 \, \texttt{weight} - 49.51222 \, \texttt{mpg} + 1946.069$$

except that it would carry out the calculation using the full, double-precision values of the coefficients. All determinations were made by Stata based on the names bordering the posted matrices.   ◁

Multiple-equation models

If the matrices posted using the `ereturn post` or `ereturn repost` commands have more than one equation name, then the estimation command is treated as a multiple-equation model.

▷ Example

Consider the following two matrices before posting:

```
. mat list b

b[1,6]
           price:       price:       price:       displ:       displ:       displ:
          weight          mpg        _cons       weight      foreign        _cons
y1     1.7417059    -50.31993    1977.9249    .09341608   -35.124241   -74.326413

. mat list V

symmetric V[6,6]
                          price:       price:       price:       displ:       displ:
                         weight          mpg        _cons       weight      foreign
price:weight         .38775906
  price:mpg          41.645165    6930.8263
price:_cons         -2057.7522   -273353.75    12116943
displ:weight          .00030351   -.01074361   -.68762197    .00005432
displ:foreign        -.18390487     -30.6065     1207.129    .05342871    152.20821
 displ:_cons         -.86175743    41.539129    1936.6875    -.1798972   -206.57691

                          displ:
                          _cons
 displ:_cons          625.79842
```

Notice that the row and column names of the matrices include equation names. Here we post these matrices to Stata, and then use the posted results:

```
. ereturn post b V

. ereturn display
```

	Coef.	Std. Err.	z	P>|z|	[95% Conf. Interval]	
price						
weight	1.741706	.622703	2.80	0.005	.5212304	2.962181
mpg	-50.31993	83.25158	-0.60	0.546	-213.49	112.8502
_cons	1977.925	3480.94	0.57	0.570	-4844.592	8800.442
displ						
weight	.0934161	.0073701	12.67	0.000	.0789709	.1078612
foreign	-35.12424	12.33727	-2.85	0.004	-59.30484	-10.94364
_cons	-74.32641	25.01596	-2.97	0.003	-123.3568	-25.29603

```
. test [price]weight

 ( 1)  [price]weight = 0.0

           chi2(  1) =      7.82
         Prob > chi2 =    0.0052

. test weight

 ( 1)  [price]weight = 0.0
 ( 2)  [displ]weight = 0.0

           chi2(  2) =    164.51
         Prob > chi2 =    0.0000
```

Stata determined that this was a multiple-equation model because equation names were present. All of Stata's equation-name features (such as those available with the `test` command) are then made available. The user could type `predict pred` to obtain linear predictions of the [price] equation (because `predict` defaults to the first equation), or the user could type `predict pred, equation(displ)` to obtain predictions of the [displ] equation:

$$.0934161\,\mathtt{weight} - 35.12424\,\mathtt{foreign} - 74.32641$$

◁

Single-equation models masquerading as multiple-equation models

Sometimes, it may be convenient to program a single-equation model as if it were a multiple-equation model. This occurs when there are ancillary parameters. Think of linear regression: in addition to the parameter estimates, there is s, which is an estimate of σ, the standard error of the residual. This can be calculated on the side in that one can calculate $\mathbf{b} = (\mathbf{X}'\mathbf{X})^{-1}\mathbf{X}'\mathbf{y}$ independently of s, and then calculate s given $\mathbf{b}$. Pretend that were not the case—think of a straightforward maximum likelihood calculation where s is just one more parameter (in most models, ancillary parameters and the coefficients must be solved for jointly). The right thing to do would be to give s its own equation:

▷ Example

```
. mat list b

b[1,4]
         price:        price:        price:         _anc:
        weight           mpg         _cons         sigma
y1    1.7465592   -49.512221    1946.0687          2514

. matrix list V
  (output omitted )

. ereturn post b V

. ereturn display
```

	Coef.	Std. Err.	z	P>|z|	[95% Conf. Interval]	
price						
weight	1.746559	.6413538	2.72	0.006	.4895288	3.003589
mpg	-49.51222	86.15604	-0.57	0.566	-218.375	119.3505
_cons	1946.069	3597.05	0.54	0.588	-5104.019	8996.156
_anc						
sigma	2514	900	2.79	0.005	750.0324	4277.968

Now consider the alternative, which would be simply to add s to the estimated parameters without equation names:

```
. matrix list b
b[1,4]
        weight        mpg       _cons       sigma
y1    1.7465592  -49.512221  1946.0687       2514
. matrix list V
  (output omitted )
. ereturn post b V
. ereturn display
```

	Coef.	Std. Err.	z	P>|z|	[95% Conf. Interval]	
weight	1.746559	.6413538	2.72	0.006	.4895288	3.003589
mpg	-49.51222	86.15604	-0.57	0.566	-218.375	119.3505
_cons	1946.069	3597.05	0.54	0.588	-5104.019	8996.156
sigma	2514	900	2.79	0.005	750.0324	4277.968

This second solution is inferior because, were the user to type `predict pred`, `predict` would attempt to form the linear combination:

$$1.746559\,\texttt{weight} - 49.51222\,\texttt{mpg} + 1946.069 + 2514\,\texttt{sigma}$$

There are only two possibilities, and neither is good: either `sigma` does not exist in the dataset—which is to be hoped—and `predict` produces the error message "variable sigma not found", or something called `sigma` does exist, and `predict` goes on to form this meaningless combination.

◁

On the other hand, if the parameter estimates are separated from the ancillary parameter (which could be parameters) by the equation names, the user can type `predict pred, equation(price)` to obtain a meaningful result. Moreover, the user can omit the `equation(price)` partly because `predict` (and Stata's other post-estimation commands) defaults to the first equation.

We recommend that ancillary parameters be collected together and given their own equation, and that the equation be called _anc.

Setting the estimation sample

In our previous examples, we did not indicate the estimation sample as specified with the `esample(varname)` option. In general, you provide this either with your initial `ereturn post` command or with a subsequent `ereturn repost` command. Some post-estimation commands automatically restrict themselves to the estimation sample, and if you do not provide this information, they will complain that there are no observations; see [U] **23.5 Specifying the estimation subsample**. Also, users of your estimation command expect to successfully use `if e(sample)` in commands that they execute after your estimation command.

▷ Example

Returning to our first example,

```
. ereturn post b V
. ereturn display
```

```
(output omitted)
. summarize price if e(sample)
    Variable |      Obs       Mean    Std. Dev.      Min       Max
    ---------+------------------------------------------------------
       price |        0
```

does not produce what the user expects. Specifying the estimation sample with the `esample()` option of `ereturn post` produces the expected result:

```
. ereturn post b V, esample(estsamp)
. ereturn display
(output omitted)
. summarize price if e(sample)
    Variable |      Obs       Mean    Std. Dev.      Min       Max
    ---------+------------------------------------------------------
       price |       74    6165.257    2949.496      3291     15906
```

◁

The `marksample` command (see [P] **mark**) is a useful programming command that aids in creating and setting up an estimation sample indicator variable, such as `estsamp`.

Reposting results

There are certain programming situations where only a small part of a previous estimation result needs to be altered. `ereturn repost` allows us to change four parts of an estimation result that was previously posted with `ereturn post`. We can change the coefficient vector, the variance–covariance matrix, the declared estimation sample by using the `esample()` option, and the variable names for the coefficients by using the `rename` option. A programmer might, for instance, simply replace the variance–covariance matrix provided by a previous `ereturn post` with a robust covariance matrix to create a new estimation result.

In some cases, a programmer might `preserve` the data, make major alterations to the data (using `drop`, `reshape`, etc.) in order to perform needed computations, post the estimation results, and then finally `restore` the data. In this case, when `ereturn post` is called, the correct estimation sample indicator variable is unavailable. `ereturn repost` with the `esample()` option allows us to set the estimation sample without changing the rest of our posted estimation results.

▷ Example

For example, inside an estimation command program, we might have

```
...
ereturn post b V
...
ereturn repost, esample(estsamp)
...
```

◁

❏ Technical Note

`ereturn repost` may only be called from within a program that has been declared an estimation class program by using the `eclass` option of the `program` statement. The same is not true of `ereturn post`. We believe that the only legitimate uses of `ereturn repost` are in a programming context. `ereturn post`, on the other hand, may be important for some non e-class programming situations.

❏

Minor details: the depname() and dof() options

Single-equation models may have a single dependent variable; in those that do, you should specify the identity of this single dependent variable in the depname() option with ereturn post. The result is simply to add a little more labeling to the output.

At the time of posting, if you do not specify the dof(#) option, normal (Z) statistics will be used to calculate significance levels and confidence intervals on subsequent ereturn display output. If you do specify dof(#), t statistics with # degrees of freedom will be used. Similarly, if dof(#) is not specified, any subsequent test commands will present a χ^2 statistic; if dof(#) is specified, subsequent test commands will use the F statistic with # denominator degrees of freedom.

▷ Example

Let's add the dependent variable name and degrees of freedom to our first example.

```
. ereturn post b V, depname(price) dof(71)
. ereturn display
```

price	Coef.	Std. Err.	t	P>|t|	[95% Conf. Interval]	
weight	1.746559	.6413538	2.72	0.008	.467736	3.025382
mpg	−49.51222	86.15604	−0.57	0.567	−221.3025	122.278
_cons	1946.069	3597.05	0.54	0.590	−5226.244	9118.382

Note the addition of the word price at the top of the table. This was produced because of the depname(price) option specification. Also note that t statistics were used instead of normal (Z) statistics because of the dof(71) option specification.

◁

Saved Results

ereturn post saves the number of observations in e(N) and saves the number of degrees of freedom, if specified, in e(df_r). With ereturn post, all previously stored estimation results—e() items—are removed. ereturn repost, however, does not remove previously stored estimation results. ereturn clear removes the current e() results.

Also See

Complementary: [P] _estimates, [P] return

Background: [U] **21 Programming Stata,**
    [U] **21.9 Accessing results calculated by estimation commands,**
    [U] **21.10.3 Saving results in s(),**
    [U] **23 Estimation and post-estimation commands**

Title

> **error** — Display generic error message and exit

Syntax

error *exp*

Description

error displays the most generic form of the error message associated with expression and sets the return code to the evaluation of the expression. If expression evaluates to 0, error does nothing. Otherwise, the nonzero return code will force an exit from the program or capture block in which it occurs. error sets the return code to 197 if there is an error in using error itself.

Remarks

error is used in two ways inside programs. In the first case, you want to display a standard error message so that users can look up your message using search:

```
if ('nvals'>100) error 134
```

According to [R] **search**, return code 134 is associated with the message "too many values". During program development, you can verify that by typing the error command interactively:

```
. error 134
too many values
r(134);
```

Below, we list the individual return codes so that you can select the appropriate one for use with error in your programs.

error is also used when you have processed a block of code in a capture block, suppressing all output. If anything has gone wrong, you want to display the error message associated with whatever the problem was:

```
capture {
        code continues
}
local rc=_rc                    preserve return code from capture
cleanup code
error 'rc'                      present error message and exit if necessary
code could continue
```

One hopes that in the majority of cases, the return code will be zero so that error does nothing.

You can interrogate the built-in variable _rc to determine the type of error that occurred, and then take the appropriate action. Also see [U] **19.1.4 Error handling in do-files**.

The return codes are numerically grouped, which is a feature that you may find useful when you are writing programs. The groups are

Return Codes	Meaning
1–99	sundry "minor" errors
100–199	syntax errors
300–399	failure to find previously stored result
400–499	statistical problems
500–599	matrix-manipulation errors
600–699	file errors
700–799	operating-system errors
900–999	insufficient-memory errors
1000–1999	system-limit-exceeded errors
2000–2999	nonerrors (continuation of 400–499)
4000–4999	class system errors
9000–9999	system-failure errors

Summary

1. You pressed *Break*. This is not considered an error.

2. `connection timed out -- see help r(2) for troubleshooting`
An Internet connection has timed out. This can happen when the initial attempt to make a connection over the Internet has not succeeded within a certain time limit. You can change the time limit that Stata uses under this condition by typing `set timeout1` *#seconds*. Or, the initial connection was successful, but a subsequent attempt to send or receive data over the Internet has timed out. You can also change this time limit by typing `set timeout2` *#seconds*.

3. `no dataset in use`
You attempted to perform a command requiring data and have no data in memory.

4. `no; data in memory would be lost`
You attempted to perform a command that would substantively alter or destroy the data and the data have not been saved, at least since the data were last changed. If you wish to continue anyway, add the `clear` option to the end of the command. Otherwise, save the data first.

5. `not sorted`
   `master data not sorted`
   `using data not sorted`
In the case of the first message, you typed `by` *varlist*: *command* but the data in memory are not sorted by *varlist*. Type `sort` *varlist* first; see [R] **sort**.

   In the second and third cases, both the dataset in memory and the dataset on disk must be sorted by the variables specified in the *varlist* of `merge` before they can be merged. If the *master* dataset is not sorted, sort it. If the *using* dataset is not sorted, use it, sort it, and then save it. See [R] **sort** and [R] **save**.

6. Return code from `confirm existence` when *string* does not exist.

7. ` '_____' found where _____ expected `
You are using a program which in turn is using the `confirm` command to verify that what you typed makes sense. The messages indicate what you typed and what the program expected to find instead of what you typed.

9. `assertion is false`
   `no action taken`
Return code and message from `assert` when the assertion is false; see [R] **assert**.
Or, you were using `mvencode` and requested that Stata change '.' to # in the specified *varlist*, but # already existed in the *varlist*, so Stata refused; see [R] **mvencode**.

18. `you must start with an empty dataset`
The command (e.g., `infile`) requires that no data be in memory—you must `drop _all` first. You are probably using `infile` to append additional data to the data in memory. Instead, save the data in memory, `drop _all`, `infile` the new data, and then append the previously saved data; see [R] **append**.

100. `varlist required`
     `= exp required`
     `using required`
     `by() option required`
     Certain commands require a *varlist* or another element of the language. The message specifies the required item that was missing from the command you gave. See the command's syntax diagram. For example, `merge` requires `using` be specified; perhaps, you meant to type `append`. Or, `ranksum` requires a `by()` option; see [R] **signrank**.

101. `varlist not allowed`
     `weights not allowed`
     `in range not allowed`
     `if not allowed`
     `= exp not allowed`
     `using not allowed`
     Certain commands do not allow an `if` *exp* or other elements of the language. The message specifies which item in the command is not allowed. See the command's syntax diagram. For example, `append` does not allow a *varlist*; perhaps you meant to type `merge`.

102. `too few variables specified`
     The command requires more variables than you specified. For instance, `stack` requires at least two variables. See the syntax diagram for the command.

103. `too many variables specified`
     The command does not allow as many variables as you specified. For example, `tabulate` takes only one or two variables. See the syntax diagram for the command.

104. `nothing to input`
     You gave the `input` command with no *varlist*. Stata will input onto the end of the dataset, but there is no existing dataset in this case. You must specify the variable names on the `input` command.

106. `_____ is _____ in using data`
     You have attempted to match-merge two datasets, and yet one of the key variables is a string in one dataset and a numeric in the other. The first blank is filled in with the variable name and the second blank with the storage type. It is logically impossible to fulfill your request. Perhaps you meant another variable.

107. `not possible with numeric variable`
     You have requested something that is logically impossible with a numeric variable, such as encoding it. Perhaps you meant another variable or typed `encode` when you meant `decode`.

108. `not possible with string variable`
     You have requested something that is logically impossible with a string variable, such as decoding it. Perhaps you meant another variable or typed `decode` when you meant `encode`.

109. `type mismatch`
     You probably attempted to `generate` a new string variable and forgot to specify its type, so Stata assumed the new variable was to be numeric. Include a `str#` before the name of the new variable in your `generate` statement. More generally, in an expression you attempted to combine a string and numeric subexpression in a logically impossible way. For instance, you attempted to subtract a string from a number or you attempted to take the substring of a number.

110. `_____ already defined`
     A variable or a value label has already been defined, and you attempted to redefine it. This occurs most often with `generate`. If you really intend to replace the values, use `replace`. If you intend to replace a value label, first give the `label drop` command. If you are attempting to alter an existing label, specify the `add` or `modify` option with the `label define` command.

111. `_____ not found`
     `no variables defined`
     The variable does not exist. You may have mistyped the variable's name.

     `variables out of order`
     You specified a *varlist* containing *varname1-varname2*, yet *varname1* occurs after *varname2*. Reverse the order of the variables if you did not make some other typographical error. Remember, *varname1-varname2* is taken by Stata to mean *varname1, varname2*, and all the variables in *dataset order* in between. Type `describe` to see the order of the variables in your dataset.

_____ not found in using data

You specified a *varlist* with `merge`, yet the variables on which you wish to merge are not found in the using dataset, so the `merge` is not possible.

_____ ambiguous abbreviation

You typed an ambiguous abbreviation for a variable in your data. The abbreviation could refer to more than one variable. Use a nonambiguous abbreviation, or, if you intend all the variables implied by the ambiguous abbreviation, append a '`*`' to the end of the abbreviation.

119. `statement out of context`

This is the generic form of this message; more likely, you will see messages such as "may not streset after . . . ". You have attempted to do something that, in this context, is not allowed or does not make sense.

120. `invalid %format`

You specified an invalid *% fmt*; see [U] **15.5 Formats: controlling how data are displayed**.

Return codes 121–127 are errors that might occur when you specify a *numlist*. For details about *numlist*, see [U] **14.1.8 numlist**.

121. `invalid numlist`

122. `invalid numlist has too few elements`

123. `invalid numlist has too many elements`

124. `invalid numlist has elements out of order`

125. `invalid numlist has elements outside of allowed range`

126. `invalid numlist has noninteger elements`

127. `invalid numlist has missing values`

130. `expression too long`
`too many SUMs`

In the first case, you specified an expression that is too long for Stata to process—the expression contains more than 255 pairs of nested parentheses or more than 66 dyadic operators. (For Small Stata, the limits are 85 pairs of nested parentheses and 22 dyadic operators.) Break the expression into smaller parts. In the second case, the expression contains more than five `sum()` functions. This expression, too, will have to be broken into smaller parts.

131. `not possible with test`

You requested a `test` of a hypothesis that is nonlinear in the variables. `test` tests only linear hypotheses. Use `testnl`.

132. `too many '(' or '['`
`too many ')' or ']'`

You specified an expression with unbalanced parentheses or brackets.

133. `unknown function _____()`

You specified a function that is unknown to Stata; see [U] **16.3 Functions**. Alternatively, you may have meant to subscript a variable and accidentally used parentheses rather than square brackets; see [U] **16.7 Explicit subscripting**.

134. `too many values`

(1) You attempted to `encode` a string variable that takes on more than 65,536 unique values. (2) You attempted to `tabulate` a variable or pair of variables that take on too many values. If you specified two variables, try interchanging them.

135. `not possible with weighted data`

You attempted to `predict` something other than the prediction or residual, yet the underlying model was weighted. Stata cannot calculate the statistic you requested using weighted data.

140. `repeated categorical variable in term`

At least one of the terms in your `anova` model or `test` statement has a repeated categorical variable, such as `reg*div*reg`. Either you forgot to specify that the variable is continuous or the second occurrence of the variable is unnecessary.

141. `repeated term`

In the list of terms in your `anova` model or `test` statement is a duplicate of another term, although perhaps ordered differently. For instance, `X*A*X` and `A*X*X`. Remove the repeated term.

142. `attempt to classify extraneous variable`
   You have specified a variable as continuous or categorical that is not contained in your `anova` model. Perhaps you inadvertently left the variable out of your model. On the other hand, if the variable does not belong in your model, then it should not appear in the `continuous()` or `category()` options.

143. `variable left unclassified`
   You can get this error only if you specify *both* the `continuous()` *and* the `category()` options. It is not necessary to do this since specifying one or the other is sufficient—Stata assumes that the remaining variables fall into the omitted class. If you do specify both, you must account for every variable in your model. You left one or more variables unclassified.

144. `variable classified inconsistently`
   Please see the explanation for return code 143. In this case, you placed the same variable in both the `continuous()` and the `category()` lists.

145. `term contains more than 8 variables`
   One of the terms in your `anova` model `test` statement contains more than 8 variables. Stata cannot estimate such models.

146. `too many variables or values  (matsize too small)`
   You can increase matsize using the `set matsize` command; see help matsize.
   Your `anova` model resulted in a specification containing more than $matsize - 2$ explanatory variables; see [R] **matsize**.

147. `term not in model`
   Your `test` command refers to a term that was not contained in your `anova` model.

148. `too few categories`
   You attempted to estimate a model such as `mlogit`, `ologit`, or `oprobit` when the number of outcomes is smaller than 3. Check that the dependent variable is the variable you intend. If it takes on exactly two values, use `logit` or `probit`.

149. `too many categories`
   You attempted to estimate a model such as `mlogit`, `ologit`, or `oprobit` with a dependent variable that takes on more than 50 outcomes (Stata/SE or Intercooled Stata) or 20 outcomes (Small Stata).

151. `non r-class program may not set r()`
   Perhaps you specified `return local` in your program, but forgot to declare the program `rclass` in the `program define` statement.

152. `non e-class program may not set e()`
   Perhaps you specified `estimates local` in your program, but forgot to declare the program `eclass` in the `program define` statement.

153. `non s-class program may not set s()`
   Perhaps you specified `sreturn local` in your program, but forgot to declare the program `sclass` in the `program define` statement.

170. `unable to chdir`
   (*Unix and Macintosh.*) `cd` was unable to change to the directory you typed because it does not exist, it is protected, or it is not a directory.

180. `invalid attempt to modify label`
   You are attempting to modify the contents of an existing *value label* using the `label define` command. If you mean to completely replace the existing label, first `label drop` it and then `label define` it. If you wish to modify the existing label, be sure to specify either the `add` option or the `modify` option on the `label define` command. `add` lets you add new entries but not change existing ones, and `modify` lets you do both. You will get this error if you specify `add` and then attempt to modify an existing entry. In that case, edit the command and substitute `modify` for the `add` option.

181. `may not label strings`
   You attempted to assign a value label to a string variable, which makes no sense.

182. `_____ not labeled`
   The indicated variable has no value label, yet your request requires a labeled variable. You may, for instance, be attempting to `decode` a numeric variable.

184. `options _____ and _____ may not be combined`
   For instance, you issued the `regress` command and tried to specify both the `beta` and the `cluster()` options.

190. `request may not be combined with by`
     Certain commands may not be combined with by, and you constructed such a combination. See the syntax diagram for the command.

191. `request may not be combined with by() option`
     Certain commands may not be combined with by() option, and you constructed such a combination. See the syntax diagram for the command.

     `in may not be combined with by`
     in may never be combined with by. Use if instead; see [U] **14.5 by varlist: construct**.

196. `could not restore sort order because variables were dropped`
     You ran an ado-file program that has an error, and the program dropped the temporary marker variables that allow the sort order to be restored.

197. `invalid syntax`
     This error is produced by syntax and other parsing commands when there is a syntax error in the use of the command itself rather than in what is being parsed.

198. `invalid syntax`
     `option _____ incorrectly specified`
     `option _____ not allowed`
     `_____ invalid`
     `range invalid`
     `_____ invalid obs no`
     `invalid filename`
     `_____ invalid varname`
     `_____ invalid name`
     `multiple by's not allowed`
     `_____ found where number expected`
     `on or off required`
     All items in this list indicate invalid syntax. These errors are often, but not always, due to typographical errors. Stata attempts to provide you with as much information as it can. Review the syntax diagram for the designated command.

     In giving the message "invalid syntax", Stata is not very helpful. Errors in specifying expressions often result in this message.

199. `unrecognized command`
     Stata failed to recognize the command, program, or ado-file name, probably because of a typographical or abbreviation error.

301. `last estimates not found`
     You typed an estimation command such as regress without arguments or attempted to perform a test or typed predict, but there were no previous estimation results.

302. `last test not found`
     You have requested the redisplay of a previous test, yet you have not run a test previously.

303. `equation not found`
     You referred to a coefficient or stored result corresponding to an equation or outcome that cannot be found. For instance, you estimated a mlogit model and the outcome variable took on the values 1, 3, and 4. You referred to [2]_b[var] when perhaps you meant [#2]_b[var] or [3]_b[var].

304. `ml model not found`
     You have used mleval, mlsum, or mlmatsum without having first used the other ml commands to define the model.

305. `ml model not found`
     Same as 304.

399. `may not drop constant`
     You issued a logistic or logit command and the constant was dropped. Your model may be underidentified; try removing one or more of the independent variables.

401. `may not use noninteger frequency weights`
     You specified an fweight frequency weight with noninteger weights, telling Stata that your weights are to be treated as replication counts. Stata encountered a weight that was not an integer, so your request made no sense. You probably meant to specify aweight analytic weights; see [U] **14.1.6 weight**.

402. `negative weights encountered`
`negative weights not allowed`
You specified a variable that contains negative values as the weighting variable, so your request made no sense. Perhaps you meant to specify another variable.

403. `may not specify norobust with pweights`
You specified one of Stata's estimation commands with both the `norobust` and the `pweight` options. You cannot do this since `robust` is a request that `pweight` be used. See [U] **23.14 Obtaining robust variance estimates**.

404. `not possible with pweighted data`
You requested a statistic that Stata cannot calculate with `pweighted` data either because of a shortcoming in Stata or because the statistics of the problem have not been worked out. For example, perhaps you requested the standard error of the survival curve, and you had previously specified `pweight` when you `stset` your data (a case where no one has worked out the statistics).

406. `not possible with analytic weights`
You specified a command that does not allow analytic weights. See the syntax diagram for the command to see which types of weights are allowed.

407. `weights must be the same for all observations in a group`
`weights not constant for same observation across repeated variables`
For some commands, weights must be the same for all observations in a group for statistical or computational reasons. For the `anova` command with the `repeated()` option, weights must be constant for an observation across the repeated variables.

409. `no variance`
You were using `lnskew0` or `bcskew0`, for instance, but the *exp* that you specified has no variance.

411. `nonpositive values encountered`
`_____ has negative values`
`time variable has negative values`
For instance, you have used `graph` with the `xlog` or `ylog` options, requesting log scales, and yet some of the data or the labeling you specified is negative or zero.
Or, perhaps you were using `ltable` and specified a time variable that has negative values.

412. `redundant or inconsistent constraints`
For instance, you are estimating a constrained model with `mlogit`. Among the constraints specified is at least one that is redundant or inconsistent. A redundant constraint might constrain a coefficient to be zero that some other constraint also constrains to be zero. An inconsistent constraint might constrain a coefficient to be 1 that some other constraint constrains to be zero. List the constraints, find the offender, and then reissue the `mlogit` command omitting it.

416. `missing values encountered`
You were using a command which requires that no values be missing.

420. `_____ groups found, 2 required`
You used a command (such as `ttest`) and the grouping variable you specified does not take on 2 unique values.

421. `could not determine between-subject error term; use bse() option`
You specified the `repeated()` option to `anova`, but Stata could not automatically determine certain terms that are needed in the calculation; see [R] **anova**.

422. `could not determine between-subject basic unit; use bseunit() option`
You specified the `repeated()` option to `anova`, but Stata could not automatically determine certain terms that are needed in the calculation; see [R] **anova**.

430. `convergence not achieved`
You have estimated a maximum-likelihood model and Stata's maximization procedure failed to converge to a solution; see [R] **maximize**. Check if the model is identified.

450. `_____ is not a 0/1 variable`
`number of successes invalid`
`p invalid`
`_____ takes on _____ values, not 2`
You have used a command, such as `bitest`, that requires the variable take on only the values 0, 1, or missing, but the variable you specified does not meet that restriction.

451. `invalid values for time variable`
For instance, you specified `mytime` as a time variable and `mytime` contains noninteger values.

459. `something that should be true of your data is not`
    This is the generic form of this message; more likely, you will see messages such as "y must be between 0 and 1" or "x not positive". You have attempted to do something that, given your data, does not make sense.

460. `only one cluster detected`
    `only one PSU detected`
    `stratum with only one PSU detected`
    `stratum with only one observation detected`
    You were using the `cluster()` option and you had only one cluster; you must have at least two clusters—preferably much more than two. Or, you were using an `svy` command, and you had only one PSU in one stratum; the `svydes` command will determine which stratum and the [SVY] **svydes** entry shows how to deal with the situation.

461. `number of obs must be greater than # for robust variance computation`
    `number of obs in subpopulation must be greater than #`
    `no observations in subpopulation`
    You had insufficient observations for the robust variance estimator. Or, you were trying to produce estimates for a subpopulation and had insufficient observations in the subpopulation.

462. `fpc must be >= 0`
    `fpc for all observations within a stratum must be the same`
    `fpc must be <= 1 if a rate, or >= no. sampled PSUs per stratum if PSU totals`
    There is a problem with your `fpc` variable; see [SVY] **svymean**.

463. `sum of weights equals zero`
    `sum of weights for subpopulation equals zero`
    When weights sum to zero, the requested statistic cannot be computed.

471. `esample() invalid`
    This concerns `estimates post`. The variable *varname* specified by the `esample(`*varname*`)` option must contain exclusively 0 and 1 values (never, for instance, 2 or missing). *varname* contains invalid values.

480. `starting values invalid or some RHS variables have missing values`
    You were using `nl` and specified starting values that were infeasible, or you have missing values for some of your independent variables.

481. `equation/system not identified`
    `cannot calculate derivatives`
    You were using `reg3`, for instance, and the system that you have specified is not identified.

    You specified an `nl` *fcn* for which derivatives cannot be calculated.

482. `nonpositive value(s) among _____, cannot log transform`
    You specified an `lnlsq` option in `nl` that attempts to take the log of a nonpositive value.

491. `could not find feasible values`
    You are using `ml` and it could not find starting values for which the likelihood function could be evaluated. You could try using `ml search` with the `repeat()` option to randomly try more values, or you could use `ml init` to specify valid starting values.

498. *various messages*
    The statistical problem described in the message has occurred. The code 498 is not helpful, but the message is supposed to be. Return code 498 is reserved for messages that are unique to a particular situation.

499. *various messages*
    The statistical problem described in the message has occurred. The code 499 is not helpful, but the message is supposed to be. Return code 499 is reserved for messages that are unique to a particular situation.

501. `matrix operation not found`
    You have issued an unknown `matrix` subcommand or used `matrix define` with a function or operator that is unknown to Stata.

503. `conformability error`
    You have issued a `matrix` command attempting to combine two matrices that are not conformable; for example, multiplying a 3×2 matrix by a 3×3 matrix. You will also get this message if you attempt an operation that requires a square matrix and the matrix is not square.

504. `matrix has missing values`
    This return code is now infrequently used since, with version 8, Stata now permits missing values in matrices.

505. matrix not symmetric

You have issued a matrix command that can only be performed on a symmetric matrix and your matrix is not symmetric. While fixing their code, programmers are requested to admire our choice of the "symmetric" number 505—it is symmetric about the zero—for this error.

506. matrix not positive definite

You have issued a matrix command that can only be performed on a positive definite matrix and your matrix is not positive definite.

507. name conflict

You have issued a matrix post command and the variance–covariance matrix of the estimators does not have the same row and column names, or, if it does, those names are not the same as for the coefficient vector.

508. matrix has zero values on diagonal
matrix has zero or negative values on diagonal

You used the matrix ty sweep() function, but the matrix had zero values on the diagonal.

509. matrix operators that return matrices not allowed in this context

Expressions returning nonmatrices, such as those in generate and replace, may use matrix functions returning scalars, such as trace(A), but may not include subexpressions evaluating to matrices, such as trace(A+B), which requires evaluating the matrix expression $A + B$. (Such subexpressions are allowed in the context of expressions returning matrices, such as those in matrix.)

601. file _____ not found

The filename you specified cannot be found. Perhaps you mistyped the name, or it may be on another CD or directory. If you are a Macintosh user, perhaps you had an unintentional blank at the beginning or ending of your filename when it was created. In Finder, click on the file to blacken the name. If you see anything other than a thin, even space on each side of the name, rename the file to eliminate the leading and trailing space characters.

602. file _____ already exists

You attempted to write over a file that already exists. Stata will never let you do this accidentally. If you really intend to overwrite the previous file, reissue the last command specifying the replace option.

603. file _____ could not be opened

This file, although found, failed to open properly. This error is unlikely to occur. You will have to review your operating system's manual to determine why it occurred.

604. log file already open

You attempted to open a log file when one is already open. Perhaps you forgot you have the file open or forgot to close it.

606. no log file open

You have attempted to close, turn on, or turn off logging when no log file was open. Perhaps you forgot to open the log file.

607. no cmdlog file open

You have attempted to close, turn on, or turn off logging when no cmdlog file was open. Perhaps you forgot to open the cmdlog file.

609. file xp format

The designated file is stored in an unsupported cross-product format.

610. file _____ not Stata format

The designated file is not a Stata-format file. This occurs most frequently with use, append, and merge. You probably typed the wrong filename.

611. record too long

You have attempted to process a record that exceeds 32,765 characters in length using formatted infile (i.e., infile with a dictionary). When reading formatted data, records may not exceed this maximum. If the records are not formatted, you can read these data using the standard infile command (i.e., without a dictionary). There is no maximum record length for unformatted data.

612. unexpected end of file

You used infile with a dictionary, and the file containing the dictionary ended before the '}' character. Perhaps you forgot to type the closing brace, or perhaps you are missing a hard return at the end of your file. You may also get this message if you issued the command #delimit ; in a do-file and then subsequently forgot to use ';' before the 'end' statement.

613. `file does not contain dictionary`
You used `infile` with a dictionary, yet the file you specified does not begin with the word 'dictionary'. Perhaps you are attempting to `infile` data without using a dictionary and forgot to specify the *varlist* on the `infile` command. Alternatively, you forgot to include the word `dictionary` at the top of the dictionary file or typed `DICTIONARY` in uppercase.

614. `dictionary invalid`
You used `infile` with a dictionary and the file appears to contain a dictionary. Nevertheless, you have made some error in specifying the dictionary and Stata does not understand your intentions. The contents of the dictionary are listed on the screen and the last line is the line that gave rise to the problem.

615. `cannot determine separator -- use tab or comma option`
You used the `insheet` command to read a file, but Stata is having trouble determining whether the file is tab- or comma-separated. Reissue the `insheet` command and specify the `comma` or `tab` option.

616. `wrong number of values in checksum file`
The checksum file being used to verify integrity of another file does not contain values in the expected checksum format.

621. `already preserved`
You specified `preserve`, but you have already `preserved` the data.

622. `nothing to restore`
You issued the `restore` command, but you have not previously specified `preserve`.

Return codes 630–696 are all messages that you might receive when executing any command with a file over the network.

631. `host not found`

632. `web filename not supported in this context`

633. `saving to web files not supported in this version of Stata`

639. `file transmission error (checksums do not match)`

640. `package file too long`

660. `proxy host not found`
The host name specified as a proxy server cannot be mapped to an IP address. Type `query` to determine the host you have set.

662. `proxy server refused request to send`
Stata was able to contact the proxy server, but the proxy server refused to send data back to Stata. The proxy host or port specified may be incorrect. Type `query` to determine your settings.

663. `remote connection to proxy failed`
Although you have set a proxy server, it is not responding to Stata. The likely problems are you specified the wrong port, you specified the wrong host, or the proxy server is down. Type `query` to determine the host and port that you have set.

665. `could not set socket nonblocking`

667. `wrong version winsock.dll`

668. `could not find a valid winsock.dll`

669. `invalid URL`

670. `invalid network port number`

671. `unknown network protocol`

672. `server refused to send file`

673. `authorization required by server`

674. `unexpected response from server`

675. `server reported server error`

676. `server refused request to send`

677. `remote connection failed`
You requested that something be done over the web, but Stata could not contact the specified host. Perhaps, the host is down; try again later.

If all of your web access results in this message, perhaps your network connection is via a proxy server. If it is, then you must tell Stata. Contact your system administrator and ask for the name and port of the "http proxy server". See *Using the Internet* in the *Getting Started* manual for details on how to inform Stata.

678. `could not open local network socket`

681. `too many open files`

691. `I/O error`
A filesystem error occurred during input or output. This typically indicates a hardware or operating system failure, although it is possible that the disk was merely full and this state was misinterpreted as an I/O error.

692. `file I/O error on read`

693. `file I/O error on write`

696. `_____ is temporarily unavailable`

699. `insufficient disk space`
You ran out of disk space while writing a file to disk. The file is now closed and is probably erased. Review your operating system documentation to determine how to proceed.

702. `op. sys. refused to start new process`

703. `op. sys. refused to open pipe`

900. `no room to add more variables`
The maximum number of variables allowed by Small Stata is 99. The maximum number of variables allowed by Intercooled Stata is 2,047. The maximum number of variables allowed by Stata/SE is 32,766. If you are using Intercooled Stata and have less than 2,047 variables (or Stata/SE and have less than 32,766 variables), you are short on memory; see [U] **7 Setting the size of memory**.

901. `no room to add more observations`
The maximum number of observations allowed by Small Stata is *approximately* 1,000. The maximum number of observations allowed by Stata/SE or Intercooled Stata is 2,147,483,647. If you are using Intercooled Stata, you are short on memory; see [U] **7 Setting the size of memory**.

902. `no room to add more variables due to width`
Try typing `compress`; see [R] **compress**.

903. `no room to promote variable (e.g., change) int to float) due to width`

908. `matsize too small`

909. `op. sys. refuses to provide memory`
You have attempted to `set memory` or `set matsize`, and, although the request seems reasonable to Stata, the operating system has refused to provide the extra memory.

910. `value too small`
You attempted to change the size of memory, but specified values for memory, maximum observations, maximum width, or maximum variables that are too small. Stata wants to allocate a minimum of 300K.

912. `value too large`
You attempted to change the size of memory, but specified values for memory, maximum observations, maximum width, or maximum variables that are too large.

913. `op. sys. refuses to provide sufficient memory`
`op. sys. provided base request, but then refused to provide`
`sufficient memory for matsize`
You attempted to `set memory` or `set matsize`, and, although the request seems reasonable to Stata, the operating system refused to provide the memory for matsize (although the operating system would provide memory for the data).

This return code has the same implications as `r(909)`. Stata allocates memory separately for the data and for matsize. `r(913)` merely indicates that it was the second rather than the first request that failed. Typically, the first request fails because it is the request for additional memory.

914. `op. sys. refused to allow Stata to open a temporary file`

920. `too many macros`
You specified a line containing too many macros, so that after expansion of the macros, the line exceeds 67,784 characters for Intercooled Stata or 8,681 characters for Small Stata. The maximum for Stata/SE is 33*c(max_k_theory) + 200, which for the default setting of 5,000 is 165,200. The line was ignored.

950. `insufficient memory`
There is insufficient memory to fulfill the request. Type `discard`, press return, and try the command again. If that fails, consider dropping value labels, variable labels, or macros.

1000. `system limit exceeded – see manual`
See [R] **limits**.

1001. `too many values`
You have attempted to create a table that has too many rows or columns. For a one-way table, the maximum number of rows is 12,000 for Stata/SE, 3,000 for Intercooled Stata, and 500 for Small Stata. For a two-way table, the maximum number of rows and columns is 1,200 by 80 for Stata/SE, 300 by 20 for Intercooled Stata, and 160 by 20 for Small Stata. Thus, `tabulate y x` may not result in too many values even if `tabulate x y` does.

1002. `too many by variables`
The number of by variables exceeded 32,766 for Stata/SE, 2,047 for Intercooled Stata, or 99 for Small Stata. You cannot exceed these maximums.

1003. `too many options`
The number of options specified exceeded 50. You cannot exceed that maximum.

1004. `command too long`
You attempted to issue a Stata command in a do-file, ado-file, or program, and the command exceeded 67,800 characters for Intercooled Stata or 8,697 for Small Stata. For Stata/SE, the limit is 33*c(max_k_theory) + 216, which for the default setting of 5,000 is 165,216.

1400. `numerical overflow`
You have attempted something that, in the midst of the necessary calculations, has resulted in something too large for Stata to deal with accurately. Most commonly, this is an attempt to estimate a model (say with `regress`) with more than 2,147,483,647 effective observations. This effective number could be reached with far fewer observations if you were running a frequency-weighted model.

2000. `no observations`
You have requested some statistical calculation and there are no observations on which to perform it. Perhaps you specified if *exp* or in *range* and inadvertently filtered all the data.

2001. `insufficient observations`
You have requested some statistical calculation, and, while there are some observations, the number is not sufficient to carry out your request.

9xxx. Various messages, all indicating an unexpected system failure. You should never see such a message. If one occurs, `save` your data and `exit` Stata immediately. Please email *tech-support@stata.com* to report the problem.

Other messages

`no observations`
`insufficient observations`
You have requested something when there are either no observations or insufficient observations in memory to carry forth your request.

`(_____ not found)`
You referred to the indicated value name in an expression and no such value label existed. A missing value was substituted.

`(eof before end of obs)`
`infile` was reading your data and encountered the end-of-file marker before it had completed reading the current observation. Missing values are filled in for the remaining variables. This message indicates that the dataset may contain more or fewer variables than you expected.

`(_____ missing values generated)`
The command resulted in the creation of the indicated number of missing values. Missing values occur when a mathematical operation is performed on a missing value or when a mathematical operation is infeasible.

(note: file _____ not found)
You specified the `replace` option on a command, yet no such file was found. The file was saved anyway.

(note: _____ is _____ in using data but will be _____ now)
Occurs during `append` or `merge`. The first blank is filled in with a variable name, and the second and third blanks with a storage type (`byte`, `int`, `long`, `float`, `double`, or `str#`). For instance, you might receive the message "myvar is str5 in using data but will be float now". This means `myvar` is of type `float` in the *master dataset*, but that a variable of the same name was found in the *using dataset* with type `str5`. You will receive this message when one variable is a string and the other is numeric.

(label _____ already defined)
Occurs during `append` or `merge`. The *using* data has a label definition for one of its variables. A label with the same name exists in the *master* dataset. Thus, you are warned that the label already exists, and the previous definition (the one from the *master* dataset) is retained.

(note: hascons false)
You specified the `hascons` option on `regress`, yet an examination of the data revealed that there is no effective constant in your *varlist*. Stata added a constant to your regression.

_____ real changes made
You used `replace`. This is the actual number of changes made to your data, not counting observations that already contained the replaced value.

_____ was _____ now _____
Occurs during `replace`, `append`, or `merge`. The first blank is filled in with a variable name and the second and third blanks are filled in with a numeric storage type (`byte`, `int`, `long`, `float`, or `double`). For instance, you might receive the message, "myvar was byte now float". Stata automatically promoted `myvar` to a `float` to prevent truncation.

Also See

Complementary:	[P] **break**, [P] **capture**,
	[R] **search**
Related:	[P] **exit**
Background:	[U] **19.1.4 Error handling in do-files**

Title

_estimates — Manage estimation results

Syntax

> _estimates <u>h</u>old *holdname* $\left[\,,\ \underline{c}opy\ \underline{rest}ore\ \underline{n}ullok\ \underline{var}name(newvar)\,\right]$
>
> _estimates <u>u</u>nhold *holdname* $\left[\,,\ not\,\right]$
>
> _estimates dir
>
> _estimates clear
>
> _estimates drop $\left\{\,holdname(s)\,|\,\_all\,\right\}$

where *holdname* is the name under which estimation results will be held.

Description

_estimates hold, _estimates unhold, _estimates dir, and _estimates drop provide a low-level mechanism for saving and later restoring up to 20 estimation results. _estimates hold moves, or copies if the copy option is specified, all information associated with the last estimation command into *holdname*. If *holdname* is a temporary name, it will automatically be deleted when you exit from the current program.

_estimates unhold restores the information from the estimation command previously moved into *holdname* and eliminates *holdname*.

_estimates dir lists the *holdname*(s) under which estimation results are currently held.

_estimates drop eliminates the estimation results stored under the specified *holdname*(s).

_estimates clear eliminates all stored results. In addition, if the restore option is specified when the estimates are held, those estimates will be automatically restored when the program concludes. It is not necessary to perform an _estimates unhold in that case.

_estimates is a programmer's command, and is designed to be used within programs. estimates is a user's command to manage multiple estimation results. estimates uses _estimates to hold and unhold results, and it adds features such as model-selection indices and looping over results. Post-estimation commands such as suest and lrtest assume that estimation results are stored using estimates rather than _estimates.

Options

copy requests that all information associated with the last estimation command be copied into *holdname*. By default, it is moved, meaning that the estimation results temporarily disappear. The default action is faster and uses less memory.

restore requests that the information in *holdname* be automatically restored when the program ends, regardless of whether that occurred because the program exited normally, the user pressed *Break*, or there was an error.

nullok specifies that it is valid to store null results. After restoring a null result, no estimation results are active.

varname(*newvar*) specifies the variable name under which esample() will be held. If varname() is not specified, *holdname* is used.

not specifies that the previous _estimates hold, restore request for automatic restoration be canceled. The previously held estimation results are discarded from memory without restoration, now or later.

Remarks

_estimates hold and _estimates unhold are typically used in programs and ado-files, although they can be used interactively. After fitting, say, a regression using regress, you can replay the regression by typing regress without arguments, you can obtain predicted values using predict, and the like; see [U] **23 Estimation and post-estimation commands**. This is because Stata stored information associated with the regression in what we will call the "last estimation results". The "last estimation results" include the coefficient vector and the variance–covariance matrix, as well as the other e() saved results.

When you type _estimates hold myreg, Stata moves the last estimation results to a holding area named myreg. After issuing this command, you can no longer replay the regression, calculate predicted values, etc. From Stata's point of view, the estimates are gone. When you type _estimates unhold myreg, however, Stata moves the estimates back. You can once again type regress without arguments, calculate predicted values, and everything else just as if the last estimation results were never disturbed.

If you instead type _estimates hold myreg, copy, Stata copies, rather than moves, the results, meaning that you can still redisplay results. Obviously, you hold estimates because you want to fit some other model and then get these estimates back, so generally, holding-by-moving works as well as holding-by-copying. Sometimes, however, you may want to hold-by-copy so that you can modify the estimates in memory and still retrieve the original.

(Continued on next page)

▷ Example

Thus, you could run a regression, hold the results, run another regression, and then unhold the original results. One method you could use is

```
regress y x1 x2 x3              ( fit first model )
_estimates hold model1         ( and save it )
regress y x1 x2 x3 x4          ( fit the second model )
_estimates hold model2         ( and save it, too )
use newdata                    ( use another dataset )
_estimates unhold model1
predict yhat1                  ( predict using first regression )
_estimates unhold model2
predict yhat2                  ( predict using second regression )
```

Understand that you are not limited to doing this with regression. You can do this with any estimation command.

◁

❏ Technical Note

Warning: Holding estimation results can tie up considerable amounts of memory, the amount depending on the kind of model and the number of variables in it. This is why there is a limit of 20 held estimation results.

❏

_estimates dir, _estimates drop, and _estimates clear are utilities associated with _estimates hold and _estimates unhold. _estimates dir lists the name(s) of held estimation results. _estimates drop drops held estimation results. _estimates clear is equivalent to _estimates drop _all.

❏ Technical Note

Despite our interactive example, _estimates hold and _estimates unhold are typically used inside programs. For instance, linktest fits a model of the dependent variable, the prediction, and the prediction squared and shows the result. Yet when it is over, the user's original model remains as the last estimation result just as if no intervening model had been estimated. linktest does this by holding the original model, performing its task, and then restoring the original model.

In addition to moving Stata's last estimation result matrices, e(b) and e(V), _estimates hold and _estimates unhold also move the other e() results. When you hold the current estimates, e(b), e(V), e(cmd), e(depvar), and the other e() results disappear. When you unhold them, they are restored.

To avoid naming conflicts, we recommend that estimates be held under a name created by tempvar or tempname; see [P] **macro**. Thus, the code fragment is

```
tempvar est
_estimates hold 'est'
( code including new estimation )
_estimates unhold 'est'
```

❏

Estimates held under a temporary name will automatically be discarded when the program ends. You can also specify _estimates hold's restore option when you hold the estimates, and then the held estimates will be restored when the program ends, too.

Saved Results

_estimates hold removes the estimation results—e() items. _estimates unhold restores the previously held e() results. _estimates clear permanently removes all held e() results. _estimates dir returns the names of the held estimation results in the local r(names), separated by single spaces. _estimates dir also returns r(varnames), which has the corresponding variable names for esample().

Also See

Complementary:	[P] **mark**, [P] **matrix**, [P] **matrix constraint**, [P] **matrix rowname**, [R] **estimates**, [R] **maximize**, [R] **ml**, [R] **predict**, [R] **test**, [R] **vce**
Related:	[P] **return**, [R] **saved results**
Background:	[U] **16.5 Accessing coefficients and standard errors**, [U] **21 Programming Stata**, [U] **23 Estimation and post-estimation commands**

Title

exit — Exit from a program or do-file

Syntax

<u>exit</u> [[=]*exp*] [, clear STATA]

Description

exit, when typed from the keyboard, causes Stata to terminate processing and returns control to the operating system. If the dataset in memory has changed since the last save command, you must specify the clear option before Stata will let you leave. Use of the command in this way is discussed in [R] **exit**.

More generally, exit causes Stata to terminate the current process and returns control to the calling process. The return code is set to the value of the expression or 0 if no expression is specified. Thus, exit can be used to exit a program or do-file and return control to Stata. With an option, exit can even be used to exit Stata from a program or do-file. Such use of exit is the subject of this entry.

Options

clear permits you to exit even if the current dataset has not been saved.

STATA exits Stata and returns control to the operating system, even when given from a do-file or program. The STATA option is implied when exit is issued from the keyboard.

Remarks

exit can be used at the terminal, from do-files, or from programs. From the terminal, it allows you to leave Stata. Given from a do-file or program without the STATA option, it causes the do-file or program to terminate and return control to the calling process, which might be the keyboard or another do-file or program.

▷ Example

Here is a useless program that will tell you whether a variable exists:

```
. program check
  1. capture confirm variable `1'
  2. if _rc!=0 {
  3.     display "`1' not found"
  4.     exit
  5. }
  6. display "The variable `1' exists."
  7. end
. check median_age
The variable median_age exists.
. check age
age not found
```

Notice that `exit` did not close Stata and cause a return to the operating system. It instead terminated the program.

◁

▷ Example

You type `exit` from the keyboard to leave Stata and return to the operating system. If the dataset in memory has changed since the last time it was saved, however, Stata will refuse. At that point, you can either `save` the data and then `exit` or type `exit, clear`:

```
. exit
no; data in memory would be lost
r(4);

. exit, clear
(Operating system prompts you for next command)
```

◁

❏ Technical Note

You can also exit Stata and return to the operating system from a do-file or program by including the line `exit, STATA` in your do-file or program. If you wish to return to the operating system regardless of whether the dataset in memory has changed, you include the line `exit, STATA clear`.

❏

❏ Technical Note

When using `exit` to force termination of a program or do-file, you may specify an expression following the `exit` and the resulting value of that expression will be used to set the return code. Not specifying an expression is equivalent to specifying `exit 0`.

❏

Also See

Complementary:	[P] **capture**, [P] **class exit**, [P] **error**,
	[R] **error messages**
Related:	[R] **exit**

Title

file — Read and write ASCII text and binary files

Syntax

file open *handle* using *filename* , {read | write | read write}

    [[text | binary] [replace | append] all]

file read *handle* [*specs*]

file write *handle* [*specs*]

file seek *handle* {query | tof | eof | #}

file set *handle* byteorder {hilo | lohi | 1 | 2}

file close {*handle* | _all}

file query

where *specs* for ASCII text output is

"*string*" or ' "*string*" '	
(*exp*)	(note that parentheses are required)
%*fmt* (*exp*)	(see [R] **format** about %*fmt*)
_skip(#)	
_column(#)	
_newline[(#)]	
_char(#)	(0 <= # <= 255)
_tab[(#)]	
_page[(#)]	
_dup(#)	

and *specs* for ASCII text input is *localmacroname*

and *specs* for binary output is

%{8|4}z	(*exp*)
%{4|2|1}b[s|u]	(*exp*)
%#s	"*text*" (1 <= # <= max_macrolen)
%#s	' "*text*" '
%#s	(*exp*)

and *specs* for binary input is

%{8|4}z	*scalarname*
%{4|2|1}b[s|u]	*scalarname*
%#s	*localmacroname* (1 <= # <= max_macrolen)

176

Description

file is a programmer's command, and should not be confused with [R] **insheet**, [R] **infile**, and [R] **infix (fixed format)**, which are the usual ways data are brought into Stata. file allows programmers to read and write both ASCII text and binary files, and so file could be used to write a program to input data in some complicated situation, but that would be an undertaking.

Files are referenced by a file *handle*. When you open a file, you specify the file handle you want to use; for example, in

        . file open myfile using example.txt, write

myfile is the file handle for the file named example.txt. From that point on, you refer to the file by its handle. Thus,

        . file write myfile "this is a test" _n

would write the line "this is a test" (without the quotes) followed by a newline into the file, and

        . file close myfile

would then close the file. You may have multiple files open at the same time, and may access them in any order.

For information on reading and writing sersets, see [P] **serset**.

Options

read, write, and read write are not optional; they specify how the file is to be opened. If the file is opened read, you can subsequently use file read but not file write; if the file is opened write, you can subsequently use file write but not file read. If the file is opened read write, you can subsequently use both.

read write is more flexible, but most programmers open files purely read or purely write because that is all that is necessary; it is safer, and it is faster.

When a file is opened read, the file must already exist or an error message will be issued. The file is positioned at the top (tof), so the first file read reads at the beginning of the file. Both local files and files over the net may be opened for read.

When a file is opened write, and the options replace or append are not specified, the file must not exist or an error message will be issued. The file is positioned at the top (tof), so the first file write writes at the beginning of the file. Net files may not be opened for write.

When a file is opened write and option replace is also specified, it does not matter whether the file already exists; the existing file, if any, is erased before hand.

When a file is opened write and option append is also specified, it also does not matter whether the file already exists; the file will be reopened or created if necessary. The file will be positioned at the append point, meaning that if the file existed, the first file write will write at the first byte past the end of the previous file; if there was no previous file, file write begins writing at the first byte in the file. file seek may not be used with write append files.

When a file is opened read write, it also does not matter whether the file exists. If the file exists, it is reopened. If the file does not exist, a new file is created. Regardless, the file will be positioned at the top of file. You can use file seek to seek to the end of the file or wherever else you desire. Net files may not be opened for read write.

Before opening a file, you can determine whether it exists using confirm file; see [P] **confirm**.

text and binary determine how the file is to be treated once it is opened. text means ASCII text files, and that is the default. In ASCII text, files are assumed to be composed of lines of characters, with each line ending in a line-end character. The character varies across operating systems, being linefeed under Unix, carriage return under Macintosh, and carriage return-line feed under Windows. file understands all the ways that lines might end when reading, and assumes that lines are to end in the way natural for the computer being used when writing.

The alternative to text is binary, meaning that the file is to be viewed merely as a stream of bytes. In binary files, there is an issue of byte order; consider the number 1 written as a 2-byte integer. On some computers (called hilo), it is written as "00 01", and on other computers (called lohi), it is written as "01 00" (with the least significant byte written first). There are similar issues for 4-byte integers, 4-byte floats, and 8-byte floats.

file assumes that the bytes are ordered in the way natural to the computer being used. file set can be used to vary this assumption. file set can be issued immediately after the file open, or later, or repeatedly.

replace and append are only allowed when the file is opened for write (which does not include read write). They determine what is to be done if the file already exists. The default is to issue an error message and not open the file. See the description of the options read, write, and read write above for more details.

all is allowed when the file is opened for write or for read write. It specifies that, if the file needs to be created, the permissions on the file are to be set so that it is readable by everybody.

ASCII text output specifications

"string" and ‘ *"string"* ’ write *string* into the file, without the surrounding quotes.

(*exp*) evaluates the expression *exp* and writes the result in the file. If the result is numeric, it is written with a %10.0g format, but with leading and trailing spaces removed. If *exp* evaluates to a string, the resulting string is written, with no extra leading or trailing blanks.

%*fmt* (*exp*) evaluates expression *exp* and writes the result with the specified %*fmt*. If *exp* evaluates to a string, %*fmt* must be a string format, and, correspondingly, if *exp* evaluates to a real, a numeric format must be specified. Do not confuse Stata's standard display formats with the binary formats %b and %z described elsewhere in this help file. file write in this case allows Stata's display formats described in [R] **format**, and also allows the centering extensions (e.g., % 20s) described in [P] **display**.

_skip(#) inserts # blanks into the file. If #<= 0, nothing is written; #<= 0 is not considered an error.

_column(#) writes a sufficient number of blanks to skip forward to column # of the line; if # refers to a prior column, nothing is output. The first column of a line is numbered 1. Referring to a column less than 1 is not considered an error; nothing is output in that case.

_newline[(#)], which may be abbreviated _n[(#)], outputs one end-of-line character if # is not specified, or outputs the specified number of end-of-line characters. The end-of-line character varies according to your operating system, being line feed under Unix, carriage return under Macintosh, and the two characters carriage return/line feed under Windows. If #<= 0, no end-of-line character is output.

_char(#) outputs one character, the character being the one given by the ASCII code # specified. # must be between 0 and 255, inclusive.

_tab⌈(#)⌉outputs one tab character if # is not specified, or outputs the specified number of tab characters. Coding _tab is equivalent to coding _char(9).

_page⌈(#)⌉outputs one pagefeed character if # is not specified, or outputs the specified number of pagefeed characters. Coding _page is equivalent to coding _char(12). The pagefeed character is often called control-L.

_dup(#) specified that the next directive is to be executed (duplicated) # times. # must be greater than or equal to 0. If # is equal to zero, the next element is not output.

Remarks

Remarks are presented under the headings

> *Use of file*
> *Use of file with tempfiles*
> *Writing ASCII text files*
> *Reading ASCII text files*
> *Use of seek when reading and writing ASCII text files*
> *Reading and writing binary files*
> *Writing binary files*
> *Reading binary files*
> *Use of seek when reading and writing binary files*
> *Appendix A.1 Useful commands and functions for use with file*
> *Appendix A.2 Actions of binary output formats with out-of-range values*

Use of file

file provides low-level access to file I/O. You open the file, use file read or file write repeatedly to read or write the file, and then close the file using file close:

```
file open ...
...
file read    or    file write ...
...
file read    or    file write ...
...
file close ...
```

Do not forget to close the file. Open files tie up system resources. In addition, in the case of files opened for write, the contents of the file probably will not be fully written until you close the file.

Typing file close _allwill close all open files, and the clear command closes all files as well. These commands, however, should not be included in programs you write; they are included to allow the user to reset Stata when programmers have been sloppy.

If you use file handles obtained from tempname, the file will be automatically closed when the ado-file terminates:

```
tempname myfile
file open 'myfile' using ...
```

This is the only case where it is appropriate not to close the file. Use of temporary names for filehandles offers considerable advantages because programs can be stopped because of errors or because the user presses *Break*.

Use of file with tempfiles

In the rare event that you file open a tempfile, you must obtain the handle from tempname. Temporary files are automatically deleted when the ado- or do-file ends. If the file is erased before it is closed, significant problems are possible. Using a tempname will guarantee that the file is properly closed beforehand:

```
tempname myfile
tempfile tfile
file open 'myfile' using "'tfile'" ...
```

Writing ASCII text files

This is easy to do:

```
file open handle using filename, write text
file write handle ...
...
file close handle
```

The syntax of file write is very similar to that of [R] **display**. The significant difference is that expressions must be bound in parentheses. In display, you can code

```
display 2+2
```

but using file write, you must code

```
file write handle (2+2)
```

The other important difference between file write and display is that display assumes that you want the end-of-line character output at the end of each display (and display provides _continue for use when you do not want this), but file write assumes that you want an end-of-line character only when you specify it. Thus, rather than coding "file write *handle* (2+2)", you probably want to code

```
file write handle (2+2) _n
```

Since end-of-line characters are output only where you specify, coding

```
file write handle "first part is " (2+2) _n
```

has the same effect as coding

```
file write handle "first part is "
file write handle (2+2) _n
```

or even

```
file write handle "first part is "
file write handle (2+2)
file write handle _n
```

There is no limit to the line length that `file write` can write since, as far as `file write` is concerned, _n is just another character. The _col(#) directive, however, will lose count if you write lines of more than 2,147,483,646 characters (_col(#) skips forward to the specified column). In general, we recommend that you do not write lines longer than 67,783 characters, because reading lines longer than that is more difficult using `file read`.

We say that _n is just another character, but we should say character or characters. _n outputs the appropriate end-of-line character for your operating system, which is the two characters carriage return followed by line feed under Windows, the one character carriage return under Macintosh, and the one character line feed under Unix.

Reading ASCII text files

The commands for reading text files are similar to those for writing them:

```
file open handle using filename, read text
file read handle localmacroname
. . .
file close handle
```

The `file read` command has exactly one syntax:

```
file read handle localmacroname
```

One line is read from the file and it is put in *localmacroname*. For instance, to read a line from the file myfile and put it in the local macro line, you code

```
file read myfile line
```

Thereafter in your code, you can refer to 'line' to obtain the contents of the line just read. The following program will do a reasonable job of displaying the contents of file, putting line numbers in front of the lines:

```
program ltype
        version 8
        local 0 '"using '0'"'
        syntax using/
        tempname fh
        local linenum = 0
        file open 'fh' using '""'using'"', read
        file read 'fh' line
        while r(eof)==0 {
                local linenum = 'linenum' + 1
                display %4.0f 'linenum' _asis '"  'macval(line)'"'
                file read 'fh' line
        }
        file close 'fh'
end
```

In the program above, notice our use of `tempname` to obtain a temporary name for the file handle. Doing that, we ensure that the file will be closed even if the user presses *Break* while our program is displaying lines, and so never executes `file close 'fh'`. In fact, our `file close 'fh'` line is unnecessary.

Also note our use of `r(eof)` to determine when the file ends. `file read` sets `r(eof)` to contain 0 before end-of-file and 1 once end-of-file is encountered; see *Saved results*, below.

As an aside, the `_asis` was included in the `display` in case the file contained braces or SMCL commands. These would be interpreted, and we wanted to suppress that interpretation so that `ltype` would display lines exactly as stored; see [P] **smcl**. We also used the `macval()` macro function to obtain what was in `'line'` without recursively expanding the contents of line.

Use of seek when reading and writing ASCII text files

You may use `file seek` when reading or writing text files, although, in fact, it is seldom used except with `read write` files and, even then, is seldom used with ASCII text files.

See *Use of seek when reading and writing binary files* below for a complete description of `file seek`—seek works the same way with both text and binary files—and then bear the following in mind:

- The # in "`file seek` *handle* #" refers to byte position, not line number. "`file seek` *handle* 5" means to seek to the fifth byte of the file, not the fifth line.

- When calculating byte offsets by hand, remember that the end-of-line character is 1 byte under Macintosh and Unix, but is 2 bytes under Windows.

- Rewriting a line of an ASCII text file works as expected only if the new and old lines are of the same length.

Reading and writing binary files

Consider whether you wish to read this section. There are lots of potential pitfalls associated with binary files and, at least in theory, a poorly written binary-I/O program can cause Stata to crash.

Binary files are made up of binary elements, of which Stata can understand:

Element	corresponding format
single- and multiple-character strings	%1s and %#s
signed and unsigned 1-byte binary integers	%1b, %1bs, and %1bu
signed and unsigned 2-byte binary integers	%2b, %2bs, and %2bu
signed and unsigned 4-byte binary integers	%4b, %4bs, and %4bu
4-byte IEEE floating point numbers	%4z
8-byte IEEE floating point numbers	%8z

The differences between all these types are only of interpretation. For instance, the decimal number 72, stored as a 1-byte binary integer, also represents the character H. If a file contained the 1-byte integer 72 and you were to read the byte using the format %1s, you would get back the character "H", and if a file contained the character "H" and you were to read the byte using the format %1bu, you would get back the number 72. 72 and H are indistinguishable in that they represent the same bit pattern. Whether that bit pattern represents 72 or H depends on the format you use, which is to say, the interpretation you give to the field.

Similar equivalence relations hold between the other elements. A binary file is nothing more than a sequence of unsigned 1-byte integers, where those integers are sometimes given different interpretations or are grouped and given an interpretation. In fact, all you need is the format %1bu to read or write anything. The other formats, however, make programming more convenient.

format	length	type	minimum	maximum	missing values?
%1bu	1	unsigned int	0	255	no
%1bs	1	signed int	-127	127	no
%1b	1	Stata int	-127	100	yes
%2bu	2	unsigned int	0	$65,474$	no
%2bs	2	signed int	$-32,767$	$32,767$	no
%2b	2	Stata int	$-32,767$	$32,740$	yes
%4bu	4	unsigned int	647	$4,294,967,296$	no
%4bs	4	signed int	$-2,147,483,647$	$2,147,483,647$	no
%4b	4	Stata int	$-2,147,483,647$	$2,147,483,620$	yes
%4z	4	float	-10^{38}	10^{38}	yes
%8z	8	float	-10^{307}	10^{307}	yes

When you write a binary file, you must decide on the format that you will use for every element that you will write. When you read a binary file, you must know ahead of time the format that was used for each of the elements.

Writing binary files

As with ASCII text files, you open the file, write repeatedly, and then close the file:

```
file open handle using filename, write binary
file write handle ...
...
file close handle
```

The file write command may be composed of the following elements:

```
%{8|4}z        (exp)
%{4|2|1}b[s|u] (exp)
%#s            "text"      (1 <= # <= max_macrolen)
%#s            ' "text" '
%#s            (exp)
```

For instance, to write "test file" followed by 2, $2 + 2$, and $3 * 2$ represented in various of its forms, you could code

```
. file write handle %9s "test file" %8z (2) %4b (2+2) %1bu (3*2)
```

or

```
. file write handle %9s "test file"
. file write handle %8z (2) %4b (2+2) %1bu (3+2)
```

or even

```
. file write handle %9s "test file"
. file write handle %8z (2)
. file write handle %4b (2+2) %1bu (3*2)
```

etc.

You write strings using the %#s format and numbers using the %b or %z formats. Concerning strings, the # in %#s should be greater than or equal to the length of the string to be written. If # is too small, only that many characters of the string will be written. Thus,

```
. file write handle %4s "test file"
```

would write "test" into the file and leave the file positioned at the fifth byte. There is nothing wrong with coding that (the "test" can be read back easily enough), but this is probably not what you intended to write.

Also concerning strings, you can output string literals—just enclose the string in quotes—or you can output the results of string expressions. Expressions, as in the case of using file write to output text files, must be enclosed in parentheses:

```
. file write handle %4s (substr(a,2,6))
```

The following program will output a user-specified matrix to a user-specified file; the syntax of the command being implemented is

$$\text{mymatout1 } matname \text{ using } filename \left[, \texttt{replace}\right]$$

and the code is

```
program mymatout1
        version 8
        gettoken mname 0 : 0
        syntax using/ [, replace]
        local r = rowsof('mname')
        local c = colsof('mname')
        tempname hdl
        file open 'hdl' using '"'using'"', 'replace' write binary
        file write 'hdl' %2b ('r') %2b ('c')
        forvalues i=1(1)'r' {
                forvalues j=1(1)'c' {
                        file write 'hdl' %8z ('mname'['i','j'])
                }
        }
        file close 'hdl'
end
```

A significant problem with mymatout1 is that, were we to write a matrix out on our Unix computer (an Intel based computer) and cart the file to a Macintosh computer, we would discover that we could not read the file. Intel computers write multiple-byte numbers with the least-significant byte first; Macintosh computers write the most-significant byte first. Who knows what your computer does? Thus, even though there is general agreement across computers on how numbers and characters are written, this byte-ordering difference is enough to stop binary files in their tracks.

file can handle this problem for you, but you have to insert a little bit of code. The recommended procedure is this: before writing any numbers in the file, write a field saying which byte order this computer uses (see byteorder() in [R] **functions**). Later, when we write the command to read the file, it will read the ordering that we recorded. We will then tell file which byte ordering the file is using, and file itself will reorder the bytes if that is necessary. There are other ways that we could handle this—such as always writing in a known byte order—but the recommended procedure is better because it is, on average, faster. Most files are read on the same computer that wrote them, and thus the computer wastes no time rearranging bytes in that case.

The improved version of `mymatout1` is

```
        program mymatout2
                version 8
                gettoken mname 0 : 0
                syntax using/ [, replace]
                local r = rowsof('mname')
                local c = colsof('mname')
                tempname hdl
                file open 'hdl' using '"'using'"', 'replace' write binary
/* new */       file write 'hdl' %1b (byteorder())
                file write 'hdl' %2b ('r') %2b ('c')
                forvalues i=1(1)'r' {
                        forvalues j=1(1)'c' {
                                file write 'hdl' %8z ('mname'['i','j'])
                        }
                }
                file close 'hdl'
        end
```

`byteorder()` returns 1 if the machine is hilo and 2 if lohi, but all that matters is that it is a small enough to fit in a byte. The important thing is that we write this number using `%1b`, about which there is no byte-ordering disagreement. What we do with this number we will deal with later.

The second significant problem with our program is that it does not write a signature. Binary files are difficult to tell apart: they all look like binary junk. It is important that we include some sort of marker at the top saying who wrote this file and in what format it was written. That is called a signature. The signature that we will use is

`mymatout 1.0.0`

We will write that 14-character long string first thing in the file so that, later when we write `mymatin`, we can read the string and verify it contains what we expect. Signature lines should always contain a generic identity (`mymatout` in this case) along with a version number, which we can change if we modify the output program to change the output format. This way, the wrong input program cannot be used with a more up-to-date file format.

Our improved program is

(Continued on next page)

```
           program mymatout3
                   version 8
                   gettoken mname 0 : 0
                   syntax using/ [, replace]
                   local r = rowsof('mname')
                   local c = colsof('mname')
                   tempname hdl
                   file open 'hdl' using '"'using'"', 'replace' write binary
/* new */          file write 'hdl' %14s "mymatout 1.0.0"
                   file write 'hdl' %1b (byteorder())
                   file write 'hdl' %2b ('r') %2b ('c')
                   forvalues i=1(1)'r' {
                           forvalues j=1(1)'c' {
                                   file write 'hdl' %8z ('mname'['i','j'])
                           }
                   }
                   file close 'hdl'
           end
```

This program works very well. After we had written the corresponding input routine (see *Reading binary files* below), however, we noticed that our restored matrices lacked their original row and column names, which led to a final round of changes:

```
           program mymatout4
                   version 8
                   gettoken mname 0 : 0
                   syntax using/ [, replace]
                   local r = rowsof('mname')
                   local c = colsof('mname')
                   tempname hdl
                   file open 'hdl' using '"'using'"', 'replace' write binary
/* changed */      file write 'hdl' %14s "mymatout 1.0.1"
                   file write 'hdl' %1b (byteorder())
                   file write 'hdl' %2b ('r') %2b ('c')
/* new */          local names : rownames 'mname'
/* new */          local len : length local names
/* new */          file write 'hdl' %4b ('len') %'len's '"'names'"'
/* new */          local names : colnames 'mname'
/* new */          local len : length local names
/* new */          file write 'hdl' %4b ('len') %'len's '"'names'"'
                   forvalues i=1(1)'r' {
                           forvalues j=1(1)'c' {
                                   file write 'hdl' %8z ('mname'['i','j'])
                           }
                   }
                   file close 'hdl'
           end
```

In this version, we added the lines necessary to write the row and column names into the file. We write the row names by coding

```
    local names : rownames 'mname'
    local len : length local names
    file write 'hdl' %4b ('len') %'len's '"'names'"'
```

and we similarly write the column names. The interesting thing here is that we need to write a string into our binary file for which the length of the string varies. One solution would be

```
    file write 'hdl' %67783s '"'mname'"'
```

but that would be inefficient since, in general, the names are a lot shorter than 67,783 characters. The solution is to obtain the length of the string to be written, and then write the length into the file. In the above code, macro 'len' contains the length, we write 'len' as a 4-byte integer, and then we write the string using a %'len's format. Consider what happens when 'len' is, say, 50. We write 50 into the file, and then we write the string using a %50s format. Later, when we read back the file, we can reverse this process, reading the length, and then using the appropriate format.

Note one other change we made: we changed the signature from "mymatout 1.0.0" to "mymatout 1.0.1", and we did that because the file format changed. Making that change ensures that an old read program does not attempt to read a more modern format (and so produce incorrect results).

❑ Technical Note

You may write strings using %#s formats that are narrower than, equal to, or wider than the length of the string being written. When the format is too narrow, only that many characters of the string are written. When the format and string are of the same width, the entire string is written. When the format is wider than the string, the entire string is written, and then the excess positions in the file are filled with binary zeros.

Binary zeros are special in strings because binary denotes the end of the string. Thus, when you read back the string, even if it was written in a field that was too wide, it will appear exactly as it appeared originally.

❑

Reading binary files

You read binary files just as you wrote them,

```
file open  handle using  filename, read binary
file read  handle ...
...
file close  handle
```

When reading them, you must be careful to specify the same formats as you did when you wrote the file.

The program that will read the matrices written by mymatout1, presented below, has syntax

```
mymatin1  matname  filename
```

and the code is

(*Continued on next page*)

```
program mymatin1
        version 8
        gettoken mname 0 : 0
        syntax using/
        tempname hdl
        file open 'hdl' using '"'using'"', read binary
        tempname val
        file read 'hdl' %2b 'val'
        local r = 'val'
        file read 'hdl' %2b 'val'
        local c = 'val'
        matrix 'mname' = J('r', 'c', 0)
        forvalues i=1(1)'r' {
                forvalues j=1(1)'c' {
                        file read 'hdl' %8z 'val'
                        matrix 'mname'['i','j'] = 'val'
                }
        }
        file close 'hdl'
end
```

When `file read` reads numeric values, they are always stored into [P] **scalar**, and you specify the name of the scalar directly after the binary numeric format. In our case, we are using the scalar named 'val', where 'val' is a name we obtained from `tempname`. We could just as well have used a fixed name, say, `myscalar`, so the first `file read` would read

```
file read 'hdl' %2b myscalar
```

and we would similarly substitute `myscalar` everywhere 'val' appears, but that would make our program less elegant. If the user had previously stored a value under the name `myscalar`, our values would replace it.

In the second version of `mymatout`, we included the byte order. The correspondingly improved version of `mymatin` is

```
            program mymatin2
                    version 8
                    gettoken mname 0 : 0
                    syntax using/
                    tempname hdl
                    file open 'hdl' using '"'using'"', read binary
                    tempname val
/* new */           file read 'hdl' %1b 'val'
/* new */           local border = 'val'
/* new */           file set 'hdl' byteorder 'border'
                    file read 'hdl' %2b 'val'
                    local r = 'val'
                    file read 'hdl' %2b 'val'
                    local c = 'val'
                    matrix 'mname' = J('r', 'c', 0)
                    forvalues i=1(1)'r' {
                            forvalues j=1(1)'c' {
                                    file read 'hdl' %8z 'val'
                                    matrix 'mname'['i','j'] = 'val'
                            }
                    }
                    file close 'hdl'
            end
```

We simply read back the value we recorded and then `file set` it. We cannot directly `file set` *handle* byteorder 'val' because 'val' is a scalar and the syntax for `file set` byteorder is

$$\text{file set } \textit{handle } \text{byteorder } \{\text{hilo}|\text{lohi}|1|2\}$$

That is, `file set` is willing to see a number (1 and `hilo` means the same thing, as do 2 and `lohi`), but that number must be a literal (the character 1 or 2), so we had to copy 'val' into a macro before we could use it. Once we set the byte order, however, we could from then on depend on `file` to reorder the bytes for us should that be necessary.

In the third version of `mymatout`, we added a signature. In the modification below, we read the signature using a `%14s` format. Strings are copied into local macros, and we must specify the name of the local macro following the format:

```
          program mymatin3
                  version 8
                  gettoken mname 0 : 0
                  syntax using/
                  tempname hdl
                  file open 'hdl' using '"'using'"', read binary
/* new */         file read 'hdl' %14s signature
/* new */         if "'signature'" != "mymatout 1.0.0" {
/* new */                 disp as err "file not mymatout 1.0.0"
/* new */                 exit 610
/* new */         }
                  tempname val
                  file read 'hdl' %1b 'val'
                  local border = 'val'
                  file set 'hdl' byteorder 'border'
                  file read 'hdl' %2b 'val'
                  local r = 'val'
                  file read 'hdl' %2b 'val'
                  local c = 'val'
                  matrix 'mname' = J('r', 'c', 0)
                  forvalues i=1(1)'r' {
                          forvalues j=1(1)'c' {
                                  file read 'hdl' %8z 'val'
                                  matrix 'mname'['i','j'] = 'val'
                          }
                  }
                  file close 'hdl'
          end
```

In the fourth and final version, we wrote the row and column names. You will remember that we wrote the names by first preceding them by a 4-byte integer recording their width:

(Continued on next page)

```
            program mymatin4
                    version 8
                    gettoken mname 0 : 0
                    syntax using/
                    tempname hdl
                    file open 'hdl' using '"'using'"', read binary
                    file read 'hdl' %14s signature
/* changed */ if "'signature'" != "mymatout 1.0.1" {
/* changed */           disp as err "file not mymatout 1.0.1"
                        exit 610
                    }
                    tempname val
                    file read 'hdl' %1b 'val'
                    local border = 'val'
                    file set 'hdl' byteorder 'border'
                    file read 'hdl' %2b 'val'
                    local r = 'val'
                    file read 'hdl' %2b 'val'
                    local c = 'val'
                    matrix 'mname' = J('r', 'c', 0)
/* new */           file read 'hdl' %4b 'val'
/* new */           local len = 'val'
/* new */           file read 'hdl' %'len's names
/* new */           matrix rownames 'mname' = 'names'
/* new */           file read 'hdl' %4b 'val'
/* new */           local len = 'val'
/* new */           file read 'hdl' %'len's names
/* new */           matrix colnames 'mname' = 'names'
                    forvalues i=1(1)'r' {
                            forvalues j=1(1)'c' {
                                    file read 'hdl' %8z 'val'
                                    matrix 'mname'['i','j'] = 'val'
                            }
                    }
                    file close 'hdl'
            end
```

Use of seek when reading and writing binary files

99% of all I/O programs are written without using `file seek`. `file seek` changes your location in the file. Ordinarily, you start at the beginning of the file and proceed sequentially through the bytes. `file seek` lets you back up or skip ahead.

`file seek` *handle* query actually does not change your location in the file; it merely returns in scalar r(loc) the current position, with the first byte in the file being numbered 0, the second 1, and so on. In fact, all the `file seek` commands return r(loc), but `file seek` query is unique because that is all it does.

`file seek` *handle* tof moves to the beginning (top) of the file. This is useful with read files when you want to read the file again, but you can seek to tof even with write files and, of course, with read write files, too. (Concerning read files, we emphasize that you can seek to top, or any point, before or after the end-of-file condition is raised.)

`file seek` *handle* eof moves to the end of the file. This is only useful with write files (or read write files), but may be used with read files, too.

`file seek` *handle* # moves to the specified position. # is measured in bytes from the beginning of the file, and is in the same units as reported in r(loc). '`file seek` *handle* 0' is equivalent to '`file seek` *handle* tof'.

❏ Technical Note

When a file is opened `write append`, you may not use `file seek`. If you need to seek in the file, open the file `read write` instead.

❏

Appendix A.1 Useful commands and functions for use with file

1. When opening a file `read write` or `write append`, `file`'s actions differ depending upon whether the file already exists. [P] **confirm** can tell you whether a file exists; use it before opening the file.

2. To obtain the length of strings when writing binary files, use the `macro length` extended function:

```
local length : length local mystr
file write handle %'length's '"'mystr'"'
```

See [P] **macro** for details.

3. To write portable binary files, we recommend writing in natural byte order and recording the byte order in the file. Then the file can be read by reading the byte order and setting it:

Writing:

```
file write handle %1b (byteorder())
```

Reading:

```
tempname mysca
file read handle %1b 'mysca'
local b_order = 'mysca'
file set handle byteorder 'b_order'
```

The `byteorder()` function returns 1 or 2, depending on whether the computer being used records data in hilo or lohi format. See [R] **functions**.

Appendix A.2 Actions of binary output formats with out-of-range values

Say you write the number 2,137 with a `%1b` format. What value will you later get back when you read the field with a `%1b` format? In this case, it turns out the answer is ., which is to say, Stata's missing value, because the `%1b` format is in fact a variation of `%1bs` that supports Stata's missing value. If you wrote 2,137 with `%1bs`, it would read back as 127; and if you wrote it with `%1bu`, it would read back as 255.

In general, in the Stata variation, missing values are supported and numbers outside of the range are written as missing. In the remaining formats, the minimum or maximum is written as

format	min value	max value	value written when value is ...	
			too small	too large
%1b	−127	100	.	.
%1bs	−127	127	−127	127
%1bu	0	255	0	255
%2b	−32,767	32,740	.	.
%2bu	−32,767	32,767	−32,767	32,767
%2bs	0	65,474	0	65,474
%4b	−2,147,483,647	2,147,483,620	.	.
%4bs	−2,147,483,647	2,147,483,647	−2,147,483,647	2,147,483,647
%4bu	0	4,294,967,296	0	4,294,967,296
%4z	-10^{38}	10^{38}	.	.
%8z	-10^{307}	10^{307}	.	.

In the above table, if you write a missing value, take that as writing a value larger than the maximum allowed for the type.

If you write a noninteger value with an integer format, the result will be truncated to an integer. For example, writing 124.75 with a %2b format is the same as writing 124.

Saved Results

file read saves in r():

Scalars
    r(eof)   1 on end-of-file; 0 otherwise

Macros
    r(status) (if text file)   win   line read, line ended in cr-lf;
                               mac   line read, line ended in cr;
                               unix   line read, line ended in lf;
                               split line read, line was too long and so split;
                               none line read, line was not terminated;
                               eof   line not read because of end-of-file

r(status)==split indicates that max_macrolen − 1 (33 maxvar + 199 for Stata/SE, 67,783 for Intercooled Stata, 8,680 for Small Stata) characters of the line were returned, and that the next file read will pick up where the last read left off.

r(status)==none indicates that the entire line was returned, that no line-end character was found, and the next file read will return r(status)==eof.

Note that if r(status)==eof (r(eof)==1), the local macro into which the line was read contains " ". The local macro containing " ", however, does not imply end-of-file, because the line might simply have been empty.

`file seek` saves in `r()`:

Scalars
    `r(loc)`   current position of the file

`file query` saves in `r()`:

Scalars
    `r(N)`   number of open files

Also See

Related: [P] **display**, [P] **hexdump**, [P] **serset**;

    [R] **infile**, [R] **infix (fixed format)**, [R] **insheet**

Title

> **file formats .dta** — Description of the .dta file format

Description

Stata's .dta datasets record data in a way generalized to work across computers that do not agree on how data are recorded. Thus, the same dataset may be used, without translation, on different computers (Windows computers, Unix computers, and Macintosh computers). Given a computer, datasets are divided into two categories: native-format and foreign-format datasets. Stata uses the following two rules:

R1. On any computer, Stata knows how to write only native-format datasets.

R2. On all computers, Stata can read foreign-format as well as native-format datasets.

Rules R1 and R2 ensure that Stata users need not be concerned with dataset formats.

Stata is also continually being updated, and these updates sometimes require changes be made to how Stata records .dta datasets. Stata can read older formats, but whenever it writes a dataset, it writes in the modern format.

Remarks

For up-to-date documentation on the Stata .dta file format, type `help dta`. You can look at the file in the Viewer by typing `whelp dta`. The online help file contains all the details a programmer will need. To obtain a copy of the help file in PostScript format, which you can then print, type

```
. which dta.hlp
. translate help_file dta.ps, translator(smcl2ps)
```

The first command will show you the where the help file is, and then you can type that name on the translate command. Even easier is

```
. findfile dta.hlp
. translate "`r(fn)'" dta.ps, translator(smcl2ps)
```

Either way, you can then print new file `dta.ps` from your current directory.

Also See

Background: [R] **translate**

Title

findfile — Find file in path

Syntax

findfile *filename* [, path(*path*) <u>nodes</u>cend all]

where *filename* and *path* may optionally be enclosed in quotes, and the default is to look over the adopath if option path() is not specified.

Description

findfile looks for a file along a specified path, and, if found, displays the fully qualified name and returns the name in r(fn). If the file is not found, the file-not-found error, r(601), is issued.

Unless told otherwise, findfile looks along the adopath, the same path Stata uses for searching for ado-files, help files, etc.

In programming contexts, findfile is usually used preceded by quietly; see [P] **quietly**.

Options

path(*path*) specifies the path over which findfile is to search. Not specifying this option is equivalent to specifying path('"'c(adopath)'"').

If specified, *path* should be a list of directory (folder) names separated by semicolons; for example,

```
path(".;/bin;/data/mine;")
path('".;\bin;"\data\my data";"')
```

The individual directory names may be enclosed in quotes, but, if any are, remember to enclose the entire path argument in compound quotes.

In addition, any of the directory names may be specified as STATA, UPDATES, BASE, SITE, PLUS, PERSONAL, or OLDPLACE, which are indirect references to directories recorded by sysdir:

```
path(UPDATES;BASE;SITE;.;PERSONAL;PLUS)
path(\bin:SITE;.;PERSONAL;PLUS)
path('"\bin;.;"\data\my data";PERSONAL;PLUS"')
path('".;'c(adopath)'"')
```

nodescend specifies that findfile should not follow Stata's normal practice of searching in letter subdirectories of directories in the path as well as in the directories themselves. nodescend is rarely specified, and, if it is specified, path() would usually be specified, too.

(Continued on next page)

all specifies that all files along the path with the specified name are to be found and listed and saved in r(fn). When all is not specified, the default is to stop the search when the first instance of the specified name is found.

When all is specified, the fully qualified names of the files found are returned in r(fn), listed one after the other, and each enclosed in quotes. Thus, when all is specified, if you subsequently need to quote the returned list, you must use compound double quotes. In addition, remember that findfile issues a file-not-found error if no files are found. If you wish to suppress that and want r(fn) returned containing nothing, precede findfile with capture. Thus, the typical usage of findfile, all is

```
. capture findfile filename, all
. local filelist '"'r(fn)'"'
```

Remarks

findfile is not a utility to search everywhere for a file that you have lost. findfile is for use in those rare ado-files that use prerecorded datasets and for which you wish to place the datasets along the adopath, along with the ado-file itself.

For instance, Stata's icd9 command performs a mapping, and that mapping is in fact stored in a dataset containing original values and mapped values. Thus, along with icd9.ado is a dataset icd9_cod.dta, and that dataset is stored along the adopath, too. Users of icd9 know nothing about the dataset. In icd9.ado, the icd9_cod.dta is merged with the data in memory. The code fragment that does that reads

```
. quietly findfile icd9_cod.dta
. merge ... using '"'r(fn)'"'
```

It would not have been possible to code simply

```
. merge ... using icd9_cod.dta
```

because icd9_cod.dta is not in the current directory.

Saved Results

findfile saves in r():

Macros
r(fn) (all not specified) name of the file found; name not enclosed in quotes
       (all specified)   names of the files found, listed one after the other,
                           each enclosed in quotes

Also See

Complementary: [P] **sysdir**, [P] **unabcmd**,
                   [R] **which**

Related: [R] **sysuse**

Title

> **foreach** — Loop over items

Syntax

```
foreach lname { in | of listtype } list {
        Stata commands referring to 'lname'
}
```

Allowed are

```
foreach lname in anylist
```

```
foreach lname of local lmacname
```

```
foreach lname of global gmacname
```

```
foreach lname of varlist varlist
```

```
foreach lname of newlist newvarlist
```

```
foreach lname of numlist numlist
```

Braces must be specified with foreach and

1. the open brace must appear on the same line as the foreach;
2. nothing may follow the open brace except, of course, comments; the first command to be executed must appear on a new line;
3. the close brace must appear on a line by itself.

(In versions prior to Stata 8, putting the open brace, command, and close brace on the same line as the foreach was allowed. Old behavior is restored under version control; see [P] **version**.)

Description

foreach repeatedly sets local macro *lname* to each element of the list and executes the commands enclosed in braces. The loop is executed zero or more times; it is executed zero times if the list is null or empty. Also see [P] **forvalues**, which is the fastest way to loop over consecutive values, such as looping over numbers from 1 to k.

foreach *lname* in *list* allows a general list. Elements are separated from each other by one or more blanks.

foreach *lname* of local *list* and foreach *lname* of global *list* obtain the list from the indicated place. This method of using foreach produces the fastest executing code.

foreach *lname* of varlist *list*, foreach *lname* of newlist *list*, and foreach *lname* of numlist *list* are very much like foreach *lname* in *list*, except that the *list* is given the appropriate interpretation. For instance,

```
foreach x in mpg weight-turn {
        ...
}
```

has two elements, "mpg" and "weight-turn", so the loop will be executed twice.

```
foreach x of varlist mpg weight-turn {
        ...
}
```

has four elements, mpg, weight, length, and turn, because *list* was given the interpretation of a varlist.

foreach *lname* of varlist *list* gives *list* the interpretation of a varlist. The *list* is expanded according to standard variable abbreviation rules, and the existence of the variables is confirmed.

foreach *lname* of newlist *list* indicates that the list is to be interpreted as new variable names; see [U] **14.4.2 Lists of new variables**. A check is performed to see that the named variables could be created, but they are not automatically created.

foreach *lname* of numlist *list* indicates a number list and allows standard number list notation; see [U] **14.1.8 numlist**.

Remarks

Remarks are presented under the headings

> *Introduction*
> *foreach . . . of local and foreach . . . of global*
> *foreach . . . of varlist*
> *foreach . . . of newlist*
> *foreach . . . of numlist*
> *Use of foreach with continue*
> *The unprocessed list elements*

Introduction

foreach has lots of forms, but it is just one command, and what it means is

```
foreach value of a list of things, set x equal to each and {
               execute these instructions once per value
               and in the loop we can refer to 'x' to refer to the value
}
```

and this is coded

```
foreach x ... {
        ... 'x' ...
}
```

We use the name x for illustration; you may use whatever name you like. The list itself can come from a variety of places and can be given a variety of interpretations, but foreach x in is easiest to understand:

```
foreach x in a b mpg 2 3 2.2 {
        ... 'x' ...
}
```

The list is a, b, mpg, 2, 3, and 2.2, and appears right in the command. In some programming instances, you might know the list ahead of time, but often what you know is that you want to do the loop for each value of the list contained in a macro; for instance, 'varlist'. In that case, you could code

```
foreach x in 'varlist' {
        ... 'x' ...
}
```

but your code will execute more quickly if you code

```
foreach x of local varlist {
        ... 'x' ...
}
```

Both work, but the second is quicker to execute. In the first, Stata has to expand the macro and substitute it into the command line, whereupon foreach must then pull back the elements one at a time and store them. In the second, all that is already done, and foreach can just grab the local macro varlist.

The two forms we have just shown,

```
foreach x in ... {
        ... 'x' ...
}
```

and

```
foreach x of local ... {
        ... 'x' ...
}
```

are the two ways foreach is most commonly used. The other forms are for special occasions.

In the event that you have something that you want to be given the interpretation of a varlist, newvarlist, or numlist before it is interpreted as a list, you can code

```
foreach x of varlist mpg weight-turn g* {
        ... 'x' ...
}
```

or

```
foreach x of newvarlist id values1-9 {
        ... 'x' ...
}
```

or

```
foreach x of numlist 1/3 5 6/10 {
        ... 'x' ...
}
```

Just as with foreach x in ..., you put the list right on the command line, and, if you have the list in a macro, you can put 'macroname' on the command line.

If you have the list in a macro, you have no alternative but to code 'macroname'; there is no special foreach x of local macroname variant for varlist, newvarlist, and numlist because, in those cases, foreach x of local macroname itself is probably sufficient. If you have the list in a macro, how did it get there? Well, it probably was something that the user typed and that your program has already parsed. In that case, the list has already been expanded, and treating the list as a general list is adequate; it need not be given the special interpretation again, at least as far as foreach is concerned.

▷ Example

foreach is generally used in programs, but it may be used interactively, and, for illustration, we will use it that way. Three files are appended to the dataset in memory. The dataset currently in memory and each of the three files have only one string observation.

```
. list

                          x
  1.          data in memory

. foreach file in this.dta that.dta theother.dta {
  2.          append using "`file'"
  3. }

. list

                          x
  1.          data in memory
  2.    data from this.dta
  3.    data from that.dta
  4. data from theother.dta
```

Quotes may be used to allow elements with blanks.

```
. foreach name in "Christi Pechacek" "Ashley Johnson" "Marsha Martinez" {
  2.          display length("`name'") " characters long -- `name'"
  3. }
16 characters long -- Christi Pechacek
14 characters long -- Ashley Johnson
15 characters long -- Marsha Martinez
```

◁

foreach ... of local and foreach ... of global

foreach *lname* of local *lmacname* obtains the blank-separated list (which may contain quotes) from local macro *lmacname*. For example,

```
foreach file of local flist {
        ...
}
```

produces the same results as typing

```
foreach file in `flist' {
        ...
}
```

except that foreach file of local flist is faster, uses less memory, and allows the list to be modified in the body of the loop.

If the contents of flist are modified in the body of foreach file in `flist', foreach will not notice and the original list will be used. The contents of flist may, however, be modified in foreach file of local flist, but only to add new elements onto the end.

foreach *lname* of global *gmacname* is the same as foreach *lname* in $*gmacname*, with the same three caveats as to speed, memory use, and modification in the loop body.

▷ Example

```
. local grains "rice wheat flax"

. foreach x of local grains {
  2.         display "`x'"
  3. }
rice
wheat
flax

. global money "Dollar Lira Pound"

. foreach y of global money {
  2.         display "`y'"
  3. }
Dollar
Lira
Pound
```
◁

foreach ... of varlist

foreach *lname* of varlist *varlist* allows specifying an existing variable list.

▷ Example

```
. foreach var of varlist pri-rep t* {
  2.         quietly summarize `var'
  3.         summarize `var' if `var' > r(mean)
  4. }
```

Variable	Obs	Mean	Std. Dev.	Min	Max
price	22	9814.364	3022.929	6229	15906

Variable	Obs	Mean	Std. Dev.	Min	Max
mpg	31	26.67742	4.628802	22	41

Variable	Obs	Mean	Std. Dev.	Min	Max
rep78	29	4.37931	.493804	4	5

Variable	Obs	Mean	Std. Dev.	Min	Max
trunk	40	17.1	2.351214	14	23

Variable	Obs	Mean	Std. Dev.	Min	Max
turn	41	43.07317	2.412367	40	51

◁

foreach *lname* of varlist *varlist* can be useful interactively, but is rarely used in programming contexts. You can code

```
syntax [varlist] ...
foreach var of varlist `varlist' {
        ...
}
```

but that is not as efficient as coding

```
syntax [varlist] ...
foreach var of local varlist {
        ...
}
```

because 'varlist' has already been expanded by the syntax command according to the macro rules.

❏ Technical Note

```
syntax [varlist] ...
foreach var of local varlist {
        ...
}
```

is also preferable to coding

```
syntax [varlist] ...
tokenize 'varlist'
while "'1'" != "" {
        ...
        macro shift
}
```

or

```
syntax [varlist] ...
tokenize 'varlist'
local i = 1
while "''i''" != "" {
        ...
        local i = 'i' + 1
}
```

not only because it is more readable, but also because it is faster.

❏

foreach ... of newlist

newlist signifies to foreach that the list is composed of new variables. foreach verifies that the list contains valid new variable names, but it does not create the variables. For instance,

```
. foreach var of newlist z1-z4 {
  2.        gen 'var' = uniform()
  3. }
```

would create variables z1, z2, z3, and z4.

foreach ... of numlist

foreach *lname* of numlist *numlist* provides a method of looping through a list of numbers. Standard number list notation is allowed; see [U] **14.1.8 numlist**. For instance,

```
. foreach num of numlist 1/4 8 103 {
  2.        display 'num'
  3. }
1
2
3
4
8
103
```

If you wish to loop over a large number of equally spaced values, do not code, for instance,

```
foreach x in 1/1000 {
        ...
}
```

Instead, code

```
forvalues x = 1/1000 {
        ...
}
```

see [P] **forvalues**. Understand that `foreach` must store the list of elements, whereas `forvalues` obtains the elements one at a time by calculation.

Use of foreach with continue

The *lname* in `foreach` is defined only in the loop body. If you code

```
foreach x ... {
        // loop body, 'x' is defined
}
// 'x' is now undefined, meaning it contains ""
```

'x' is defined only within the loop body, and this is the case even if you use `continue`, `break` (see [P] **continue**) to exit the loop early:

```
foreach x ... {
        ...
        if ... {
                continue, break
        }
}
// 'x' is still undefined, even if continue, break is executed
```

If you subsequently need the value of 'x', code

```
foreach x ... {
        ...
        if ... {
                local lastx '"'x'"'
                continue, break
        }
}
// 'lastx' defined
```

The unprocessed list elements

The macro 'ferest()' may be used in the body of the `foreach` loop to obtain the unprocessed list elements.

(Continued on next page)

▷ Example

```
. foreach x in alpha "one two" three four {
  2.          display
  3.          display `"        x is |`x'|"'
  4.          display `""ferest() is |`ferest()'|"'
  5. }

        x is |alpha|
ferest() is |"one two" three four|

        x is |one two|
ferest() is |three four|

        x is |three|
ferest() is |four|

        x is |four|
ferest() is ||
```
◁

`ferest()` is only available within the body of the loop; outside of that, `ferest()` evaluates
to "". Thus, you might code,

```
foreach x ... {
        ...
        if ... {
                local lastx `""`x'""'
                local rest `""`ferest()'""'
                continue, break
        }
}
// `lastx' and `rest' are defined
```

Also See

Complementary:	[P] **continue**
Related:	[P] **forvalues**, [P] **if**, [P] **while**
Background:	[U] **21 Programming Stata**,
	[U] **21.3 Macros**

Title

> **forvalues** — Loop over consecutive values

Syntax

<u>forv</u>alues *lname* = *range* {
           Stata commands referring to '*lname*'
}

where *range* is

$\#_1(\#_d)\#_2$	meaning $\#_1$ to $\#_2$ in steps of $\#_d$
$\#_1/\#_2$	meaning $\#_1$ to $\#_2$ in steps of 1
$\#_1\ \#_t$ to $\#_2$	meaning $\#_1$ to $\#_2$ in steps of $\#_t - \#_1$
$\#_1\ \#_t : \#_2$	meaning $\#_1$ to $\#_2$ in steps of $\#_t - \#_1$

The loop is executed as long as calculated values of '*lname*' are $\leq \#_2$, assuming $\#_d > 0$.

Braces must be specified with forvalues and

1. the open brace must appear on the same line as the forvalues;

2. nothing may follow the open brace except, of course, comments; the first command to be executed must appear on a new line;

3. the close brace must appear on a line by itself.

(In versions prior to Stata 8, putting the open brace, command, and close brace on the same line as the forvalues was allowed. Old behavior is restored under version control; see [P] **version**.)

Description

forvalues repeatedly sets local macro *lname* to each element of *range* and executes the commands enclosed in braces. The loop is executed zero or more times.

Remarks

forvalues is the fastest way to execute a block of code for different numeric values of *lname*.

▷ Example

With forvalues *lname* = $\#_1(\#_d)\#_2$, the loop is executed zero or more times, once for *lname* = $\#_1$, once for *lname* = $\#_1 + \#_d$, once for *lname* = $\#_1 + \#_d + \#_d$, and so on, as long as *lname* $\leq \#_2$ (assuming $\#_d$ is positive) or as long as *lname* $\geq \#_2$ (assuming $\#_d$ is negative). Specifying $\#_d$ as 0 is an error.

```
. forvalues i = 1(1)5 {
  2.         display 'i'
  3. }
1
2
3
4
5
```

lists the numbers 1 to 5, stepping by 1, while

```
. forvalues i = 10(-2)1 {
  2.          display 'i'
  3. }
10
8
6
4
2
```

lists the numbers starting from 10, stepping down by 2 until it reaches 2. Notice that it stops at 2 instead of at 1 or 0.

```
. forvalues i = 1(1)1 {
  2.          display 'i'
  3. }
1
```

displays 1, while

```
. forvalues i = 1(1)0 {
  2.          display 'i'
  3. }
```

displays nothing.

◁

forvalues *lname* = $\#_1/\#_2$ is the same as using forvalues *lname* = $\#_1(1)\#_2$. Note that using / does not allow counting backwards.

▷ Example

```
. forvalues i = 1/3 {
  2.          display 'i'
  3. }
1
2
3
```

lists the three values from 1 to 3, but

```
. forvalues i = 3/1 {
  2.          display 'i'
  3. }
```

lists nothing, since using this form of the forvalues command only allows incrementing by 1.

◁

The forvalues *lname* = $\#_1$ $\#_t$ to $\#_2$ and forvalues *lname* = $\#_1$ $\#_t$: $\#_2$ forms of the forvalues command are equivalent to computing $\#_d = \#_t - \#_1$ and then using the forvalues *lname* = $\#_1(\#_d)\#_2$ form of the command.

▷ Example

```
. forvalues i = 5 10 : 25 {
  2.          display 'i'
  3. }
5
10
15
20
25
. forvalues i = 25 20 to 5 {
  2.          display 'i'
  3. }
25
20
15
10
5
```

◁

❑ Technical Note

The values of the loop bounds are determined once and for all the first time the loop is executed. Changing the loop bounds will have no effect. For instance,

```
. local n 3
. forvalues i = 1(1)'n' {
  2.          local n = 'n' + 1
  3.          display 'i'
  4. }
1
2
3
```

will not create an infinite loop. With 'n' originally equal to 3, the loop will be performed three times.

Similarly, modifying the loop counter will not affect forvalues' subsequent behavior. For instance,

```
. forvalues i = 1(1)3 {
  2.          display "Top of loop  i = 'i'"
  3.          local i = 'i' * 4
  4.          display "After change i = 'i'"
  5. }
Top of loop  i = 1
After change i = 4
Top of loop  i = 2
After change i = 8
Top of loop  i = 3
After change i = 12
```

will still execute three times, setting 'i' to 1, 2, and 3 at the beginning of each iteration.

❑

Also See

Complementary:	[P] **continue**
Related:	[P] **foreach**, [P] **if**, [P] **while**
Background:	[U] **21 Programming Stata**,
	[U] **21.3 Macros**

Title

gettoken — Low-level parsing

Syntax

gettoken *emname1* [*emname2*] : *emname3* [, p̲arse(*pchars*) q̲uotes qed(*lmacname*)

m̲atch(*lmacname*) bind]

where *pchars* are the parsing characters, *lmacname* is a local macro name, and *emname* is described
in the following table:

emname is:	refers to a:
macroname	local macro
(local) *macroname*	local macro
(global) *macroname*	global macro

Description

The gettoken command is a low-level parsing command designed for programmers who wish
to parse input for themselves. The syntax command (see [P] **syntax**) is an easier-to-use, high-level
parsing command.

gettoken obtains the next token from the macro *emname3* and stores it in the macro *emname1*.
If macro *emname2* is specified, the remainder of the string from *emname3* is stored in the *emname2*
macro. *emname1* and *emname3*, or *emname2* and *emname3*, may be the same name. The first token
is determined based on the parsing characters *pchars* which default to a space if not specified.

Options

parse("*pchars*") specifies the parsing characters. If parse() is not specified, parse(" ") is
assumed.

quotes indicates that the outside quotes are not to be stripped in what is stored in *emname1*. This
option has no effect on what is stored in *emname2*, because it always retains outside quotes.
quotes is a rarely specified option; in most cases, you want the quotes stripped. You would not
want the quotes stripped if you wanted to make a perfect copy of the contents of the original
macro for parsing at a later time.

qed(*lmacname*) specifies a local macroname that is to be filled in with 1 or 0 according to whether
the returned token was enclosed in quotes in the original string. qed() does not change how
parsing is done; it merely returns additional information.

match(*lmacname*) specifies that parentheses are to be matched in determining the token. The outer
level of parentheses, if any, are removed before the token is stored in *emname1*. The local macro
lmacname is set to "(" if parentheses were found; otherwise, it is set to an empty string.

bind specifies that expressions within parentheses and those within brackets are to be bound together
even when not parsing on () and [].

Remarks

Often we apply `gettoken` to the macro '0' (see [U] **21.4.6 Parsing nonstandard syntax**), as in

```
gettoken first : 0
```

which obtains the first token (with spaces as token delimiters) from '0' and leaves '0' unchanged. Or, alternatively,

```
gettoken first 0 : 0
```

which obtains the first token from '0' and saves the rest back in '0'.

▷ Example

Even though `gettoken` is typically used as a programming command, we demonstrate its use interactively:

```
. local str "cat+dog   mouse++horse"
. gettoken left : str
. display '"'left'"'
cat+dog
. display '"'str'"'
cat+dog   mouse++horse
. gettoken left str : str, parse(" +")
. display '"'left'"'
cat
. display '"'str'"'
+dog   mouse++horse
. gettoken next str : str, parse(" +")
. display '"'next'"'
+
. display '"'str'"'
dog   mouse++horse
```

Both global and local variables may be used with `gettoken`. Strings with nested quotes are also allowed, and the `quotes` option may be specified if desired. For more information on compound double quotes, see [U] **21.3.5 Double quotes**.

```
. global weird '"'""some" strings"' are '"within "strings""'"'
. gettoken (local)left (global)right : (global)weird
. display '"'left'"'
"some" strings
. display '"$right"'
 are '"within "strings""'
. gettoken left (global)right : (global)weird , quotes
. display '"'left'"'
'""some" strings"'
. display '"$right"'
 are '"within "strings""'
```

The `match` option is illustrated below.

```
. local pstr "(a (b c)) ((d e f) g h)"
. gettoken left right : pstr
. display `"`left'"'
(a
. display `"`right'"'
 (b c)) ((d e f) g h)
. gettoken left right : pstr , match(parns)
. display `"`left'"'
a (b c)
. display `"`right'"'
 ((d e f) g h)
. display `"`parns'"'
(
```

◁

▷ Example

One use of `gettoken` is to process two-word commands. For example, `mycmd list` does one thing and `mycmd generate` does another. We wish to obtain the word following `mycmd`, examine it, and call the appropriate subroutine with a perfect copy of what followed.

```
program mycmd
        version 8.0
        gettoken subcmd 0 : 0
        if "`subcmd'" == "list" {
                mycmd_l `0'
        }
        else if "`subcmd'" == "generate" {
                mycmd_g `0'
        }
        else    error 199
end

program mycmd_l
        ...
end

program mycmd_g
        ...
end
```

◁

▷ Example

Suppose that we wish to create a general prefix command with syntax

```
newcmd ... : stata_command
```

where the ... is some possibly complicated syntax. We want to split this entire command line on colon, making a perfect copy of what precedes the colon—which will be parsed by our program—and what follows the colon—which will be passed along to *stata_command*.

```
program newcmd
        version 8.0
        gettoken part 0 : 0, parse(" :") quotes
        while '"'part'"' != ":" & '"'part'"' != "" {
                local left '"'left' 'part'"'
                gettoken part 0 : 0, parse(" :") quotes
        }

        ('left' now contains what followed newcmd up to the colon)
        ('0' now contains what followed the colon)

        ...

end
```

Notice the use of the quotes option. Also notice that we used compound double quotes when accessing 'part' and 'left' because these macros might contain embedded quotation marks.

◁

❑ Technical Note

We strongly encourage you to specify space as one of your parsing characters. For instance, with the last example, you may have been tempted to use gettoken, but to parse only on colon instead of on colon and space as in

```
gettoken left 0 : 0, parse(":") quotes
gettoken colon 0 : 0, parse(":")
```

and thereby avoid the while loop. This is not guaranteed to work for two reasons. First, if the length of the string up to the colon is large, you run the risk of having it truncated. Second, if 'left' begins with a quotation mark, the result will not be what you expect.

Our recommendation is always to specify a space as one of your parsing characters and to grow your desired macro as was demonstrated in our last example.

❑

Also See

Complementary:	[P] **display**, [P] **while**
Related:	[P] **syntax**, [P] **tokenize**
Background:	[U] **21 Programming Stata**

Title

hexdump — Display hexadecimal report on file

Syntax

hexdump *filename* $\big[$, <u>a</u>nalyze <u>tab</u>ulate <u>noex</u>tended <u>res</u>ults <u>f</u>rom(#) <u>to</u>(#) $\big]$

Description

hexdump displays a hexadecimal dump of a file, or, optionally, a report analyzing the dump.

Although hexdump is not a programming command, it is included in this manual because it is highly technical.

Options

analyze specifies that a report on the dump, rather than the dump itself, is to be presented.

tabulate specifies in the analyze report that a full tabulation of the ASCII characters is also to be presented.

noextended states that your screen cannot display printable extended ASCII characters, characters in the range 161–254, or, equivalently, 0xa1–0xfe. (hexdump does not display characters 128–160 and 255.)

results is for programmers. It specifies that in addition to other saved results, hexdump is to save r(c0), r(c1), ..., r(c255), containing the frequency with which each character code was observed.

from(#) specifies the first byte of the file to be dumped or analyzed. The default is to start at the first byte of the file, from(0).

to(#) specifies the last byte of the file to be analyzed. The default is to continue to the end of the file.

Remarks

hexdump is useful when you are having difficulty reading a file using infile, infix, or insheet. Sometimes, the reason for the difficulty is that the file does not contain what you think it contains, or that it does contain the format you have been told, and looking at the file in text mode is either not possible or not sufficiently revealing.

Pretend we had the file myfile.raw containing

```
Datsun 210      4589  35  5  1
VW Scirocco     6850  25  4  1
Merc. Bobcat    3829  22  4  0
Buick Regal     5189  20  3  0
VW Diesel       5397  41  5  1
Pont. Phoenix   4424  19  .  0
Merc. Zephyr    3291  20  3  0
Olds Starfire   4195  24  1  0
BMW 320i        9735  25  4  1
```

This file has no problems. hexdump produces output that looks like

```
. hexdump myfile.raw
```

address	hex representation 0 1 2 3 4 5 6 7 8 9 a b c d e f	character representation 0123456789abcdef
0	4461 7473 756e 2032 3130 2020 2020 2034	Datsun 210 4
10	3538 3920 2033 3520 2035 2020 310d 0a56	589 35 5 1..V
20	5720 5363 6972 6f63 636f 2020 2020 3638	W Scirocco 68
30	3530 2020 3235 2020 3420 2031 0d0a 4d65	50 25 4 1..Me
40	7263 2e20 426f 6263 6174 2020 2033 3832	rc. Bobcat 382
50	3920 2032 3220 2034 2020 300d 0a42 7569	9 22 4 0..Bui
60	636b 2052 6567 616c 2020 2020 3531 3839	ck Regal 5189
70	2020 3230 2020 3320 2030 0d0a 5657 2044	20 3 0..VW D
80	6965 7365 6c20 2020 2020 2035 3339 3720	iesel 5397
90	2034 3120 2035 2020 310d 0a50 6f6e 742e	41 5 1..Pont.
a0	2050 686f 656e 6978 2020 3434 3234 2020	Phoenix 4424
b0	3139 2020 2e20 2030 0d0a 4d65 7263 2e20	19 . 0..Merc.
c0	5a65 7068 7972 2020 2033 3239 3120 2032	Zephyr 3291 2
d0	3020 2033 2020 300d 0a4f 6c64 7320 5374	0 3 0..Olds St
e0	6172 6669 7265 2020 3431 3935 2020 3234	arfire 4195 24
f0	2020 3120 2030 0d0a 424d 5720 3332 3069	1 0..BMW 320i
100	2020 2020 2020 2039 3733 3520 2032 3520	9735 25
110	2034 2020 310d 0a	4 1..

But, it can also produce output that looks like

```
. hexdump myfile.raw, analyze
```

Line-end characters			Line length (tab=1)	
\r\n	(DOS)	9	minimum	30
\r by itself (Mac)		0	maximum	30
\n by itself (Unix)		0		
Space/separator characters			Number of lines	9
[blank]		99	EOL at EOF?	yes
[tab]		0		
[comma] (,)		0	Length of first 5 lines	
Control characters			Line 1	30
binary 0		0	Line 2	30
CTL excl. \r, \n, \t		0	Line 3	30
DEL		0	Line 4	30
Extended (128-159,255)		0	Line 5	30
ASCII printable				
A-Z		20		
a-z		61	File format	ASCII
0-9		77		
Special (!@#$ etc.)		4		
Extended (160-254)		0		

```
Total                   279

Observed were:
    \n \r blank . 0 1 2 3 4 5 6 7 8 9 B D M O P R S V W Z a b c d e f g h i
    k l n o p r s t u x y
```

Of the two forms of output, the second is often the more useful because it summarizes the file and the length of the summary is not a function of the length of the file. Here is the summary for a file that is just over 4 megabytes long,

```
. hexdump bigfile.raw, analyze
   Line-end characters                  Line length (tab=1)
     \r\n        (DOS)      147,456        minimum               29
     \r by itself (Mac)          0        maximum               30
     \n by itself (Unix)         2
   Space/separator characters           Number of lines      147,458
     [blank]            1,622,039          EOL at EOF?            yes
     [tab]                      0
     [comma] (,)                0        Length of first 5 lines
   Control characters                     Line 1                30
     binary 0                   0         Line 2                30
     CTL excl. \r, \n, \t       0         Line 3                30
     DEL                        0         Line 4                30
     Extended (128-159,255)     0         Line 5                30
   ASCII printable
     A-Z                  327,684
     a-z                  999,436        File format          ASCII
     0-9                1,261,587
     Special (!@#$ etc.)   65,536
     Extended (160-254)         0
                         _____
   Total                4,571,196

   Observed were:
     \n \r blank . 0 1 2 3 4 5 6 7 8 9 B D M O P R S V W Z a b c d e f g h i
     k l n o p r s t u x y
```

and here is the same file, but with a subtle problem:

```
. hexdump badfile.raw, analyze
   Line-end characters                  Line length (tab=1)
     \r\n        (DOS)      147,456        minimum               30
     \r by itself (Mac)          0        maximum               90
     \n by itself (Unix)         0
   Space/separator characters           Number of lines      147,456
     [blank]            1,622,016          EOL at EOF?            yes
     [tab]                      0
     [comma] (,)                0        Length of first 5 lines
   Control characters                     Line 1                30
     binary 0                   8         Line 2                30
     CTL excl. \r, \n, \t       4         Line 3                30
     DEL                        0         Line 4                30
     Extended (128-159,255)    24         Line 5                30
   ASCII printable
     A-Z                  327,683
     a-z                  999,426        File format          BINARY
     0-9                1,261,568
     Special (!@#$ etc.)   65,539
     Extended (160-254)        16
                         _____
   Total                4,571,196

   Observed were:
     \0 ^C ^D ^G \n \r ^U blank & . 0 1 2 3 4 5 6 7 8 9 B D E M O P R S U V W
     Z a b c d e f g h i k l n o p r s t u v x y } ~ E^A E^C E^I E^M E^P
     ë é ö 255
```

In the above, note that the line length varies between 30 and 90 (we were told that each line would be 30 characters long). Also note that the file contains what hexdump, analyze labeled control characters. Finally, note that hexdump, analyze declared the file to be BINARY rather than ASCII.

We created the second file by removing two valid lines from bigfile.raw (60 characters) and substituting 60 characters of binary junk. We would defy you to find the problem without using hexdump, analyze. You would succeed, but only after a lot of work. Remember, this file has 147,456 lines, and only 2 of them are bad. Printing 1,000 lines at random from the file, your chances of listing the bad part is only .013472. To have a 50% chance of finding the bad lines, you would have to list 52,000 lines, which is to say, review about 945 pages of output. On those 945 pages, each line would need to be drawn at random. More likely, you would list lines in groups, and that would greatly reduce your chances of encountering the bad lines.

The situation is not quite as dire as we make out because, were you to read badfile.raw using infile, it would complain, and, in this case, it would tell you exactly where it was complaining. Still, at that point you might wonder whether the problem was with how you were using infile or with the data. Moreover, our 60 bytes of binary junk experiment corresponds to transmission error. If the problem were instead that the person who constructed the file constructed two of the lines differently, infile might not complain, but later you would notice some odd values in your data (because obviously you would review the summary statistics, right?). In this case, hexdump, analyze might be the only way you could prove to yourself and others that the raw data need to be reconstructed.

❏ Technical Note

In the full hexadecimal dump,

```
. hexdump myfile.raw
```

								character
	hex representation							representation
address	0 1	2 3	4 5	6 7	8 9	a b	c d	e f	0123456789abcdef
0	4461	7473	756e	2032	3130	2020	2020	2034	Datsun 210 4
10	3538	3920	2033	3520	2035	2020	310d	0a56	589 35 5 1..V
20	5720	5363	6972	6f63	636f	2020	2020	3638	W Scirocco 68
30	3530	2020	3235	2020	3420	2031	0d0a	4d65	50 25 4 1..Me

(output omitted)

addresses (listed on the left) are listed in hexadecimal. 10 means decimal 16, 20 means decimal 32, and so on. Sixteen characters are listed across each line.

In some other dump, you might see something like

```
. hexdump myfile2.raw
```

								character
	hex representation							representation
address	0 1	2 3	4 5	6 7	8 9	a b	c d	e f	0123456789abcdef
0	4461	7473	756e	2032	3130	2020	2020	2034	Datsun 210 4
10	3538	3920	2033	3520	2035	2020	3120	2020	589 35 5 1
20	2020	2020	2020	2020	2020	2020	2020	2020	
*									
160	2020	2020	2020	0a56	5720	5363	6972	6f63	.VW Sciroc
170	636f	2020	2020	3638	3530	2020	3235	2020	co 6850 25

(output omitted)

The * in the address field indicates that the previous line is repeated, and repeated, and repeated, until we get to hexadecimal address 160 (decimal 352).

❏

Saved Results

hexdump, analyze and hexdump, results save in r():

Scalars

r(DOS)	number of \r\n
r(Mac)	number of \r by itself
r(Unix)	number of \n by itself
r(blank)	number of blanks
r(tab)	number of tab characters
r(comma)	number comma (,) characters
r(ctl)	number of binary 0s; A–Z, excluding \r, \n, \t; DELs; and 128–159, 255
r(uc)	number of A–Z
r(lc)	number of a–z
r(digit)	number of 0–9
r(special)	number of printable special characters (!@# etc.)
r(extended)	number of printable extended characters (160–254)
r(filesize)	number of characters
r(lmin)	minimum line length
r(lmax)	maximum line length
r(lnum)	number of lines
r(eoleof)	1 if EOL at EOF, otherwise 0
r(l1)	length of 1st line
r(l2)	length of 2nd line
r(l3)	length of 3rd line
r(l4)	length of 4th line
r(l5)	length of 5th line
r(c0)	number of binary 0s (results only)
r(c1)	number of binary 1s (^A) (results only)
r(c2)	number of binary 2s (^B) (results only)
...	...
r(c255)	number of binary 255s (results only)

Macros

r(format)	ASCII, EXTENDED ASCII, or BINARY

Also See

Complementary: [R] **type**

Title

> **if** — if programming command

Syntax

if *exp* {   or   if *exp single_command*
     multiple_commands
}

which, in either case, may be followed by

else {   or   else *single_command*
     multiple_commands
}

If you put braces following the if or else,

    1. the open brace must appear on the same line as the if or else;

    2. nothing may follow the open brace except, of course, comments; the first command to be executed must appear on a new line;

    3. the close brace must appear on a line by itself.

(In versions prior to Stata 8, putting the open brace, command, and close brace on the same line as the if or else was allowed, but omitting the braces altogether was not. Old behavior is preserved under version control; see [P] **version**.)

Description

The if command (not to be confused with the if qualifier; see [U] **14.1.3 if exp**) evaluates *exp*. If the result is *true* (nonzero), the commands inside the braces are executed. If the result is *false* (zero), those statements are ignored, and the statement (or statements if enclosed in braces) following the else is executed.

Remarks

The if command is intended for use inside programs and do-files; see [U] **21.3.4 Macros and expressions** for examples of its use.

▷ Example

Do not confuse the if command with the if qualifier. Typing if age>21 {summarize age} will summarize *all* the observations on age if the first observation on age is greater than 21. Otherwise, it will do nothing. Typing summarize age if age>21, on the other hand, summarizes all the observations on age that are greater than 21.

◁

▷ Example

if is typically used in do-files and programs. For instance, let's write a program to calculate the Tukey (1977, 90–91) "power" function of a variable x:

```
. program power
      if '2'>0 {
            generate z='1'^'2'
            label variable z "'1'^'2'"
      }
      else if '2'==0 {
            generate z=log('1')
            label variable z "log('1')"
      }
      else {
            generate z=-('1'^('2'))
            label variable z "-'1'^('2')"
      }
      end
```

This program takes two arguments. The first argument is the name of an existing variable, x. The second argument is a number, which we will call n. The program creates a new variable z. If $n > 0$, z is x^n; if $n = 0$, z is $\log x$; and if $n < 0$, z is $-x^n$. No matter which path the program follows through the code, it labels the variable appropriately:

```
. power age 2
. describe z
```

variable name	storage type	display format	value label	variable label
z	float	%9.0g		age^2

◁

❑ Technical Note

If the expression refers to any variables, their values in the first observation are used unless explicit subscripts are specified.

❑

References

Tukey, J. W. 1977. *Exploratory Data Analysis.* Reading, MA: Addison–Wesley Publishing Company.

Also See

Related:	[P] **while**
Background:	[U] **21 Programming Stata**

Title

> **macro** — Macro definition and manipulation

Syntax

$\underline{g}$lobal *mname* $\big[$ =*exp* | :*extended_fcn* | "$\big[$*string*$\big]$" | ' "$\big[$*string*$\big]$" ' $\big]$

$\underline{loc}$al *lclname* $\big[$ =*exp* | :*extended_fcn* | "$\big[$*string*$\big]$" | ' "$\big[$*string*$\big]$" ' $\big]$

tempvar *lclname* $\big[$*lclname* $\big[$...$\big]$$\big]$

tempname *lclname* $\big[$*lclname* $\big[$...$\big]$$\big]$

tempfile *lclname* $\big[$*lclname* $\big[$...$\big]$$\big]$

$\underline{loc}$al $\big\{$ ++*lclname* | --*lclname* $\big\}$

$\underline{ma}$cro $\underline{dir}$

$\underline{ma}$cro $\underline{drop}$ $\big\{$ *mname* $\big[$*mname* $\big[$...$\big]$$\big]$ | *mname** | _all $\big\}$

$\underline{ma}$cro $\underline{list}$ $\big[$ *mname* $\big[$*mname* $\big[$...$\big]$$\big]$ | _all $\big]$

$\underline{ma}$cro $\underline{shift}$ $\big[$#$\big]$

$\big[$...$\big]$ '*expansion_optr*' $\big[$...$\big]$

where *extended_fcn* is any of

$\big\{$ $\underline{type}$ | $\underline{f}$ormat | $\underline{value}$ $\underline{l}$abel | $\underline{var}$iable $\underline{l}$abel $\big\}$ *varname*

data $\underline{l}$abel

$\underline{sort}$edby

$\underline{l}$abel $\big\{$ *valuelabelname* | (*varname*) $\big\}$ $\big\{$ maxlength | # $\big[$#$\big]$ $\big\}$

constraint $\big\{$ dir | # $\big\}$

char $\big\{$ *varname*[] | *varname*[*charname*] $\big\}$ or   char $\big\{$ _dta[] | _dta[*charname*] $\big\}$

permname *suggested_name* $\big[$, $\underline{l}$ength(#) $\big]$

dir $\big[$"$\big]$*dir*$\big[$"$\big]$ $\big\{$ $\underline{files}$ | $\underline{dirs}$ | other $\big\}$ $\big[$"$\big]$*pattern*$\big[$"$\big]$ $\big[$, nofail $\big]$

sysdir $\big[$ STATA | UPDATES | BASE | SITE | PLUS | PERSONAL | *dirname* $\big]$

$\underline{env}$ironment *name*

220

r(scalars | macros | matrices | functions)

e(scalars | macros | matrices | functions)

s(macros)

<u>dis</u>play ...   (see *Macro extended function*
                                                                  for formatting results below)

list ...   (see [P] **macro lists**)

{ <u>rown</u>ames | <u>col</u>names | <u>rowe</u>q | <u>cole</u>q | <u>rowf</u>ullnames | <u>colf</u>ullnames } *matname*

tsnorm *string* [, <u>var</u>name]

word { count | # of } *string*

piece #*piece_number* #*length_of_pieces* of ['] "*string*" ['] [, <u>nob</u>reak]

length { <u>loc</u>al *lclname* | <u>gl</u>obal *mname* }

subinstr { <u>gl</u>obal *mname2* | <u>loc</u>al *lclname2* } { "*from*" | ' "*from*" ' }

    { "*to*" | ' "*to*" ' } [, all <u>c</u>ount(<u>gl</u>obal *mname3* | <u>loc</u>al *lclname3*) <u>w</u>ord]

<u>tempv</u>ar | <u>tempf</u>ile

and *expansion_optr* is

    lclname | ++*lclname* | *lclname*++ | --*lclname* | *lclname*-- | =*exp* |

       :*extended_fcn* | .*class_directive* | macval(*lclname*)

Description

global assigns strings to specified global macro names (*mnames*). local assigns strings to local macro names (*lclnames*). Both regular quotes (" and ") and compound double quotes (' " and " ') are allowed; see [U] **21.3.5 Double quotes**. If the *string* has embedded quotes, then compound double quotes are needed.

tempvar assigns names to the specified local macro names that may be used as temporary variable names in the dataset. When the program or do-file concludes, any variables in the dataset with these assigned names are dropped.

tempname assigns names to the specified local macro names that may be used as temporary scalar or matrix names. When the program or do-file concludes, any scalars or matrices in active memory with these assigned names are dropped.

tempfile assigns names to the specified local macro names that may be used as names for temporary files. When the program or do-file concludes, any datasets created with these assigned names are erased.

macro manipulates global and local macros.

See [U] **21.3 Macros** for information on macro substitution.

Remarks

Remarks are presented under the headings

> *Formal definition of a macro*
> *Global and local macro names*
> *Macro assignment*
> *Macro extended functions*
> *Macro extended functions for extracting data attributes*
> *Macro extended function for naming variables*
> *Macro extended functions for filenames and file paths*
> *Macro extended functions for accessing operating-system parameters*
> *Macro extended functions for names of saved results*
> *Macro extended function for formatting results*
> *Macro extended function for manipulating lists*
> *Macro extended functions related to matrices*
> *Macro extended functions related to time-series operators*
> *Macro extended functions for parsing*
> *Macro expansion operators and function*
> *The tempvar, tempname, and tempfile commands*
> *Temporary variables*
> *Temporary scalars and matrices*
> *Temporary files*
> *Manipulation of macros*
> *Macros as arguments*

Macros are a tool used in programming Stata, and this entry assumes that you have read [U] **21 Programming Stata** and especially [U] **21.3 Macros**. This entry concerns advanced issues not previously covered.

Formal definition of a macro

A *macro* has a *macro name* and *macro contents*. Everywhere a punctuated macro name appears in a command—punctuation is defined below—the macro contents are substituted for the macro name.

Macros come in two types, called global and local macros. Macro names are up to 32 characters long for global macros and up to 31 characters long for local macros. The contents of global macros are defined with the `global` command and local macros with the `local` command. Global macros are just that. Local macros exist solely within the program or do-file in which they are defined. If that program or do-file calls another program or do-file, the local macros previously defined temporarily cease to exist, and their existence is re-established when the calling program regains control. When a program or do-file ends, its local macros are permanently deleted.

To substitute the macro contents of a global macro name, the macro name is typed (punctuated) with a dollar sign ($) in front. To substitute the macro contents of a local macro name, the macro name is typed (punctuated) with surrounding left and right single quotes (' '). In either case, braces ({ }) can be used to clarify meaning and to form nested constructions. When the contents of an undefined macro are substituted, the macro name (and punctuation) is removed, and nothing is substituted in its place.

For example,

The input . . .	is equivalent to . . .
`global a "myvar"`	
`gen $a = oldvar`	`gen myvar = oldvar`
`gen a = oldvar`	`gen a = oldvar`
`local a "myvar"`	
`gen 'a' = oldvar`	`gen myvar = oldvar`
`gen a = oldvar`	`gen a = oldvar`

```
global a "newvar"
global i = 2
gen $a$i = oldvar                        gen newvar2 = oldvar

local a "newvar"
local i = 2
gen 'a''i' = oldvar                      gen newvar2 = oldvar

global b1 "newvar"
global i=1
gen ${b$i} = oldvar                      gen newvar = oldvar

local b1 "newvar"
local i=1
gen 'b'i'' = oldvar                      gen newvar = oldvar

global b1 "newvar"
global a "b"
global i = 1
gen ${$a$i} = oldvar                     gen newvar = oldvar

local b1 "newvar"
local a "b"
local i = 1
gen ''a''i'' = oldvar                    gen newvar = oldvar
```

Global and local macro names

What we next say is an exceedingly fine point: Global macro names that begin with an underscore
are really local macros; this is why local macro names can have only 31 characters. The command
local is formally defined as equivalent to global _. Thus, the following are equivalent:

```
local x                      global _x
local i=1                    global _i=1
local name "Bill"            global _name "Bill"
local fmt : format myvar     global _fmt : format myvar
local 3 '2'                  global _3 $_2
```

tempvar is formally defined as equivalent to local *name* : tempvar for each name specified
after tempvar. Thus,

```
tempvar a b c
```

is equivalent to

```
local a : tempvar
local b : tempvar
local c : tempvar
```

which in turn is equivalent to

```
global _a : tempvar
global _b : tempvar
global _c : tempvar
```

tempfile is defined similarly.

Macro assignment

When you type

```
. local name "something"
```

or

```
. local name '"something"'
```

something becomes the contents of the macro. The compound double quotes (' " and " ') are needed when *something* itself contains quotation marks. When you type

```
. local name = something
```

something is evaluated as an expression, and the result becomes the contents of the macro. Note the presence and lack of the equal sign. That is, if you type

```
. local problem "2+2"
. local result = 2+2
```

then `problem` contains 2+2, whereas `result` contains 4.

Finally, when you type

```
. local name : something
```

something is interpreted as an extended macro function. (Note the colon rather than nothing or the equal sign.) Of course, all of this applies to `global` as well as to `local`.

`local ++`*lclname*, or `local --`*lclname*, is used to increment, or decrement, *lclname*.

For instance, typing

```
. local ++x
```

is equivalent to typing

```
. local x = 'x' + 1
```

Macro extended functions

Macro extended functions are of the form

```
. local macname : ...
```

For instance,

```
. local x : type mpg
. local y : matsize
. local z : display %9.4f sqrt(2)
```

We document the macro extended functions below. Macro extended functions are typically used in programs, but you can experiment with them interactively. For instance, if you are unsure what 'local x : type mpg' does, you could type

```
. local x : type mpg
. display "'x'"
int
```

Macro extended functions for extracting data attributes

type *varname*
   returns the storage type of variable *varname*, which might be "int", "long", "float", "double", "str1", "string2", etc.

format *varname*
   returns the display format associated with *varname*; for instance, "%9.0g", "%12s", etc.

value label *varname*
   returns the name of the value label associated with *varname*, which might be " " (meaning no label), or, for example, "make", meaning the value label's name is make.

variable label *varname*
   returns the variable label associated with *varname*, which might be " " (meaning no label), or, for example, "Repair Record 1978".

data label
   returns the dataset label associated with the dataset currently in memory, which might be " " (meaning no label), or, for example, "1978 Automobile Data".

sortedby
   returns the names of the variables by which the data in memory are currently sorted, which might be " " (meaning not sorted), or, for example, "foreign mpg", meaning the data are in the order of the variable foreign, and, within that, in the order of mpg (the order that would be obtained from the Stata command sort foreign mpg).

label *valuelabelname* # [#₂] { maxlength | # [#] }
   returns the label value of # in *valuelabelname*. For instance, 'label forlab 1' might return "Foreign cars" if forlab were the name of a value label and 1 mapped to "Foreign cars". If 1 did not correspond to any mapping within the value label, or if the value label forlab were not defined, then "1" (the # itself) would be returned.

   #₂ optionally specifies the maximum length of the of the label to be returned. If 'label forlab 1' would return "Foreign cars", then 'label forlab 1 6' would return "Foreig".

   maxlength specifies that, rather than looking up a number in a value label, label is to return the maximum length of the labelings.

label (*varname*) # [#₂] { maxlength | # [#] }
   works exactly as the above, except that rather than specifying the *valuelabelname* directly, one indirectly specifies. The value label name associated with *varname* is used, if there is one. If not, it is treated just as if *valuelabelname* were undefined, and the number itself is returned.

   maxlength specifies that, rather than looking up a number in a value label, label is to return the maximum length of the labelings.

constraint { dir | # } gives information on constraints.

   constraint # puts constraint # in *macroname*. constraint # when constraint # is not defined returns " "; it is not an error. constraint # for # < 0 is an error

   constraint dir returns the numbers of the constraints. The list is not sorted.

   For example,

```
. constraint define 1 price = weight
. constraint define 2 mpg > 20
. local myname : constraint 2
. macro list _myname
_myname         mpg > 20
```

```
. local aname : constraint dir
. macro list _aname
_aname:    2 1
```

char $\big\{$ *varname* [] | *varname* [*charname*] $\big\}$ or   char $\big\{$ _dta[] | _dta[*charname*] $\big\}$
returns information on the characteristics of a dataset; see [P] **char**. For instance,

```
. use http://www.stata-press.com/data/r8/auto
(1978 Automobile Data)
. char mpg[one] "this"
. char mpg[two] "that"
. local x : char mpg[one]
. di "`x'"
this
. local x : char mpg[nosuch]
. di "`x'"

. local x : char mpg[]
. di "`x'"
two one
```

Macro extended function for naming variables

permname *suggested_name* $\big[$, length(#) $\big]$ returns a valid new variable name based on *suggested_name* in *mname*. *suggested_name* must follow naming conventions, but may be too long or may be a variable that already exists.

length(#) specifies the maximum length of the returned variable name, which must be between 8 and 32. length(32) is the default.

For instance,

```
. local myname : permname foreign
. macro list _myname
_myname:        foreign1
.local aname : permname displacement, length(8)
. macro list _aname
_aname:         displace
```

Macro extended functions for filenames and file paths

dir "*dir*" $\big\{$ files | dirs | other $\big\}$ "*pattern*" $\big[$, nofail $\big]$ puts in *macroname* the specified files, directories, or entries that are neither files nor directories, from directory *dir*. *pattern* is as defined by Stata's match(s_1, s_2) function; see [R] **functions**. The quotes in the command are optional, but recommended, and they are nearly always required surrounding *pattern*. The returned string will contain each of the names, separated one from the other by spaces, and each enclosed in double quotes. If *macroname* is subsequently used in a quoted context, it must be enclosed in compound compound double quotes: ` "`*macroname*'" ' .

The nofail option specifies that if the directory contains too many filenames to fit into a macro, rather than issuing an error, the filenames that fit into *macroname* should be returned. nofail should rarely, if ever, be specified.

For example,

`local list : dir . files "*"` makes a list of all regular files in the current directory. In `list` might be returned `""subjects.dta" "step1.do" "step2.do" "reest.ado"`.

`local list : dir . dirs "*"` makes a list of all subdirectories of the current directory. In `list` might be returned `""notes" "subpanel"`.

`local list : dir . other "*"` makes a list of all things that are neither regular files nor directories. These files rarely occur, and might be, for instance, Unix device drivers.

`local list : dir "\mydir\data" files "*"` makes a list of all regular files that are to be found in `\mydir\data`. Returned might be `""example.dta" "make.do" "analyze.do"`.

Note that it is the names of the files that are returned, not their full path names.

`local list : dir "subdir" files "*"` makes a list of all regular files that are to be found in `subdir` of the current directory.

sysdir [STATA | UPDATES | BASE | SITE | PLUS | PERSONAL | *dirname*]
returns the various Stata system directory path names; see [P] **sysdir**. The name is always returned with a trailing path separator; e.g., 'sysdir STATA' might return "D:\PROGRAMS\STATA\".

sysdir *dirname*
returns *dirname*. This function is used to code 'local x : sysdir 'dir'', where 'dir' might contain the name of a directory specified by a user or a keyword, such as STATA, UPDATES, etc. The appropriate directory name will be returned. The name is always returned with a trailing path separator.

Macro extended functions for accessing operating-system parameters

environment *name*
returns the contents of the operating system's environment variable named *name*, or "" if *name* is undefined.

Macro extended functions for names of saved results

e(scalars)
returns the names of all the saved results in e() that are scalars, with the names listed one after the other and separated by one space. For instance, e(scalars) might return "N ll_0 ll df_m chi2 r2_p", meaning scalar saved results e(N), e(ll_0), ... exist.

e(macros)
returns the names of all the saved results in e() that are macros.

e(matrices)
returns the names of all the saved results in e() that are matrices.

e(functions)
returns the names of all the saved results in e() that are functions. e(functions) might return "sample", meaning that the function e(sample) exists.

r(scalars), r(macros), r(matrices), r(functions)
does the same for the r() that the extended macro functions e() do for the saved results in e().

s(macros)
returns the names of all the saved results in s() that are macros. (Results saved in s() can only be macros.)

Macro extended functions for formatting results

display ...
  returns the results from the display command. The display extended function is the display command, except that the output is rerouted, not appearing on the screen, but instead placed into the contents of a macro.

  You can use all the features of display that make sense, which is to say, you may not set styles with as *style* because macros do not have colors, you may not use _continue to suppress going to a new line on the real display (it is not being displayed), you may not use _newline (for the same reason), and you may not use _request to obtain input from the console (because input and output have nothing to do with macro definition). With those exceptions, everything else works. See [P] **display**.

  Example:
  local x : display %9.4 sqrt(2)

Macro extended functions related to matrices

  In understanding the functions below, remember that the *fullname* of a matrix row or column is defined as *eqname*:*name*. For instance, *fullname* might be outcome:weight, and then the *eqname* is outcome and the *name* is weight. Or, the *fullname* might be gnp:L.cpi, and then the *eqname* is gnp and the *name* is L.cpi. Or, the *fullname* might be mpg, in which case the *eqname* is " " and the *name* is mpg. For more information, see [P] **matrix define**.

rowfullnames *matname*
  returns the *fullnames* of the rows of *matname*, listed one after another and separated by one space. As many *fullnames* are listed as rows of *matname*.

colfullnames *matname*
  is like rowfullnames, but returns the *fullnames* of the columns.

rownames *matname*
  returns the *names* of the rows of *matname*, listed one after another and separated by one space. As many names are listed as rows of *matname*.

colnames *matname*
  is like rownames, but returns the *names* of the columns.

roweq *matname*
  returns the *eqnames* of the columns of *matname*, listed one after another and separated by one space. As many names are listed as columns of *matname*. If the eqname of a column is blank, _ (underscore) is substituted. Thus, roweq might return "Poor Poor Poor Average Average Average" for one matrix and "_ _ _ _ _ _" for another.

coleq *matname*
  is like roweq, but returns the *eqnames* of the columns.

Macro extended functions related to time-series operators

tsnorm *string*
  returns the canonical form of *string* when *string* is interpreted as a time-series operator. For instance, if *string* is 1d1, "L2D" is returned, and if string is 1.1d1, L3D is returned. If *string* is nothing, " " is returned.

`tsnorm` *string*, `varname`

returns the canonical form of *string* when *string* is interpreted as a time-series operated variable. For instance, if *string* is `1d1.gnp`, "`L2D.gnp`" is returned, and if string is `1.1d1.gnp`, "`L3D.gnp`" is returned. If string is just a variable name, the variable name is returned.

Macro extended functions for parsing

`word count` *string*

returns the number of tokens in *string*. A token is a word (characters separated by spaces) or set of words enclosed in quotes. Do *not* enclose *string* in double quotes, because then `word count` will return "1".

`word #` `of` *string*

returns the #th token from *string*. Do not enclose *string* in double quotes.

`piece #`$_1$ `#`$_2$ `of "`*string*`"` $\left[\,,\,\underline{\text{nobreak}}\,\right]$

returns a piece of *string*. This macro extended function provides a smart method of breaking a string into pieces of roughly the specified length. #$_1$ specifies which piece to obtain. #$_2$ specifies the maximum length of each piece. Each piece is built trying to fill to the maximum length without breaking in the middle of a word. However, when a word is longer than #$_2$, the word will be split unless `nobreak` is specified. `nobreak` specifies that words are not to be broken even if that would result in a string longer than #$_2$ characters.

Compound double quotes may be used around *string*, and must be used when *string* itself might contain double quotes.

`length` $\left\{\,\texttt{local}\ \textit{macroname}\,|\,\texttt{global}\ \textit{macroname}\,\right\}$ returns the length of *macroname* in characters. If *macroname* is undefined, 0 is returned.

For instance,

```
. constraint define 1 price = weight
. local myname : constraint 1
. macro list _myname
_myname          price = weight
. local lmyname : length local myname
. macro list _lmyname
_lmyname:       14
```

`subinstr local` *mname* `"`*from*`" "`*to*`"`

returns the contents of *'mname'*, with the first occurrence of "*from*" changed to "*to*".

`subinstr local` *mname* `"`*from*`" "`*to*`"`, `all`

does the same thing, but changes all occurrences of "*from*" to "*to*".

`subinstr local` *mname* `"`*from*`" "`*to*`"`, `word`

returns the contents of *'mname'*, with the first occurrence of the word "*from*" changed to "*to*". A word is defined as a space-separated token or a token at the beginning or end of the string.

`subinstr local` *mname* `"`*from*`" "`*to*`"`, `word all`

does the same thing, but changes all occurrences of the word "*from*" to "*to*".

`subinstr global` *mname* `...`

is the same as the above, but obtains the original string from the global macro `$mname` rather than from the local macro *'mname'*.

`subinstr ... global` *mname* `...,` `...` `count({`global`|`local`}` *mname2*`)`

in addition to what is specified, places a count of the number of substitutions in the specified global or in local macro *mname2*.

▷ Example

```
. local string "a or b or c or d"
. global newstr : subinstr local string "c" "sand"
. display "$newstr"
a or b or sand or d
. local string2 : subinstr global newstr "or" "and", all count(local n)
. display "`string2'"
a and b and sand and d
. display "`n'"
3
. local string3: subinstr local string2 "and" "x", all word
. display "`string3'"
a x b x sand x d
```

Notice that the "and" in "sand" did not get replaced by "x" since the word option was specified.

◁

Macro expansion operators and function

There exist five macro expansion operators that may be used within references to local (not global) macros.

'*lclname*++' and '++*lclname*' provide inline incrementation of local macro *lclname*. For example,

```
. local x 5
. display "`x++'"
5
. display "`x'"
6
```

or ++ can be place before *lclname* in which case *lclname* is incremented *before* '*lclname*' is evaluated.

```
. local x 5
. display "`++x'"
6
. display "`x'"
6
```

'*lclname*--' and '--*lclname*' provide inline decrementation of local macro *lclname*.

'=*exp*' provides inline access to Stata's expression evaluator. The Stata expression *exp* is evaluated, and substituted is a string containing the results. For example,

```
. local alpha = 0.05
. regress mpg weight, level(`=100*(1-`alpha')')
```

':*extended_fcn*' provides inline access to Stata's extended macro functions. ':*extended_fcn*' evaluates to the results of the extended macro function *extended_fcn*. For example,

```
. format `:format gear_ratio' headroom
```

will set the display format of headroom to that of gear_ratio, which was obtained via the extended macro function format.

'.*class_directive*' provides inline access to class-object values. See [P] **class** for details.

The macro expansion function '`macval(name)`' expands local macro `name` but not any macros contained within `name`. For instance, if `name` contained "example '`of`' macval" then '`name`' would expand to "example macval" (assuming that '`of`' is not defined), whereas '`macval(name)`' would expand to "example '`of`' name". The '`of`' would be left just as it is.

The tempvar, tempname, and tempfile commands

The `tempvar`, `tempname`, and `tempfile` commands generate names that may be used for temporary variables, temporary scalars and matrices, and temporary files. A temporary something exists while the program or do-file is running, but, once it concludes, automatically ceases to exist.

Temporary variables

You are writing a program, and, in the middle of it, you need to calculate a new variable equal to $var1^2 + var2^2$ for use in the calculation. You might be tempted to write

```
( code omitted )
gen sumsq = var1^2 + var2^2
( code continues )
( code uses sumsq  in subsequent calculations )
drop sumsq
```

This would be a poor idea. First, users of your program might already have a variable called `sumsq`, and if they did, your program will break at the `generate` statement with the error "sumsq already defined". Second, your program in the subsequent code might call some other program, and perhaps that program (poorly) also attempts to create a variable `sumsq`. Third, even if nothing goes wrong, if users press *Break* after your code executes the `generate` but before the `drop`, you would confuse them by leaving behind the `sumsq` variable.

The way around these problems is to use temporary variables. Your code should read as

```
( code omitted )
tempvar sumsq
gen 'sumsq' = var1^2 + var2^2
( code continues )
( code uses 'sumsq'  in subsequent calculations )
( you do not bother to drop 'sumsq' )
```

The `tempvar sumsq` command created a local macro called `sumsq` and stored in it a name that is different from any name currently in the data. Subsequently, you then use '`sumsq`' with single quotes around it rather than `sumsq` in your calculation, so that rather than naming your temporary variable `sumsq`, you are naming it whatever Stata wants you to name it. With that small change, your program works just as before.

Another advantage of temporary variables is that you do not have to drop them—Stata will do that for you when your program terminates, regardless of the reason for your program terminating. So, if users press *Break* after the `generate`, your program is stopped, the temporary variables are dropped, and things really are just as if the user had never run your program.

❑ Technical Note

So, what do these temporary variable names assigned by Stata look like? It should not matter to you; however they look, they are guaranteed to be unique (`tempvar` will not hand out the same name to more than one concurrently executing program). Nevertheless, to satisfy your curiosity,

```
. tempvar var1 var2
. display "'var1' 'var2'"
__000009 __00000A
```

Although we reveal the style of the names created by `tempvar`, you should not depend on this style. All that is important is that

1. The names are unique; they differ from one call to the next.

2. You should not prefix or suffix them with additional characters.

3. Stata keeps track of any names created by `tempvar`, and, when the program or do-file ends, searches the data for those names. Any variables found with those names are automatically dropped. This happens regardless of whether your program ends with an error.

❑

Temporary scalars and matrices

`tempname` is the equivalent of `tempvar` for obtaining names for scalars and matrices. This use is explained, with examples, in [P] **scalar**.

❑ Technical Note

The temporary names created by `tempname` look just like those created by `tempvar`. The same cautions and features apply to `tempname` as `tempvar`:

1. The names are unique; they differ from one call to the next.

2. You should not prefix or suffix them with additional characters.

3. Stata keeps track of any names created by `tempname`, and, when the program or do-file ends, searches for scalars or matrices with those names. Any scalars or matrices so found are automatically dropped; see [P] **scalar**. This happens regardless of whether your program ends with an error.

❑

Temporary files

`tempfile` is the equivalent of `tempvar` for obtaining names for disk files. Before getting into that, let us discuss how you should not use `tempfile`. Sometimes, in the midst of your program, you will find it necessary to destroy the user's data to obtain your desired result. You do not want to change the data, but it cannot be helped, and therefore you would like to arrange things so that the user's original data are restored at the conclusion of your program.

In such a case, you might be tempted to save the user's data in a (temporary) file, do your damage, and then restore the data. You can do this, but it is complicated, because you then have to worry about the user pressing *Break* after you have stored the data and done the damage but have not yet restored the data. Working with `capture` (see [P] **capture**), you can program all of this, but you do not have to. Stata's `preserve` command (see [P] **preserve**) will handle saving and restoring the user's data, regardless of how your program ends.

Still, there may be times when you need temporary files. For example,

```
( code omitted )
preserve                            // preserve user's data
keep var1 var2 xvar
save master, replace
drop var2
save part1, replace
use master, clear
drop var1
rename var2 var1
append using part1
erase master.dta
erase part1.dta
( code continues )
```

This is poor code, even though it does use `preserve` so that, regardless of how this code concludes, the user's original data will be restored. It is poor because datasets called `master.dta` and `part1.dta` might already exist, and, if they do, this program will replace the user's (presumably valuable) data. It is also poor because, if the user presses *Break* before both (temporary) datasets are erased, they will be left behind to consume (presumably valuable) disk space.

Here is how the code should read:

```
( code omitted )
preserve                            // preserve user's data
keep var1 var2 xvar
tempfile master part1               // declare temporary files
save "'master'"
drop var2
save "'part1'"
use "'master'", clear
drop var1
rename var2 var1
append using "'part1'"
( code continues, temporary files are not erased )
```

In this draft, Stata was asked to provide the names of temporary files in local macros named `master` and `part1`. We then put single quotes around `master` and `part1` wherever we referred to them so that, rather than using the names `master` and `part1`, we used the names Stata handed us. At the end of our program, we no longer bother to erase the temporary files. Since Stata gave us the temporary filenames, it knows they are temporary, and will erase them for us if our program completes, has an error, or the user presses *Break*.

❑ Technical Note

So what do the temporary filenames look like? Again, it should not matter to you, but for the curious,

```
. tempfile file1 file2
. display "'file1' 'file2'"
/tmp/St13310.0001 /tmp/St13310.0002
```

We were using the Unix version of Stata; had we been using the Windows version, the last line might read as

```
. display "'file1' 'file2'"
C:\WIN\TEMP\__000003.tmp C:\WIN\TEMP\__000004.tmp
```

Under Windows, Stata uses the environment variable `TEMP` to determine where temporary files are to be located. This variable is typically set in your `autoexec.bat` file. Ours is set to `C:\WIN\TEMP`. If the variable is not defined, Stata places temporary files in your current directory.

Under Unix, Stata uses the environment variable TMPDIR to determine where temporary files are to be located. If the variable is not defined, Stata locates temporary files in /tmp.

Although we reveal the style of the names created by tempfile, just as with tempvar, you should not depend on it. tempfile produces names the operating system finds pleasing, and all that is important is that

1. The names are unique; they differ from one call to the next.

2. You should assume that they are so long that you cannot prefix or suffix them with additional characters and make use of them.

3. Stata keeps track of any names created by tempfile, and, when your program or do-file ends, looks for files with those names. Any files found are automatically erased. This happens regardless of whether your program ends with an error.

❑

Manipulation of macros

macro dir and macro list list the names and contents of all defined macros; both do the same thing:

```
. macro list
_file2:         /tmp/St27844.0002
_file1:         /tmp/St27844.0001
_var2:          __00000A
_var1:          __000009
_str3:          a x b x sand x d
S_FNDATE:        7 Jul 2002 13:51
S_FN:           auto.dta
_dl:            Employee Data
_lbl:           Employee name
_vl:            sexlbl
_fmt:           tofname:        str18
F1:             help
F2:             #review;
F3:             describe;
F7:             save
F8:             use
S_ADO:          UPDATES;BASE;SITE;.;PERSONAL;PLUS;OLDPLACE
S_FLAVOR:       Intercooled
S_OS:           Unix
S_MACH:         PC
S_level:        95
```

macro drop eliminates macros from memory, although it is rarely used since most macros are local and automatically disappear when the program ends. Macros can also be eliminated by defining their contents to be nothing using global or local, but macro drop is more convenient.

Typing macro drop base* drops all global macros whose names begin with base.

Typing macro drop _all eliminates all macros except system macros—macros that begin with "S_".

Typing macro drop S_* does not drop all system macros that begin with S_. It leaves certain macros in place that should not be casually deleted.

▷ Example

```
. macro drop _var* _lbl tofname _fmt
. macro list
_file2:         /tmp/St27844.0002
_file1:         /tmp/St27844.0001
_str3:          a x b x sand x d
S_FNDATE:        7 Jul 2002 13:51
S_FN:           auto.dta
_dl:            Employee Data
_vl:            sexlbl
F1:             help
F2:             #review;
F3:             describe;
F7:             save
F8:             use
S_ADO:          UPDATES;BASE;SITE;.;PERSONAL;PLUS;OLDPLACE
S_FLAVOR:       Intercooled
S_OS:           Unix
S_MACH:         PC
S_level:        95
. macro drop _all
. macro list
S_FNDATE:        7 Jul 2002 13:51
S_FN:           auto.dta
S_ADO:          UPDATES;BASE;SITE;.;PERSONAL;PLUS;OLDPLACE
S_FLAVOR:       Intercooled
S_OS:           Unix
S_MACH:         PC
S_level:        95
. macro drop S_*
. macro list
S_FNDATE:        7 Jul 2002 13:51
S_FN:           auto.dta
S_ADO:          UPDATES;BASE;SITE;.;PERSONAL;PLUS;OLDPLACE
S_FLAVOR:       Intercooled
S_OS:           Unix
S_MACH:         PC
S_level:        95
```

◁

❑ Technical Note

Stata usually requires that you explicitly drop something before redefining it. For instance, before redefining a value label with the `label define` command or redefining a program with the `program define` command, you must type `label drop` or `program drop`. This way, you are protected from accidentally replacing something that might require considerable effort to reproduce.

Macros, however, may be redefined freely. It is *not* necessary to `drop` a macro before redefining it. Macros typically consist of short strings that could be easily reproduced if necessary. The inconvenience of the protection is not justified by the small benefit.

❑

Macros as arguments

Sometimes programs have in a macro a list of things—numbers, variable names, etc.—that you wish to access one at a time. For instance, after parsing (see [U] **21.4 Program arguments**), you might have in the local macro 'varlist' a list of variable names. The tokenize command (see [P] **tokenize**) will take any macro containing a list and assign the elements to local macros named '1', '2', and so on. That is, if 'varlist' contained "mpg weight displ", then coding

```
tokenize 'varlist'
```

will make '1' contain "mpg", '2' contain "weight", '3' contain "displ", and '4' contain "" (nothing). The empty fourth macro marks the end of the list.

macro shift can be used to work through these elements one at a time in constructs like

```
while "'1'" != "" {
        do something based on '1'
        macro shift
}
```

macro shift discards '1', shifts '2' to '1', '3' to '2', and so on. For instance, in our example, after the first macro shift, '1' will contain "weight", '2' will contain "displ", and '3' will contain "" (nothing).

Better to avoid macro shift, and instead code

```
local i = 1
while "''i''" != "" {
        do something based on ''i''
        local i = 'i' + 1
}
```

The second has the advantage that it is faster. In addition, what is in '1', '2', ... remains unchanged so that one can pass through the list multiple times without resetting it (coding "tokenize 'varlist'" again).

It is even better to avoid tokenize and the numbered macros altogether, and instead loop over the variables in 'varlist' directly:

```
foreach var of local varlist {
        do something based on 'var'
}
```

This is easier to understand and executes even more quickly; see [P] **foreach**.

macro shift # performs multiple macro shifts, or, if # is 0, none at all. That is, macro shift 2 is equivalent to two macro shift commands. macro shift 0 does nothing.

Also see [P] **macro lists** for other list-processing commands.

Also See

Complementary:	[P] **char**, [P] **display**, [P] **gettoken**, [P] **macro lists**, [P] **numlist**, [P] **return**, [P] **syntax**, [P] **tokenize**
Related:	[P] **matrix define**, [P] **preserve**, [P] **scalar**
Background:	[U] **15.8 Characteristics**, [U] **21 Programming Stata**, [U] **21.3 Macros**, [P] **creturn**

Title

macro lists — Manipulate lists

Syntax

{<u>lo</u>cal | <u>gl</u>obal} *macname* :   list uniq *macname*

{<u>lo</u>cal | <u>gl</u>obal} *macname* :   list dups *macname*

{<u>lo</u>cal | <u>gl</u>obal} *macname* :   list sort *macname*

{<u>lo</u>cal | <u>gl</u>obal} *macname* :   list <u>reto</u>kenize *macname*

{<u>lo</u>cal | <u>gl</u>obal} *macname* :   list clean *macname*

{<u>lo</u>cal | <u>gl</u>obal} *macname* :   list *macname* | *macname*

{<u>lo</u>cal | <u>gl</u>obal} *macname* :   list *macname* & *macname*

{<u>lo</u>cal | <u>gl</u>obal} *macname* :   list *macname* - *macname*

{<u>lo</u>cal | <u>gl</u>obal} *macname* :   list *macname* == *macname*

{<u>lo</u>cal | <u>gl</u>obal} *macname* :   list *macname* === *macname*

{<u>lo</u>cal | <u>gl</u>obal} *macname* :   list *macname* in *macname*

{<u>lo</u>cal | <u>gl</u>obal} *macname* :   list sizeof *macname*

{<u>lo</u>cal | <u>gl</u>obal} *macname* :   list posof "*element*" in *macname*

Note: In the above where *macname* appears, it is the name of macros and *not* their contents that you are to type. For example, you are to type

```
local result : list list1 | list2
```

and not

```
local result : list "'list1'" | "'list2'"
```

*macname*s that appear to the right of the colon are assumed to be the names of local macros. You may type local(*macname*) to emphasize that fact. Type global(*macname*) if you wish to refer to a global macro.

Description

The extended macro function list manipulates lists.

uniq A returns A with duplicate elements removed. The resulting list has the same ordering of its elements as A; duplicate elements are removed from their rightmost position. If $A =$ "$a\ b\ a\ c\ a$", **uniq** returns "$a\ b\ c$".

dups A returns the duplicate elements of A. If $A =$ "$a\ b\ a\ c\ a$", **uniq** returns "$a\ a$".

sort A returns A with its elements placed in alphabetical (ascending ASCII) order.

retokenize A returns A with single spaces between elements. Logically speaking, it makes no difference how many spaces a list has between elements, and thus **retokenize** leaves the list logically unchanged.

clean A returns A retokenized and with each element adorned minimally. An element is said to be unadorned if it is not enclosed in quotes (e.g., a). Alternatively, an element may be adorned in simple or compound quotes (e.g., $"a"$ or $‘"a"’$). Logically speaking, it makes no difference how elements are adorned, assuming they are adorned adequately. The list

$$‘"a’"\ ‘"b\ c"’\ ‘"b\ "c"\ d"’$$

is equal to

$$a\ "b\ c"\ ‘"b\ "c"\ d’"$$

clean, in addition to performing the actions of **retokenize**, adorns each element minimally: not at all if the element contains no spaces or quotes, in simple quotes (" and ") if it contains spaces but not quotes, and in compound quotes (‘" and "’) otherwise.

$A \mid B$ returns the union of A and B, the result being equal to A with elements of B not found in A added to the tail. For instance, if $A =$ "$a\ b\ c$" and $B =$ "$b\ d\ e$", $A \mid B$ is "$a\ b\ c\ d\ e$". If you instead want list concatenation, you code,

$$\text{local } newlist\ ‘"‘A’\ ‘B’"’$$

In the example above, this would return "$a\ b\ c\ b\ d\ e$".

$A\ \&\ B$ returns the intersection of A and B. If $A =$ "$a\ b\ c\ d$" and $B =$ "$b\ c\ f\ g$", then $A\ \&\ B =$ "$b\ c$".

$A - B$ returns a list containing elements of A with the elements of B removed, with the resulting elements in the same order as A. For instance, if $A =$ "$a\ b\ c\ d$" and $B =$ "$b\ e$", the result is "$a\ c\ d$".

$A == B$ returns 0 or 1; it returns 1 if A is equal to B, that is, if A has the same elements as B and in the same order. Otherwise, 0 is returned.

$A === B$ returns 0 or 1; it returns 1 if A is equivalent to B, that is, if A has the same elements as B regardless of the order in which the elements appear. Otherwise, 0 is returned.

A **in** B returns 0 or 1; it returns 1 if all elements of A are found in B. If A is empty, **in** returns 1.

sizeof A returns the number of elements of A. If $A =$ "$a\ b\ c$", **sizeof** A is 3. (Note that **sizeof** returns the same result as the extended macro function **word count**.)

posof "*element*" **in** A returns the location of *macname* in A or returns 0 if not found. For instance, if A contains "$a\ b\ c\ d$", then **posof** "b" **in** A returns 2. (**word # of** may be used to extract positional elements from lists, as can **tokenize** and **gettoken**.)

Note that it is the element itself and not a macroname that you type as the first argument. In a program where macro **tofind** contained an element to be found in list (macro) **variables**, you might code

```
local i : list posof ‘"‘tofind’"’ in variables
```

Note that *element* must be enclosed in quotes, and may be either simple or compound.

Remarks

A *list* is a space-separated set of elements listed one after the other. The individual elements may be enclosed in quotes, and elements containing spaces obviously must be enclosed in quotes. The following are examples of lists:

```
this that what
"first element" second "third element" 4
this that what this that
```

In addition, a *list* could be empty.

Do not confuse *varlist* with *list*. Varlists are a special notation, such as `"id m* pop*"`, which is a shorthand way of specifying a list of variables. Once expanded, however, a *varlist* is a *list*.

Treatment of adornment

An element of a list is said to be adorned if it is enclosed in quotes. Adornment, however, plays no role in the substantive interpretation of lists. The list

a $"b"$ c

is identical to the list

a b c

Treatment of duplicate elements in lists

With the exception of `uniq` and `dups`, all list functions treat duplicates as being distinct. For instance, consider the list A,

$$a\ b\ c\ b$$

Note that b appears twice in this list. You want to think of the list as containing a, the first occurrence of b, c, and the second occurrence of b:

$$a\ b_1\ c\ b_2$$

Do the same thing with the duplicate elements of all lists, carry out the operation on the now unique elements, and then erase the subscripts from the result.

If you were to ask whether $B =$ "$b\ b$" is `in` A, the answer would be yes, because A contains two occurrences of b. If B contained "$b\ b\ b$", however, the answer would be no because A does not contain three occurrences of b.

Similarly, if $B =$ "$b\ b$", then $A \mid B =$ "$a\ b\ c\ b$", but if $B =$ "$b\ b\ b$", then $A \mid B =$ "$a\ b\ c\ b\ b$".

Also See

Background: [P] **macro**

Title

mark — Mark observations for inclusion

Syntax

marksample *lmacname* [, <u>nova</u>rlist <u>s</u>trok <u>zero</u>weight noby]

mark *newmarkvar* [*weight*] [if *exp*] [in *range*] [, <u>zero</u>weight noby]

markout *markvar* [*varlist*] [, <u>s</u>trok]

markin [if *exp*] [in *range*] [, <u>n</u>ame(*lclname*) noby]

aweights, fweights, iweights, and pweights are allowed; see [U] **14.1.6 weight**.
varlist may contain time-series operators; see [U] **14.4.3 Time-series varlists**.

Description

marksample, mark, and markout are for use in Stata programs. They create a 0/1 variable recording which observations are to be used in subsequent code. The idea is to determine the relevant sample early in the code:

```
program ...
        (parse the arguments)
        (determine which observations are to be used)
        rest of code ... if  to be used
end
```

marksample, mark, and markout assist in this.

```
program ...
        (parse the arguments)
        (use mark* to create temporary variable 'touse' containing 0 or 1)
        rest of code ... if 'touse'
end
```

marksample is for use in programs where the arguments are parsed using the syntax command; see [P] **syntax**. marksample creates a temporary byte variable, stores the name of the temporary variable in *lmacname*, and fills in the temporary variable with 0s and 1s according to whether the observation should be used. This determination is made by accessing information stored by syntax concerning the *varlist*, if *exp*, etc. allowed by the program. Its typical use is

```
program ...
        syntax ...
        marksample touse
        rest of code ... if 'touse'
end
```

mark starts with an already created temporary variable name. It fills in *newmarkvar* with 0s and 1s according to whether the observation should be used according to the *weight*, if *exp*, and in *range* specified. markout modifies the variable created by mark by resetting it to contain 0 in observations that have missing values recorded for any of the variables in *varlist*. These commands are typically used as

```
program ...
        (parse the arguments)
        tempvar touse
        mark 'touse' ...
        markout 'touse' ...
        rest of code ... if 'touse'
end
```

`marksample` is better than `mark` because there is less chance of your forgetting to include some part of the sample restriction. `markout` can be used after `mark` or `marksample` when there are variables other than the varlist, and when observations that contain missing values of those variables are also to be excluded. For instance, the following code is common:

```
program ...
        syntax ... [, Denom(varname) ... ]
        marksample touse
        markout 'touse' 'denom'
        rest of code ... if 'touse'
end
```

Regardless of whether you use `mark` or `marksample`, followed or not by `markout`, the following rules apply:

1. The marker variable is set to 0 in observations for which *weight* is 0 (but see option `zeroweight`).

2. The appropriate error message is issued, and all stops if *weight* is invalid (such as being less than 0 in some observation, or being a noninteger in the case of frequency weights, etc.).

3. The marker variable is set to 0 in observations for which the `if` *exp* is not satisfied.

4. The marker variable is set to 0 in observations outside of the `in` *range*.

5. The marker variable is set to 0 in observations for which any of the numeric variables in *varlist* contain a numeric missing value.

6. The marker variable is set to 0 in *all* observations if any of the variables in *varlist* are strings; see option `strok` below for an exception.

7. The marker variable is set to 1 in the remaining observations.

Employing the name `touse` is a convention, not a rule, but it is recommended for consistency between programs.

❑ Technical Note

`markin` is for use after `marksample`, `mark`, and `markout`, and should be used only with extreme caution. Its use is never necessary, but, in the case where it is known that the specified `if` *exp* will select a small subset of the observations (small being, for example, 6 out of 750,000), `markin`'s use can result in code that executes more quickly. `markin` creates local macro '*lclname*' (or '`in`' if `name()` is not specified) containing the smallest `in` *range* that contains the `if` *exp*.

❑

(Continued on next page)

Options

novarlist is for use with marksample. It specifies that missing values among variables in *varlist* are not to cause the marker variable to be set to 0. Specify novarlist if you previously specified

        syntax newvarlist ...

or

        syntax newvarname ...

In addition, specify novarlist in instances where missing values are not to cause observations to be excluded (perhaps you are analyzing the pattern of missing values).

strok is used with marksample or markout. Specify this option if string variables in *varlist* are to be allowed. strok changes Rule 6 above to read

"The marker variable is set to 0 in observations for which any of the string variables in *varlist* contain "".

zeroweight is for use with marksample or mark. It deletes Rule 1 above, meaning that observations will not be excluded because the weight is zero.

noby is used rarely and only in byable(recall) programs. It specifies that, in identifying the sample, the restriction to the by-group is to be ignored. mark and marksample are to create the marker variable as they would had the user not specified the by... : prefix. If the user did not specify the by prefix, specifying noby has no effect. noby provides a way for byable(recall) programs to identify the overall sample. For instance, if the program needed to calculate the percentage of observations in the by-group, the program would need to know both the sample to be used on this call and the overall sample. The program might be coded as

```
program ..., byable(recall)
        ...
        marksample touse
        marksample alluse, noby
        ...
        quietly count if 'touse'
        local curN = r(N)
        quietly count if 'alluse'
        local totN = r(N)
        local frac = 'curN'/'totN'
        ...
end
```

See [P] **byable**.

name(*lclname*) (markin only) specifies the name of the macro to be created. If name() is not specified, the name in is used.

Remarks

By far the most common programming error—made by us at StataCorp and others—is to use different samples in different parts of a Stata program. We strongly recommend that programmers identify the sample at the outset. This is easy with marksample (or alternatively, mark and markout). Consider a Stata program that begins

```
program myprog
        version 8.0
        syntax varlist [if] [in]
        ...
end
```

Pretend that this program makes a statistical calculation based on the observations specified in *varlist* that do not contain missing values (such as a linear regression). The program must identify the observations that it will use. Moreover, since the user can specify if *exp* or in *range*, these restrictions must also be taken into account. `marksample` makes this easy:

```
                version 8.0
                syntax varlist [if] [in]
                marksample touse
                . . .
        end
```

To produce the same result, we could create the temporary variable `touse`, and then use `mark` and `markout` as follows:

```
        program myprog
                version 8.0
                syntax varlist [if] [in]
                tempvar touse
                mark 'touse' 'if' 'in'
                markout 'touse' 'varlist'
                . . .
        end
```

The result will be the same.

The `mark` command creates temporary variable `'touse'` (temporary because of the preceding `tempvar`; see [P] **macro**) based on the if *exp* and in *range*. If there is no if *exp* or in *range*, `'touse'` will contain 1 for every observation in the data. If `if price>1000` was specified by the user, only observations for which `price` is greater than 1,000 will have `touse` set to 1; the remaining observations will have `touse` set to zero.

The `markout` command updates the `'touse'` marker created by `mark`. For observations where `'touse'` is 1—observations that might potentially be used—the variables in *varlist* are checked for missing values. If such an observation has any of the variables equal to missing, the observation's `'touse'` value is reset to 0.

Thus, observations to be used all have `'touse'` set to 1. Including if `'touse'` at the end of statistical or data-management commands will restrict the command to operate on the appropriate sample.

▷ Example

Let's write a program to do the same thing as `summarize`, except that our program will also engage in casewise deletion—if an observation has a missing value in any of the variables, it is to be excluded from all the calculations.

```
        program cwsumm
                version 8.0
                syntax [varlist(ts)] [if] [in] [aweight fweight] [, Detail noFormat]
                marksample touse
                summarize 'varlist' ['weight''exp'] if 'touse', 'detail' 'format'
        end
```

◁

❏ Technical Note

Let us now turn to `markin`. `markin` is for use in those rare instances where you, as a programmer, know that only a small number of the observations are going to be selected, that those small number of observations probably occur close together in terms of observation number, and that speed is important. All of this is to say, the use of `markin` is never required and a certain caution is required in its use, so in most circumstances it is best to avoid it. On the other hand, when the requirements are met, `markin` can speed programs considerably.

The safe way to use `markin` is to first write the program without it, and then splice in its use. Form a `touse` variable in the usual way by using `marksample`, `mark`, and `markout`. Once you have identified the `touse` sample, use `markin` to construct an in *range* from it. Then add `'in'` on every command in which `if 'touse'` appears, without removing the `if 'touse'`.

That is, pretend that our original code reads like the following:

```
program ...
        syntax ...
        marksample touse
        mark 'touse' ...               // touse now fully set
        gen ... if 'touse'
        replace ... if 'touse'
        summarize ... if 'touse'
        replace ... if 'touse'
        ...
    end
```

We now change our code to read as follows:

```
program ...
        syntax ...
        marksample touse
        mark 'touse' ...               // touse now fully set
        markin if 'touse'              // <- new
                                       // we add 'in':
        gen ... if 'touse' 'in'
        replace ... if 'touse' 'in'
        summarize ... if 'touse' 'in'
        replace ... if 'touse' 'in'
        ...
    end
```

This new version will, under certain conditions, run faster. Why? Consider the case where the program is called when there are 750,000 observations in memory. Let's imagine that the 750,000 observations are a panel dataset containing 20 observations each on 37,500 individuals. Let's further imagine that the dataset is sorted by `subjectid`, the individual identifier, and let's imagine that the user calls our program and includes the restriction `if subject_id==4225`.

Thus, our program must select 20 observations from the 750,000. That's fine, but think about the work that `generate`, `replace`, `summarize`, and `replace` must each go to in our original program. Each must thumb through 750,000 observations asking themselves whether `'touse'` is true, and 759,980 times, the answer is no. That will happen four times.

`markin` in this instance will save Stata work. It creates a macro named `'in'` of the form "in j_1/j_2", where j_1 to j_2 is the narrowest range that contains all the `'touse'` $\neq 0$ values. Under the assumptions we made, that range will be exactly 20 long; perhaps it will be `in 84500/84520`. Now the `generate`, `replace`, `summarize`, and `replace` commands will each restrict themselves to those 20 observations. This will save them a lot of work and the user a lot of time.

Since there is a speed advantage, why not always use `markin` in our programs? Assume that between the `summarize` and the `replace` there was a `sort` command in our program. The in *range* constructed by `markin` would be inappropriate for our last `replace`; we would break our program. If we use `markin`, we must make sure that the in *range* constructed continues to be valid throughout our program (our construct a new one when it changes). So, that is the first answer: you cannot add `markin` without thinking. The second answer is that `markin` takes time to execute, albeit just a little, and in most circumstances that time is wasted because the in *range* will not improve performance since the data are not ordered as required. Taking the two reasons together, it is simply not worth the effort to add `markin` to most programs.

In those cases where it is worth the effort, you may wonder why, when we added 'in' to the subsequent commands, we did not simultaneously remove the `if` 'touse'. The answer is that 'in' is not a guaranteed substitute for `if`. In our example, under the assumptions made, the 'in' happens to substitute perfectly, but that was just an assumption, and we have no guarantees that the user happens to have his or her data sorted in the desired way. If, in our program, we sorted the data, and then we used `markin` to produce the range, we could omit the `if` 'touse', but even in that case, we do not recommend it. We always recommend programming defensively, and the cost of evaluating the `if` 'touse', when 'in' really does restrict the sample to the relevant observations, is barely measurable.

❑

Also See

Complementary:	[P] **byable**, [P] **syntax**
Background:	[U] **21 Programming Stata**

Title

> **matrix** — Introduction to matrix commands

Description

An introduction to matrices in Stata is found in [U] **17 Matrix expressions**. This entry provides an overview of the `matrix` commands, and provides additional background information on matrices in Stata.

Remarks

An overview of the `matrix` commands is presented below. This is followed by information on matrices not covered elsewhere.

Overview of matrix commands

Documentation on matrices in Stata are grouped below into three categories — Basics, Programming, and Specialized. We recommend that you begin with [U] **17 Matrix expressions** and then read [P] **matrix define**. After that, feel free to skip around.

Basics

[U] **17 Matrix expressions**	Introduction to matrices in Stata
[P] **matrix define**	Matrix definition, operators, and functions
[P] **matrix utility**	List, rename, and drop matrices

Programming

[P] **matrix accum**	Form cross-product matrices
[R] **ml**	Maximum likelihood estimation
[P] **ereturn**	Post estimation results
[P] **matrix rowname**	Name rows and columns
[P] **matrix score**	Score data from coefficient vectors

Specialized

[P] **matrix constraint**	Constrained estimation
[P] **matrix mkmat**	Convert variables to matrix and vice versa
[P] **matrix svd**	Singular value decomposition
[P] **matrix symeigen**	Eigenvalues and eigenvectors of symmetric matrices
[P] **matrix eigenvalues**	Eigenvalues of nonsymmetric matrices
[P] **matrix get**	Access system matrices

Creating and replacing matrices

In general, matrices do not have to be preallocated or dimensioned prior to creation, but the exception is when you want to create an $r \times c$ matrix and then fill in each element one-by-one; see the description of the J() function in [P] **matrix define**. Matrices are typically created by `matrix define` or `matrix accum`; see [P] **matrix accum**.

Stata takes a high-handed approach to redefining matrices. You know that, when dealing with data, you must distinguish between creating a new variable or replacing the contents of an existing variable—Stata has two commands for this: `generate` and `replace`. For matrices, there is no such distinction. If you define a new matrix, it is created. If you give the same command and the matrix already exists, the currently existing matrix is destroyed and then the new one is defined. This treatment is the same as that given to macros and scalars.

❑ Technical Note

Beginning with Stata 8, matrices are allowed to contain missing values. If `version` is set less than 8 (see [P] **version**), in some cases, missing values cannot be assigned to matrices; this was done to keep old code working.

❑

Name space

The term "name space" refers to how names are interpreted. For instance, the variables in your dataset occupy one name space—other things, such as value labels, macros, and scalars, can have the same name and not cause confusion.

Macros also have their own name space; macros can have the same names as other things, and Stata can still tell by context when you are referring to a macro because of the punctuation. When you type `gen newvar=myname`, myname must refer to a variable. When you type `gen newvar='myname'`—note the single quotes around `myname`—myname must refer to a local macro. When you type `gen newvar=$myname`, myname must refer to a global macro.

Scalars and matrices share the same name space, which is to say, scalars and matrices may have the same names as variables in the dataset, etc., but they cannot have the same names as each other. Thus, when you define a matrix called, say, `myres`, if a scalar by that name already exists, it is destroyed, and the matrix replaces it. Correspondingly, if you define a scalar called `myres`, if a matrix by that name exists, it is destroyed, and the scalar replaces it.

Naming conventions in programs

If you are writing Stata programs or ado-files using matrices, you may have some matrices that you wish to leave behind for other programs to build upon, but you will certainly have other matrices that are nothing more than leftovers from calculations. Such matrices are called *temporary*. You should use Stata's `tempname` facility (see [P] **macro**) to name such matrices. These matrices will automatically be discarded when your program ends. For example, a piece of your program might read

```
tempname YXX XX
matrix accum 'YXX' = price weight mpg
matrix 'XX' = 'YXX'[2...,2...]
```

Note the single quotes around the names after they are obtained from `tempname`; see [U] **21.3 Macros**.

❑ Technical Note

Let us consider writing a regression program in Stata. (There is actually no need for such a program since Stata already has the `regress` command.) A well-written estimation command would allow the `level()` option for specifying the width of confidence intervals, and it would replay results when the command is typed without arguments. Here is a well-written version:

```
program myreg, eclass
        version 8.0
        if !replay() {
                syntax varlist(min=2 numeric) [if] [in] [, Level(integer 'c(level)')]

                marksample touse       // mark the sample

                tempname YXX XX Xy b hat V

                // compute cross products YXX = (Y'Y , Y'X \ X'Y , X'X)
                quietly matrix accum 'YXX' = 'varlist' if 'touse'
                local nobs = r(N)
                local df = 'nobs' - (rowsof('YXX') - 1)
                matrix 'XX' = 'YXX'[2...,2...]
                matrix 'Xy' = 'YXX'[1,2...]

                // compute the beta vector
                matrix 'b' = 'Xy' * syminv('XX')

                // compute the covariance matrix
                matrix 'hat' = 'b' * 'Xy''
                matrix 'V' = syminv('XX') * ('YXX'[1,1] - 'hat'[1,1])/'df'

                // post the beta vector and covariance matrix
                ereturn post 'b' 'V', dof('df') obs('nobs') depname('1') /*
                                */ esample('touse')

                // save estimation information
                tokenize "'varlist'"  // put varlist into numbered arguments

                ereturn local depvar "'1'"
                ereturn local cmd "myreg"
        }
        else {  // replay
                syntax [, Level(integer 'c(level)')]
        }

        if "'e(cmd)'"!="myreg" error 301

        if 'level' < 10 | 'level' > 99 {
                di as err "level() must be between 10 and 99 inclusive"
                exit 198
        }

        // print the regression table
        ereturn display, level('level')
end
```

The syntax of our new command is

$$\texttt{myreg} \; depvar \; indepvars \; \big[\,\texttt{if} \; exp\,\big] \; \big[\,\texttt{in} \; range\,\big] \; \big[\, , \texttt{level}(\#) \, \big]$$

myreg, typed without arguments, redisplays the output of the last myreg command. After estimation with myreg, the user may use correlate to display the covariance matrix of the estimators, predict to obtain predicted values or standard errors of the prediction, and test to test linear hypotheses about the estimated coefficients. The command is indistinguishable from any other Stata estimation command.

Despite the excellence of our work, we do have some criticisms:

1. myreg does not display the ANOVA table, R^2, etc.; it should and could be made to, although we would have to insert our own display statements before the ereturn display instruction.

2. The program makes copious use of matrices with different names, resulting in extra memory use while the estimation is being made; the code could be made more economical, if less readable, by reusing matrices.

3. `myreg` makes the least-squares calculation using the absolute cross-product matrix, an invitation to numerical problems if the data are not consistently scaled. Stata's own `regress` command is more careful, and we could be, too: `matrix accum` does have an option for forming the cross-product matrix in deviation form, but its use would complicate this program. This does not overly concern us, although we should make a note of it when we document `myreg`. Nowadays, users expect to be protected in linear regression, but have no such expectations for more complicated estimation schemes because avoiding the problem can be difficult to nearly impossible.

There is one nice feature of our program that did not occur to us when we wrote it. We use `syminv()` to form the inverse of the cross-product matrix, and `syminv()` can handle singular matrices. If there is a collinearity problem, `myreg` behaves just like `regress`: it drops the offending variables and notes that they are dropped when it displays the output (at the `ereturn display` step).

❏

❏ Technical Note

Our linear regression program is quite a bit longer than one might have written in an exclusively matrix programming language. After all, the coefficients can be obtained from $(\mathbf{X}'\mathbf{X})^{-1}\mathbf{X}'\mathbf{y}$, and in a dedicated matrix language, one would type nearly that, and obtaining the standard errors would require only a couple more matrix calculations. In fact, we did type nearly that to make the calculation; the extra lines in our program mostly have to do with syntax issues and linking to the rest of Stata. In writing your own programs, you might be tempted not to bother linking to the rest of Stata. Fight this temptation.

Linking to the rest of Stata pays off: in this case, we do not merely display the numerical results, we display them in a readable form, complete with variable names. We made a command that is indistinguishable from Stata's other estimation commands. If the user wants to test `_b[denver]=_b[la]`, the user types literally that; there is no need to remember the matrix equation and to count variables (such as constrain the third minus the fifteenth variable to sum to zero).

❏

Also See

Related:	[P] **ereturn**, [P] **matrix define**,
	[R] **ml**
Background:	[U] **17 Matrix expressions**,
	[U] **21 Programming Stata**

Title

> **matrix accum** — Form cross-product matrices

Syntax

<u>mat</u>rix <u>ac</u>cum **A** = *varlist* [*weight*] [if *exp*] [in *range*] [, <u>noc</u>onstant

   <u>d</u>eviations <u>m</u>eans(**m**)]

<u>mat</u>rix <u>gls</u>accum **A** = *varlist* [*weight*] [if *exp*] [in *range*] , <u>gr</u>oup(*groupvar*)

   <u>gl</u>smat(**W** | *stringvarname*) <u>r</u>ow(*rowvar*) [<u>noc</u>onstant]

<u>mat</u>rix <u>op</u>accum **A** = *varlist* [if *exp*] [in *range*] , <u>gr</u>oup(*groupvar*)

   <u>op</u>var(*opvar*) [<u>noc</u>onstant]

<u>mat</u>rix <u>vec</u>accum **a** = *varlist* [*weight*] [if *exp*] [in *range*] [, <u>noc</u>onstant]

aweights, fweights, iweights, and pweights are allowed; see [U] **14.1.6 weight**.

varlist may contain time-series operators; see [U] **14.4.3 Time-series varlists**.

Description

matrix accum accumulates cross-product matrices from the data to form $\mathbf{A} = \mathbf{X'X}$.

matrix glsaccum accumulates cross-product matrices from the data using a specified inner weight matrix to form $\mathbf{A} = \mathbf{X'BX}$, where $\mathbf{B}$ is a block diagonal matrix.

matrix opaccum accumulates cross-product matrices from the data using an inner weight matrix formed from the outer product of a variable in the data to form

$$\mathbf{A} = \mathbf{X}_1' \mathbf{e}_1 \mathbf{e}_1' \mathbf{X}_1 + \mathbf{X}_2' \mathbf{e}_2 \mathbf{e}_2' \mathbf{X}_2 + \cdots + \mathbf{X}_K' \mathbf{e}_K \mathbf{e}_K' \mathbf{X}_K$$

where $\mathbf{X}_i$ is a matrix of observations from the ith group of the *varlist* variables and $\mathbf{e}_i$ is a vector formed from the observations in the ith group of the *opvar* variable.

matrix vecaccum accumulates the first variable against remaining variables in *varlist* to form a row vector of accumulated inner products to form $\mathbf{a} = \mathbf{x}_1' \mathbf{X}$, where $\mathbf{X} = (\mathbf{x}_2, \mathbf{x}_3, \ldots)$.

(Continued on next page)

251

Options

noconstant suppresses the addition of a "constant" to the $\mathbf{X}$ matrix. If noconstant is not specified, it is as if a column of 1s is added to $\mathbf{X}$ before the accumulation begins. For instance, in the case of accum without noconstant, $\mathbf{X}'\mathbf{X}$ is really $(\mathbf{X}, \mathbf{1})'(\mathbf{X}, \mathbf{1})$, resulting in

$$\begin{pmatrix} \mathbf{X}'\mathbf{X} & \mathbf{X}'\mathbf{1} \\ \mathbf{1}'\mathbf{X} & \mathbf{1}'\mathbf{1} \end{pmatrix}$$

Thus, the last row and column contain the sums of the columns of $\mathbf{X}$, and the element in the last row and column contains the number of observations. If p variables are specified in the *varlist*, the resulting matrix is $(p+1) \times (p+1)$. Specifying noconstant suppresses the addition of this row and column (or just the column in the case of vecaccum).

deviations, allowed only with matrix accum, causes the accumulation to be performed in terms of deviations from the mean. If noconstant is not specified, the accumulation of $\mathbf{X}$ is done in terms of deviations, but the added row and column of sums are *not* in deviation format (in which case, they would be zeros). With noconstant specified, the resulting matrix, divided through by $N-1$ where N is the number of observations, is a covariance matrix.

means(m), allowed only with accum, creates matrix m: $1 \times (p+1)$ or $1 \times p$ (depending on whether noconstant is also specified) containing the means of $\mathbf{X}$.

group(*groupvar*) is required with glsaccum and opaccum and is not allowed otherwise. In the two cases where it is required, it specifies the name of a variable that identifies groups of observations. The data must be sorted by *groupvar*.

In glsaccum, *groupvar* identifies the observations to be individually weighted by glsmat().

In opaccum, *groupvar* identifies the observations to be weighted by the outer product of opvar().

glsmat(**W** | *stringvarname*), required with glsaccum and not allowed otherwise, specifies the name of the matrix or the name of a string variable in the dataset that contains the name of the matrix that is to be used to weight the observations in the group(). *stringvarname* must be str8 or less.

row(*rowvar*), required with glsaccum and not allowed otherwise, specifies the name of a numeric variable containing the row numbers that specify the row and column of the glsmat() matrix to use in the inner-product calculation.

opvar(*opvar*), required by opaccum, specifies the variable used to form the vector whose outer product forms the weighting matrix.

Remarks

Remarks are presented under the headings

> *accum*
> *glsaccum*
> *opaccum*
> *vecaccum*
> *Treatment of user-specified weights*

accum

`matrix accum` is a straightforward command that accumulates a single matrix that holds $\mathbf{X'X}$ and $\mathbf{X'y}$, which is typically used in $\mathbf{b} = (\mathbf{X'X})^{-1}\mathbf{X'y}$. Say we wish to run a regression of the variable `price` on `mpg` and `weight`. We can begin by accumulating the full cross-product matrix for all three variables:

```
. matrix accum A = price weight mpg
(obs=74)

. matrix list A

symmetric A[4,4]
               price       weight         mpg       _cons
 price     3.448e+09
weight     1.468e+09    7.188e+08
   mpg       9132716      4493720       36008
 _cons        456229       223440        1576          74
```

In our accumulation, `accum` automatically added a constant; we specified three variables and got back a 4×4 matrix. The constant term is always added last. In terms of our regression model, the matrix we just accumulated has $\mathbf{y} = \texttt{price}$ and $\mathbf{X} = (\texttt{weight}, \texttt{mpg}, \_\texttt{cons})$, and can be written as

$$\mathbf{A} = (\mathbf{y}, \mathbf{X})'(\mathbf{y}, \mathbf{X}) = \begin{pmatrix} \mathbf{y'y} & \mathbf{y'X} \\ \mathbf{X'y} & \mathbf{X'X} \end{pmatrix}$$

Thus, we can extract $\mathbf{X'X}$ from the submatrix of $\mathbf{A}$ beginning at the second row and column, and we can extract $\mathbf{X'y}$ from the first column of $\mathbf{A}$, omitting the first row:

```
. matrix XX = A[2...,2...]

. matrix list XX

symmetric XX[3,3]
              weight         mpg       _cons
weight     7.188e+08
   mpg       4493720       36008
 _cons        223440        1576          74

. matrix Xy = A[2...,1]

. matrix list Xy

Xy[3,1]
               price
weight     1.468e+09
   mpg       9132716
 _cons        456229
```

We can now calculate $\mathbf{b} = (\mathbf{X'X})^{-1}\mathbf{X'y}$:

```
. matrix b = syminv(XX)*Xy

. matrix list b

b[3,1]
               price
weight     1.7465592
   mpg    -49.512221
 _cons     1946.0687
```

The same result could have been obtained directly from $\mathbf{A}$:

```
. matrix b = syminv(A[2...,2...])*A[2...,1]
```

□ Technical Note

matrix accum, with the deviations and noconstant options, can also be used to obtain covariance matrices. The covariance between variables x_i and x_j is defined as

$$C_{ij} = \frac{\sum_{k=1}^{n}(x_{ik} - \overline{x}_i)(x_{jk} - \overline{x}_j)}{n - 1}$$

Without the deviations option, matrix accum calculates a matrix with elements

$$R_{ij} = \sum_{k=1}^{n} x_{ik}x_{jk}$$

and with the deviations option,

$$A_{ij} = \sum_{k=1}^{n}(x_{ik} - \overline{x}_i)(x_{jk} - \overline{x}_j)$$

Thus, the covariance matrix $\mathbf{C} = \mathbf{A}/(n - 1)$.

```
. matrix accum Cov = price weight mpg, deviations noconstant
(obs=74)
. matrix Cov = Cov/(r(N)-1)
. matrix list Cov
symmetric Cov[3,3]
              price       weight          mpg
price       8699526
weight    1234674.8    604029.84
   mpg   -7996.2829   -3629.4261    33.472047
```

In addition to calculating the cross-product matrix, matrix accum records the number of observations in r(N), a feature we use in calculating the normalizing factor. With the corr() matrix function defined in [P] **matrix define**, we can convert the covariance matrix into a correlation matrix:

```
. matrix P = corr(Cov)
. matrix list P
symmetric P[3,3]
              price       weight          mpg
price             1
weight    .53861146            1
   mpg   -.46859669   -.80717486            1
```
◁

glsaccum

matrix glsaccum is a generalization of matrix accum useful in producing GLS-style weighted accumulations. Whereas matrix accum produces matrices of the form $\mathbf{X}'\mathbf{X}$, glsaccum produces matrices of the form $\mathbf{X}'\mathbf{B}\mathbf{X}$, where

$$B = \begin{pmatrix} \mathbf{W}_1 & 0 & \cdots & 0 \\ 0 & \mathbf{W}_2 & \cdots & 0 \\ \vdots & \vdots & \ddots & \vdots \\ 0 & 0 & \cdots & \mathbf{W}_K \end{pmatrix}$$

The matrices $\mathbf{W}_k$, $k = 1, \ldots, K$ are called the weighting matrices for observation group k. In the above, each of the $\mathbf{W}_k$ matrices is square, but there is no assumption that they are all the same dimension. Note that by writing

$$\mathbf{X} = \begin{pmatrix} \mathbf{X}_1 \\ \mathbf{X}_2 \\ \vdots \\ \mathbf{X}_K \end{pmatrix}$$

the accumulation made by `glsaccum` can be written as

$$\mathbf{X}'\mathbf{B}\mathbf{X} = \mathbf{X}_1'\mathbf{W}_1\mathbf{X}_1 + \mathbf{X}_2'\mathbf{W}_2\mathbf{X}_2 + \cdots + \mathbf{X}_K'\mathbf{W}_K\mathbf{X}_K$$

`glsaccum` requires you to specify three options: `group(`*groupvar*`)`, `glsmat(`*matname*`)` or `glsmat(`*matvar*`)`, and `row(`*rowvar*`)`. Observations sharing the same value of *groupvar* are said to be in the same observation group—this specifies the group k in which they are to be accumulated. How $\mathbf{W}_k$ is assembled is the subject of the other two options.

Think of there being a super weighting matrix for the group, which we will call $\mathbf{V}_k$. $\mathbf{V}_k$ is specified by `glsmat()`—the same super matrix can be used for all observations by specifying a *matname* as the argument to `glsmat`, or, if a variable name is specified, different super matrices can be specified—the contents of the variable will be used to obtain the particular name of the super matrix. (More correctly, the contents of the variable for the first observation in the group will be used: super matrices can vary across groups, but must be the same within group.)

Weighting matrix $\mathbf{W}_k$ is made from the super matrix $\mathbf{V}_k$ by selecting the rows and columns specified in `row(`*rowvar*`)`. In the simple case, $\mathbf{W}_k = \mathbf{V}_k$. This happens when there are m observations in the group and the first observation in the group has *rowvar* $= 1$, the second *rowvar* $= 2$, and so on. To fix ideas, let $m = 3$ and write

$$\mathbf{V}_1 = \begin{pmatrix} v_{11} & v_{12} & v_{13} \\ v_{21} & v_{22} & v_{23} \\ v_{31} & v_{32} & v_{33} \end{pmatrix}$$

$\mathbf{V}$ need not be symmetric. Let's pretend that the first four observations in our dataset contain

obs. no.	*groupvar*	*rowvar*
1	1	1
2	1	2
3	1	3
4	2	...

In these data, the first three observations are in the first group because they share an equal *groupvar*. It is not important that *groupvar* happens to equal 1; it is important that the values are equal. The *rowvars* are, in order, 1, 2, and 3, so $\mathbf{W}_1$ is formed by selecting the first row and column of $\mathbf{V}_1$, then the second row and column of $\mathbf{V}_1$, and finally the third row and column of $\mathbf{V}_1$; to wit,

$$\mathbf{W}_1 = \begin{pmatrix} v_{11} & v_{12} & v_{13} \\ v_{21} & v_{22} & v_{23} \\ v_{31} & v_{32} & v_{33} \end{pmatrix}$$

or $\mathbf{W}_1 = \mathbf{V}_1$. Now, consider the same data, but reordered:

obs. no.	*groupvar*	*rowvar*
1	1	2
2	1	1
3	1	3
4	2	. . .

$\mathbf{W}_1$ is now formed by selecting the second row and column, then the first row and column, and finally the third row and column of $\mathbf{V}_1$. These steps can be performed sequentially, reordering first the rows and then the columns; the result is

$$\mathbf{W}_1 = \begin{pmatrix} v_{22} & v_{21} & v_{23} \\ v_{12} & v_{11} & v_{13} \\ v_{32} & v_{31} & v_{33} \end{pmatrix}$$

This reorganization of the $\mathbf{W}_1$ matrix exactly undoes the reorganization of the $\mathbf{X}_1$ matrix, so $\mathbf{X}_1'\mathbf{W}_1\mathbf{X}_1$ remains unchanged. Given how $\mathbf{W}_k$ is assembled from $\mathbf{V}_k$, the order of the row numbers in the data does not matter.

glsaccum is willing to carry this concept even further. Consider the following data:

obs. no.	*groupvar*	*rowvar*
1	1	1
2	1	3
3	1	3
4	2	. . .

Note that now *rowvar* equals 1 followed by 3 twice, so the first row and column of $\mathbf{V}_1$ are selected, followed by the third row and column twice; the second column is never selected. The resulting weighting matrix is

$$\mathbf{W}_1 = \begin{pmatrix} v_{11} & v_{13} & v_{13} \\ v_{31} & v_{33} & v_{33} \\ v_{31} & v_{33} & v_{33} \end{pmatrix}$$

Such odd weighting would not occur in, say, time-series analysis, where the matrix might be weighting lags and leads. It could very well occur in an analysis of individuals in families, where 1 might indicate head of household, 2 a spouse, and 3 a child. In fact, such a case could be handled with a 3×3 super weighting matrix V, even if the family became quite large: the appropriate weighting matrix $\mathbf{W}_k$ would be assembled, on a group-by-group (family-by-family) basis, from the underlying super matrix.

opaccum

opaccum is a special case of glsaccum. Recall that glsaccum calculates results of the form

$$\mathbf{A} = \mathbf{X}_1'\mathbf{W}_1\mathbf{X}_1 + \mathbf{X}_2'\mathbf{W}_2\mathbf{X}_2 + \cdots + \mathbf{X}_K'\mathbf{W}_K\mathbf{X}_K$$

Often $\mathbf{W}_i$ is simply the outer product of another variable in the dataset; i.e.,

$$\mathbf{W}_i = \mathbf{e}_i\mathbf{e}_i'$$

where $\mathbf{e}_i$ is the $n_i \times 1$ vector formed from the n_i groupvar() observations of the variable specified in opvar().

▷ Example

Suppose that we have a panel dataset that contains five variables: id, t, e (a residual), and covariates x1 and x2. Further suppose that we need to compute

$$\mathbf{A} = \mathbf{X}_1'\mathbf{e}_1\mathbf{e}_1'\mathbf{X}_1 + \mathbf{X}_2'\mathbf{e}_2\mathbf{e}_2'\mathbf{X}_2 + \cdots + \mathbf{X}_K'\mathbf{e}_K\mathbf{e}_K'\mathbf{X}_K$$

where $\mathbf{X}_i$ contains the observations on x1 and x2 when id==i and $\mathbf{e}_i$ contains the observations on e when id==i.

Below is the output from xtdes for our example data. Note that there are 11 groups and that the number of observations per group is not constant.

```
. xtdes, i(id) t(t) patterns(11)
     id:  1, 2, ..., 11                              n =          11
      t:  1, 2, ..., 15                              T =          15
           Delta(t) = 1; (15-1)+1 = 15
           (id*t uniquely identifies each observation)

Distribution of T_i:    min     5%     25%      50%     75%     95%     max
                          5       5       7       10      13      15      15

     Freq.  Percent    Cum.  |  Pattern
  ---------------------------+-----------------
        1     9.09     9.09  |  11111..........
        1     9.09    18.18  |  111111.........
        1     9.09    27.27  |  1111111........
        1     9.09    36.36  |  11111111.......
        1     9.09    45.45  |  111111111......
        1     9.09    54.55  |  1111111111.....
        1     9.09    63.64  |  11111111111....
        1     9.09    72.73  |  111111111111...
        1     9.09    81.82  |  1111111111111..
        1     9.09    90.91  |  11111111111111.
        1     9.09   100.00  |  111111111111111
  ---------------------------+-----------------
       11   100.00          |  XXXXXXXXXXXXXXX
```

If we were to calculate $\mathbf{A}$ using glsaccum, we would need to form 11 matrices and store their names in a string variable prior to calling glsaccum. Note that this is the step that slows down glsaccum when there are many groups. Also note that all the information contained in the $\mathbf{W}_i$ matrices is contained in the variable e. It is this structure that opaccum exploits to make a faster command for this type of problem:

```
. mat opaccum  A = x1 x2, group(id) opvar(e)
```

◁

vecaccum

The first variable in the *varlist* is treated differently from the others by vecaccum. Think of the first variable as specifying a vector $\mathbf{y}$ and the remaining variables as specifying matrix $\mathbf{X}$. vecaccum makes the accumulation $\mathbf{y}'\mathbf{X}$ to return a row vector with elements

$$a_i = \sum_{k=1}^{n} y_k x_{ki}$$

Like accum, vecaccum adds a constant _cons to $\mathbf{X}$ unless noconstant is specified.

vecaccum serves two purposes. First, terms like $\mathbf{y}'\mathbf{X}$ often occur in calculating derivatives of likelihood functions; vecaccum provides a fast way of calculating them. Second, it is useful in time-series accumulations of the form

$$\mathbf{C} = \sum_{t=1}^{T} \sum_{\delta=-k}^{k} \mathbf{x}'_{t-\delta}\mathbf{x}_t W_\delta r_{t-\delta} r_t$$

In this calculation, $\mathbf{X}$ is an observation matrix with elements x_{tj}, with t indexing time (observations) and j variables $t = 1, \ldots, T$ and $j = 1, \ldots, p$. $\mathbf{x}_t$ ($1 \times p$) refers to the tth row of this matrix. Thus, $\mathbf{C}$ is a $p \times p$ matrix.

The Newey–West covariance matrix uses the definition $W_\delta = 1 - |\delta|/(k+1)$ for $\delta \le k$. To make the calculation, the user (programmer) cycles through each of the j variables, forming

$$z_{tj} = \sum_{\delta=-k}^{k} x_{(t-\delta)j} W_\delta r_{t-\delta} r_t$$

Writing $\mathbf{z}_j = (z_{1j}, z_{2j}, \ldots, z_{Tj})'$, $\mathbf{C}$ is then

$$\mathbf{C} = \sum_{j=1}^{p} \mathbf{z}'_j \mathbf{X}$$

In this derivation, the user must decide in advance the maximum lag length k such that observations that are far apart in time must have increasingly small covariances in order to establish the convergence results.

The Newey–West estimator is in the class of generalized methods of moments (GMM) estimators. The choice of a maximum lag length k is a reflection of the length in time beyond which the autocorrelation becomes negligible for the purposes of estimating the variance matrix. The code fragment given below is merely for illustration of the matrix commands, as Stata includes estimation with the Newey–West covariance matrix in the newey command. See [TS] **newey** or Greene (2003, 200–201) for details on this estimator.

Note that it is calculations like $\mathbf{z}'_j\mathbf{X}$ that are made by vecaccum. Also note that $\mathbf{z}_j$ can be treated as a temporary variable in the dataset.

```
        assume '1','2', etc. contain the x's including constant
        assume 'r' contains the r variable
        assume 'k' contains the k range
        tempname C factor t c
        tempvar z

        local p : word count '*'
        matrix 'C' = J('p','p',0)
        gen double 'z' = 0
        forvalues d = 0/'k' {
                            /* Add each submatrix twice except for
                               the lag==0 case */
                    scalar 'factor' = cond('d'>0, 1, .5)
```

```
                local w = (1 - 'd'/('k'+1))
                capture mat drop 't'
                forvalues j = 1/'p' {
                        replace 'z' = ''j''[_n-'d']*'w'*'r'[_n-'d']*'r'
                        mat vecaccum 'c' = 'z' '*', nocons
                        mat 't' = 't' \ 'c'
                }
                mat 'C' = 'C' + ('t' + 't'')*'factor'
        }
        local 'p' = "_cons"                    // Rename last var to _cons
        mat rownames 'C' = '*'
        mat colnames 'C' = '*'
        assume inverse and scaling for standard error reports
```

Treatment of user-specified weights

accum, glsaccum, and vecaccum all allow weights. Here is how they are treated:

All three commands can be thought of as returning something of the form $\mathbf{X}_1'\mathbf{B}\mathbf{X}_2$. In the case of accum, $\mathbf{X}_1 = \mathbf{X}_2$ and $\mathbf{B} = \mathbf{I}$; in the case of glsaccum, $\mathbf{X}_1 = \mathbf{X}_2$; and in the case of vecaccum, $\mathbf{B} = \mathbf{I}$, $\mathbf{X}_1$ is a column vector and $\mathbf{X}_2$ is a matrix.

In point of fact, the commands really calculate $\mathbf{X}_1'\mathbf{W}^{1/2}\mathbf{B}\mathbf{W}^{1/2}\mathbf{X}_2$, where $\mathbf{W}$ is a diagonal matrix. If no weights are specified, $\mathbf{W} = \mathbf{I}$. Now assume that weights are specified, and let $\mathbf{v}: 1 \times n$ be the specified weights. If fweights or pweights are specified, then $\mathbf{W} = \text{diag}(\mathbf{v})$. If aweights are specified, then $\mathbf{W} = \text{diag}\{\mathbf{v}/(\mathbf{1}'\mathbf{v})(\mathbf{1}'\mathbf{1})\}$, which is to say, the weights are normalized to sum to the number of observations. If iweights are specified, they are treated like fweights, except that the elements of $\mathbf{v}$ are not restricted to be positive integers.

Saved Results

matrix accum, glsaccum, opaccum, and vecaccum save the number of observations in r(N). glsaccum (with aweights) and vecaccum also store the sum of the weight in r(sum_w), but accum does not.

References

Greene, W. H. 2003. *Econometric Analysis*. 5th ed. Upper Saddle River, NJ: Prentice–Hall.

Also See

Complementary:	[R] **ml**
Background:	[U] **17 Matrix expressions**,
	[P] **matrix**

Title

> **matrix constraint** — Constrained estimation

Syntax

<u>mat</u>rix makeCns [*clist* | *matname*]

<u>mat</u>rix dispCns [, r]

matcproc **T a C**

where *clist* is a list of constraint numbers, separated by commas or dashes and *matname* is an existing matrix representing the constraints and must have one more column than the e(b) and e(V) matrices.

T, **a**, and **C** are names of new or existing matrices.

Description

matrix makeCns makes a constraint matrix; the matrix can be obtained by the matrix get(Cns) function (see [P] **matrix get**).

matrix dispCns displays the system-stored constraint matrix in readable form.

matcproc returns matrices helpful for performing constrained estimation, including the constraint matrix.

Options

r (matrix dispCns only) specifies that the readable forms should be saved in r() instead of displayed.

Remarks

Remarks are presented under the headings

> *Introduction*
> *Overview*
> *Mathematics*
> *Linkage of the mathematics to Stata*

Introduction

Users of estimation commands that allow constrained estimation define constraints using the constraint command; they indicate which constraints they want to use by specifying the constraints(*clist*) option to the estimation command. This entry concerns programming such sophisticated estimators. If you are programming using ml, you can ignore this entry. Constraints are handled automatically (and if you were to look inside the ml code, you would find that it uses matrix makeCns).

Before reading this entry, you should be familiar with constraints from a user's perspective; see [R] **constraint**. You should also be familiar with programming estimation commands that do not include constraints; see [P] **ereturn**.

Overview

You have an estimation command and wish to allow a set of linear constraints to be specified for the parameters by the user and then to produce estimates subject to those constraints. Stata will do most of the work for you. First, it will collect the constraints—all you have to do is add an option to your estimation command to allow the user to specify which constraints to use. Second, it will process those constraints, converting them from algebraic form (such as `group1=group2`) to a constraint matrix. Third, it will convert the constraint matrix into two almost magical matrices that will, in the case of maximum likelihood estimation, allow you to write your routine almost as if there were no constraints.

There will be a "reduced-form" parameter vector $\mathbf{b}_c$, which your likelihood-calculation routine will receive. That vector, multiplied by one of the almost magical matrices and then added to the other, can be converted into a regular parameter vector with the constraints applied, so, other than the few extra matrix calculations, you can calculate the likelihood function as if there were no constraints. You can do the same thing with respect to the first and second derivatives (if you are calculating them), except that, after getting them, you will need to perform another matrix multiplication or two to convert them into the reduced form.

Once the optimum is found, you will have reduced-form parameter vector $\mathbf{b}_c$ and variance–covariance matrix $\mathbf{V}_c$. Both can be easily converted into full-form-but-constrained $\mathbf{b}$ and $\mathbf{V}$.

Finally, you will `post` the results along with the constraint matrix Stata made up for you in the first place. You can, with a few lines of program code, arrange it so that, every time results are replayed, the constraints under which they were produced are redisplayed in standard algebraic format.

Mathematics

Let $\mathbf{Rb}' = \mathbf{r}$ be the constraint for $\mathbf{R}$, a $c \times p$ constraint matrix imposing c constraints on p parameters; $\mathbf{b}$, a $1 \times p$ parameter vector; and $\mathbf{r}$, a $c \times 1$ vector of constraint values.

We wish to construct a $p \times k$ matrix $\mathbf{T}$ that takes $\mathbf{b}$ into a reduced-rank form, where $k = p - c$. There are obviously lots of $\mathbf{T}$ matrices that will do this; we choose one with the properties

$$\mathbf{b}_c = \mathbf{b}_0 \mathbf{T}$$
$$\mathbf{b} = \mathbf{b}_c \mathbf{T}' + \mathbf{a}$$

where $\mathbf{b}_c$ is a reduced-form projection of any solution $\mathbf{b}_0$; i.e., $\mathbf{b}_c$ is a vector of lesser dimension ($1 \times k$ rather than $1 \times p$) that can be treated as if it were unconstrained. The second equation says that $\mathbf{b}_c$ can be mapped back into a higher-dimensioned, properly constrained $\mathbf{b}$; $1 \times p$ vector $\mathbf{a}$ is a constant that depends only on $\mathbf{R}$ and $\mathbf{r}$.

With such a $\mathbf{T}$ matrix and $\mathbf{a}$ vector, one can engage in unconstrained optimization of $\mathbf{b}_c$. If the estimate $\mathbf{b}_c$ with variance–covariance matrix $\mathbf{V}_c$ is produced, it can be mapped back into $\mathbf{b} = \mathbf{b}_c \mathbf{T}' + \mathbf{a}$ and $\mathbf{V} = \mathbf{T} \mathbf{V}_c \mathbf{T}'$. The resulting $\mathbf{b}$ and $\mathbf{V}$ can then be posted.

❏ Technical Note

So, how did we get so lucky? This happy solution arises if

$$\mathbf{T} = \text{first } k \text{ eigenvectors of } \mathbf{I} - \mathbf{R}'(\mathbf{RR}')^{-1}\mathbf{R} \quad (p \times k)$$
$$\mathbf{L} = \text{last } c \text{ eigenvectors of } \mathbf{I} - \mathbf{R}'(\mathbf{RR}')^{-1}\mathbf{R} \quad (p \times c)$$
$$\mathbf{a} = \mathbf{r}'(\mathbf{L}'\mathbf{R}')^{-1}\mathbf{L}'$$

because
$$\left(\mathbf{b}_c, \mathbf{r}'\right) = \mathbf{b}\!\left(\mathbf{T}, \mathbf{R}'\right)$$

If $\mathbf{R}$ consists of a set of consistent constraints, then it is guaranteed to have rank c. Thus, $\mathbf{RR}'$ is a $c \times c$ invertible matrix.

We will now show that $\mathbf{RT} = \mathbf{0}$ and $\mathbf{R}(\mathbf{LL}') = \mathbf{R}$.

Since $\mathbf{R}$: $c \times p$ is assumed to be of rank c, the first k eigenvalues of $\mathbf{P} = \mathbf{I} - \mathbf{R}'(\mathbf{RR}')^{-1}\mathbf{R}$ are positive and the last c are zero. Break $\mathbf{R}$ into a basis spanned by these components. If $\mathbf{R}$ had any components in the first k, they could not be annihilated by $\mathbf{P}$, contradicting
$$\mathbf{RP} = \mathbf{R} - \mathbf{RR}'(\mathbf{RR}')^{-1}\mathbf{R} = \mathbf{0}$$

Therefore, $\mathbf{T}$ and $\mathbf{R}$ are orthogonal to each other. Since $(\mathbf{T}, \mathbf{L})$ is an orthonormal basis, $(\mathbf{T}, \mathbf{L})'$ is its inverse, so $(\mathbf{T}, \mathbf{L})(\mathbf{T}, \mathbf{L})' = \mathbf{I}$. Thus,

$$\mathbf{TT}' + \mathbf{LL}' = \mathbf{I}$$
$$(\mathbf{TT}' + \mathbf{LL}')\mathbf{R}' = \mathbf{R}'$$
$$(\mathbf{LL}')\mathbf{R}' = \mathbf{R}'$$

So, we conclude that $\mathbf{r} = \mathbf{bR}(\mathbf{LL}')$. $\mathbf{RL}$ is an invertible $c \times c$ matrix, so
$$\left\{\mathbf{b}_c, \mathbf{r}'(\mathbf{L}'\mathbf{R})^{-1}\right\} = \mathbf{b}\!\left(\mathbf{T}, \mathbf{L}\right)$$

Remember, $(\mathbf{T}, \mathbf{L})$ is a set of eigenvectors, meaning $(\mathbf{T}, \mathbf{L})^{-1} = (\mathbf{T}, \mathbf{L})'$, so $\mathbf{b} = \mathbf{b}_c\mathbf{T}' + \mathbf{r}'(\mathbf{L}'\mathbf{R}')^{-1}\mathbf{L}'$. ❏

If a solution is found by likelihood methods, the reduced form parameter vector will be passed to the maximizer, and from there to the program that computes a likelihood value from it. In order to find the likelihood value, the inner routines can compute $\mathbf{b} = \mathbf{b}_c\mathbf{T}' + \mathbf{a}$. The routine may then go on to produce a set of $1 \times p$ first derivatives $\mathbf{d}$ and $p \times p$ second derivatives $\mathbf{H}$, even though the problem is of lesser dimension. These matrices can be reduced to the k-dimensional space via

$$\mathbf{d}_c = \mathbf{dT}$$
$$\mathbf{H}_c = \mathbf{T}'\mathbf{HT}$$

❏ Technical Note

Alternatively, if a solution were to be found by direct matrix methods, then the programmer must derive a new solution based on $\mathbf{b} = \mathbf{b}_c\mathbf{T}' + \mathbf{a}$. For example, the least-squares normal equations come from differentiating $(\mathbf{y} - \mathbf{Xb})^2$. Setting the derivative with respect to $\mathbf{b}$ to zero results in

$$\mathbf{T}'\mathbf{X}'\left\{\mathbf{y} - \mathbf{X}(\mathbf{Tb}_c' + \mathbf{a}')\right\} = 0$$

yielding

$$\mathbf{b}_c' = (\mathbf{T}'\mathbf{X}'\mathbf{XT})^{-1}(\mathbf{T}'\mathbf{X}'\mathbf{y} - \mathbf{T}'\mathbf{X}'\mathbf{Xa}')$$
$$\mathbf{b}' = \mathbf{T}\left\{(\mathbf{T}'\mathbf{X}'\mathbf{XT})^{-1}(\mathbf{T}'\mathbf{X}'\mathbf{y} - \mathbf{T}'\mathbf{X}'\mathbf{Xa}')\right\} + \mathbf{a}'$$

Using the matrices $\mathbf{T}$ and $\mathbf{a}$, the solution is not merely to constrain the $\mathbf{b}'$ obtained from an unconstrained solution $(\mathbf{X}'\mathbf{X})^{-1}\mathbf{X}'\mathbf{y}$, even though you might know that, in this case, with further substitutions this could be reduced to

$$\mathbf{b}' = (\mathbf{X}'\mathbf{X})^{-1}\mathbf{X}'\mathbf{y} + (\mathbf{X}'\mathbf{X})^{-1}\mathbf{R}'\{\mathbf{R}(\mathbf{X}'\mathbf{X})^{-1}\mathbf{R}'\}^{-1}\{\mathbf{r} - \mathbf{R}(\mathbf{X}'\mathbf{X})^{-1}\mathbf{X}'\mathbf{y}\}$$

❏

Linkage of the mathematics to Stata

Users define constraints using the `constraint` command; see [R] **constraint**. The constraints are numbered and Stata stores them in algebraic format—the same format in which the user typed them. Stata does this because, until the estimation problem is defined, it cannot know how to interpret the constraint. Think of the constraint `_b[group1]=_b[group2]`, meaning two coefficients are to be constrained to equality, along with the constraint `_b[group3]=2`. The constraint matrices $\mathbf{R}$ and $\mathbf{r}$ are defined so that $\mathbf{R}\mathbf{b}' = \mathbf{r}$ imposes the constraint. The matrices *might* be

$$\begin{pmatrix} 0 & 0 & 1 & -1 & 0 & 0 \\ 0 & 0 & 0 & 0 & 1 & 0 \end{pmatrix} \begin{pmatrix} b_1 \\ b_2 \\ b_3 \\ b_4 \\ b_5 \\ b_6 \end{pmatrix} = \begin{pmatrix} 0 \\ 2 \end{pmatrix}$$

if it just so happened that the third and fourth coefficients corresponded to `group1` and `group2` and the fifth corresponded to `group3`. Then again, it might look different if the coefficients were organized differently.

Therefore, Stata must wait until estimation begins to define the $\mathbf{R}$ and $\mathbf{r}$ matrices. Stata learns about the organization of a problem from the names bordering the coefficient vector and variance–covariance matrix. Therefore, Stata requires you to `post` a dummy estimation result that has the correct names. Based on that, it can now determine the organization of the constraint matrix and make it for you. Once an (dummy) estimation result has been posted, `makeCns` can make the constraint matrices, and, once they are built, you can obtain copies of them using `matrix` *mname*`=get(Cns)`. Stata stores the constraint matrices $\mathbf{R}$ and $\mathbf{r}$ as a single, $c \times (p+1)$ matrix $\mathbf{C} = (\mathbf{R}, \mathbf{r})$. Putting them together makes it easier to pass them to subroutines.

The second step in the process is to convert the constrained problem to a reduced-form problem. We outlined the mathematics above; the `matcproc` command will produce the $\mathbf{T}$ and $\mathbf{a}$ matrices. If you are performing maximum likelihood, your likelihood, gradient, and Hessian calculation subroutines can still work in the full metric by using the same $\mathbf{T}$ and $\mathbf{a}$ matrices to translate the reduced-format parameter vector back to the original metric. If you do this, and if you are calculating gradients or Hessians, you must remember to compress them to reduced form using the $\mathbf{T}$ and $\mathbf{a}$ matrices.

When you have a reduced-form solution, you translate this back to a constrained solution using $\mathbf{T}$ and $\mathbf{a}$. You then `post` the constrained solutions, along with the original Cns matrix, and use `ereturn display` to display the results.

Thus, the outline of a program to perform constrained estimation is

(Continued on next page)

```
program myest, eclass
       version 8.0
       if !replay() {
              syntax whatever [, whatever Constraints(clist)   ///
                     Level(integer 'c(level)')];
              any other parsing of the user's estimation request
              tempname b V C T a bc Vc
              local p=number of parameters
              define the model ( set the row and column names)  in 'b'
              if "'constraints'"!="" {
                     matrix 'V'='b''*'b'
                     ereturn post 'b' 'V'            // a dummy solution
                     matrix makeCns 'constraints'
                     matrix dispCns               // display constraints
                     local shown "yes"
                     matcproc 'T' 'a' 'C'
                     obtain solution in 'bc' and 'Vc'
                     matrix 'b' = 'bc'*'T' + 'a'
                     matrix 'V' = 'T'*'Vc'*'T''   // note prime
                     ereturn post 'b' 'V' 'C', options
              }
              else {
                     obtain standard solution in 'b' and 'V'
                     ereturn post 'b' 'V', options
              }
              store whatever else you want in e()
              ereturn local cmd "myest"
       }
       else {    // replay
              if "'e(cmd)'"!="myest" error 301
              syntax [, Level(integer 'c(level)')]
       }
       if 'level'<10 | 'level'>99 {
              di as err "level() must be between 10 and 99 inclusive"
              exit 198
       }
       if "'shown'"!="yes" {
              matrix dispCns  // display any constraints on replay
       }
       output any header above the coefficient table
       ereturn display, level('level')
   end
```

There is one point that might escape your attention: Immediately after obtaining the constraint, we display the constraints even before we undertake the estimation. This way, a user who has made a mistake may press *Break* rather than waiting until the estimation is complete to discover the error.

Our code also redisplays the constraints every time the problem output is repeated (by typing *myest* without arguments). So that the constraints are not shown twice at the time of estimation, we set the local macro shown to contain yes. If the output is ever repeated, the local macro shown will never be defined (and so will not contain yes), and we will redisplay the constraints along with the results of our estimation.

(Continued on next page)

Saved Results

matrix dispCns, r saves in r():

Scalars
  r(k)   the number of system constraints (k)
Macros
  r(cns1)   system constraint number 1
  r(cns2)   system constraint number 2
            . . .
  r(cnsk)   system constraint number k

Also See

Complementary:	[P] **ereturn**, [P] **matrix get**,
	[R] **constraint**
Related:	[R] **cnsreg**, [R] **ml**
Background:	[U] **17 Matrix expressions**,
	[U] **21 Programming Stata**,
	[U] **23 Estimation and post-estimation commands**,
	[P] **matrix**

Title

> **matrix define** — Matrix definition, operators, and functions

Syntax

<u>matrix</u> [<u>define</u>] *matname* = *matrix_expression*

<u>matrix</u> [<u>input</u>] *matname* = (# [,# ...] [\ # [, # ...] [\ [...]]])

Description

matrix **define** performs matrix computations. The word **define** may be omitted.

matrix **input** provides a method of inputting matrices. The word **input** may be omitted (see discussion that follows).

For an introduction and overview of matrices in Stata, see [U] **17 Matrix expressions**.

Remarks

matrix **define** calculates matrix results from other matrices. For instance,

```
. matrix define D = A + B + C
```

creates D containing the sum of A, B, and C. The word **define** may be omitted,

```
. matrix D = A + B + C
```

and the command may be further abbreviated:

```
. mat D=A+B+C
```

The same matrix may appear on both the left and the right of the equals sign in all contexts, and Stata will not become confused. Complicated matrix expressions are allowed.

With **matrix** **input** you define the matrix elements rowwise; commas are used to separate elements within a row and backslashes are used to separate the rows. Spacing does not matter.

```
. matrix input A = (1,2\3,4)
```

The above would also work if you omitted the **input** subcommand.

```
. matrix A = (1,2\3,4)
```

There is a subtle difference: The first method uses the **matrix** **input** command, and the second uses the matrix expression parser. Omitting **input** allows expressions in the command. For instance,

```
. matrix X = (1+1, 2*3/4 \ 5/2, 3)
```

is understood but

. matrix input X = (1+1, 2*3/4 \ 5/2, 3)

would produce an error.

matrix input, however, has two advantages. First, it allows input of very large matrices. (The expression parser is limited because it must "compile" the expressions, and, if the result is too long, will produce an error.) Second, matrix input allows you to omit the commas.

Further remarks are presented under the headings

> *Inputting matrices by hand*
> *Matrix operators*
> *Matrix functions returning matrices*
> *Matrix functions returning scalars*
> *Subscripting and element-by-element definition*
> *Name conflicts in expressions (name spaces)*
> *Macro extended functions*

Inputting matrices by hand

Before turning to operations on matrices, let's examine how matrices are created. Typically, at least in programming situations, you obtain matrices by accessing one of Stata's internal matrices (e(b) and e(V); see [P] **matrix get**) or by accumulating it from the data (see [P] **matrix accum**). Nevertheless, the easiest way to create a matrix is to enter it using matrix input—this may not be the normal way one creates matrices, but it is useful for performing small, experimental calculations.

▷ Example

To create the matrix

$$\mathbf{A} = \begin{pmatrix} 1 & 2 \\ 3 & 4 \end{pmatrix}$$

type

. matrix A = (1,2 \ 3,4)

The spacing does not matter. To define the matrix

$$\mathbf{B} = \begin{pmatrix} 1 & 2 & 3 \\ 4 & . & 6 \end{pmatrix}$$

type

. matrix B = (1,2,3 \ 4,.,6)

To define the matrix

$$\mathbf{C} = \begin{pmatrix} 1 & 2 \\ 3 & 4 \\ 5 & 6 \end{pmatrix}$$

type

. matrix C = (1,2 \ 3,4 \ 5,6)

If you need more than one line and are working interactively, you merely keep typing; Stata will wrap the line around the screen. If you are working in a do- or ado-file, see [U] **19.1.3 Long lines in do-files**.

So, how do you create vectors? You enter the elements, separating them by commas or backslashes. To create the row vector

$$\mathbf{D} = (\,1 \quad 2 \quad 3\,)$$

type

    . matrix D = (1,2,3)

To create the column vector

$$\mathbf{E} = \begin{pmatrix} 1 \\ 2 \\ 3 \end{pmatrix}$$

type

    . matrix E = (1\2\3)

To create the 1×1 matrix $\mathbf{F} = (\,2\,)$, type

    . matrix F = (2)

In these examples, we have omitted the `input` subcommand. They would work either way.

◁

Matrix operators

In what follows, uppercase letters $\mathbf{A}$, $\mathbf{B}$, ... stand for matrix names. The matrix operators are

+ meaning addition. `matrix` $\mathbf{C=A+B}$, $\mathbf{A}$: $r \times c$ and $\mathbf{B}$: $r \times c$, creates $\mathbf{C}$: $r \times c$ containing the elementwise addition $\mathbf{A} + \mathbf{B}$. An error is issued if the matrices are not conformable. Row and column names are obtained from $\mathbf{B}$.

- meaning subtraction or negation. `matrix` $\mathbf{C=A-B}$, $\mathbf{A}$: $r \times c$ and $\mathbf{B}$: $r \times c$, creates $\mathbf{C}$ containing the elementwise subtraction $\mathbf{A} - \mathbf{B}$. An error is issued if the matrices are not conformable. `matrix` $\mathbf{C=-A}$ creates $\mathbf{C}$ containing the elementwise negation of $\mathbf{A}$. Row and column names are obtained from $\mathbf{B}$.

* meaning multiplication. `matrix` $\mathbf{C=A*B}$, $\mathbf{A}$: $a \times b$ and $\mathbf{B}$: $b \times c$, returns $\mathbf{C}$: $a \times c$ containing the matrix product $\mathbf{AB}$; an error is issued if $\mathbf{A}$ and $\mathbf{B}$ are not conformable. The row names of $\mathbf{C}$ are obtained from the row names of $\mathbf{A}$, and the column names of $\mathbf{C}$ from the column names of $\mathbf{B}$.

  `matrix` $\mathbf{C=A*}s$ or `matrix` $\mathbf{C=}s\mathbf{*A}$, $\mathbf{A}$: $a \times b$ and s a Stata scalar (see [P] **scalar**) or a literal number, returns $\mathbf{C}$: $a \times b$ containing the elements of $\mathbf{A}$ each multiplied by s. The row and column names of $\mathbf{C}$ are obtained from $\mathbf{A}$. For example, `matrix VC=MYMAT*2.5` multiplies each element of `MYMAT` by 2.5 and stores the result in `VC`.

/ meaning matrix division by scalar. `matrix` $\mathbf{C=A/}s$, $\mathbf{A}$: $a \times b$ and s a Stata scalar (see [P] **scalar**) or a literal number, returns $\mathbf{C}$: $a \times b$ containing the elements of $\mathbf{A}$ each divided by s. The row and column names of $\mathbf{C}$ are obtained from $\mathbf{A}$.

meaning Kronecker product. `matrix` $\mathbf{C=A\#B}$, $\mathbf{A}$: $a \times b$ and $\mathbf{B}$: $c \times d$, returns $\mathbf{C}$: $ac \times bd$ containing the Kronecker product $\mathbf{A} \otimes \mathbf{B}$, all elementwise products of $\mathbf{A}$ and $\mathbf{B}$. The upper-left submatrix of $\mathbf{C}$ is the product $A_{1,1}\mathbf{B}$; the submatrix to the right is $A_{1,2}\mathbf{B}$; and so on. Row and column names are obtained by using the subnames of $\mathbf{A}$ as resulting equation names and the subnames of $\mathbf{B}$ for the subnames of $\mathbf{C}$ in each submatrix.

Nothing meaning copy. `matrix B=A` copies $\mathbf{A}$ into $\mathbf{B}$. The row and column names of $\mathbf{B}$ are obtained from $\mathbf{A}$. The `matrix rename` command (see [P] **matrix utility**) will rename instead of copy a matrix.

' meaning transpose. $\texttt{matrix } \mathbf{B=A'}$, $\mathbf{A}$: $r \times c$, creates $\mathbf{B}$: $c \times r$ containing the transpose of $\mathbf{A}$. The row names of $\mathbf{B}$ are obtained from the column names of $\mathbf{A}$ and the column names of $\mathbf{B}$ from the row names of $\mathbf{A}$.

, meaning join columns by row. $\texttt{matrix } \mathbf{C=A,B}$, $\mathbf{A}$: $a \times b$ and $\mathbf{B}$: $a \times c$, returns $\mathbf{C}$: $a \times (b+c)$ containing $\mathbf{A}$ in columns 1 through b and $\mathbf{B}$ in columns $b+1$ through $b+c$ (the columns of $\mathbf{B}$ are appended to the columns of $\mathbf{A}$). An error is issued if the matrices are not conformable. The row names of $\mathbf{C}$ are obtained from $\mathbf{A}$. The column names are obtained from $\mathbf{A}$ and $\mathbf{B}$.

\ meaning join rows by column. $\texttt{matrix } \mathbf{C=A \backslash B}$, $\mathbf{A}$: $a \times b$ and $\mathbf{B}$: $c \times b$, returns $\mathbf{C}$: $(a+c) \times b$ containing $\mathbf{A}$ in rows 1 through a and $\mathbf{B}$ in rows $a+1$ through $a+c$ (the rows of $\mathbf{B}$ are appended to the rows of $\mathbf{A}$). An error is issued if the matrices are not conformable. The column names of $\mathbf{C}$ are obtained from $\mathbf{A}$. The row names are obtained from $\mathbf{A}$ and $\mathbf{B}$.

$\texttt{matrix define}$ allows complicated matrix expressions. Parentheses may be used to control order of evaluation. The default order of precedence for the matrix operators (from highest to lowest) is

Matrix operator precedence

Operator	symbol
parentheses	()
transpose	'
negation	–
Kronecker product	#
division by scalar	/
multiplication	*
subtraction	–
addition	+
column join	,
row join	\

▷ Example

The following examples are artificial but informative:

```
. matrix A = (1,2\3,4)
. matrix B = (5,7\9,2)
. matrix C = A+B
. matrix list C
C[2,2]
     c1   c2
r1   6    9
r2   12   6
. matrix B = A-B
. matrix list B
B[2,2]
     c1   c2
r1   -4   -5
r2   -6   2
. matrix X = (1,1\2,5\8,0\4,5)
. matrix C = 3*X*A'*B
```

```
. matrix list C

C[4,2]
        c1    c2
r1   -162    -3
r2   -612   -24
r3   -528    24
r4   -744   -18

. matrix D = (X'*X - A'*A)/4

. matrix rownames D = dog cat        // see [P] matrix rowname

. matrix colnames D = bark meow      // see [P] matrix rowname

. matrix list D

symmetric D[2,2]
        bark    meow
dog  18.75
cat   4.25    7.75

. matrix rownames A = aa bb          // see [P] matrix rowname

. matrix colnames A = alpha beta     // see [P] matrix rowname

. matrix list A

A[2,2]
      alpha   beta
aa       1      2
bb       3      4

. matrix D=A#D

. matrix list D

D[4,4]
          alpha:   alpha:   beta:   beta:
           bark     meow    bark    meow
aa:dog    18.75     4.25    37.5     8.5
aa:cat     4.25     7.75     8.5    15.5
bb:dog    56.25    12.75      75      17
bb:cat    12.75    23.25      17      31

. matrix G=A,B\D

. matrix list G

G[6,4]
          alpha    beta     c1      c2
     aa       1       2     -4      -5
     bb       3       4     -6       2
 aa:dog   18.75    4.25    37.5     8.5
 aa:cat    4.25    7.75     8.5    15.5
 bb:dog   56.25   12.75      75      17
 bb:cat   12.75   23.25      17      31

. matrix Z = (B - A)'*(B + A'*-B)/4

. matrix list Z

Z[2,2]
          c1      c2
alpha    -81    -1.5
 beta  -44.5     8.5
```

◁

❏ Technical Note

Programmers: Watch out for confusion when combining ', meaning transpose with local macros, where ' is one of the characters that enclose macro names: `'mname'`. Stata will not become confused, but you might. Compare:

```
. matrix 'new1' = 'old'
```

and

```
. matrix 'new2' = 'old''
```

Note that matrix 'new2' contains matrix 'old', transposed. Stata will become confused if you type

```
. matrix 'C' = 'A'\'B'
```

because the backslash in front of the 'B' makes the macro processor take the left quote literally. No substitution is ever made for 'B'. Even worse, the macro processor assumes that the backslash was meant for it, and so removes the character! Pretend that 'A' contained a, 'B' contained b, and 'C' contained c. After substitution, the line would read

```
. matrix c = a'B'
```

which is not at all what was intended. To make your meaning clear, put a space after the backslash,

```
. matrix 'C' = 'A'\ 'B'
```

which would then be expanded to read

```
. matrix c = a\ b
```

❏

Matrix functions returning matrices

In addition to matrix operators, Stata has matrix functions. The matrix functions allow expressions to be passed as arguments. The following matrix functions are provided:

matrix $\mathbf{A}$=I(dim) defines $\mathbf{A}$ as the $dim \times dim$ identity matrix, where dim is a scalar expression and will be rounded to the nearest integer. matrix $\mathbf{A}$=I(3) defines $\mathbf{A}$ as the 3×3 identity matrix.

matrix $\mathbf{A}$=J(r,c,z) defines $\mathbf{A}$ as an $r \times c$ matrix containing elements z. r, c, and z are scalar expressions with r and c rounded to the nearest integer. matrix $\mathbf{A}$=J(2,3,0) returns a 2×3 matrix containing 0 for each element.

matrix $\mathbf{L}$=cholesky($mexp$) performs Cholesky decomposition. An error is issued if the matrix expression $mexp$ does not evaluate to a square, symmetric matrix. matrix $\mathbf{L}$=cholesky($\mathbf{A}$) produces the lower-triangular (square root) matrix $\mathbf{L}$ such that $\mathbf{LL}' = \mathbf{A}$. The row and column names of $\mathbf{L}$ are obtained from $\mathbf{A}$.

matrix $\mathbf{B}$=syminv($mexp$), for $mexp$ evaluating to a square, symmetric, and positive definite matrix, returns the inverse. If $mexp$ does not evaluate to a positive definite matrix, rows will be inverted until the diagonal terms are zero or negative; the rows and columns corresponding to these terms will be set to 0, producing a g2 inverse. The row names of $\mathbf{B}$ are obtained from the column names of $mexp$, and the column names of $\mathbf{B}$ are obtained from the row names of $mexp$.

matrix $\mathbf{B}$=inv($mexp$), for $mexp$ evaluating to a square but not necessarily symmetric or positive definite matrix, returns the inverse. A singular matrix will result in an error. The row names of $\mathbf{B}$ are obtained from the column names of $mexp$, and the column names of $\mathbf{B}$ are obtained from the row names of $mexp$. syminv() should be used in preference to inv(), which is less accurate, whenever possible. (Also see [P] **matrix svd** for singular value decomposition.)

(Continued on next page)

`matrix` **B**=`sweep`(*mexp*,*n*) applies the sweep operator to the *n*th row and column of the square matrix resulting from the matrix expression *mexp*. *n* is a scalar expression, and will be rounded to the nearest integer. The names of **B** are obtained from *mexp*, except that the *n*th row and column names are interchanged. For **A**: $n \times n$, **B** = sweep$(\mathbf{A}, k)$ produces **B**: $n \times n$, defined as

$$B_{kk} = \frac{1}{A_{kk}}$$

$$B_{ik} = -\frac{A_{ik}}{A_{kk}}, \qquad i \neq k \qquad \textit{(kth column)}$$

$$B_{kj} = \frac{A_{ij}}{A_{kk}}, \qquad j \neq k \qquad \textit{(jth row)}$$

$$B_{ij} = A_{ij} - \frac{A_{ik}A_{kj}}{A_{kk}}, \qquad i \neq k, j \neq k$$

`matrix` **B**=`corr`(*mexp*), for *mexp* evaluating to a covariance matrix, stores the corresponding correlation matrix in **B**. The row and column names are obtained from *mexp*.

`matrix` **B**=`diag`(*mexp*), for *mexp* evaluating to a row or column vector ($1 \times c$ or $c \times 1$), creates **B**: $c \times c$ with diagonal elements from *mexp* and off-diagonal elements 0. The row and column names are obtained from the column names of *mexp* if *mexp* is a row vector or the row names if *mexp* is a column vector.

`matrix` **B**=`vec`(*mexp*), for *mexp* evaluating to a $r \times c$ matrix, creates **B**: $rc \times 1$ containing the elements of *mexp* starting with the first column, and proceeding column by column.

`matrix` **B**=`vecdiag`(*mexp*), for *mexp* evaluating to a square $c \times c$ matrix, creates **B**: $1 \times c$ containing the diagonal elements from *mexp*. `vecdiag()` is the opposite of `diag()`. The row name is set to r1. The column names are obtained from the column names of *mexp*.

`matrix` **B**=`matuniform`(*r*,*c*) creates **B**: $r \times c$ containing uniformly distributed pseudo-random numbers on the interval $[0, 1]$.

`matrix` **B**=`hadamard`(*mexp*, *nexp*), where *mexp* and *nexp* evaluate to $r \times c$ matrices, creates a matrix whose i, j element is $mexp[i, j] \cdot nexp[i, j]$. If *mexp* and *nexp* do not evaluate to matrices of the same size, this function reports a conformability error.

`nullmat`(**B**) may only be used with the row-join (,) and column-join (\) operators, and informs Stata that **B** might not exist. If **B** does not exist, the row-join or column-join operator simply returns the other matrix operator argument. An example of the use of `nullmat()` is given in [R] **functions**.

`matrix` **B**=`get`(*systemname*) returns in **B** a copy of the Stata internal matrix *systemname*; see [P] **matrix get**. You can obtain the coefficient vector and variance–covariance matrix after an estimation command either with `matrix get` or by reference to `e(b)` and `e(V)`.

(Continued on next page)

▷ Example

The examples are, once again, artificial but informative.

```
. matrix myid = I(3)
. matrix list myid
symmetric myid[3,3]
     c1  c2  c3
r1   1
r2   0   1
r3   0   0   1
. matrix new = J(2,3,0)
. matrix list new
new[2,3]
     c1  c2  c3
r1   0   0   0
r2   0   0   0
. matrix A = (1,2\2,5)
. matrix Ainv = syminv(A)
. matrix list Ainv
symmetric Ainv[2,2]
     r1  r2
c1   5
c2   -2   1
. matrix L = cholesky(4*I(2) + A'*A)
. matrix list L
L[2,2]
             c1          c2
c1            3           0
c2            4    4.1231056
. matrix B = (1,5,9\2,1,7\3,5,1)
. matrix Binv = inv(B)
. matrix list Binv
Binv[3,3]
             r1          r2          r3
c1   -.27419355   .32258065   .20967742
c2    .15322581  -.20967742   .08870968
c3    .05645161   .08064516  -.07258065
. matrix C = sweep(B,1)
. matrix list C
C[3,3]
     r1   c2   c3
c1   1    5    9
r2   -2   -9   -11
r3   -3   -10  -26
. matrix C = sweep(C,1)
. matrix list C
C[3,3]
     c1  c2  c3
r1   1   5   9
r2   2   1   7
r3   3   5   1
. matrix Cov = (36.6598,-3596.48\-3596.48,604030)
. matrix R = corr(Cov)
```

```
. matrix list R

symmetric R[2,2]
            c1          c2
r1        1
r2  -.7642815              1

. matrix d = (1,2,3)

. matrix D = diag(d)

. matrix list D

symmetric D[3,3]
     c1  c2  c3
c1   1
c2   0   2
c3   0   0   3

. matrix e = vec(D)

. matrix list e

e[9,1]
        c1
c1:c1   1
c1:c2   0
c1:c3   0
c2:c1   0
c2:c2   2
c2:c3   0
c3:c1   0
c3:c2   0
c3:c3   3

. matrix f = vecdiag(D)

. matrix list f

f[1,3]
     c1  c2  c3
r1   1   2   3

. * matrix function arguments can be other matrix functions and expressions
. matrix G = diag(inv(B) * vecdiag(diag(d) + 4*sweep(B+J(3,3,10),2)'*I(3))')

. matrix list G

symmetric G[3,3]
            c1          c2          c3
c1  -3.2170088
c2          0    -7.686217
c3          0           0   2.3548387

. matrix U = matuniform(3,4)

. matrix list U

U[3,4]
           c1          c2          c3          c4
r1  .13698408   .64322067    .5578017   .60479494
r2  .68417598   .10866794   .61845813   .06106378
r3  .55523883   .87144908   .25514988    .0445188

. matrix H = hadamard(B,C)

. matrix list H

H[3,3]
     c1   c2   c3
r1    1   25   81
r2   -4   -9  -77
r3   -9  -50  -26
```

Matrix functions returning scalars

In addition to the above functions used with `matrix define`, functions that can be described as matrix functions returning matrices, there are matrix functions that return mathematical scalars. The list of functions that follow should be viewed as a continuation of [U] **16.3 Functions**. If the functions listed below are used in a scalar context (for example used with `display` or `generate`) then **A**, **B**, ..., below stand for matrix names (possibly as a string literal or string variable name—details later). If the functions below are used in a matrix context (in `matrix define` for instance), then **A**, **B**, ... may also stand for matrix expressions.

`rowsof(`**A**`)` and `colsof(`**A**`)` return the number of rows or columns of **A**.

`rownumb(`**A**`,`*string*`)` and `colnumb(`**A**`,`*string*`)` return the row or column number associated with the name specified by *string*. For instance, `rownumb(MYMAT,"price")` returns the row number (say, 3) in `MYMAT` that has name `price` (subname `price` and equation name blank). `colnumb(MYMAT,"out2:price")` returns the column number associated with name `out2:price` (subname `price` and equation name `out2`). If row or column name is not found, missing is returned.

`rownumb()` and `colnumb()` can also return the first row or column number associated with an equation name. For example, `colnumb(MYMAT,"out2:")` returns the first column number in `MYMAT` that has equation name `out2`. Missing is returned if the equation name `out2` is not found.

`trace(`**A**`)` returns the sum of the diagonal elements of square matrix **A**. If **A** is not square, missing is returned.

`det(`**A**`)` returns the determinant of square matrix **A**. The determinant is the volume of the $p - 1$ dimensional manifold described by the matrix in p-dimensional space. If **A** is not square, missing is returned.

`diag0cnt(`**A**`)` returns the number of zeros on the diagonal of the square matrix **A**. If **A** is not square, missing is returned.

`issym(`**A**`)` returns 1 if the matrix is symmetric, and 0 otherwise.

`matmissing(`**A**`)` returns 1 if any elements of the matrix are missing, and 0 otherwise.

`mreldif(`**A**`,`**B**`)` returns the relative difference of matrix **A** and **B**. If **A** and **B** do not have the same dimensions, missing is returned. The matrix relative difference is defined as

$$\max_{i,j} \left(\frac{|\mathbf{A}[i,j] - \mathbf{B}[i,j]|}{|\mathbf{B}[i,j]| + 1} \right)$$

`el(`**A**`,`i`,`j`)` and **A**`[`i`,`j`]` return the i, j element of **A**. In most cases, either construct may be used; `el(MYMAT,2,3)` and `MYMAT[2,3]` are equivalent, although `MYMAT[2,3]` is more readable. In the case of the second construct, however, **A** must be a matrix name—it cannot be a string literal or string variable. The first construct allows **A** to be a matrix name, string literal, or string variable. For instance, assume `mymat` (as opposed to `MYMAT`) is a string variable in the dataset containing matrix names. `mymat[2,3]` refers to the $(2,3)$ element of the matrix named `mymat`, a matrix that probably does not exist, and so produces an error. `el(mymat,2,3)` refers to the data variable `mymat`; the contents of that variable will be taken to obtain the matrix name, and `el()` will then return the $(2,3)$ element of that matrix. If that matrix does not exist, Stata will not issue an error; because you referred to it indirectly, the `el()` function will return missing.

In either construct, i and j may be any expression (an *exp*) evaluating to a real. `MYMAT[2,3+1]` returns the $(2,4)$ element. In programs that loop, you might refer to `MYMAT['i','j'+1]`.

In a matrix context (like `matrix define`), the first argument of `el()` may be a matrix expression. For instance, `matrix A = B*el(B-C,1,1)` is allowed, but `display el(B-C,1,1)` would be an error since `display` is in a scalar context.

The matrix functions returning scalars defined above can be used in any context that allows an expression—what is abbreviated *exp* in the syntax diagrams throughout this manual. For instance, `trace()` returns the (scalar) trace of a matrix. Say you have a matrix called MYX. You could type

```
. generate tr = trace(MYX)
```

although this would be a silly thing to do. It would be silly because it would force Stata to evaluate the trace of the matrix many times, once for each observation in the data, and it would then store that same result over and over again in the new data variable `tr`. But you could do it because, if you examine the syntax diagram for `generate` (see [R] **generate**), `generate` allows an *exp*.

If you just wanted to see the trace of MYX, you could type

```
. display trace(MYX)
```

because the syntax diagram for `display` also allows an *exp*; see [P] **display**. More usefully, you could do either of the following:

```
. local tr = trace(MYX)
. scalar tr = trace(MYX)
```

This is more useful because it will evaluate the trace only once and then store the result. In the first case, the result will be stored in a local macro (see [P] **macro**); in the second, it will be stored in a Stata scalar (see [P] **scalar**).

▷ Example

Storing the number as a scalar is better for two reasons: it is more accurate (scalars are stored in double precision) and it is faster (macros are stored as printable characters, and this conversion is a time-consuming operation). Not too much should be made of the accuracy issue; macros are stored with at least 13 digits, but it can make a difference in some cases.

In any case, let us demonstrate that both methods work with the simple trace function:

```
. matrix A = (1,6\8,4)
. local tr = trace(A)
. display 'tr'
5
. scalar sctr = trace(A)
. scalar list sctr
     sctr =          5
```
◁

❑ Technical Note

The use of a matrix function returning scalar with `generate` does not have to be silly because, instead of specifying a matrix name, you may specify a string variable in the dataset. If you do, in each observation the contents of the string variable will be taken as a matrix name, and the function will be applied to that matrix for that observation. If there is no such matrix, missing will be returned. Thus, if your dataset contained

```
. list
```

	matname
1.	X1
2.	X2
3.	Z

you could type

```
. generate tr = trace(matname)
(1 missing value generated)
. list
```

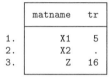

	matname	tr
1.	X1	5
2.	X2	.
3.	Z	16

Evidently, we have no matrix called X2 stored. All the matrix functions returning scalars allow you to specify either a matrix name directly or a string variable that indirectly specifies the matrix name. When you indirectly specify the matrix and the matrix does not exist—as happened above—the function evaluates to missing. When you directly specify the matrix and it does not exist, you get an error:

```
. display trace(X2)
X2 not found
r(111);
```

This is true not only for `trace()`, but for every matrix function that returns a scalar described above.

❑

Subscripting and element-by-element definition

matrix **B**=**A**$[r_1,r_2]$, for range expressions r_1 and r_2 (defined below), extracts a submatrix from **A** and stores it in **B**. Row and column names of **B** are obtained from the extracted rows and columns of **A**. In what follows, assume that **A** is $a \times b$.

A range expression can be a literal number. matrix **B**=**A**[1,2] would return a 1×1 matrix containing $A_{1,2}$.

A range expression can be a number followed by two periods followed by another number, meaning the rows or columns from the first number to the second. matrix **B**=**A**[2..4,1..5] would return a 3×5 matrix containing the second through fourth rows and the first through fifth columns of **A**.

A range expression can be a number followed by three periods, meaning all the remaining rows or columns from that number. matrix **B**=**A**[3,4...] would return a $1 \times b - 3$ matrix (row vector) containing the fourth through last elements of the third row of **A**.

A range expression can be a quoted string, in which case it refers to the row or column with the specified name. matrix **B**=**A**["price","mpg"] returns a 1×1 matrix containing the element whose row name is `price` and column name mpg, which would be the same as matrix **B**=**A**[2,3] if the second row were named `price` and the third column mpg. matrix **B**=**A**["price",1...]

would return the $1 \times b$ vector corresponding to the row named `price`. In either case, if there is no matrix row or column with the specified name, an error is issued and the return code is set to 111. If the row and/or column names include both an equation name and a subname, the fully qualified name must be specified, as in `matrix B=A["eq1:price",1...]`.

A range expression can be a quoted string containing only an equation name, in which case it refers to all rows or columns with the specified equation name. `matrix B=A["eq1:","eq1:"]` would return the submatrix of rows and columns that have equation names `eq1`.

A range expression containing a quoted string referring to an element (not to an entire equation) can be combined with the .. and ... syntaxes above: `matrix B=A["price"...,"price"...]` would define **B** as the submatrix of **A** beginning with the rows and columns corresponding to `price`. `matrix B=A["price".."mpg","price".."mpg"]` would define **B** as the submatrix of **A** starting at rows and columns corresponding to `price` and continuing through the rows and columns corresponding to `mpg`.

A range expression can be mixed. `matrix B=A[1.."price",2]` defines **B** as the column vector extracted from the second column of **A** containing the first element through the element corresponding to `price`.

Scalar expressions may be used in place of literal numbers. The resulting number will be rounded to the nearest integer. Subscripting with scalar expressions may be used in any expression context (such as `generate`, `replace`, etc.). Subscripting with row and column names may only be used in a matrix expression context. This is really not a constraint; see the `rownumb()` and `colnumb()` functions discussed previously in the section titled *Matrix functions returning scalars*.

`matrix A[r,c]=`*exp* changes the *r,c* element of **A** to contain the result of the evaluated scalar expression, as defined in [U] **16 Functions and expressions**, and as further defined in *Matrix functions returning scalars*. *r* and *c* may be scalar expressions, and will be rounded to the nearest integer. The matrix **A** must already exist; the matrix function `J()` can be used to achieve this.

`matrix A[r,c]=`*mexp* places the matrix resulting from the *mexp* matrix expression into the already existing matrix **A** with the upper left corner of the *mexp* matrix located at the *r,c* element of **A**. If there is not enough room to place the *mexp* matrix at that location, a conformability error will be issued and the return code will be set to 503. *r* and *c* may be scalar expressions, and will be rounded to the nearest integer.

▷ Example

Continuing with our artificial but informative examples,

```
. matrix A = (1,2,3,4\5,6,7,8\9,10,11,12\13,14,15,16)

. matrix rownames A = mercury venus earth mars

. matrix colnames A = poor average good exc

. matrix list A

A[4,4]
              poor   average     good      exc
mercury          1         2        3        4
  venus          5         6        7        8
  earth          9        10       11       12
   mars         13        14       15       16

. matrix b = A[1,2..3]

. matrix list b

b[1,2]
           average      good
mercury          2         3
```

```
. matrix b = A[2...,1..3]

. matrix list b

b[3,3]
          poor   average    good
venus       5        6        7
earth       9       10       11
 mars      13       14       15

. matrix b = A["venus".."earth","average"...]

. matrix list b

b[2,3]
        average    good     exc
venus       6        7        8
earth      10       11       12

. matrix b = A["mars",2...]

. matrix list b

b[1,3]
        average    good     exc
mars       14       15       16

. matrix b = A[sqrt(9)+1..substr("xmars",2,4),2.8..2*2] /* strange but valid */

. mat list b

b[1,2]
        good     exc
mars     15       16

. matrix rownames A = eq1:alpha eq1:beta eq2:alpha eq2:beta

. matrix colnames A = eq1:one eq1:two eq2:one eq2:two

. matrix list A

A[4,4]
            eq1:   eq1:   eq2:   eq2:
            one    two    one    two
eq1:alpha     1      2      3      4
 eq1:beta     5      6      7      8
eq2:alpha     9     10     11     12
 eq2:beta    13     14     15     16

. matrix b = A["eq1:","eq2:"]

. matrix list b

b[2,2]
            eq2:   eq2:
            one    two
eq1:alpha     3      4
 eq1:beta     7      8

. matrix A[3,2] = sqrt(9)

. matrix list A

A[4,4]
            eq1:   eq1:   eq2:   eq2:
            one    two    one    two
eq1:alpha     1      2      3      4
 eq1:beta     5      6      7      8
eq2:alpha     9      3     11     12
 eq2:beta    13     14     15     16

. matrix X = (-3,0\-1,-6)

. matrix A[1,3] = X
```

```
. matrix list A
A[4,4]
             eq1:   eq1:   eq2:   eq2:
             one    two    one    two
  eq1:alpha    1      2     -3      0
   eq1:beta    5      6     -1     -6
  eq2:alpha    9      3     11     12
   eq2:beta   13     14     15     16
```

◁

❑ Technical Note

matrix A[i,j]=*exp* can be used to implement matrix formulas that perhaps Stata does not have built in. Let's pretend that Stata could not multiply matrices. We could still multiply matrices, and after some work, we could do so conveniently. Given two matrices, **A**: $a \times b$ and **B**: $b \times c$, the (i, j) element of **C** = **AB**, **C**: $a \times c$, is defined as

$$C_{ij} = \sum_{k=1}^{b} A_{ik} B_{kj}$$

Here is a Stata program to make that calculation:

```
program matmult                          // arguments A B C, creates C=A*B
        version 8.0
        args A B C                       // unload arguments into better names
        if colsof('A')!=rowsof('B') {    // check conformability
                error 503
        }
        local a = rowsof('A')            // obtain dimensioning information
        local b = colsof('A')            //     see Matrix functions returning
        local c = colsof('B')            //     scalars above
        matrix 'C' = J('a','c',0)        // create result containing 0s
        forvalues i = 1/'a' {
                forvalues 'j' = 1/'c' {
                        forvalues 'k' = 1/'b' {
                                matrix 'C'['i','j'] = 'C'['i','j'] + /*
                                */ 'A'['i','k']*'B'['k','j']
                        }
                }
        }
end
```

Now, if in some other program, we needed to multiply matrix XXI by Xy to form result beta, we could type matmult XXI Xy beta and never use Stata's built-in method for multiplying matrices (matrix beta=XXI*Xy). If we typed the program matmult into a file named matmult.ado, we would not even have to bother to load matmult before using it—it would be loaded automatically; see [U] **20 Ado-files**.

❑

Name conflicts in expressions (name spaces)

See [P] **matrix** for a description of name spaces. A matrix might have the same name as a variable in the dataset, and, if it does, Stata might appear confused when evaluating an expression (an *exp*). When the names conflict, Stata uses the rule that it always takes the data-variable interpretation. You can override this.

First, when working interactively, you can avoid the problem by simply naming your matrices differently from your variables.

Second, when writing programs, you can avoid name conflicts by obtaining names for matrices from `tempname`; see [P] **macro**.

Third, whether working interactively or writing programs, when using names that might conflict, you can use the `matrix()` pseudo-function to force Stata to take the matrix name interpretation.

`matrix(`*name*`)` says that *name* is to be interpreted as a matrix name. For instance, consider the statement `local new=trace(xx)`. This might work and it might not. If `xx` is a matrix and there is no variable named `xx` in your dataset, it will work. If there is also a numeric variable named `xx` in your dataset, it will not. Typing the statement will produce a type-mismatch error—Stata assumes when you type `xx` that you are referring to the data variable `xx` because there is a data variable `xx`. Typing `local new=trace(matrix(xx))` will produce the desired result in that case. When writing programs using matrix names not obtained from `tempname`, you are strongly advised to state explicitly that all matrix names are matrix names by using the `matrix()` function.

The only exception to this recommendation has to do with the construct $\mathbf{A}[i,j]$. The two subscripts key Stata that $\mathbf{A}$ must be a matrix name and not an attempt to subscript a variable, and so `matrix()` is not needed. This exception applies only to $\mathbf{A}[i,j]$; it does not apply to `el(`$\mathbf{A},i,j$`)`, which would be more safely written as `el(matrix(`$\mathbf{A}$`),`i,j`)`.

❑ Technical Note

The `matrix()` and `scalar()` pseudo-functions (see [P] **scalar**) are really the same function, but you do not need to understand this fine point to program Stata successfully. Understanding might, however, lead to producing more readable code. The formal definition is this:

`scalar(`*exp*`)` (and therefore `matrix(`*exp*`)`) evaluates *exp*, but restricts Stata to interpreting all names in *exp* as scalar or matrix names. Recall that scalars and matrices share the same name space.

Ergo, since `scalar()` and `matrix()` are the same function, you can type `trace(matrix(xx))` or `trace(scalar(xx))`: both do the same thing, even though the second looks wrong. Since `scalar()` and `matrix()` allow an *exp*, you could also type `scalar(trace(xx))` and achieve the same result. `scalar()` evaluates the *exp* inside the parentheses: it merely restricts how names are interpreted, so now `trace(xx)` clearly means the trace of the matrix named `xx`.

How can you make your code more readable? Pretend you wanted to calculate the trace plus the determinant of matrix `xx` and store it in the Stata scalar named `tpd` (no, there is no reason you would ever want to make such a silly calculation). You are writing a program, and want to protect yourself from `xx` also existing in the dataset. One solution would be

```
scalar tpd = trace(matrix(xx)) + det(matrix(xx))
```

Knowing the full interpretation rule, however, you realize you can shorten this to

```
scalar tpd = matrix(trace(xx) + det(xx))
```

and then, to make it more readable, you substitute `scalar()` for `matrix()`:

```
scalar tpd = scalar(trace(xx) + det(xx))
```

❑

Macro extended functions

The following macro extended functions (see [P] **macro**) are also defined:

rownames **A** and colnames **A** return the list of all the row or column subnames (with time-series operators if applicable) of **A**, separated by single blanks. Note that the equation names, even if present, are not included.

roweq **A** and coleq **A** return the list of all row equation names or column equation names of **A**, separated by single blanks, and with each name appearing however many times it appears in the matrix.

rowfullnames **A** and colfullnames **A** return the list of all the row or column names, including equation names of **A**, separated by single blanks.

▷ Example

These functions are provided as macro functions and standard expression functions because Stata's expression evaluator is limited to working with strings of no more than 80 characters in length, something not true of Stata's macro parser. A matrix with many rows or columns can produce an exceedingly long list of names.

In sophisticated programming situations, you sometimes want to process the matrices by row and column names rather than by row and column number. For instance, assume you are programming and have two matrices, xx and yy. You know that they contain the same column names, but they might be in a different order. You want to reorganize yy to be in the same order as xx. The following code fragment will create 'newyy' (a matrix name obtained from tempname) containing yy in the same order as xx:

```
tempname newyy newcol
local names : colfullnames(xx)
foreach name of local names {
        local j = colnumb(yy,"'name'")
        if 'j'>=. {
                display as error "column for 'name' not found"
                exit 111
        }
        matrix 'newcol' = yy[1...,'j']
        matrix 'newyy' = nullmat('newyy'),'newcol'
}
```

◁

References

Cox, N. J. 1999. dm69: Further new matrix commands. *Stata Technical Bulletin* 50: 5–9. Reprinted in *Stata Technical Bulletin Reprints*, vol. 9, pp. 29–34.

——. 2000. dm79: Yet more new matrix commands. *Stata Technical Bulletin* 56: 4–8.

Weesie, J. 1997. dm49: Some new matrix commands. *Stata Technical Bulletin* 39: 17–20. Reprinted in *Stata Technical Bulletin Reprints*, vol. 7, pp. 43–48.

Also See

Complementary:	[P] **macro**, [P] **matrix get**, [P] **matrix utility**, [P] **scalar**
Background:	[U] **16.3 Functions**,
	[U] **17 Matrix expressions**,
	[P] **matrix**

Title

Syntax

`matrix eigenvalues` r c = **A**

Description

Given an $n \times n$ nonsymmetric (real) matrix **A**, `matrix eigenvalues` returns the real part of the eigenvalues in the $1 \times n$ row vector **r** and the imaginary part of the eigenvalues in the $1 \times n$ row vector **c**. Thus, the jth eigenvalue is `r[1,j]` $+ i *$ `c[1,j]`.

The eigenvalues are sorted by their moduli; `r[1,1]` $+ i *$ `c[1,1]` has the largest modulus, and `r[1,n]` $+ i *$ `c[1,n]` has the smallest modulus.

If you want the eigenvalues for a symmetric matrix, see [P] **matrix symeigen**.

Remarks

Typing `matrix eigenvalues` r c = **A** for **A** $n \times n$ returns

$$\mathbf{r} = \left(r_1, r_2, \ldots, r_n \right)$$
$$\mathbf{c} = \left(c_1, c_2, \ldots, c_n \right)$$

where $\mathbf{r}_j$ is the real part and $\mathbf{c}_j$ the imaginary part of the jth eigenvalue. The eigenvalues are part of the solution to the problem

$$\mathbf{A}\mathbf{x}_j = \lambda_j \mathbf{x}_j$$

and, in particular,

$$\lambda_j = \mathbf{r}_j + i * \mathbf{c}_j$$

The corresponding eigenvectors $\mathbf{x}_j$ are not saved by `matrix eigenvalue`. The returned **r** and **c** are ordered so that $|\lambda_1| \geq |\lambda_2| \geq \cdots \geq |\lambda_n|$, where $|\lambda_j| = \sqrt{\mathbf{r}_j^2 + \mathbf{c}_j^2}$.

▷ Example

In time-series analysis, researchers frequently use eigenvalues to verify the stability of the fitted model.

Suppose that we have fitted a univariate time-series model and that the stability condition requires that the moduli of all the eigenvalues of a matrix **A** be less 1. (See Hamilton 1994 for a discussion of these models and conditions.)

First, let's look at the matrix **A**.

```
. mat list A
A[5,5]
               L.          L2.          L3.          L4.          L5.
            value        value        value        value        value
   y1     .66151492    .2551595    .35603325   -.15403902   -.12734386
   r1             1           0            0            0            0
   r2             0           1            0            0            0
   r3             0           0            1            0            0
   r4             0           0            0            1            0
```

Next, we use `matrix eigenvalues` to obtain the eigenvalues, which we will then list.

```
. matrix eigenvalues re im = A

. mat list re
re[1,5]
               L.          L2.          L3.          L4.          L5.
            value        value        value        value        value
   re     .99121823    .66060005   -.29686008   -.29686008   -.39658321

. mat list im
im[1,5]
               L.          L2.          L3.          L4.          L5.
            value        value        value        value        value
   im             0            0    .63423776   -.63423776            0
```

Finally, we compute and list the moduli, which are all less than 1, although the first is very close.

```
. forvalues i = 1/5 {
  2.         di sqrt(re[1,`i']^2 + im[1,`i']^2)
  3. }
.99121823
.66060005
.70027384
.70027384
.39658321
```

◁

Methods and Formulas

Stata's internal eigenvalue extraction routine for nonsymmetric matrices is based on the public domain LAPACK routine DGEEV. Anderson et al. (1999) provides an excellent introduction to these routines. Stata's internal routine also uses, with permission, **f2c** ©1990–1997 by AT&T, Lucent Technologies and Bellcore.

References

Anderson, E., et al. 1999. *LAPACK Users' Guide*. 3d ed. Philadelphia: Society for Industrial and Applied Mathematics.

Hamilton, J. 1994. *Time Series Analysis*. Princeton: Princeton University Press.

Also See

Related:	[P] **matrix symeigen**
Background:	[U] **17 Matrix expressions**,
	[P] **matrix**

Title

> **matrix get** — Access system matrices

Syntax

<u>matrix</u> [<u>define</u>] *matname* = get(*internal_Stata_matrix_name*)

where *internal_Stata_matrix_name* is

_b	coefficients after any estimation command
VCE	covariance matrix of estimators after any estimation command
Rr	constraint matrix after test
Cns	constraint matrix after any estimation command
Ld	factor loadings after factor or pca
L	rotated factor loadings after rotate
Ev	eigenvalues after factor or pca
Psi	uniquenesses after factor
Co	correlation matrix after factor or pca
SD	standard deviations after factor or pca
Mean	means after factor or pca

mat_put_rr *matname*

Description

The get() matrix function obtains a copy of an internal Stata system matrix. Some system matrices can also be obtained more easily by directly referring to the returned result after a command. In particular, the coefficient vector can be referred to as e(b) and the variance–covariance matrix of estimators as e(V) after an estimation command.

mat_put_rr is a programmer's command that posts *matname* as the internal **Rr** matrix. *matname* must have one more than the number of columns in the e(b) or e(V) matrices. The extra column contains the r vector and the earlier columns contain the **R** matrix for the Wald test

$$Rb = r$$

The matrix ... get(Rr) command provides a way to obtain the current **Rr** system matrix.

Remarks

get() obtains copies of matrices containing coefficients and the covariance matrix of the estimators after estimation commands (such as regress, probit, etc.) and obtains copies of matrices left behind by other Stata commands. The other side of get() is ereturn post, which allows ado-file estimation commands to post results to Stata's internal areas; see [P] **ereturn**.

▷ Example

After any model fitting command, the coefficients are available in _b and the variance–covariance matrix of the estimators in VCE.

```
. regress price weight mpg
```
(*output omitted*)

In this case we can directly use e(b) and e(V) to obtain the matrices.

```
. matrix list e(b)
e(b)[1,3]
          weight        mpg       _cons
y1    1.7465592  -49.512221   1946.0687
. matrix list e(V)
symmetric e(V)[3,3]
            weight         mpg        _cons
weight   .41133468
   mpg   44.601659    7422.863
 _cons  -2191.9032  -292759.82    12938766
```

We can also use the matrix get command to obtain these matrices.

```
. matrix b = get(_b)
. matrix V = get(VCE)
. matrix list b
b[1,3]
          weight        mpg       _cons
y1    1.7465592  -49.512221   1946.0687
. matrix list V
symmetric V[3,3]
            weight         mpg        _cons
weight   .41133468
   mpg   44.601659    7422.863
 _cons  -2191.9032  -292759.82    12938766
```

Note that the columns of b and both dimensions of V are properly labeled.

◁

▷ Example

After test, the restriction matrix is available in Rr. Having just estimated a regression of price on weight and mpg, we will run a test and then get the restriction matrix:

(*Continued on next page*)

```
. test weight=1, notest
( 1)  weight = 1.0
. test mpg=40, accum
( 1)  weight = 1.0
( 2)  mpg = 40.0
        F( 2,    71) =    6.29
            Prob > F =   0.0030
. matrix rxtr=get(Rr)
. matrix list rxtr
rxtr[2,4]
    c1  c2  c3  c4
r1   1   0   0   1
r2   0   1   0  40
```

◁

Also See

Background: [U] **16.5 Accessing coefficients and standard errors**,
[U] **17 Matrix expressions**,
[P] **matrix**

Title

> **matrix mkmat** — Convert variables to matrix and vice versa

Syntax

mkmat *varlist* [if *exp*] [in *range*] [, matrix(*matname*) nomissing]

svmat [*type*] **A** [, names(col | eqcol | matcol | *string*)]

matname **A** *namelist* [, rows(*range*) columns(*range*) explicit]

where **A** is the name of an existing matrix, *type* is a storage type for the new variables, and *namelist* is one of (1) a *varlist*, i.e., names of existing variables possibly abbreviated; (2) _cons and the names of existing variables possibly abbreviated; or (3) arbitrary names when the explicit option is specified.

Description

mkmat stores the variables listed in *varlist* in column vectors of the same name; that is, $N \times 1$ matrices, where $N = $ _N, the number of observations in the dataset. Optionally, they can be stored as a $N \times k$ matrix, where k is the number of variables in *varlist*.

svmat takes a matrix and stores its columns as new variables. It is the reverse of the mkmat command, which creates a matrix from existing variables.

matname renames the rows and columns of a matrix. matname differs from the matrix rownames and matrix colnames commands in that matname expands varlist abbreviations and also allows a restricted range for the rows or columns. See [P] **matrix rowname**.

Options

matrix() requests that the vectors be combined in a matrix, instead of creating the column vectors.

nomissing specifies that observations with missing values are excluded.

names(col | eqcol | matcol | *string*) specifies how the new variables are to be named.
  names(col) uses the column names of the matrix to name the variables.
  names(eqcol) uses the equation names prefixed to the column names.
  names(matcol) uses the matrix name prefixed to the column names.
  names(*string*) names the variables *string*1, *string*2, ..., *string*n, where *string* is a user-specified *string* and *n* is the number of columns of the matrix.
  If names() is not specified, the variables are named **A**1, **A**2, ..., **A**n, where **A** is the name of the matrix.

(Continued on next page)

288

rows(*range*) and columns(*range*) specify the rows and columns of the matrix to rename. The number of rows or columns specified must be equal to the number of names in *namelist*. If both rows() and columns() are given, then the specified rows are named *namelist* and the specified columns are also named *namelist*. The range must be given in one of the following forms:

rows(.)   renames all the rows;
rows(2..8)   renames rows 2 through 8;
rows(3)   renames only row 3; and
rows(4...)   renames row 4 to the last row.

If neither rows() nor columns() is given, then rows(.) columns(.) is the default. That is, the matrix must be square, and both the rows and the columns are named *namelist*.

explicit suppresses the expansion of varlist abbreviations and omits the verification that the names are those of existing variables. That is, the names in *namelist* are used explicitly, and can be any valid row or column names.

Remarks

mkmat

Although cross-products of variables can be loaded into a matrix using the matrix accum command, in some instances, programmers may find it more convenient to work with the variables in their datasets as vectors instead of as cross products. mkmat allows the user a simple way to load specific variables into matrices in Stata's memory.

▷ Example

mkmat uses the variable name to name the single column in the vector. This feature guarantees that the variable name will be carried along in any additional matrix calculations. This feature is also useful when vectors are combined in a general matrix.

```
. describe
Contains data from test.dta
  obs:            10
  vars:            3                      19 Jul 2000 11:24
  size:          160 (99.9% of memory free)

              storage  display    value
variable name   type   format     label      variable label

x             float   %9.0g
y             float   %9.0g
z             float   %9.0g

Sorted by:
```

```
. list
```

	x	y	z
1.	1	10	2
2.	2	9	4
3.	3	8	3
4.	4	7	5
5.	5	6	7
6.	6	5	6
7.	7	4	8
8.	8	3	10
9.	9	2	1
10.	10	1	9

```
. mkmat x y z, matrix(xyzmat)

. matrix list xyzmat

xyzmat[10,3]
        x    y    z
  r1    1   10    2
  r2    2    9    4
  r3    3    8    3
  r4    4    7    5
  r5    5    6    7
  r6    6    5    6
  r7    7    4    8
  r8    8    3   10
  r9    9    2    1
 r10   10    1    9
```

If the variables contain missing values, so will the corresponding matrix or matrices. Many matrix commands, for instance, the matrix inversion functions `inv` and `syminv`, do not allow missing values in matrices. By specifying the option `nomissing`, `mkmat` will exclude observations with missing values, so that subsequent matrix computations will not be hampered by missing values. Listwise deletion parallels missing value handling in most Stata commands.

◁

❏ Technical Note

`mkmat` provides a useful addition to Stata's matrix commands, but it will work only with small datasets.

Stata limits matrices to being no more than matsize × matsize, which, by default, means 40×40, and, even with Intercooled Stata, this can be increased to a maximum of 800×800. In Stata/SE, these limits are much higher. Such limits appear to contradict Stata's claims of being able to process large datasets. By limiting Stata's matrix capabilities to matsize × matsize, has not Stata's matrix language itself been limited to datasets no larger than matsize? It would certainly appear so; in the simple matrix calculation for regression coefficients $(\mathbf{X}'\mathbf{X})^{-1}\mathbf{X}'\mathbf{y}$, $\mathbf{X}$ is an $n \times k$ matrix (n being the number of observations and k the number of variables) and, given the matsize constraint, n must certainly be less than 800 (or up to 11,000 in Stata/SE).

Our answer is as follows: Yes, $\mathbf{X}$ is limited in the way stated, but note that $\mathbf{X}'\mathbf{X}$ is a mere $k \times k$ matrix, and, similarly, $\mathbf{X}'\mathbf{y}$ only $k \times 1$. Both these matrices are well within Stata's matrix-handling capabilities, and Stata's `matrix accum` command (see [P] **matrix accum**) can directly create both of them.

Moreover, even if Stata could hold the $n \times k$ matrix $\mathbf{X}$, it would still be more efficient to use matrix accum to form $\mathbf{X}'\mathbf{X}$. $\mathbf{X}'\mathbf{X}$, interpreted literally, says to load a copy of the dataset, transpose it, load a second copy of the dataset, and then form the matrix product. Thus, two copies of the dataset occupy memory, in addition to the original copy Stata already had available (and from which matrix accum could directly form the result with no additional memory use). For small n, the inefficiency is not important, but, for large n, the inefficiency could make the calculation infeasible. For instance, with $n = 12{,}000$ and $k = 6$, the additional memory use is 1,125K bytes.

More generally, matrices in statistical applications tend to have dimension $k \times k$, $n \times k$, and $n \times n$, with k small and n large. Terms dealing with the data are of the generic form $\mathbf{X}'_{k_1 \times n} \mathbf{W}_{n \times n} \mathbf{Z}_{n \times k_2}$. ($\mathbf{X}'\mathbf{X}$ fits the generic form with $\mathbf{X} = \mathbf{X}$, $\mathbf{W} = \mathbf{I}$, and $\mathbf{Z} = \mathbf{X}$.) Matrix programming languages are not capable of dealing with the deceivingly simple calculation $\mathbf{X}'\mathbf{W}\mathbf{Z}$ because of the staggering size of the $\mathbf{W}$ matrix. For $n = 12{,}000$, storing $\mathbf{W}$ requires a little more than a gigabyte of memory. In statistical formulas, however, $\mathbf{W}$ is given by formula, and, in fact, never needs to be stored in its entirety. Exploitation of this fact is all that is needed to resurrect the use of a matrix programming language in statistical applications. Matrix programming languages may be inefficient because of copious memory use, but in statistical applications, the inefficiency is minor for matrices of size $k \times k$ or smaller. Our design of the various matrix accum commands allow calculating terms of the form $\mathbf{X}'\mathbf{W}\mathbf{Z}$, and this one feature is all that is necessary to allow efficient and robust use of matrix languages.

Programs for creating data matrices such as that offered by mkmat are useful for pedagogical purposes, and for a specific application where Stata's matsize constraint is not binding, it seems so natural. On the other hand, it is important that general tools not be implemented by forming data matrices because such tools will be drastically limited in terms of the dataset size. Coding the problem in terms of the various matrix accum commands (see [P] **matrix accum**) is admittedly more tedious, but, by abolishing data matrices from your programs, you will produce tools suitable for use on large datasets.

❑

svmat

▷ Example

Let us get the vector of coefficients from a regression and use svmat to save the vector as a new variable, save the dataset, load the dataset back into memory, use mkmat to create a vector from the variable, and finally, use matname to rename the columns of the row vector.

```
. quietly regress mpg weight gear_ratio foreign
. matrix b = e(b)
. matrix list b

b[1,4]
        weight   gear_ratio      foreign       _cons
y1  -.00613903    1.4571134   -2.2216815   36.101353

. matrix c = b'
. svmat double c, name(bvector)
```

```
. list bvector1 in 1/5

     |  bvector1  |
     |------------|
  1. | -.00613903 |
  2. |  1.4571134 |
  3. | -2.2216815 |
  4. |  36.101353 |
  5. |      .     |

. save example
file example.dta saved

. use example

. mkmat bvector1 if bvector1< .

. matrix list bvector1
bvector1[4,1]
      bvector1
r1  -.00613903
r2   1.4571134
r3  -2.2216815
r4   36.101353

. matrix d = bvector1'

. matname d wei gear for _cons, c(.)

. matrix list d
d[1,4]
              weight    gear_ratio     foreign      _cons
bvector1  -.00613903    1.4571134   -2.2216815   36.101353
```

◁

Methods and Formulas

mkmat, svmat, and matname are implemented as ado-files.

Acknowledgment

mkmat was written by Ken Heinecke of CIMCO, Madison, Wisconsin.

References

Gould, W. W. 1994. ip6.1: Data and matrices. *Stata Technical Bulletin* 20: 10. Reprinted in *Stata Technical Bulletin Reprints*, vol. 4, pp. 70–71.

Heinecke, K. 1994. ip6: Storing variables in vectors and matrices. *Stata Technical Bulletin* 20: 8–9. Reprinted in *Stata Technical Bulletin Reprints*, vol. 4, pp. 68–70.

Sribney, W. M. 1995. ip6.2: Storing matrices as variables. *Stata Technical Bulletin* 24: 9–10. Reprinted in *Stata Technical Bulletin Reprints*, vol. 4, pp. 71–73.

Also See

Related:	[P] **matrix accum**
Background:	[U] **17 Matrix expressions,**
	[P] **matrix**

Title

> **matrix rowname** — Name rows and columns

Syntax

<u>matrix</u> <u>rown</u>ames **A** = *name(s)*

<u>matrix</u> <u>coln</u>ames **A** = *name(s)*

<u>matrix</u> <u>roweq</u> **A** = *name(s)*

<u>matrix</u> <u>coleq</u> **A** = *name(s)*

Description

`matrix rownames` and `colnames` reset the row and column names of an already existing matrix. Row and column names may have three parts: *equation_name:ts_operator.subname*. Here, *name* can be *subname*, *ts_operator.subname*, *equation_name:*, *equation_name:subname*, or *equation_name:ts_operator.subname*.

`matrix roweq` and `coleq` also reset the row and column names of an already existing matrix, but, if a simple name is specified (a name without a colon), it is interpreted as an equation name.

In either case, the part of the name not specified is left unchanged.

Remarks

See [U] **17.2 Row and column names** for a description of the row and column names bordering a matrix.

▷ Example

In general, the names bordering matrices are set correctly by Stata due to the tracking of the matrix algebra, and you will not need to reset them. Nevertheless, imagine that you have formed $X'X$ in the matrix named XX and that it corresponds to the underlying variables price, weight, and mpg:

```
. matrix list XX
symmetric XX[3,3]
            c1          c2          c3
r1   3.448e+09
r2   1.468e+09   7.188e+08
r3     9132716     4493720       36008
```

You did not form this matrix with `matrix accum` because, had you done so, the rows and columns would already be correctly named. However you formed it, you now want to reset the names:

```
. matrix rownames XX = price weight mpg

. matrix colnames XX = price weight mpg

. matrix list XX

symmetric XX[3,3]
              price       weight         mpg
 price    3.448e+09
weight    1.468e+09    7.188e+08
   mpg     9132716       4493720       36008
```

◁

▷ Example

We now demonstrate setting the equation names, time-series operator, and subnames.

```
. matrix list AA

symmetric AA[4,4]
            c1           c2          c3          c4
r1    .2967663
r2    .03682017   .57644416
r3   -.87052852   .32713601   20.274957
r4   -1.572579   -.63830843  -12.150097   26.099582

. matrix rownames AA = length L3D2.length mpg L.mpg

. matrix colnames AA = length L3D2.length mpg L.mpg

. matrix roweq AA = eq1 eq1 eq2 eq2

. matrix coleq AA = eq1 eq1 eq2 eq2

. matrix list AA

symmetric AA[4,4]
                        eq1:         eq1:        eq2:        eq2:
                                    L3D2.                     L.
                      length       length         mpg         mpg
    eq1:length      .2967663
eq1:L3D2.length      .03682017   .57644416
      eq2:mpg       -.87052852   .32713601   20.274957
      eq2:L.mpg     -1.572579   -.63830843  -12.150097   26.099582
```

◁

❏ Technical Note

`matrix rownames` and `colnames` sometimes behave in surprising ways. Among the surprises are

1. If your list of names includes no colons—does not mention the equation names—whatever equation names are in place are left in place; they are not changed.

2. If your list of names has every name ending in a colon—so that it mentions only the equation names and not the subnames—whatever subnames are in place are left in place; they are not changed.

3. If your list of names has fewer names than are required to label all the rows or columns, the last name in the list is replicated. (If you specify too many names, you will get the conformability error message, and no names will be changed.)

These surprises have their uses, but, if you make a mistake, the result really may surprise you. For instance, rule 3, by itself, is just odd. Combined with rule 2, however, rule 3 allows you to set all the equation names in a matrix easily. If you type 'matrix rownames XX = myeq:', all the equation names in the row are reset while the subnames are left unchanged:

```
. matrix rownames XX = myeq:
. matrix list XX
symmetric XX[3,3]
                    price        weight           mpg
  myeq:price    3.448e+09
 myeq:weight    1.468e+09    7.188e+08
    myeq:mpg      9132716      4493720         36008
```

Setting equation names is often done before forming a partitioned matrix so that, when the components are assembled, each has the correct equation name.

Thus, to review, to get the result above, we could have typed

```
. matrix rownames XX = myeq:price myeq:weight myeq:mpg
```

or

```
. matrix rownames XX = price weight mpg
. matrix rownames XX = myeq:
```

or even

```
. matrix rownames XX = myeq:
. matrix rownames XX = price weight mpg
```

All would have resulted in the same outcome. The real surprise comes, however, when you make a mistake:

```
. matrix rownames XX = myeq:
. matrix rownames XX = price weight
. matrix list XX
symmetric XX[3,3]
                    price        weight           mpg
  myeq:price    3.448e+09
 myeq:weight    1.468e+09    7.188e+08
 myeq:weight      9132716      4493720         36008
```

Our mistake above is that we listed only two names for the subnames of the rows of XX and `matrix rownames` and then labeled both of the last rows with the subname `weight`.

❑

❑ Technical Note

The equation name _: by itself is special; it means the null equation name. For instance, as of the last technical note, we were left with

```
. matrix list XX
symmetric XX[3,3]
                    price        weight           mpg
  myeq:price    3.448e+09
 myeq:weight    1.468e+09    7.188e+08
 myeq:weight      9132716      4493720         36008
```

Let's fix it:

```
. matrix rownames XX = price weight mpg

. matrix rownames XX = _:

. matrix list XX

symmetric XX[3,3]
              price       weight        mpg
  price   3.448e+09
 weight   1.468e+09    7.188e+08
    mpg     9132716      4493720      36008
```

❑

❑ Technical Note

`matrix roweq` and `coleq` are really the same commands as `matrix rownames` and `colnames`. They differ in only one respect: If a specified name does not contain a colon, `roweq` and `coleq` interpret that name as if it did end in a colon.

`matrix rownames`, `colnames`, `roweq`, and `coleq` are often used in conjunction with the `rowfullnames`, `colfullnames`, `rownames`, `colnames`, `roweq`, and `coleq` macro extended functions introduced in [P] **matrix define**. It is important to remember that the `rownames` and `colnames` extended macro functions return only the subname and, if present, the time-series operator:

```
. matrix list AA

symmetric AA[4,4]
                         eq1:        eq1:       eq2:        eq2:
                                    L3D2.                    L.
                       length      length        mpg         mpg
    eq1:length      .2967663
eq1:L3D2.length      .03682017   .57644416
       eq2:mpg     -.87052852    .32713601  20.274957
     eq2:L.mpg     -1.572579    -.63830843  -12.150097   26.099582

. local rsubs : rownames AA

. display "The row subnames of AA are -- `rsubs' --"
The row subnames of AA are -- length L3D2.length mpg L.mpg --
```

Similarly, the `roweq` extended macro function returns only the equation names without the trailing colon:

```
. local reqs : roweq AA

. display "The row equations of AA are -- `reqs' --"
The row equations of AA are -- eq1 eq1 eq2 eq2 --
```

Thus, now consider the problem that you have two matrices named A and B that have the same number of rows. A is correctly labeled and includes equation names. You want to copy the names of A to B. You might be tempted to type

```
. local names : rownames A

. matrix rownames B = `names'
```

This is not adequate. You will have copied the subnames but not the equation names. To copy both parts of the names, you can type

```
. local subs : rownames A

. local eqs : roweq A

. matrix rownames B = `subs'

. matrix roweq B = `eqs'
```

This method can be used even when there might not be equation names. The equation name _ is special; not only does setting an equation to that name remove the equation name, but, when there is no equation name, the `roweq` and `coleq` macro extended functions return that name.

A better way to copy the names is to use the `rowfullnames` and `colfullnames` extended macro functions (see [P] **matrix define** and [P] **macro**). You can more compactly type

```
. local rname : rowfullnames A
. matrix rownames B = 'rname'
```

❏

Also See

Complementary:	[P] **macro**, [P] **matrix define**
Background:	[U] **17 Matrix expressions**, [P] **matrix**

Title

matrix score — Score data from coefficient vectors

Syntax

<u>mat</u>rix <u>sco</u>re [*type*] *newvar* = **b** [if *exp*] [in *range*]

[, [<u>eq</u>uation(*##*) | <u>eq</u>uation(*eqname*)] <u>mi</u>ssval(*#*) replace forcezero]

where **b** is a $1 \times p$ matrix.

Description

matrix score creates $newvar_j = x_j b'$ (**b** a row vector), where x_j is the row vector of values of the variables specified by the column names of **b**. The name _cons is treated as a variable equal to 1.

Options

equation(*##*) or equation(*eqname*) specify the equation—by either number or name—for selecting coefficients from **b** to use in scoring. See [U] **17.2 Row and column names** and [P] **matrix rowname** for more on equation labels with matrices.

missval(*#*) specifies the value to be assumed if any values are missing from the variables referenced by the coefficient vector. By default, this value is taken to be missing (.), and any missing value among the variables produces a missing score.

replace specifies that *newvar* already exists. In this case, observations not included by if *exp* and in range are left unchanged; that is, they are not changed to missing. Be warned that replace does not promote the storage type of the existing variable; if the variable was stored as an int, the calculated scores would be truncated to integers when stored.

forcezero specifies that, should a variable described by the column names of *b* not exist, the calculation treats the missing variable as if it did exist and was equal to zero for all observations. In other words, it contributes nothing to the summation. By default, a missing variable would produce an error message.

Remarks

Scoring refers to forming linear combinations of variables in the data with respect to a coefficient vector. For instance, consider the vector coefs:

```
. matrix list coefs

coefs[1,3]
          weight          mpg        _cons
y1     1.7465592   -49.512221    1946.0687
```

298

Scoring the data with this vector would create a new variable equal to the linear combination:

$$1.7465592\,\text{weight} - 49.512221\,\text{mpg} + 1946.0687$$

The vector is interpreted as coefficients; the corresponding names of the variables are obtained from the column names (row names if `coefs` were a column vector). To form this linear combination, we type

```
. matrix score lc = coefs

. summarize lc
```

Variable	Obs	Mean	Std. Dev.	Min	Max
lc	74	6165.257	1597.606	3406.46	9805.269

If the coefficient vector has equation names, `matrix score` with the `eq()` option selects the appropriate coefficients for scoring. `eq(#1)` is assumed if no `eq()` option is specified.

```
. matrix list coefs
coefs[1,5]
        price:     price:     price:     displ:     displ:
        weight        mpg      _cons     weight      _cons
y1   1.7358275  -51.298249  2016.5101  .10574552  -121.99702
. matrix score lcnoeq = coefs

. matrix score lca = coefs, eq(price)

. matrix score lc1 = coefs, eq(#1)

. matrix score lcb = coefs, eq(displ)

. matrix score lc2 = coefs, eq(#2)

. summarize lcnoeq lca lc1 lcb lc2
```

Variable	Obs	Mean	Std. Dev.	Min	Max
lcnoeq	74	6165.257	1598.264	3396.859	9802.336
lca	74	6165.257	1598.264	3396.859	9802.336
lc1	74	6165.257	1598.264	3396.859	9802.336
lcb	74	197.2973	82.18474	64.1151	389.8113
lc2	74	197.2973	82.18474	64.1151	389.8113

❏ Technical Note

If the same equation name is scattered in different sections of the coefficient vector, the results may not be what you expect.

```
. matrix list bad
bad[1,5]
        price:     price:     displ:     price:     displ:
        weight        mpg     weight      _cons      _cons
y1   1.7358275  -51.298249  .10574552  2016.5101  -121.99702
. matrix score badnoeq = bad

. matrix score bada = bad, eq(price)

. matrix score bad1 = bad, eq(#1)

. matrix score badb = bad, eq(displ)

. matrix score bad2 = bad, eq(#2)

. matrix score bad3 = bad, eq(#3)

. matrix score bad4 = bad, eq(#4)
```

```
. summarize bad*
    Variable |     Obs       Mean    Std. Dev.       Min        Max
-------------+--------------------------------------------------------
     badnoeq |      74   4148.747    1598.264   1380.349   7785.826
        bada |      74   4148.747    1598.264   1380.349   7785.826
        bad1 |      74   4148.747    1598.264   1380.349   7785.826
        badb |      74   319.2943    82.18474   186.1121   511.8083
        bad2 |      74   319.2943    82.18474   186.1121   511.8083
        bad3 |      74    2016.51           0    2016.51    2016.51
        bad4 |      74   -121.997           0   -121.997   -121.997
```

Coefficient vectors created by Stata estimation commands will have equation names together.

❏

Also See

Background: [U] **17 Matrix expressions,**

                        [P] **matrix**

Title

matrix svd — Singular value decomposition

Syntax

<u>mat</u>rix svd **U** w **V** = **A**

where **U**, **w**, and **V** are matrix names (the matrices may exist or not) and **A** is the name of an existing $m \times n, m \geq n$ matrix.

Description

The svd matrix command produces the singular value decomposition (SVD) of **A**.

Remarks

The singular value decomposition of $m \times n$ matrix **A**, $m \geq n$, is defined as

$$\mathbf{A} = \mathbf{U} \operatorname{diag}(\mathbf{w}) \mathbf{V}'$$

U: $m \times n$, **w**: $1 \times n$ ($\operatorname{diag}(\mathbf{w})$: $n \times n$), and **V**: $n \times n$, where **U** is column orthogonal ($\mathbf{U}'\mathbf{U} = \mathbf{I}$ if $m = n$), all the elements of **w** are positive or zero, and $\mathbf{V}'\mathbf{V} = \mathbf{I}$.

Singular value decomposition can be used to obtain a g2-inverse of **A** ($\mathbf{A}^*$: $n \times m$, such that $\mathbf{A}\mathbf{A}^*\mathbf{A} = \mathbf{A}$ and $\mathbf{A}^*\mathbf{A}\mathbf{A}^* = \mathbf{A}^*$—the first two Moore–Penrose conditions) via $\mathbf{A}^* = \mathbf{V}\{\operatorname{diag}(1/w_j)\}\mathbf{U}'$, where $1/w_j$ refers to individually taking the reciprocal of the elements of **w** and substituting 0 if $w_j = 0$ or is small. If **A** is square and of full rank, $\mathbf{A}^* = \mathbf{A}^{-1}$.

▷ Example

Singular value decomposition is used to obtain accurate inverses of nearly singular matrices and to obtain g2-inverses of matrices that are singular, to construct orthonormal bases, and to develop approximation matrices. Our example will prove that **matrix svd** works:

```
. matrix A = (1,2,9\2,7,5\2,4,18)

. matrix svd U w V = A

. matrix list U
U[3,3]
            c1          c2          c3
r1  -.42313293    .89442719   -.1447706
r2   -.3237169   -6.016e-17   .94615399
r3  -.84626585   -.4472136   -.2895412

. matrix list w
w[1,3]
            c1          c2          c3
r1   21.832726   2.612e-16   5.5975071
```

```
. matrix list V

V[3,3]
            c1           c2           c3
c1  -.12655765   -.96974658     .2087456
c2  -.29759672    .23786237    .92458514
c3  -.94626601    .05489132   -.31869671

. matrix newA = U*diag(w)*V'

. matrix list newA

newA[3,3]
     c1  c2  c3
r1    1   2   9
r2    2   7   5
r3    2   4  18
```

As claimed, **newA** is equal to our original **A**.

The g2-inverse of **A** is computed below. The second element of **w** is small, so we decide to set the corresponding element of $\text{diag}(1/w_j)$ to zero. We then show that the resulting **Ainv** matrix has the properties of a g2-inverse for **A**.

```
. matrix Winv = J(3,3,0)

. matrix Winv[1,1] = 1/w[1,1]

. matrix Winv[3,3] = 1/w[1,3]

. matrix Ainv = V*Winv*U'

. matrix list Ainv

Ainv[3,3]
            r1           r2           r3
c1   -.0029461    .03716103    -.0058922
c2   -.0181453    .16069635   -.03629059
c3    .02658185   -.0398393    .05316371

. matrix AAiA = A*Ainv*A

. matrix list AAiA

AAiA[3,3]
     c1  c2  c3
r1    1   2   9
r2    2   7   5
r3    2   4  18

. matrix AiAAi = Ainv*A*Ainv

. matrix list AiAAi

AiAAi[3,3]
            r1           r2           r3
c1   -.0029461    .03716103    -.0058922
c2   -.0181453    .16069635   -.03629059
c3    .02658185   -.0398393    .05316371
```

◁

Also See

Complementary:	[P] **matrix define**
Background:	[U] **17 Matrix expressions**,
	[P] **matrix**

Title

> **matrix symeigen** — Eigenvalues and eigenvectors of symmetric matrices

Syntax

<u>mat</u>rix <u>sym</u>eigen **X** **v** = **A**

Description

Given an $n \times n$ symmetric matrix **A**, `matrix symeigen` returns the eigenvectors in the columns of **X**: $n \times n$ and the corresponding eigenvalues in **v**: $1 \times n$. The eigenvalues are sorted; **v**[1,1] contains the largest eigenvalue (and **X**[1...,1] its corresponding eigenvector) and **v**[1,n] contains the smallest eigenvalue (and **X**[1...,n] its corresponding eigenvector).

If you want the eigenvalues for a nonsymmetric matrix, see [P] **matrix eigenvalues**.

Remarks

Typing `matrix symeigen` **X** **v** = **A** for **A** $n \times n$ returns

$$\mathbf{v} = \left(\lambda_1, \lambda_2, \ldots, \lambda_n \right)$$

$$\mathbf{X} = \left(\mathbf{x}_1, \mathbf{x}_2, \ldots, \mathbf{x}_n \right)$$

where $\lambda_1 \geq \lambda_2 \geq \ldots \geq \lambda_n$. Each $\mathbf{x}_i$ and λ_i is a solution to

$$\mathbf{A}\mathbf{x}_i = \lambda_i \mathbf{x}_i$$

or, more compactly,

$$\mathbf{A}\mathbf{X} = \mathbf{X} \operatorname{diag}(\mathbf{v})$$

▷ Example

Eigenvalues and eigenvectors have many uses. We will demonstrate that `symeigen` returns matrices meeting the definition:

```
. matrix list A
symmetric A[3,3]
              weight         mpg        length
weight      44094178
   mpg    -264948.11   2443.4595
length     1195077.3  -7483.5135    36192.662
. matrix symeigen X lambda = A
. matrix list lambda
lambda[1,3]
             e1          e2          e3
r1     44128163   3830.4869   820.73955
. matrix list X
X[3,3]
                   e1          e2          e3
weight      .99961482  -.02756261   .00324179
   mpg     -.00600667   -.1008305   .99488549
length      .02709477   .99452175   .10095722
```

303

```
. matrix AX = A*X

. matrix XLambda = X*diag(lambda)

. matrix list AX

AX[3,3]
                e1          e2          e3
weight    44111166   -105.57823   2.6606641
   mpg    -265063.5   -386.22991   816.54187
length   1195642.6    3809.5025   82.859585

. matrix list XLambda

XLambda[3,3]
                e1          e2          e3
weight    44111166   -105.57823   2.6606641
   mpg    -265063.5   -386.22991   816.54187
length   1195642.6    3809.5025   82.859585
```

◁

Methods and Formulas

Stata's internal eigenvalue and eigenvector extraction routines are translations of the public domain EISPACK routines, Smith et al. (1976), which are in turn based on Wilkinson and Reinsch (1971). EISPACK was developed under contract for the Office of Scientific and Technical Information, U.S. Department of Energy, by Argonne National Laboratory and supported by funds provided by the Nuclear Regulatory Commission. Stata's use of these routines is by permission of the National Energy Software Center of the Argonne National Laboratory. A brief but excellent introduction to the techniques employed by these routines can be found in Press et al. (1992, 456–495).

References

Press, W. H., S. A. Teukolsky, W. T. Vetterling, and B. P. Flannery. 1992. *Numerical Recipes in C: The Art of Scientific Computing*. 2d ed. Cambridge University Press.

Smith, B. T., et al. 1976. *Matrix Eigen System Routines—EISPACK Guide*. 2d ed. vol. 6 of Lecture Notes in Computer Science. New York: Springer.

Wilkinson, J. H. and C. Reinsch. 1971. *Linear Algebra*, vol. 2 of *Handbook for Automatic Computation*. New York: Springer.

Also See

Related: [P] **matrix eigenvalues**

Background: [U] **17 Matrix expressions**,
                   [P] **matrix**

Title

> **matrix utility** — List, rename, and drop matrices

Syntax

<u>mat</u>rix <u>d</u>ir

<u>mat</u>rix <u>list</u> *mname* $\Big[$, <u>nobl</u>ank <u>noha</u>lf <u>noh</u>eader <u>nona</u>mes <u>f</u>ormat(%*fmt*)

   <u>t</u>itle(*string*) nodotz $\Big]$

<u>mat</u>rix <u>ren</u>ame *oldname newname*

<u>mat</u>rix drop $\big\{$ _all | *mname(s)* $\big\}$

Description

matrix dir lists the names of currently existing matrices. **matrix list** lists the contents of a matrix. **matrix rename** changes the name of a matrix. **matrix drop** eliminates a matrix.

Options

noblank suppresses printing a blank line before printing the matrix. This is useful in programs.

nohalf specifies that, even if the matrix is symmetric, the full matrix is to be printed. The default is to print only the lower triangle in such cases.

noheader suppresses the display of the matrix name and dimension before the matrix itself. This is useful in programs.

nonames suppresses the display of the bordering names around the matrix.

format(%*fmt*) specifies the format to be used to display the individual elements of the matrix. The default is **format(%10.0g)**.

title(*string*) adds the specified title *string* to the header displayed before the matrix itself. If **noheader** is specified, **title()** does nothing because displaying the header is suppressed.

nodotz specifies that .z missing values should be displayed as blanks.

Remarks

▷ Example

Little needs to be said by way of introduction. In the example below, however, note that **matrix list** normally displays only the lower half of symmetric matrices. **nohalf** prevents this.

```
. matrix dir
            a[2,2]
            b[3,3]
. matrix rename a z
```

```
. matrix dir
            z[2,2]
            b[3,3]
. matrix list b

symmetric b[3,3]
       c1  c2  c3
r1    2
r2    5   8
r3    4   6   3
. matrix list b, nohalf

symmetric b[3,3]
       c1  c2  c3
r1    2   5   4
r2    5   8   6
r3    4   6   3
. matrix drop b
. matrix dir
            z[2,2]
. matrix drop _all
. matrix dir
```
◁

❏ Technical Note

When writing programs and using matrix names obtained through `tempname` (see [P] **macro**), it is not necessary to explicitly drop matrices; the matrices are removed automatically at the conclusion of the program.

```
. program example
   1.          tempname a
   2.          matrix 'a' = (1,2\3,4)              // this is temporary
   3.          matrix b = (5,6\7,8)                // and this permanent
   4.          display "The temporary matrix a contains"
   5.          matrix list 'a', noheader
   6. end
. example
The temporary matrix a contains
       c1  c2
r1    1   2
r2    3   4
. matrix dir
            b[2,2]
```

Nevertheless, dropping matrices with temporary names in programs when they are no longer needed is recommended unless the program is about to exit (when they will be dropped anyway). Matrices consume memory; dropping them frees memory.

❏

Also See

Background: [U] **17 Matrix expressions**,
                   [P] **matrix**

Title

> **more** — Pause until key is pressed

Syntax

<u>more</u>

Description

more causes Stata to display —more— and pause until any key is pressed if more is set on and does nothing if more is set off.

The current value of set more is stored in c(more); see [P] **creturn**.

See [R] **more** for information on set more on and set more off.

Remarks

Ado-file programmers need take no special action to have —more— conditions arise when the screen is full. Stata handles that automatically.

If, however, you wish to force a —more— condition early, you can include the more command in your program. The syntax of more is

more

more takes no arguments.

Also See

Complementary: [R] **query**

Background: [U] **10** —more— **conditions**

Title

numlist — Parse numeric lists

Syntax

numlist *"numlist"* $\big[$, <u>as</u>cending <u>desc</u>ending <u>int</u>eger <u>miss</u>ingokay min(*#*) max(*#*)

<u>r</u>ange(*operator #* $\big[$*operator #*$\big]$) sort $\big]$

where *operator* is   < | <= | > | >=

there is no space between *operator* and *#*

and where *numlist* consists of one or more *numlist_elements* shown below.

numlist_element	Example	Expands to	Definition
#	3.82	3.82	a number
.	.	.	a missing value
$\#_1/\#_2$	4/6 2.3/5.7	4 5 6 2.3 3.3 4.3 5.3	starting at $\#_1$ increment by 1 to $\#_2$
$\#_1(\#_2)\#_3$	2(3)10 4.8(2.1)9.9	2 5 8 4.8 6.9 9	starting at $\#_1$ increment by $\#_2$ to $\#_3$
$\#_1[\#_2]\#_3$	2[3]10 4.8[2.1]9.9	2 5 8 4.8 6.9 9	starting at $\#_1$ increment by $\#_2$ to $\#_3$
$\#_1 \ \#_2 : \#_3$	5 7:13 1.1 2.4:5.8	5 7 9 11 13 1.1 2.4 3.7 5	starting at $\#_1$ increment by $(\#_2 - \#_1)$ to $\#_3$
$\#_1 \ \#_2$ to $\#_3$	5 7 to 13 1.1 2.4 to 5.8	same	same

Description

The `numlist` command expands the numeric list supplied as a string argument and performs error checking based on the options specified. Any numeric sequence operators in the *numlist* string are evaluated, and the expanded list of numbers is returned in r(numlist). See [U] **14.1.8 numlist** for a discussion of numeric lists.

Options

ascending indicates that the user must give the numeric list in ascending order without repeated values. This is different from the sort option.

descending indicates that the numeric list must be given in descending order without repeated values.

integer specifies that the user may only give integer values in the numeric list.

missingokay indicates that missing values are allowed in the numeric list. By default, missing values are not allowed.

min(#) specifies the minimum number of elements allowed in the numeric list. The default is min(1). If you want to allow empty numeric lists, specify min(0).

max(#) specifies the maximum number of elements allowed in the numeric list. The default is max(1600), which is the largest allowed maximum.

range(*operator* # [*operator* #]) specifies the acceptable range for the values in the numeric list. The *operators* are < (less than), <= (less than or equal to), > (greater than), and >= (greater than or equal to). No space is allowed between the *operator* and the #.

sort specifies that the returned numeric list is to be sorted. This is different from the ascending option. ascending places the responsibility for providing a sorted list on the user who will not be allowed to enter a nonsorted list. sort, on the other hand, puts no restriction on the user and will take care of sorting the list. Repeated values are also allowed with sort.

Remarks

Programmers rarely use the numlist command because syntax will also expand numeric lists, and it will handle the rest of the parsing problem, too, at least if the command being parsed follows standard syntax. numlist is used for expanding numeric lists when what is being parsed does not follow standard syntax.

▷ Example

We demonstrate the numlist command interactively.

```
. numlist "5.3 1.0234 3 6:18 -2.0033 5.3/7.3"
. display "`r(numlist)'"
5.3 1.0234 3 6 9 12 15 18 -2.0033 5.3 6.3 7.3
. numlist "5.3 1.0234 3 6:18 -2.0033 5.3/7.3", integer
invalid numlist has noninteger elements
r(126);
. numlist "1 5 8/12 15", integer descending
invalid numlist has elements out of order
r(124);
. numlist "1 5 8/12 15", integer ascending
. display "`r(numlist)'"
1 5 8 9 10 11 12 15
```

```
. numlist "100 1 5 8/12 15", integer ascending
invalid numlist has elements out of order
r(124);
. numlist "100 1 5 8/12 15", integer sort
. display "`r(numlist)'"
1 5 8 9 10 11 12 15 100
. numlist "3 5 . 28 -3(2)5"
invalid numlist has missing values
r(127);
. numlist "3 5 . 28 -3(2)5", missingokay min(3) max(25)
. display "`r(numlist)'"
3 5 . 28 -3 -1 1 3 5
. numlist "28 36", min(3) max(6)
invalid numlist has too few elements
r(122);
. numlist "28 36 -3 5 2.8 7 32 -8", min(3) max(6)
invalid numlist has too many elements
r(123);
. numlist "3/6 -4 -1 to 5", range(>=1)
invalid numlist has elements outside of allowed range
r(125);
. numlist "3/6", range(>=0 <30)
. display "`r(numlist)'"
3 4 5 6
```

◁

Saved Results

numlist saves in r():

Macros
r(numlist)   the expanded numeric list

Also See

Related: [P] **syntax**

Background: [U] **14.1.8 numlist**

Title

pause — Program debugging command

Syntax

pause { on | off | [*message*] }

Description

If pause is on, 'pause [*message*]' command displays *message* and temporarily suspends execution of the program, returning control to the keyboard. Execution of keyboard commands continues until you type end or q, at which time execution of the program resumes. Typing BREAK in pause mode (as opposed to pressing the *Break* key) also resumes program execution, but the break signal is sent to the calling program.

If pause is off, pause does nothing.

Pause is off by default. Type pause on to turn pause on. Type pause off to turn it back off.

Remarks

pause assists in debugging Stata programs. The line pause or 'pause *message*' is placed in the program where problems are suspected (more than one pause may be placed in a program). For instance, you have a program that is not working properly. A piece of this program reads

```
gen 'tmp'=exp('1')/'2'
summarize 'tmp'
local mean=r(mean)
```

You think the error may be in the creation of 'tmp'. You change the program to read

```
gen 'tmp'=exp('1')/'2'
pause Just created tmp          /* this line is new */
summarize 'tmp'
local mean=r(mean)
```

Let's pretend your program is named myprog; interactively, you now type

```
. myprog
( output from your program appears )
```

That is, pause does nothing because pause is off, so pauses in your program are ignored. If you turn pause on,

```
. pause on
. myprog
( any output myprog creates up to the pause appears )
pause:  Just created tmp
-> . describe
  (output omitted )
-> . list
  (output omitted )
-> . end
execution resumes...
( remaining output from myprog appears)
```

The "->" is called the pause-mode prompt. You can give any Stata command. You can examine variables, and, if you wish, even change them. If while in pause mode, you wish to terminate execution of your program, you type BREAK (in capitals):

```
. myprog
( any output myprog creates up to the pause appears )
pause:  Just created tmp
-> . list
  (output omitted )
-> . BREAK
sending Break to calling program...
--Break--
r(1);

. _
```

The results are the same as if you pressed *Break* while your program were executing. If you press the *Break* key in pause mode (as opposed to typing BREAK), however, it means only that the execution of the command you have just given interactively is to be interrupted.

Notes:

1. You may put many pauses in your programs.

2. By default, pause is off, so the pauses will not do anything. Even so, you should remove the pauses after your program is debugged because each execution of a do-nothing pause will slow your program slightly.

3. pause is implemented as an ado-file; this means the definitions of local macros in your program are unavailable to you. To see the value of local macros, display them in the pause message; for instance,

           pause Just created tmp, i='i'

   Then, when the line is executed, you will see something like

```
pause:  Just created tmp, i=1
-> . _
```

4. Remember, temporary variables (e.g., tempvar tmp ... gen 'tmp'=...) are assigned real names such as __00424 by Stata; see [P] **macro**. Thus, in pause mode you want to examine __00424 and not tmp. Generally, you can determine the real name of your temporary variables from describe's output, but in the example above, it would be better had pause been invoked with

           pause Just created tmp, called 'tmp', i='i'

   Then, when the line is executed, you will see something like

```
pause:  Just created tmp, called __00424, i=1
-> . _
```

5. When giving commands that include double quotes, you may occasionally see the error message "type mismatch", but then the command will work properly:

```
pause:  Just created tmp, called __00424, i=1
-> . list if __00424=="male"
type mismatch
( output from request appears as if nothing is wrong)
-> . _
```

Methods and Formulas

pause is implemented as an ado-file.

References

Becketti, S. 1993. ip4: Program debugging command. *Stata Technical Bulletin* 13: 13–14. Reprinted in *Stata Technical Bulletin Reprints*, vol. 3, pp. 57–58.

Also See

Complementary:	[P] **program**
Related:	[P] **more**, [P] **trace**
Background:	[U] **21 Programming Stata**

Title

postfile — Save results in Stata dataset

Syntax

postfile *postname newvarlist* using *filename* [, <u>e</u>very(*#*) replace]

post *postname* (*exp*) (*exp*) ... (*exp*)

postclose *postname*

postutil dir

postutil clear

Description

These commands are utilities to assist Stata programmers in performing Monte Carlo-type experiments. postfile declares the variable names and the filename of a (new) Stata dataset where results will be stored. post adds a new observation to the declared dataset. postclose declares an end to the posting of observations. postutil dir lists all open postfiles. postutil clear closes all open postfiles. All five commands manipulate the new dataset without disturbing the data in memory. After postclose, the new dataset contains the posted results and may be loaded with use; see [R] **save**.

filename, if specified without a suffix, is taken to mean *filename*.dta.

Options

every(*#*) specifies results are to be written to disk every *#*th call to post. post temporarily holds results in memory and periodically opens the Stata dataset being built to append the stored results. every() should typically not be specified, as you are unlikely to choose a value for *#* that is as efficient as the number post chooses on its own, which is a function of the number of results being written and their storage type.

replace indicates that the file specified may already exist, and, if it does, postfile may erase the file and create a new one.

Remarks

The typical use of the post commands is

```
tempname memhold
tempfile results
...
postfile 'memhold' ... using "'results'"
...
while ... {
        ...
        post 'memhold' ...
        ...
}
```

```
postclose 'memhold'
...
use "'results'", clear
...
```

Two names are specified with `postfile`, *postname* and *filename*. *postname* is a name assigned to internal memory buffers, and *filename* is the name of the file to be created. Subsequent `post`s and the `postclose` are followed by *postname* so Stata will know to what file they refer.

In our sample, we obtain both names from Stata's temporary name facility (see [P] **macro**), although, in some programming situations, you may wish to substitute a hard-coded *filename*. We recommend that *postname* always be obtained from `tempname`. This ensures that your program can be nested within any other program and ensures that the memory used by `post` is freed if anything goes wrong. Using a temporary filename, too, ensures that the file will be erased if the user presses *Break*. In some cases, however, you may wish to leave the file of incomplete results behind. That is okay, but remember that the file is not fully up to date if `postclose` has not been executed. `post` buffers results in memory and only periodically updates the file.

Note that since `postfile` accepts a *newvarlist*, storage types may be interspersed, so you could have

```
postfile 'memhold' a b str20 c double(d e f) using "'results'"
```

▷ Example

We wish to write a program to collect means and variances from 10,000 randomly constructed 100-observation samples of lognormal data and store the results in `results.dta`. Suppose we are evaluating the coverage of the 95%, *t*-based confidence interval when applied to lognormal data. As background, we can obtain a single 100-observation lognormal sample by typing

```
drop _all
set obs 100
gen z = exp(invnorm(uniform()))
```

We can obtain the mean and standard deviation by then typing

```
summarize z
```

Moreover, `summarize` stores the sample mean in `r(mean)` and variance in `r(Var)`. It is those two values we wish to collect. Our program is

```
program lnsim
        version 8.0
        tempname sim
        postfile 'sim' mean var using results, replace
        quietly {
                forvalues i = 1/10000 {
                        drop _all
                        set obs 100
                        gen z = exp(invnorm(uniform()))
                        summarize z
                        post 'sim' (r(mean)) (r(Var))
                }
        }
        postclose 'sim'
end
```

The command `postfile` begins the accumulation of results. `'sim'` is the name assigned to the internal memory buffers where results will be held; `mean` and `var` are the names to be given to the two variables that will contain the information we collect; and variables will be stored in the file named `results.dta`. Since two variable names were specified on the `postfile`, two expressions must be specified following the `post`. In this case, the expressions are simply `r(mean)` and `r(Var)`. Had we wanted, however, to save the mean divided by the standard deviation and the standard deviation, we could have typed

```
post 'sim' (r(mean)/r(sd)) (r(sd))
```

Finally, `postclose 'sim'` concluded the simulation. The dataset `results.dta` is now complete.

```
. lnsim

. use results, clear

. describe
Contains data from results.dta
  obs:          10,000
  vars:              2                          23 Sep 2000 12:59
  size:        120,000 (88.4% of memory free)

              storage  display     value
variable name   type   format      label      variable label

mean            float  %9.0g
var             float  %9.0g

Sorted by:

. summarize
    Variable |      Obs        Mean    Std. Dev.       Min        Max

        mean |     10000    1.649879    .216586    1.069133   2.896868
         var |     10000    4.689451   4.458131    .7389911   106.0029
```

References

Gould, W. 1994. ssi6: Routines to speed Monte Carlo experiments. *Stata Technical Bulletin* 20: 18–22. Reprinted in *Stata Technical Bulletin Reprints*, vol. 4, pp. 202–207.

Also See

Related: [R] **bootstrap**, [R] **simulate**

Title

> **_predict** — Obtain predictions, residuals, etc. after estimation programming command

Syntax

After regress

    _predict [*type*] *newvarname* [if *exp*] [in *range*] [, xb stdp stdf

       stdr hat cooksd residuals rstandard rstudent

       nooffset nolabel]

After single-equation (SE) *estimators*

    _predict [*type*] *newvarname* [if *exp*] [in *range*] [, xb stdp

       nooffset nolabel]

After multiple-equation (ME) *estimators*

    _predict [*type*] *newvarname* [if *exp*] [in *range*] [, xb stdp stddp

       nooffset nolabel equation(*eqno*[, *eqno*])]

If no prediction options are specified, the following are calculated:

after logit	probability of a positive outcome
after probit	probability of a positive outcome
after mlogit	probability of a positive outcome
after stcox	relative hazard
after other commands	linear prediction

Description

    _predict is for use by programmers as a subroutine for implementing the predict command for use after estimation; see [R] **predict**.

Options

    xb calculates the linear prediction from the estimated model. That is, all models can be thought of as estimating a set of parameters b_1, b_2, ..., b_k, and the linear prediction is $\widehat{y}_j = b_1 x_{1j} + b_2 x_{2j} + \cdots + b_k x_{kj}$, often written in matrix notation as $\widehat{\mathbf{y}}_j = \mathbf{x}_j \mathbf{b}$. In the case of linear regression, the values $\widehat{y}_j$ are called the predicted values, or, for out-of-sample predictions, the forecast. In the case of logit and probit, for example, $\widehat{y}_j$ is called the logit or probit index.

It is important to understand that the x_{1j}, x_{2j}, ..., x_{kj} used in the calculation are obtained from the data currently in memory and do not have to correspond to the data on the independent variables used in estimating the model (obtaining the b_1, b_2, ..., b_k).

stdp calculates the standard error of the prediction after any estimation command. Here, the prediction is understood to mean the same thing as the "index", namely $\mathbf{x}_j\mathbf{b}$. The statistic produced by stdp can be thought of as the standard error of the predicted expected value, or mean index, for the observation's covariate pattern. This is also commonly referred to as the standard error of the fitted value.

stdf calculates the standard error of the forecast. This is the standard error of the point prediction for a single observation. It is commonly referred to as the standard error of the future or forecast value. By construction, the standard errors produced by stdf are always larger than those by stdp; see *Methods and Formulas* in [R] **predict**.

stdr calculates the standard error of the residuals.

stddp is allowed only after you have previously estimated a multiple-equation model. The standard error of the difference in linear predictions $(\mathbf{x}_{1j}\mathbf{b} - \mathbf{x}_{2j}\mathbf{b})$ between equations 1 and 2 is calculated.

hat or leverage calculates the diagonal elements of the projection hat matrix.

cooksd calculates the Cook's D influence statistic (Cook 1977).

residuals calculates the residuals.

rstandard calculates the standardized residuals.

rstudent calculates the studentized (jackknifed) residuals.

nooffset may be combined with most statistics and specifies that the calculation should be made ignoring any offset or exposure variable specified when the model was estimated.

This option is available, even if not documented, for predict after a specific command. If neither the offset(*varname*) option nor the exposure(*varname*) option was specified when the model was estimated, specifying nooffset does nothing.

nolabel prevents _predict from labeling the newly created variable.

equation(*eqno*[, *eqno*]) is relevant only when you have previously estimated a multiple-equation model. It specifies to which equation you are referring.

equation() is typically filled in with one *eqno*—it would be filled in that way with options xb and stdp, for instance. equation(#1) would mean the calculation is to be made for the first equation, equation(#2) would mean the second, and so on. Alternatively, you could refer to the equations by their names. equation(income) would refer to the equation named income and equation(hours) to the equation named hours.

If you do not specify equation(), the results are as if you specified equation(#1).

Other statistics refer to between-equation concepts; stddp is an example. In those cases, you might specify equation(#1,#2) or equation(income,hours). When two equations must be specified, equation() is not optional.

Methods and Formulas

See *Methods and Formulas* in [R] **predict** and [R] **regress**.

References

Cook, R. D. 1977. Detection of influential observations in linear regression. *Technometrics* 19: 15–18.

Also See

Related: [R] **predict**

Background: [U] **23 Estimation and post-estimation commands**

Title

preserve — Preserve and restore data

Syntax

preserve [, changed]

restore [, not preserve]

Description

preserve preserves the data, guaranteeing a restore on program termination.

restore forces a restore of the data now.

Options

changed instructs preserve to preserve only the data-has-changed-since-last-save flag. Use of this option is strongly discouraged, as explained below.

not instructs restore to cancel the previous preserve.

preserve instructs restore to restore the data now, but not to cancel the restoration of the data again at program conclusion. If preserve is not specified, the scheduled restoration at program conclusion is canceled.

Remarks

preserve and restore deal with the programming problem where the user's data must be changed in order to achieve the desired result but, when the program concludes, the programmer wishes to undo the damage done to the data. When preserve is issued, the user's data are preserved. The data in memory remain unchanged. When the program or do-file concludes, the user's data are automatically restored.

Alternatively, after a preserve, the programmer can instruct Stata to restore the data now with the restore command. This is useful when the programmer needs the original data back and knows no more damage will be done to the data. restore, preserve can be used when the programmer needs the data back but plans further damage. restore, not can be used when the programmer wishes to cancel the previous preserve and to have the data currently in memory returned to the user.

▷ Example

In most cases, preserve is used by itself and is used early in the program. You are writing a program to report some statistic, but the statistic cannot be calculated without changing the user's data. Here, changing does not mean merely adding a variable or two; that could be done with temporary variables as described in [P] **macro**. Changing means that the data really must be changed: observations might be discarded, the contents of existing variables changed, and the like. Although the programmer could just ignore the destruction of the user's data, the programmer might actually want to use the program herself, and knows she will become exceedingly irritated when she uses it without remembering to first save her data. In other words, the programmer wishes to write a programmingly correct, or PC, command. It is not difficult:

```
program myprog
        ( code for interpreting — parsing — the user's request )
        preserve
        ( code that destroys the data )
        ( code that makes the calculation )
        ( code that reports the result )
end
```

To preserve the data, `preserve` must make a copy of it on disk. Therefore, our programmer smartly performs all the parsing and setup, where errors are likely, before the `preserve`. Once she gets to the point in the code where the damage must be done, however, she preserves the data. After that, she forgets the problem. Stata will handle restoring the user's data even if the user presses *Break* in the middle of the program.

◁

▷ Example

Now let's consider a program that must destroy the user's data but needs the data back again, and, once the data are recovered, will do no more damage. The outline is

```
program myprog
        ( code for interpreting — parsing — the user's request )
        preserve
        ( code that destroys the data )
        ( code that makes the first part of the calculation )
        restore
        ( code that makes the second part of the calculation )
        ( code that reports the result )
end
```

While there are other ways the programmer could have arranged to save the data and get the data back (`save` and `use` with temporary files as described in [P] **macro** comes to mind), this method is better because should the user press *Break* after the data are damaged but before the data are restored, Stata will handle restoring the data.

◁

▷ Example

This time the program must destroy the user's data, bring the data back and destroy the data again, and finally report its calculation. The outline is

```
program myprog
        ( code for interpreting — parsing — the user's request )
        preserve
        ( code that destroys the data )
        ( code that makes the first part of the calculation )
        restore, preserve
        ( code that makes the second part of the calculation )
        ( code that reports the result )
end
```

Alternatively, the programmer could have coded a `restore` on one line and a `preserve` on the next. It would have the same result but would be inefficient, since Stata would then rewrite the data to disk. `restore, preserve` tells Stata to reload the data but to leave the copy on disk for ultimate restoration.

◁

▷ Example

   You are writing a program that intends to change the user's data in memory—the damage you are about to do is not damage at all. Nevertheless, were the user to press *Break* while you are in the midst of your machinations, what would be left in memory would be useless. The programmingly correct outline is

```
program myprog
           ( code for interpreting—parsing—the user's request )
           preserve
           ( code that reforms the data )
           restore, not
    end
```

   Before undertaking the reformation, the programmer smartly preserves the data. Then, when everything is complete, the programmer cancels the restoration by saying `restore, not`.

                                                                                                              ◁

❑ Technical Note

   `preserve, changed` is best avoided, although it is very fast. `preserve, changed` does not preserve the data: it merely records whether the data have changed since the data were last saved (as mentioned by `describe` and as checked by `exit` and `use` when the user does not also say `clear`), and restores the flag at the conclusion of the program. It is the programmer's responsibility to ensure that the data really have not changed.

   As long as your programs use temporary variables as created by `tempvar` (see [P] **macro**), the changed-since-last-saved flag would not be changed anyway—Stata is able to track such temporary changes to the data that it will, itself, be able to undo. In fact, we cannot think of a single use for `preserve, changed`, and included it only to preserve the happiness of our more imaginative users.

                                                                                                              ❑

Also See

   Background: [P] **macro**

Title

program — Define and manipulate programs

Syntax

program [define] program_name [, [nclass | rclass | eclass | sclass]

byable(recall[, noheader]|onecall)

sortpreserve]

program dir

program drop { program_name [program_name [...]] | _all }

program list [program_name [program_name [...]] | _all]

Description

program defines and manipulates programs. define is required if program_name is any of the words define, dir, drop, list, or plugin.

See [U] **21 Programming Stata** for a complete description of programs. The remarks below address only the use of the program dir, program drop, and program list commands.

See [P] **trace** for information on debugging programs.

See the Subject Table of Contents, which immediately follows the Table of Contents, for a subject summary of the programming commands.

Options

nclass states that the program being defined does not return results in r(), e(), or s(), and is the default.

rclass states that the program being defined returns results in r(). This is done using the return command; see [P] **return**. If the program is not explicitly declared to be rclass, then it may not change or replace results in r().

eclass states that the program being defined returns results in e() or modifies already existing results in e(). This is done using the ereturn command, but still see [P] **return** because that is where it is documented. If the program is not explicitly declared to be eclass, then it may not replace or change results in e().

sclass states that the program being defined returns results in s(). This is done using the sreturn command; see [P] **return**. If the program is not explicitly declared to be sclass, then it may not change or replace results in s(), but it still may clear s() using 'sreturn clear'; see [P] **return**.

byable() states that the program is to allow Stata's by varlist: prefix. There are two styles for writing byable programs: byable(recall) and byable(onecall). The writing of byable programs is discussed in [P] **byable**; see [P] **byable** for a discussion of this important option.

sortpreserve states that the program will change the sort order of the data and that Stata is to restore the original sort order of the data upon the program's conclusion. See [P] **sortpreserve** for a discussion of this important option.

Remarks

The program dir command lists the names of all the programs stored in memory. program list lists contents of the program or programs.

▷ Example

When you start Stata, there are no programs stored in memory. If you type program dir, Stata displays an empty list:

```
. program dir

.
```

Later during the session,

```
. program dir
ado       720   _pred_se
ado       336   logit_p.GetRhs
ado      3728   logit_p
ado       272   predict
ado      1456   logistic
         ─────
         6512
```

The ado after the program name indicates that the program was automatically loaded, and thus is eligible to be automatically dropped should memory become scarce; see [U] **20 Ado-files**. The number is the size, in bytes, of the program. The total amount of memory occupied by programs is currently 6,464 bytes. Notice the logit_p.GetRhs entry. The GetRhs program is defined in the logit_p.ado file, and was loaded when logit_p was loaded.

Let's now create two of our own programs using program:

```
. program rng
  1. args n a b
  2. if "`b'"=="" {
  3.     display "You must type three arguments: n a b"
  4.     exit
  5. }
  6. drop _all
  7. set obs `n'
  8. generate x = (_n-1)/(_N-1)*(`b'-`a')+`a'
  9. end
. program smooth
  1. args v1 v2
  2. confirm variable `v1'
  3. confirm new variable `v2'
  4. generate `v2' = cond(_n==1|_n==_N,`v1',(`v1'[_n-1]+`v1'+`v1'[_n+1])/3)
  5. end
```

After typing program, lines are collected until you type a line with the word end. For our purposes, it does not matter what these programs do. If we were now to type program dir, we would see

```
. program dir
        256    smooth
        288    rng
ado     720    _pred_se
ado     336    logit_p.GetRhs
ado    3728    logit_p
ado     272    predict
ado    1456    logistic
       ─────
       7056
```

We can list a program using the `program list` command:

```
. program list smooth
smooth:
  1. args v1 v2
  2. confirm variable 'v1'
  3. confirm new variable 'v2'
  4. generate 'v2' = cond(_n==1|_n==_N,'v1',(('v1'[_n-1]+'v1'+'v1'[_n+1])/3)
```

If we do not specify the program that we want listed, `program list` lists all the programs stored in memory.

The `program drop` command eliminates programs from memory. Typing `program drop` *program_name* eliminates *program_name* from memory. Typing `program drop _all` eliminates *all* programs from memory.

```
. program drop smooth
. program dir
        288    rng
ado     720    _pred_se
ado     336    logit_p.GetRhs
ado    3728    logit_p
ado     272    predict
ado    1456    logistic
       ─────
       6800
. program drop _all
. program dir
.
```

◁

Also See

Complementary: [P] **byable**, [P] **discard**, [P] **sortpreserve**, [P] **trace**
                        [R] **query**

Background: [U] **21 Programming Stata**

Title

quietly — Quietly and noisily perform Stata command

Syntax

<u>qu</u>ietly *command*

<u>n</u>oisily *command*

<u>set</u> <u>ou</u>tput { <u>p</u>roc | <u>inform</u> | <u>e</u>rror }

Description

quietly suppresses all terminal output for the duration of *command*.

noisily turns back on terminal output, if appropriate, for the duration of *command*. It is useful only in programs.

set output specifies the output to be displayed.

Remarks

quietly used interactively

▷ Example

quietly is useful in situations where you are using Stata interactively and want to temporarily suppress the terminal output. For instance, to estimate a regression of mpg on the variables weight, weightsq, and foreign and to suppress the terminal output, type

```
. quietly regress mpg weight weightsq foreign
. _
```

Admittedly, it is unlikely that you would ever want to do this in real life.

◁

quietly used in programs

❑ Technical Note

quietly is often used in programs. For instance, let's say you have the following program to run a regression of y on x, calculate the residuals, and then list the outliers, defined as points with residuals below the fifth percentile or above the 95th percentile:

```
program myprog
        regress '1' '2'
        predict resid, resid
        sort resid
        summarize resid, detail
        list '1' '2' resid if resid< r(p5) | resid> r(p95)
        drop resid
end
```

While the program will work, it will also fill the screen with the regression output, any notes predict feels obligated to mention, and the detailed output from summarize. A better version of this program might read

```
program myprog
        quietly regress '1' '2'
        quietly predict resid, resid
        quietly sort resid
        quietly summarize resid, detail
        list '1' '2' resid if resid< r(p5) | resid> r(p95)
        drop resid
end
```

You can also combine quietly with { }:

```
program myprog
        quietly {
                regress '1' '2'
                predict resid, resid
                sort resid
                summarize resid, detail
        }
        list '1' '2' resid if resid< r(p5) | resid> r(p95)
        drop resid
end
```

❑

❑ Technical Note

noisily is the antonym of quietly, and it too can be used in programs and do-files. In fact, that is its only real use. We could recode our example program to read as follows:

```
program myprog
        quietly {
                regress '1' '2'
                predict resid, resid
                sort resid
                summarize resid, detail
                noisily list '1' '2' resid if resid< r(p5) | resid> r(p95)
                drop resid
        }
end
```

In this case, we have not improved readability.

❑

❏ Technical Note

noisily is not really the antonym of quietly. If the user types quietly myprog yvar xvar, the output will be suppressed because that is what the user wanted. In this case, a noisily inside myprog will not display the output—noisily means noisily only if the program was allowed to be noisy when it was invoked.

❏

❏ Technical Note

If you think you understand all of this, take the following test. Is there any difference between quietly do *filename* and run *filename*? How about noisily run *filename* and do *filename*? What would happen if you typed quietly noisily summarize *myvar*? If you typed noisily quietly summarize *myvar*?

When you are ready, we will tell you the answers.

quietly do *filename* is equivalent to run *filename*. Typing run is easier, however.

noisily run *filename* is not at all the same as do *filename*. run produces no output, and no matter how noisily you run run, it is still quiet.

Typing quietly noisily summarize *myvar* is the same as typing summarize myvar. Think of it as quietly {noisily summarize *myvar*}. It is the inside noisily that takes precedence.

Typing noisily quietly summarize *myvar* is the same as typing quietly summarize *myvar*—it does nothing but burn computer time. Again, it is the inside term, quietly this time, that takes precedence.

❏

❏ Technical Note

set output proc means that all output, including procedure (command) output, is displayed. inform suppresses procedure output, but displays informative messages and error messages. error suppresses all output except error messages. In practice, set output is seldom used.

❏

Also See

Background: [U] **21 Programming Stata**

Title

_**return** — Preserve saved results

Syntax

_return hold *name*

_return restore *name* [, hold]

_return drop {*name* | _all}

_return dir

Description

_return saves and restores the contents of r().

_return hold saves under *name* the contents of r() and clears r(). If *name* is a name obtained from *tempname*, *name* will be automatically dropped at the program's conclusion, if it is not automatically or explicitly dropped before that.

_return restore restores from *name* the contents of r(), and, unless option hold is specified, drops *name*.

_return drop removes from memory (drops) *name*, or, if _all is specified, all _return names currently saved.

_return dir lists the names currently saved by _return.

Options

hold, specified with _return restore, specifies that results are to continue to be held so that they can be _return restored later, as well. If the option is not specified, the specified results are restored and *name* is dropped.

Remarks

_return is rarely necessary. Most programs open with

```
program example
        version 8
        syntax ...
        marksample touse
        if '"'exp'"' != "" {
                tempvar e
                qui gen double 'e' = 'exp' if 'touse'
        }
        ... (code to calculate final results)...
end
```

329

In the program above, no commands are given that change the contents of r() until all parsing is complete and the if *exp* and =*exp* are evaluated. Thus, the user can type

```
. summarize myvar
. example ... if myvar>r(mean) ...
```

and the results will be as the user expects.

Some programs, however, have nonstandard and complicated syntax, and, in the process of deciphering that syntax, other r-class commands might be run before the user-specified expressions are evaluated. Consider a command that reads

```
program example2
        version 8
        ...(commands that parse)...
        ...(r() might be reset at this stage)...
        ... commands that evaluate user-specified expressions...
        tempvar touse
        mark 'tempvar' 'if'
        tempvar v1 v2
        gen double 'v1' = 'exp1' if 'touse'
        // 'exp1' specified by user
        gen double 'v2' = 'exp2' if 'touse'
        // 'exp2' specified by user
        ...(code to calculate final results)...
end
```

In this case, it would be a disaster if the user were to type

```
. summarize myvar
. example2 ... if myvar>r(mean) ...
```

because r(mean) would not mean what the user expected it to mean, which is the mean of myvar. The solution to this problem to code the following:

```
program example2
        version 8
                                        // save r()
        tempname myr
        _return hold 'myr'
        ...(commands that parse)...
        ...(r() might be reset at this stage)...
        ... commands that evaluate user-specified expressions...
                                        // restore r()
        _return restore 'myr'
        tempvar touse
        mark 'tempvar' 'if'
        tempvar v1 v2
        gen double 'v1' = 'exp1' if 'touse'
        // 'exp1' specified by user
        gen double 'v2' = 'exp2' if 'touse'
        // 'exp2' specified by user
        ...(code to calculate final results)...
end
```

In the above example, we save the contents of r() in 'myr', and then later bring them back.

Saved Results

_return restore resaves in r() what was saved in r() at the time _return hold was executed.

Also See

Complimentary: [P] **return**; [P] **_estimates**

Title

---
return — Return saved results

Syntax

<pre>
<u>re</u>turn clear

<u>re</u>turn <u>sca</u>lar name = exp

<u>re</u>turn <u>loc</u>al name = exp

<u>re</u>turn <u>loc</u>al name [["]]string[["]]

<u>re</u>turn <u>mat</u>rix name [=] matname [, copy]

<u>re</u>turn add

<u>sre</u>turn clear

<u>sre</u>turn <u>loc</u>al name = exp

<u>sre</u>turn <u>loc</u>al name [["]]string[["]]

<u>ere</u>turn clear

<u>ere</u>turn post b V [C] [, <u>dep</u>name(string) <u>o</u>bs(#) <u>d</u>of(#) <u>e</u>sample(varname)]

<u>ere</u>turn <u>sca</u>lar name = exp

<u>ere</u>turn <u>loc</u>al name = exp

<u>ere</u>turn <u>loc</u>al name [["]]string[["]]

<u>ere</u>turn <u>mat</u>rix name [=] matname [, copy]

<u>ere</u>turn repost [b = b] [V = V] [, <u>e</u>sample(varname) <u>ren</u>ame]
</pre>

where b, V, and C are *matnames*.

Description

Results of calculations are saved by many Stata commands so that they can be easily accessed and substituted into subsequent commands. This entry summarizes for programmers how to save results. If your interest is in using previously saved results, see [R] **saved results**.

return saves results in r().

sreturn saves results in s().

ereturn saves results in e().

Stata also has the values of system parameters and certain constants such as pi stored in c(). Since these values may be referenced, but not assigned, the c-class is discussed in a different entry; see [P] **creturn**.

Programmers of earlier versions of Stata: note that e-results are no longer saved via the estimates command. The functionality of the 'old' estimates is now subsumed by the new commands ereturn and _estimates, while estimates is a new nonprogrammer's command.

Options

copy specified with `return matrix` or `ereturn matrix` indicates that the matrix is to be copied; that is, the original matrix should be left in place. The default is to "steal" or "rename" the existing matrix, which is both fast and conserves memory.

depname(*string*) is for use with `ereturn post`. It supplies the name of the dependent variable to appear in the estimation output. The name specified need not be the name of an existing variable.

obs(#) is for use with `ereturn post`. It specifies the number of observations on which the estimation was performed. This number is stored in `e(N)`, and `obs()` is provided simply for convenience. Results are no different than `ereturn post` followed by `ereturn scalar N = #`.

dof(#) is for use with `ereturn post`. It specifies the number of denominator degrees of freedom to be used with t and F statistics, and so is used in calculating significance levels and confidence intervals. The number specified is saved in `e(df_r)`, and `dof()` is provided simply for convenience. Results are no different than `ereturn post` followed by `ereturn scalar df_r = #`.

esample(*varname*) is for use with `ereturn post` and `ereturn repost`. It specifies the name of a 0/1 variable that is to become the `e(sample)` function. *varname* must contain 0 and 1 values only, with 1 indicating that the observation is in the estimation subsample. `ereturn post` and `ereturn repost` will be able to execute a little more quickly if *varname* is stored as a `byte` variable.

varname is dropped from the dataset, or, more correctly, it is stolen and stashed in a secret place.

rename is for use with the b = b syntax of `ereturn repost`. All numeric estimation results remain unchanged, but the labels of **b** are substituted for the variable and equation names of the already posted results.

Remarks

This entry summarizes information that is presented in greater detail in other parts of the Stata documentation. Most particularly, we recommend you read [U] **21 Programming Stata**. The commands listed above are used by programmers to save results, which are accessed by others using `r()`, `e()`, and `s()`; see [R] **saved results**.

The commands listed above may be used only in programs—see [U] **21 Programming Stata** and [P] **program**—and then only when the program is declared explicitly as being `rclass`, `eclass`, or `sclass`:

```
program ..., rclass
        ...
        return ...
        ...
end

program ..., eclass
        ...
        ereturn ...
        ...
end

program ..., sclass
        ...
        sreturn ...
        ...
end
```

Saving results in r()

1. The program must be declared explicitly to be r-class: `program ... , rclass`.

2. Distinguish between `r()` (returned results) and `return()` (results being assembled that will be returned). The program you write actually stores results in `return()`. Then, when your program completes, whatever is in `return()` is copied to `r()`. Thus, the program you write can consume `r()` results from other programs, and there is no conflict.

3. `return clear` clears the `return()` class. This command is seldom used because `return()` starts out empty when your program begins. `return clear` is for those instances when you have started assembling results and all is going well, but given the problem at hand, you need to start all over again.

4. `return scalar` *name* = *exp* evaluates *exp* and stores the result in the scalar `return(`*name*`)`. *exp* must evaluate to a numeric result or missing. If your code has previously stored something in `return(`*name*`)`, whether that be a scalar, matrix, or whatever else, the previous value is discarded and this result replaces it.

5. `return local` *name* = *exp* evaluates *exp* and stores the result in the macro `return(`*name*`)`. *exp* may evaluate to a numeric or string result. If your code has previously stored something in `return(`*name*`)`, whether that be a scalar, matrix, or whatever else, the previous value is discarded and this result replaces it.

   Be careful with this syntax: do not code

   ```
   return local name = 'mymacro'
   ```

   because that will copy just the first 244 (or 80) characters of '*mymacro*'. Instead, code

   ```
   return local name '"'mymacro'"'
   ```

6. `return local` *name string* copies *string* to macro `return(`*name*`)`. If your code has previously stored something in `return(`*name*`)`, whether that be a scalar, matrix, or whatever else, the previous value is discarded and this result replaces it.

   If you do not enclose *string* in double quotes, multiple blanks in *string* are compressed into single blanks.

7. `return matrix` *name matname* destructively copies `matname` into matrix `return(`*name*`)`, which is to say, *matname* is erased. What actually occurs is that *matname* is renamed `return(`*name*`)`. If your code has previously stored something in `return(`*name*`)`, whether that be a scalar, matrix, or whatever else, the previous value is discarded and this result replaces it.

8. `return add` copies everything new in `r()` into `return()`. For instance, say your program performed a `summarize`. `return add` lets you add everything just returned by `summarize` to the to-be-returned results of your program. The emphasis is on add. If your program had already set `return(N)`, `summarize`'s `r(N)` would not replace the previously set result. The remaining `r()` results set by `summarize` would be copied.

Saving results in s()

1. The program must be declared explicitly to be s-class: `program ... , sclass`.

2. The s-class is not cleared automatically. It is a static, single-level class. Results are posted to `s()` the instant they are saved.

3. `sreturn clear` clears `s()`. It is recommended that this command be used near the top of s-class routines. `sreturn clear` may be used in non s-class programs, too.

4. The s-class provides macros only. The s-class is intended for returning results of subroutines that parse input. At the parsing step, it is important that the r-class not be changed or cleared because some of what still awaits being parsed might refer to r(), and the user expects those results to substitute according to what was in r() at the time he or she typed the command.

5. `sreturn local` *name* = *exp* evaluates *exp* and stores the result in the macro s(*name*). *exp* may evaluate to a numeric or string result. If your code has previously stored something else in s(*name*), the previous value is discarded and this result replaces it.

   Be careful with this syntax: do not code

   ```
   sreturn local name = 'mymacro'
   ```

   because that will copy just the first 244 (or 80) characters of '*mymacro*'. Instead, code

   ```
   sreturn local name '"'mymacro'"'
   ```

6. `sreturn local` *name string* copies *string* to macro s(*name*). If your code has previously stored something else in s(*name*), the previous value is discarded and this result replaces it.

   If you do not enclose *string* in double quotes, multiple blanks in *string* are compressed into single blanks.

Saving results in e()

For detailed guidance on saving in e(), see [P] **ereturn**. What follows is a quick summary.

1. The program must be declared explicitly to be e-class: `program ... , eclass`.

2. The e-class is cleared whenever an `ereturn post` is executed. The e-class is a static, single-level class, meaning results are posted to the class the instant they are stored.

3. `ereturn clear` clears e(). This is a rarely used command.

4. `ereturn post` is how you must begin saving results in e(). Because `ereturn post` clears e(), anything saved in e() prior to the `ereturn post` is lost.

   `ereturn post` saves matrix (vector, really) e(b), matrix e(V), and function e(sample). The recommended syntax is

   ```
   ereturn post 'b' 'V', esample('touse') ...
   ```

   where 'b' is a row vector containing the parameter estimates, 'V' is a symmetric matrix containing the variance estimates, and 'touse' is a 0/1 variable recording 1 in observations that appear in the estimation subsample.

   The result of this command will be that 'b', 'V', and 'touse' will all disappear. In fact, `ereturn post` examines what you specify, and, if it is satisfied with them, renames them e(b), e(V), and e(sample).

(Continued on next page)

In terms of `ereturn post`'s other options,

   a. We recommend that you specify `depname`(*string*) if there is a single dependent variable name that you want to appear on the output. Whether you specify `depname()` or not, remember later to define macro `e(depvar)` to contain the name(s) of the dependent variable(s).

   b. Specify `obs(#)`, or remember later to define scalar `e(N)` to contain the number of observations.

   c. Few models require specifying `dof(#)`, or, if that is not done, remembering to later define scalar `e(df_r)`. This all has to do with substituting t and F statistics based on # (denominator) degrees of freedom for asymptotic z and χ^2 statistics in the estimation output.

5. `ereturn scalar` *name* = *exp* evaluates *exp* and stores the result in the scalar `e(`*name*`)`. *exp* must evaluate to a numeric result or missing. If your code has previously stored something in `e(`*name*`)`, whether that be a scalar, matrix, or whatever else, the previous value is discarded and this result replaces it.

6. `ereturn local` *name* = *exp* evaluates *exp* and stores the result in the macro `e(`*name*`)`. *exp* may evaluate to a numeric or string result. If your code has previously stored something in `e(`*name*`)`, whether that be a scalar, matrix, or whatever else, the previous value is discarded and this result replaces it.

   Be careful with this syntax: do not code

   ```
   ereturn local name = `mymacro'
   ```

   because that will copy just the first 244 (or 80) characters of `` `mymacro' ``. Instead, code

   ```
   ereturn local name `"`mymacro'"'
   ```

7. `ereturn local` *name string* copies *string* to macro `e(`*name*`)`. If your code has previously stored something in `e(`*name*`)`, whether that be a scalar, matrix, or whatever else, the previous value is discarded and this result replaces it.

   If you do not enclose *string* in double quotes, multiple blanks in *string* are compressed into single blanks.

8. `ereturn matrix` *name* = *matname* destructively copies `matname` into matrix `e(`*name*`)`, which is to say, *matname* is erased. At least, that is what happens if you do not specify the `copy` option. What actually occurs is that *matname* is renamed `e(`*name*`)`. If your code has previously stored something in `e(`*name*`)`, whether that be a scalar, matrix, or whatever else, the previous value is discarded and this result replaces it, with two exceptions:

   `ereturn matrix` cannot be used to save in `e(b)` or `e(V)`. The only way to post matrices to these special names is `ereturn post` and `ereturn repost`. The reason for that is so that various tests can be run on them before they are made official. Other Stata commands will use `e(b)` and `e(V)` and expect to see a valid estimation result. If `e(b)` is $1 \times k$, they expect `e(V)` to be $k \times k$. They expect that the names of rows and columns will be the same, so that the ith column of `e(b)` corresponds to the ith row and column of `e(V)`. They expect `e(V)` to be symmetric. They expect `e(V)` to have positive or zero elements along its diagonal, and so on. `ereturn post` and `ereturn repost` check these assumptions.

9. `ereturn repost` allows changing `e(b)`, `e(V)`, and `e(sample)` without clearing the estimation results and starting all over again. As with `ereturn post`, specified matrices and variables disappear after reposting because they are renamed `e(b)`, `e(V)`, or `e(sample)` as appropriate.

10. Programmers posting estimation results should remember to save

    a. Macro e(cmd) containing the name of the estimation command. Make this the last thing you save in e().

    b. Macro e(depvar) containing the name(s) of the dependent variable(s).

    c. Scalar e(N) containing the number of observations.

    d. Scalar e(df_m) containing the model degrees of freedom.

    e. Scalar e(df_r) containing the "denominator" degrees of freedom if estimates are nonasymptotic; otherwise, do not define this result.

    f. Scalar e(ll) containing the log-likelihood value, if relevant.

    g. Scalar e(ll_0) containing the log-likelihood value for the constant-only model, if relevant.

    h. Scalar e(chi2) containing the χ^2 test of the model against the constant-only model, if relevant.

    i. Macro e(chi2type) containing "LR", "Wald", or other depending on how e(chi2) was obtained.

    j. Scalar e(r2_p) containing the value of the pseudo-R^2 if it is calculated.

    k. Macro e(vcetype) containing the text to appear above standard errors in estimation output; typically "Robust" or it is undefined.

    l. Macro e(clustvar) containing the name of the cluster variable, if any.

    m. Scalar e(N_clust) containing the number of clusters.

    n. Macro e(predict) containing the name of the command that predict is to use; if this is blank, predict uses the default _predict.

Recommended names for saved results

Users will appreciate it if you use predictable names for your saved results. The rules we use are

1. Mathematical and statistical concepts such as number of observations, degrees of freedom, etc. are given short mathematical-style names. Subscripting is indicated with '_'. Names are to proceed from the general to the specific. If N means number of observations, then N_1 might be the number of observations in the first group.

Suffixes are to be avoided where possible. For instance, a χ^2 statistic would be recorded in a variable starting with chi2. If, in the context of the command, a statement about "the χ^2 statistic" would be understood as referring to this statistic, then the name would be chi2. If it required further modification, such as χ^2 for the comparison test, then the name might be chi2_c.

Common prefixes are

N	number of observations
df	degrees of freedom
k	count of variables
n	generic count
lb and ub	lower- and upper-bound of confidence interval
chi2	χ^2 statistic
t	t statistic
F	F statistic
p	significance
p and pr	probability
ll	log likelihood
D	deviance
r2	R^2

2. Programming concepts such as lists of variable names, etc. are given English-style names. Names should proceed from the specific to the general. The name of the dependent variable is depvar, not vardep.

Some examples are

depvar	dependent variable name(s)
eqnames	equation names
model	name of model estimated
xvar	x variable
title	title used

3. Popular usage takes precedence over the rules. For example,

    a. mss is model's sum of squares, even though, per Rule 1, it ought to be ss_m.

    b. mean is used as the prefix to record means.

    c. Var is used as the prefix to mean variance.

    d. The returned results from most Stata commands follow Rule 3.

Also See

Related: [P] **creturn**, [P] **ereturn**, [P] **_estimates**, [P] **_return**,
        [R] **saved results**

Background: [U] **21 Programming Stata**,
        [U] **21.10 Saving results**

Title

> **_rmcoll** — Remove collinear variables

Syntax

> _rmcoll *varlist* [in *range*] [if *exp*] [*weight*] [, <u>nocons</u>tant]
>
> _rmdcoll *depvar varlist* [in *range*] [if *exp*] [*weight*] [, <u>nocons</u>tant <u>nocoll</u>in]

fweights, aweights, iweights, and pweights are allowed; see [U] **14.1.6 weight**.

Description

> _rmcoll returns in r(varlist) the names of the variables from the varlist that form a noncollinear set.

> If any variables are collinear, in addition to each not being included in r(varlist), a message is displayed for each:

>> Note: _____ dropped due to collinearity.

> ml users: It is not necessary to call _rmcoll because ml removes the collinear variables for you, assuming that you do not specify ml model's collinear option. Even so, ml programmers sometimes use _rmcoll because they need the noncollinear set of variables, and, in such cases, they specify ml model's collinear option so that ml does not waste time looking for collinearity again.

> _rmdcoll identifies collinearity, including collinearity with the dependent variable. _rmdcoll returns in r(varlist) a variable list from which collinear variables have been removed and displays the message

>> _____ collinear with _____

with an error code 459 when the dependent variable is collinear with the independent variables.

Options

> noconstant specifies that, in looking for collinearity, an intercept should not be included. That is, a variable that contains the same nonzero value in every observation should not be considered collinear.

> nocollin specifies that collinear variables have already been removed from the varlist. Otherwise, _rmcoll is called first to remove any such collinearity.

Remarks

> _rmcoll and _rmdcoll are typically used when writing estimation commands.

> _rmcoll is used if the programmer wants to drop the collinear variables from the independent variables.

> _rmdcoll is used if the programmer wants to detect the collinearity of the dependent variable with the independent variables.

A code fragment for the caller of _rmcoll might read as

```
...
syntax varlist [fweight iweight] ... [, noCONStant ... ]
marksample touse
if "`weight'" != ""
        tempvar w
        quietly gen double `w' = `exp' if `touse'
        local wgt [`weight'=`w']
else    local wgt /* is nothing */
tokenize `varlist'
local depvar `1'
mac shift
_rmcoll `*' `wgt' if `touse', `constant'
local xvars `r(varlist)'
...
```

In this code fragment, *varlist* contains a single dependent and zero or more independent variables. The dependent variable is split off and stored in *depvar*, and then the remaining variables are passed through _rmcoll and the resulting noncollinear set stored in *xvars*.

Saved Results

_rmcoll and _rmdcoll save in r():

r(varlist)   names of noncollinear variables

Also See

Complementary: [R] **ml**

Background: [U] **21 Programming Stata**

Title

rmsg — Return messages

Syntax

set rmsg { on | off } [, permanently]

Description

set rmsg determines whether the return message is to be displayed at the completion of each command. The initial setting is off.

Remarks

See [U] **11 Error messages and return codes** for a description of return messages and for use of this command.

Also See

Complementary: [P] **error**,

                       [R] **query**

Background: [U] **11 Error messages and return codes**

Title

_robust — Robust variance estimates

Syntax

_robust *varlist* [*weight*] [if *exp*] [in *range*] [, <u>v</u>ariance(*matname*) minus(*#*)

    <u>strata</u>(*varname*) psu(*varname*) <u>cl</u>uster(*varname*) fpc(*varname*)

    <u>subp</u>op(*varname*) vsrs(*matname*) <u>srss</u>ubpop <u>zero</u>weight]

varlist may contain time-series operators; see [U] **14.4.3 Time-series varlists**.
pweights, aweights, fweights, and iweights are allowed; see [U] **14.1.6 weight**.

Description

    _robust is a programmer's command. It computes a robust variance estimator based on a *varlist* of scores and a covariance matrix. It produces estimators for ordinary data (each observation independent), clustered data (data not independent within groups, but independent across groups), and complex survey data with stratified cluster sampling.

    The robust variance estimator goes by many names: Huber/White/sandwich are typically used in the context of robustness against heteroskedasticity. Survey statisticians often refer to this variance calculation as a first-order Taylor-series linearization method. Despite the different names, the estimator is the same.

    The score *varlist* consists of a single variable for single-equation models or multiple variables for multiple-equation models—one variable for each equation. The "covariance" matrix before adjustment is either posted using ereturn post (see [P] **ereturn**) or specified with the variance(*matname*) option. In the former case, _robust replaces the covariance in the post with the robust covariance matrix. In the latter case, the matrix *matname* is overwritten with the robust covariance matrix. Note: The robust covariance formula is $\mathbf{V} = \mathbf{DMD}$, where $\mathbf{D}$ is what we are calling the "covariance" matrix before adjustment; this is not always a true covariance. See *Remarks* below.

    Before tackling this section, readers should be familiar with [U] **23.14 Obtaining robust variance estimates** and the *Methods and Formulas* section of [R] **regress**. It is presumed that readers have already programmed an estimator in Stata and now wish to have it compute robust variance estimates. If you have not yet programmed your estimator, see [U] **21 Programming Stata**, [R] **ml**, and [P] **ereturn**. Users who wish to program an estimator for survey data should be intimately familiar with [SVY] **svymean** and [SVY] **svy estimators**. See [R] **estimation commands** for a complete list of commands that compute robust variance estimators.

Options

    variance(*matname*) specifies a matrix containing the unadjusted "covariance" matrix; i.e., the $\mathbf{D}$ in $\mathbf{V} = \mathbf{DMD}$. The matrix must have its rows and columns labeled with the appropriate corresponding variable names; i.e., the names of the x's in $\mathbf{x}\beta$. If there are multiple equations, the matrix must have equation names; see [P] **matrix rowname**. The $\mathbf{D}$ matrix is overwritten with the robust covariance matrix $\mathbf{V}$. If this option is not specified, it is assumed that $\mathbf{D}$ has been posted using ereturn post; _robust will then automatically post the robust covariance matrix $\mathbf{V}$ and replace $\mathbf{D}$.

minus(*#*) specifies $k = \#$ for the multiplier $n/(n-k)$ of the robust variance estimator. Stata's maximum likelihood commands use $k = 1$, as do all the svy commands. regress, robust uses, by default, this multiplier with k equal to the number of explanatory variables in the model including the constant. The default is $k = 1$. See *Methods and Formulas* for details.

strata(*varname*) specifies the name of a variable (numeric or string) that contains stratum identifiers.

psu(*varname*) specifies the name of a variable (numeric or string) that contains identifiers for the primary sampling unit (PSU). psu() and cluster() are synonyms; they both specify the same thing.

cluster(*varname*) is a synonym for psu().

fpc(*varname*) requests a finite population correction for the variance estimates. If the variable specified has values less than or equal to 1, it is interpreted as a stratum sampling rate $f_h = n_h/N_h$, where n_h = number of PSUs sampled from stratum h and N_h = total number of PSUs in the population belonging to stratum h. If the variable specified has values greater than 1, it is interpreted as containing N_h.

subpop(*varname*) specifies that estimates be computed for the single subpopulation defined by the observations for which *varname* $\neq 0$ (and not missing). This option would typically be used only with survey data.

vsrs(*matname*) creates a matrix containing $\widehat{V}_{\text{srswor}}$, an estimate of the variance that would have been observed had the data been collected using simple random sampling without replacement. This is used for the computation of deff and deft for survey data; see [SVY] **svymean** for details.

srssubpop can only be specified if vsrs() and subpop() are specified. srssubpop requests that the estimate of simple-random-sampling variance vsrs() be computed assuming sampling within a subpopulation. If srssubpop is not specified, it is computed assuming sampling from the entire population.

zeroweight specifies whether observations with weights equal to zero should be omitted from the computation. This option does not apply to frequency weights; observations with zero frequency weights are always omitted. If zeroweight is specified, observations with zero weights are included in the computation. If zeroweight is not specified (the default), observations with zero weights are omitted. Including the observations with zero weights affects the computation in that it may change the counts of PSUs (clusters) per stratum. Stata's svy commands include observations with zero weights; all other commands exclude them. This option would typically be used only with survey data.

Remarks

We will proceed to explain the formulas behind the robust variance estimator and how to use _robust through an informal development with some simple examples. For an alternative discussion, see [U] **23.14 Obtaining robust variance estimates**. See the references cited at the end of this entry for more formal expositions.

Let us first consider ordinary least-squares regression. The estimator for the coefficients is

$$\widehat{\beta} = (\mathbf{X}'\mathbf{X})^{-1}\mathbf{X}'\mathbf{y}$$

where $\mathbf{y}$ is an $n \times 1$ vector representing the dependent variable, and $\mathbf{X}$ is an $n \times k$ matrix of covariates.

Since we consider everything conditional on $\mathbf{X}$, $(\mathbf{X}'\mathbf{X})^{-1}$ can be regarded as a constant matrix. Hence, the variance of $\widehat{\beta}$ is

$$V(\widehat{\beta}) = (\mathbf{X}'\mathbf{X})^{-1} V(\mathbf{X}'\mathbf{y}) (\mathbf{X}'\mathbf{X})^{-1}$$

What is the variance of $\mathbf{X}'\mathbf{y}$, a $k \times 1$ vector? Let's look at its first element; it is

$$\mathbf{X}_1'\mathbf{y} = x_{11}y_1 + x_{21}y_2 + \cdots + x_{n1}y_n$$

where $\mathbf{X}_1$ is the first column of $\mathbf{X}$. Since $\mathbf{X}$ is treated as a constant, we can write the variance as

$$V(\mathbf{X}_1'\mathbf{y}) = x_{11}^2 V(y_1) + x_{21}^2 V(y_2) + \cdots + x_{n1}^2 V(y_n)$$

The only assumption that we have made here is that the y_j are independent.

The obvious estimate for $V(y_j)$ is $\hat{e}_j^2$, the square of the residual $\hat{e}_j = y_j - \mathbf{x}_j\hat{\beta}$, where $\mathbf{x}_j$ is the jth row of $\mathbf{X}$. We must estimate the off-diagonal terms of the covariance matrix for $\mathbf{X}'\mathbf{y}$ as well. Working this out, we have

$$\hat{V}(\mathbf{X}'\mathbf{y}) = \sum_{j=1}^{n} \hat{e}_j^2 \, \mathbf{x}_j'\mathbf{x}_j$$

Note that we defined $\mathbf{x}_j$ as a row vector, so that $\mathbf{x}_j'\mathbf{x}_j$ is a $k \times k$ matrix.

We have just derived the robust variance estimator for linear regression coefficient estimates for independent observations:

$$\hat{V}(\hat{\beta}) = (\mathbf{X}'\mathbf{X})^{-1} \left(\sum_{j=1}^{n} \hat{e}_j^2 \, \mathbf{x}_j'\mathbf{x}_j \right) (\mathbf{X}'\mathbf{X})^{-1}$$

You can see why it is called the "sandwich" estimator.

❏ Technical Note

The only detail that we have overlooked is the multiplier. We will see later that survey statisticians like to view the center of the sandwich as a variance estimator for totals. As such, they use a multiplier of $n/(n-1)$, just as $1/(n-1)$ is used for the variance estimator of a mean. However, for survey data, n is no longer the total number of observations, but the number of clusters in a stratum. See *Methods and Formulas* at the end of this entry.

The case of linear regression is, however, special. If we assume homoskedasticity and normality, we can derive the expectation of $\hat{e}_j^2$ for finite n. This is discussed in [R] **regress**. Under the assumptions of homoskedasticity and normality, $n/(n-k)$ is a better multiplier than $n/(n-1)$.

If you specify the minus(#) option, _robust will use $n/(n-\#)$ as the multiplier. regress, robust also gives two other options for the multiplier: hc2 and hc3. Since these multipliers are special to linear regression, _robust does not compute them.

❏

▷ Example

Before we show how _robust is used, let's compute the robust variance estimator "by hand" for linear regression for the case in which observations are independent (i.e., no clusters).

We need to compute $\mathbf{D} = (\mathbf{X}'\mathbf{X})^{-1}$ and the residuals $\hat{e}_j$. regress with the mse1 option will allow us to compute both easily; see [R] **regress**.

```
. use http://www.stata-press.com/data/r8/auto
(1978 Automobile Data)
. quietly regress mpg weight gear_ratio foreign, mse1
. matrix D = e(V)
. predict double e, residual
```

We can write the center of the sandwich as

$$\mathbf{M} = \sum_{j=1}^{n} \widehat{e}_j^2 \mathbf{x}_j' \mathbf{x}_j = \mathbf{X}' \mathbf{W} \mathbf{X}$$

where $\mathbf{W}$ is a diagonal matrix with $\widehat{e}_j^2$ on the diagonal. `matrix accum` with `iweights` can be used to calculate this (see [P] **matrix accum**):

```
. matrix accum M = weight gear_ratio foreign [iweight=e^2]
(obs=813.7814109)
```

We now assemble the sandwich. In order to match `regress, robust`, we use a multiplier of $n/(n-k)$.

```
. matrix V = 74/70 * D*M*D

. matrix list V

symmetric V[4,4]
                  weight   gear_ratio      foreign        _cons
    weight     3.788e-07
 gear_ratio    .00039798    1.9711317
    foreign    .00008463   -.55488334    1.4266939
      _cons   -.00236851   -6.9153285    1.2149035    27.536291
```

The result is exactly the same as that from `regress, robust`:

```
. quietly regress mpg weight gear_ratio foreign, robust

. matrix Vreg = e(V)

. matrix list Vreg

symmetric Vreg[4,4]
                  weight   gear_ratio      foreign        _cons
    weight     3.788e-07
 gear_ratio    .00039798    1.9711317
    foreign    .00008463   -.55488334    1.4266939
      _cons   -.00236851   -6.9153285    1.2149035    27.536291
```

If we use `_robust`, the initial steps are the same. We still need $\mathbf{D}$, the "bread" of the sandwich, and the residuals. The residuals `e` are the *varlist* for `_robust`. $\mathbf{D}$ is passed via the `variance()` option (abbreviation `v()`). $\mathbf{D}$ is overwritten, and contains the robust variance estimate.

```
. quietly regress mpg weight gear_ratio foreign, mse1

. matrix D = e(V)

. predict double e, residual

. _robust e, v(D) minus(4)

. matrix list D

symmetric D[4,4]
                  weight   gear_ratio      foreign        _cons
    weight     3.788e-07
 gear_ratio    .00039798    1.9711317
    foreign    .00008463   -.55488334    1.4266939
      _cons   -.00236851   -6.9153285    1.2149035    27.536291
```

Rather than specifying the `variance()` option, $\mathbf{D}$ and the point estimates can be first posted using `ereturn post`. `_robust` alters the post, substituting the robust variance estimates.

```
. quietly regress mpg weight gear_ratio foreign, mse1
. gen byte samp = e(sample)
. matrix D = e(V)
. matrix b = e(b)
. local n = e(N)
. local k = colsof(D)
. local dof = 'n' - 'k'
. predict double e, residual
. ereturn post b D, dof('dof') esample(samp)
. _robust e, minus('k')
. ereturn display
```

	Coef.	Robust Std. Err.	t	P>|t|	[95% Conf. Interval]	
weight	-.006139	.0006155	-9.97	0.000	-.0073666	-.0049115
gear_ratio	1.457113	1.40397	1.04	0.303	-1.343016	4.257243
foreign	-2.221682	1.194443	-1.86	0.067	-4.603923	.1605597
_cons	36.10135	5.247503	6.88	0.000	25.63554	46.56717

Again, what we did matches `regress, robust`:

```
. regress mpg weight gear_ratio foreign, robust
```

Regression with robust standard errors

```
Number of obs =      74
F(  3,    70) =   48.30
Prob > F      =  0.0000
R-squared     =  0.6670
Root MSE      =  3.4096
```

mpg	Coef.	Robust Std. Err.	t	P>|t|	[95% Conf. Interval]	
weight	-.006139	.0006155	-9.97	0.000	-.0073666	-.0049115
gear_ratio	1.457113	1.40397	1.04	0.303	-1.343016	4.257243
foreign	-2.221682	1.194443	-1.86	0.067	-4.603923	.1605597
_cons	36.10135	5.247503	6.88	0.000	25.63554	46.56717

◁

❏ Technical Note

Note the simple ways in which _robust was called. When we used the variance() option, we called it by typing

```
. _robust e, v(D) minus(4)
```

As we described, _robust computed

$$\widehat{V}(\widehat{\beta}) = \mathbf{D} \left(\frac{n}{n-k} \sum_{j=1}^{n} \widehat{e}_j^2 \mathbf{x}_j' \mathbf{x}_j \right) \mathbf{D}$$

We passed $\mathbf{D}$ to _robust using the option v(D), and specified $\widehat{e}_j$ as the variable e. So how did _robust know what variables to use for $\mathbf{x}_j$? It got them from the row and column names of the matrix D. Recall how we generated D initially:

```
. quietly regress mpg weight gear_ratio foreign, mse1
. matrix D = e(V)
. matrix list D

symmetric D[4,4]
                  weight   gear_ratio      foreign       _cons
    weight     5.436e-08
gear_ratio     .00006295    .20434146
   foreign     .00001032   -.08016692     .1311889
     _cons    -.00035697     -.782292     .17154326   3.3988878
```

Stata's estimation commands and the `ml` commands produce matrices with appropriately labeled rows and columns. So, if that is how you generate your **D**, this will be taken care of automatically. But if you generate **D** in another manner, be sure that you label it appropriately; see [P] **matrix rowname**.

When _robust is used after `ereturn post`, it gets the variable names from the row and column names of the posted matrices. So again, the matrices must be labeled appropriately.

Let us make another rather obvious comment. _robust uses the variables from the row and column names of the **D** matrix at the time _robust is called. It is the programmer's responsibility to ensure that the data in these variables have not changed, and that _robust selects the appropriate observations for the computation, using an `if` restriction if necessary (for instance, `if e(sample)`).

❑

Clustered data

To get robust variance estimates for clustered data or for complex survey data, simply use the `cluster()`, `strata()`, etc. options when you call _robust.

The first steps are the same as before. For clustered data, the number of degrees of freedom of the t statistic is the number of clusters minus one (we will discuss this later).

```
. quietly regress mpg weight gear_ratio foreign, mse1
. gen byte samp = e(sample)
. matrix D = e(V)
. matrix b = e(b)
. predict double e, residual
. local k = colsof(D)
. tabulate rep78
```

Repair Record 1978	Freq.	Percent	Cum.
1	2	2.90	2.90
2	8	11.59	14.49
3	30	43.48	57.97
4	18	26.09	84.06
5	11	15.94	100.00
Total	69	100.00	

```
. local nclust = r(r)
. di 'nclust'
5
. local dof = 'nclust' - 1
. ereturn post b D, dof('dof') esample(samp)
```

```
. _robust e, minus('k') cluster(rep78)
. ereturn display
                             (standard errors adjusted for clustering on rep78)
```

	Coef.	Robust Std. Err.	t	P>|t|	[95% Conf.	Interval]
weight	-.006139	.0008399	-7.31	0.002	-.008471	-.0038071
gear_ratio	1.457113	1.801311	0.81	0.464	-3.544129	6.458355
foreign	-2.221682	.8144207	-2.73	0.053	-4.482876	.0395129
_cons	36.10135	3.39887	10.62	0.000	26.66458	45.53813

What we get is, of course, the same as `regress, robust cluster()`. Wait a minute, it is not the same!

```
. regress mpg weight gear_ratio foreign, robust cluster(rep78)
Regression with robust standard errors          Number of obs =       69
                                                F( 3,    4) =    78.61
                                                Prob > F      =   0.0005
                                                R-squared     =   0.6631
Number of clusters (rep78) = 5                  Root MSE      =   3.4827
```

mpg	Coef.	Robust Std. Err.	t	P>|t|	[95% Conf.	Interval]
weight	-.005893	.0008214	-7.17	0.002	-.0081735	-.0036126
gear_ratio	1.904503	2.18322	0.87	0.432	-4.157088	7.966093
foreign	-2.149017	1.20489	-1.78	0.149	-5.49433	1.196295
_cons	34.09959	4.215275	8.09	0.001	22.39611	45.80307

Not even the point estimates are the same. We made the classic programmer's mistake of not using the same sample for our initial `regress, mse1` call as we did with `_robust`. Our cluster variable `rep78` is missing for 5 observations. `_robust` omitted these observations, but `regress, mse1` did not.

`_robust` is best used only in programs for just this reason. So, let's write a program and use `marksample` and `markout` (see [P] **mark**) to determine the sample in advance of running `regress` and `_robust`.

(Continued on next page)

```
                                                   ——— top of myreg.ado ———
program myreg, eclass
        version 8.0
        syntax varlist [if] [in] [, CLuster(varname) ]
        marksample touse
        markout `touse' `cluster', strok

        tempvar e count
        tempname D b

        quietly {
                regress `varlist' if `touse', mse1
                matrix `D' = e(V)
                matrix `b' = e(b)
                local n = e(N)
                local k = colsof(`D')
                predict double `e' if `touse', residual

                if "`cluster'"!="" {
                        sort `touse' `cluster'
                        by `touse' `cluster': gen byte `count' = 1 if _n==1 & `touse'
                        summarize `count', meanonly
                        local nclust =  r(sum)
                        local dof = `nclust' - 1
                        local clopt "cluster(`cluster')"
                }
                else    local dof = `n' - `k'

                ereturn post `b' `D', dof(`dof') esample(`touse')

                _robust `e' if e(sample), minus(`k') `clopt'
        }
        ereturn display
end
                                                   ——— end of myreg.ado ———
```

When we run this program, we do get the same results as `regress, robust cluster()`.

```
. myreg mpg weight gear_ratio foreign, cluster(rep78)
                     (standard errors adjusted for clustering on rep78)
```

	Coef.	Robust Std. Err.	t	P>|t|	[95% Conf. Interval]	
weight	-.005893	.0008214	-7.17	0.002	-.0081735	-.0036126
gear_ratio	1.904503	2.18322	0.87	0.432	-4.157088	7.966093
foreign	-2.149017	1.20489	-1.78	0.149	-5.49433	1.196295
_cons	34.09959	4.215275	8.09	0.001	22.39611	45.80307

Survey data

We will now modify our `myreg` command so that it handles complex survey data. Our new version will allow `pweights` and `iweights`, stratification, and clustering.

(Continued on next page)

```
                                                ── top of myreg.ado ──────
    program myreg, eclass
        version 8.0
        syntax varlist [if] [in] [pweight iweight] [, /*
            */ STRata(varname) CLuster(varname) ]
        marksample touse, zeroweight
        markout 'touse' 'cluster' 'strata', strok

        if "'weight'"!="" {
            tempvar w
            quietly gen double 'w' 'exp' if 'touse'
            local iwexp "[iw='w']"
            if "'weight'" == "pweight" {
                capture assert 'w' >= 0 if 'touse'
                if _rc error 402
            }
        }
        if "'cluster'"!="" {
            local clopt "cluster('cluster')"
        }
        if "'strata'"!="" {
            local stopt "strata('strata')"
        }
        tempvar e
        tempname D b

        quietly {
            regress 'varlist' 'iwexp' if 'touse', mse1
            matrix 'D' = e(V)
            matrix 'b' = e(b)
            predict double 'e' if 'touse', residual
            _robust 'e' 'iwexp' if 'touse', v('D') 'clopt' 'stopt' zeroweight

            local dof = r(N_clust) - r(N_strata)
            local depn : word 1 of 'varlist'
            ereturn post 'b' 'D', depn('depn') dof('dof') esample('touse')
        }
        di
        ereturn display
    end
                                                ── end of myreg.ado ──────
```

Note the following details about our version of myreg for survey data:

1. We called _robust before we posted the matrices with ereturn post, whereas in our previous version of myreg, we called ereturn post and then _robust. Here, we called _robust first so that we could use its r(N_strata), containing the number of strata, and r(N_clust), containing the number of clusters; see *Saved Results* at the end of this entry. We did this so that we could pass the correct degrees of freedom (= number of clusters − number of strata) to ereturn post.

   Note that this works even if the strata() and cluster() options are not specified: r(N_strata) = 1 if strata() is not specified (there truly is one stratum); and r(N_clust) = number of observations if cluster() is not specified (each observation is a cluster).

2. The call to _robust was made with iweights regardless of whether myreg was called with pweights or iweights. Computationally, _robust treats pweights and iweights exactly the same. The only difference is that it puts out an error message if it encounters a negative pweight, whereas negative iweights are allowed. As good programmers, we put out the error message early before any time-consuming computations are done.

3. We used the `zeroweight` option with the `marksample` command so that zero weights would not be excluded from the sample. We gave the `zeroweight` option with _robust so that it, too, would not exclude zero weights.

Observations with zero weights affect final results only by their effect (if any) on the counts of the clusters. Setting some weights temporarily to zero will, for example, produce subpopulation estimates. If subpopulation estimates are desired, however, it would be better to implement _robust's `subpop()` option and restrict the call to `regress, mse1` to this subpopulation.

4. Stata's `svy` commands always use `psu` rather than `cluster`. This is only a matter of style. They are synonyms as far as _robust is concerned.

Our program gives the same results as `svyregress`. Indeed, `svyregress` is implemented as an ado-file that calls `regress, mse1` and then _robust.

```
. myreg mpg weight gear_ratio foreign [pw=displ], strata(strata) cluster(psu)
```

mpg	Coef.	Std. Err.	t	P>|t|	[95% Conf. Interval]	
weight	-.0057248	.0004042	-14.16	0.000	-.0066055	-.0048441
gear_ratio	.7775839	1.084891	0.72	0.487	-1.586191	3.141359
foreign	-1.86776	1.242491	-1.50	0.159	-4.574914	.8393952
_cons	36.64061	3.912454	9.37	0.000	28.1161	45.16511

```
. svyset [pweight=displ], strata(strata) psu(psu)
pweight is displ
strata is strata
psu is psu

. svyregress mpg weight gear_ratio foreign

Survey linear regression
```

pweight:	displacement			Number of obs	=	74
Strata:	strata			Number of strata	=	3
PSU:	psu			Number of PSUs	=	15
				Population size	=	14600
				F(3, 10)	=	77.04
				Prob > F	=	0.0000
				R-squared	=	0.6900

mpg	Coef.	Std. Err.	t	P>|t|	[95% Conf. Interval]	
weight	-.0057248	.0004042	-14.16	0.000	-.0066055	-.0048441
gear_ratio	.7775839	1.084891	0.72	0.487	-1.586191	3.141359
foreign	-1.86776	1.242491	-1.50	0.159	-4.574914	.8393952
_cons	36.64061	3.912454	9.37	0.000	28.1161	45.16511

Controlling the header display

Compare the output for our survey version of `myreg` with the earlier version that only handled clustering. The header for the earlier version was

(standard errors adjusted for clustering on rep78)

	Robust					
Coef.	Std. Err.	t	P>|t|	[95% Conf. Interval]		

The header for the survey version lacked the word "Robust" above "Std. Err.", and it also lacked the banner "(standard errors adjusted for clustering on . . .)".

Both of these headers were produced by `ereturn display`, and programmers can control what it produces. The word above "Std. Err." is controlled by setting `e(vcetype)`. The banner "(standard errors adjusted for clustering on . . .)" is controlled by setting `e(clustvar)` to the cluster variable name. These can be set using the `ereturn local` command; see [P] **ereturn**.

When `_robust` is called after `ereturn post` (as it did in the earlier version that produced the above header), it automatically sets these macros. If you do not want the banner displayed, your code should read

```
ereturn post ...
_robust ...
ereturn local clustvar ""
```

You can also change the phrase displayed above "Std. Err." by resetting `e(vcetype)`. If you want nothing there, reset `e(vcetype)` to empty—`ereturn local vcetype ""`.

For our survey version of `myreg`, we called `_robust` before calling `ereturn post`. In this case, `_robust` does not set these macros. Trying to do so would be futile since `ereturn post` clears all previous estimation results, including all `e()` macros, but you can set them yourself after calling `ereturn post`. We make this addition to our survey version of `myreg`:

```
_robust ...
ereturn post ...
ereturn local vcetype "Design-based"
```

The output is

```
. myreg mpg weight gear_ratio foreign [pw=displ], strata(strata) cluster(psu)
```

mpg	Coef.	Design-based Std. Err.	t	P>|t|	[95% Conf. Interval]	
weight	-.0057248	.0004042	-14.16	0.000	-.0066055	-.0048441
gear_ratio	.7775839	1.084891	0.72	0.487	-1.586191	3.141359
foreign	-1.86776	1.242491	-1.50	0.159	-4.574914	.8393952
_cons	36.64061	3.912454	9.37	0.000	28.1161	45.16511

Maximum likelihood estimators

Maximum likelihood estimators are basically no different from linear regression when it comes to the use of `_robust`. We will first do a little statistics, and then give a simple example.

We can write our maximum-likelihood estimation equation as

$$\mathbf{G}(\boldsymbol{\beta}) = \sum_{j=1}^{n} \mathbf{S}(\boldsymbol{\beta}; y_j, \mathbf{x}_j) = \mathbf{0}$$

where $\mathbf{S}(\boldsymbol{\beta}; y_j, \mathbf{x}_j) = \partial l_j / \partial \boldsymbol{\beta}$ is the score vector and l_j the log likelihood for the jth observation. Here, $\boldsymbol{\beta}$ represents all the parameters in the model, including any auxiliary parameters. We will discuss how to use `_robust` when there are auxiliary parameters or multiple equations in the next section. But for now, all the theory works out fine for any set of parameters.

Using a first-order Taylor-series expansion (i.e., the delta method), we can write the variance of $\mathbf{G}(\beta)$ as

$$\widehat{V}\{\mathbf{G}(\beta)\}\big|_{\beta=\widehat{\beta}} = \frac{\partial \mathbf{G}(\beta)}{\partial \beta}\bigg|_{\beta=\widehat{\beta}} \widehat{V}(\widehat{\beta}) \frac{\partial \mathbf{G}(\beta)}{\partial \beta\prime}\bigg|_{\beta=\widehat{\beta}}$$

Solving for $\widehat{V}(\widehat{\beta})$ gives

$$\widehat{V}(\widehat{\beta}) = \left[\left\{\frac{\partial \mathbf{G}(\beta)}{\partial \beta}\right\}^{-1} \widehat{V}\{\mathbf{G}(\beta)\} \left\{\frac{\partial \mathbf{G}(\beta)}{\partial \beta\prime}\right\}^{-1}\right]\bigg|_{\beta=\widehat{\beta}}$$

but

$$\mathbf{H} = \frac{\partial \mathbf{G}(\beta)}{\partial \beta}$$

is the Hessian (matrix of second-derivatives) of the log likelihood. Thus, we can write

$$\widehat{V}(\widehat{\beta}) = \mathbf{D}\,\widehat{V}\{\mathbf{G}(\beta)\}\big|_{\beta=\widehat{\beta}}\,\mathbf{D}$$

where $\mathbf{D} = -\mathbf{H}^{-1}$ is the traditional covariance estimate.

Now $\mathbf{G}(\beta)$ is simply a sum, and we can estimate its variance just as we would the sum of any other variable—it is n^2 times the standard estimator of the variance of a mean:

$$\frac{n}{n-1}\sum_{j=1}^{n}\left(z_j - \overline{z}\right)^2$$

But, here, the scores $\mathbf{u}_j = \mathbf{S}(\widehat{\beta}; y_j, \mathbf{x}_j)$ are (row) vectors. Also note that their sum, and thus their mean, is zero. So, we have

$$\widehat{V}\{\mathbf{G}(\beta)\}\big|_{\beta=\widehat{\beta}} = \frac{n}{n-1}\sum_{j=1}^{n}\mathbf{u}_j'\mathbf{u}_j$$

Putting it all together, our robust variance estimator is

$$\widehat{V}(\widehat{\beta}) = \mathbf{D}\left(\frac{n}{n-1}\sum_{j=1}^{n}\mathbf{u}_j'\mathbf{u}_j\right)\mathbf{D}$$

so we see that the robust variance estimator is just the delta method combined with a simple estimator for totals!

The above estimator for the variance of the total (the center of the sandwich) is only appropriate when observations are independent. For clustered data and complex survey data, this estimator is replaced by one appropriate for the independent units of the data. Clusters (or PSUs) are independent, so we can sum the scores within a cluster to create a "super-observation" and then use the standard formula for a total on these independent super-observations. Our robust variance estimator thus becomes

$$\widehat{V}(\widehat{\beta}) = \mathbf{D}\left\{\frac{n_{\mathrm{c}}}{n_{\mathrm{c}}-1}\sum_{i=1}^{n_{\mathrm{c}}}\left(\sum_{j\in C_i}\mathbf{u}_j\right)'\left(\sum_{j\in C_i}\mathbf{u}_j\right)\right\}\mathbf{D}$$

where C_i contains the indices of the observations belonging to the ith cluster for $i = 1, 2, \ldots, n_c$, with n_c the total number of clusters.

See [SVY] **svymean** for the variance estimator for a total that is appropriate for complex survey data. Our development here has been quite heuristic. We have, for instance, purposefully omitted sampling weights from our discussion; see [SVY] **svy estimators** for a better treatment.

See Gould and Sribney (1999) for a discussion of maximum likelihood and of Stata's ml command.

❏ Technical Note

It is easy to see where the appropriate degrees of freedom for the robust variance estimator come from: the center of the sandwich is n^2 times the standard estimator of the variance for the mean of n observations. A mean divided by its standard error has exactly a Student's t distribution with $n - 1$ degrees of freedom for normal iid variables, but also has approximately this distribution under many other conditions. Thus, a point estimate divided by the square root of its robust variance estimate is approximately distributed as a Student's t with $n - 1$ degrees of freedom.

More importantly, this also applies to clusters, where each cluster is considered a "super-observation". Here, the degrees of freedom are $n_c - 1$, where n_c is the number of clusters (super-observations). Note that if there are only a small number of clusters, confidence intervals using t statistics can become quite large. It is just like estimating a mean with only a small number of observations.

When there are strata, the degrees of freedom are $n_c - L$, where L is the number of strata; see [SVY] **svymean** for details.

Note that not all of Stata's maximum likelihood estimators that produce robust variance estimators for clustered data use t statistics. Obviously, it only matters when the number of clusters is small. Users who want to be rigorous in their handling of clustered data should use the svy commands, where t statistics and adjusted Wald tests (see [SVY] **test for svy**) are always used. Programmers who want to inflict similar rigor should do likewise.

❏

We have not yet given any details about the functional form of our scores $\mathbf{u}_j = \partial l_j / \partial \boldsymbol{\beta}$. In many cases, the log likelihood l_j is a function of $\mathbf{x}_j \boldsymbol{\beta}$ (the "index"). Logistic regression, probit, and poisson regression are examples. There are no auxiliary parameters, and there is only one equation.

In these cases, we can write $\mathbf{u}_j = \widehat{s}_j \mathbf{x}_j$, where

$$\widehat{s}_j = \frac{\partial l_j}{\partial(\mathbf{x}_j \boldsymbol{\beta})}\bigg|_{\beta = \widehat{\beta}}$$

We refer to s_j as the score index. Our formula for the robust estimator when observations are independent becomes

$$\widehat{V}(\widehat{\boldsymbol{\beta}}) = \mathbf{D} \left(\frac{n}{n-1} \sum_{j=1}^{n} \widehat{s}_j^2 \, \mathbf{x}_j' \mathbf{x}_j \right) \mathbf{D}$$

This is precisely the formula that we used for linear regression, with $\widehat{e}_j$ replaced by $\widehat{s}_j$ and $k = 1$ in the multiplier.

Before we discuss auxiliary parameters, let's show how to implement _robust for single-equation models.

▷ Example

The robust variance implementation for single-equation maximum-likelihood estimators with no auxiliary parameters is almost exactly the same as it is for linear regression. The only differences are that **D** is now the traditional covariance matrix (the negative of the inverse of the matrix of second derivatives) and that the variable passed to _robust is the score index $\widehat{s}_j$ rather than the residuals $\widehat{e}_j$.

Let's alter our last myreg program for survey data to make a program that does logistic regression for survey data. We only have to change a few lines of the program.

```
───────────────────────────────────────────────────── top of mylogit.ado ─────────────
program mylogit, eclass
        version 8.0
        syntax varlist [if] [in] [pweight] [, /*
                */ STRata(varname) CLuster(varname) ]
        marksample touse, zeroweight
        markout 'touse' 'strata' 'cluster', strok

        if "'weight'"!="" {
                tempvar w
                quietly gen double 'w' 'exp' if 'touse'
                local awexp "[aw='w']"
                capture assert 'w' >= 0 if 'touse'
                if _rc error 402
        }
        if "'cluster'"!="" {
                local clopt "cluster('cluster')"
        }
        if "'strata'"!="" {
                local stopt "strata('strata')"
        }
        tempvar s
        tempname D b

        quietly {
                logit 'varlist' 'awexp' if 'touse'
                matrix 'D' = e(V)
                matrix 'b' = e(b)

                predict double 's' if e(sample)
                local depn : word 1 of 'varlist'
                replace 's' = ('depn'!=0) - 's' if e(sample)

                _robust 's' 'awexp' if e(sample), v('D') 'clopt' 'stopt' zeroweight

                local dof = r(N_clust) - r(N_strata)

                replace 'touse' = e(sample)
                ereturn post 'b' 'D', depn('depn') dof('dof') esample('touse')
                ereturn local vcetype "Design-based"
        }
        di // display blank line
        ereturn display
end
───────────────────────────────────────────────────── end of mylogit.ado ─────────────
```

(Continued on next page)

Note the following about our program:

1. This time we used `aweights` in both the call to `logit` and the call to `_robust`. Unfortunately, `logit` does not allow `iweights`; otherwise, we would have used them. If you examine the robust estimator formula $\mathbf{V} = \mathbf{DMD}$, you will see that $\mathbf{D} \propto w^{-1}$ and $\mathbf{M} \propto w^2$, where w represents the weights (any weights other than frequency weights). `logit` scales the weights when it computes $\mathbf{D}$, and `_robust` scales the weights when it computes $\mathbf{M}$; thus, these two scalings cancel each other out, and we are left with what we would have computed had we used unscaled weights. See *Methods and Formulas* at the end of this entry.

2. Since `logit` only allows nonnegative weights, so must `mylogit`. Negative weights are, admittedly, a rather odd item; they only arise when using some very specialized techniques.

3. We obtained the scores by first calling `predict` to compute the predicted probabilities and then doing the necessary computation ourselves. `logit` has a `score()` option that computes the scores. This would have been a better way to get the scores, but using `predict` is a more typical procedure.

4. `logit` is a unique command in that it will drop observations in some cases for reasons (e.g., when success or failure is predicted perfectly) other than missing values, so our `'touse'` variable may not represent the true estimation sample. That is why we used the `if e(sample)` condition with the `predict`, `replace`, and `_robust` commands. Then, to provide `ereturn post` with an appropriate `esample()` option, we set the `'touse'` variable equal to the `e(sample)` from the `logit` command and then use this `'touse'` variable in the `esample()` option.

Our `mylogit` program gives the same results as `svylogit`:

```
. mylogit foreign mpg weight gear_ratio [pw=displ], strata(strata) cluster(psu)
```

foreign	Coef.	Design-based Std. Err.	t	P>|t|	[95% Conf. Interval]	
mpg	-.3489011	.1263689	-2.76	0.017	-.6242353	-.0735669
weight	-.0040789	.001226	-3.33	0.006	-.00675	-.0014077
gear_ratio	6.324169	1.263861	5.00	0.000	3.570453	9.077886
_cons	-2.189748	7.220947	-0.30	0.767	-17.92284	13.54334

```
. svyset [pweight=displ], strata(strata) psu(psu)
pweight is displ
strata is strata
psu is psu

. svylogit foreign mpg weight gear_ratio
Survey logistic regression
```

pweight: displacement		Number of obs	=	74
Strata: strata		Number of strata	=	3
PSU: psu		Number of PSUs	=	15
		Population size	=	14600
		F(3, 10)	=	11.14
		Prob > F	=	0.0016

foreign	Coef.	Std. Err.	t	P>|t|	[95% Conf. Interval]	
mpg	-.3489011	.1263689	-2.76	0.017	-.6242353	-.0735669
weight	-.0040789	.001226	-3.33	0.006	-.00675	-.0014077
gear_ratio	6.324169	1.263861	5.00	0.000	3.570453	9.077886
_cons	-2.189748	7.220947	-0.30	0.767	-17.92284	13.54334

◁

❑ Technical Note

The theory developed here applies to full-information maximum-likelihood estimators. Conditional likelihoods such as conditional (fixed-effects) logistic regression (clogit) and Cox regression (stcox) use variants on this theme. The robust option on stcox uses a similar, but different, formula; see [ST] **stcox** and Lin and Wei (1989) for details.

On the other hand, the theory developed here applies to more estimators than just maximum likelihood estimators. The theory can also be applied to general estimating equations

$$\mathbf{G}(\beta) = \sum_{j=1}^{n} \mathbf{g}(\beta; y_j, \mathbf{x}_j) = \mathbf{0}$$

See, for example, Binder (1983) for a formal development of the theory.

Programmers are cautioned that they are responsible for the theory behind their implementation.

❑

Multiple-equation estimators

The theory for auxiliary parameters and multiple-equation models is no different from what we described in the previous section. For independent observations, just as before, our robust variance estimator is

$$\widehat{V}(\widehat{\beta}) = \mathbf{D}\left(\frac{n}{n-1}\sum_{j=1}^{n}\mathbf{u}_j'\mathbf{u}_j\right)\mathbf{D}$$

where $\mathbf{u}_j = \partial l_j / \partial \beta$ is the score (row) vector and $\mathbf{D}$ is the traditional covariance estimate (the negative of the inverse of the matrix of second derivatives).

With auxiliary parameters and/or multiple equations, we simply view β as the vector of all the parameters in the model. Without loss of generality, we can write the log likelihood as

$$l_j = l_j(\mathbf{x}_j^{(1)}\beta^{(1)}, \mathbf{x}_j^{(2)}\beta^{(2)}, \ldots, \mathbf{x}_j^{(p)}\beta^{(p)})$$

An auxiliary parameter is regarded as $\mathbf{x}_j^{(i)}\beta^{(i)}$ with $\mathbf{x}_j \equiv 1$ and $\beta^{(i)}$ a scalar. Our score vector becomes

$$\mathbf{u}_j = [\, s_j^{(1)}\mathbf{x}_j^{(1)} \quad s_j^{(2)}\mathbf{x}_j^{(2)} \quad \ldots \quad s_j^{(p)}\mathbf{x}_j^{(p)} \,]$$

where $s_j^{(i)} = \partial l_j / \partial(\mathbf{x}_j\beta^{(i)})$ is the score index for the ith equation.

This notation has been introduced so that it is clear how to call _robust. You use

. _robust $s_j^{(1)}$ $s_j^{(2)}$ ... $s_j^{(p)}$, *options*

where $s_j^{(1)}$, etc., are variables that contain the score indexes. The $\mathbf{D}$ matrix that you pass to _robust or post with ereturn post must be labeled with exactly p equation names.

_robust takes the first score index $s_j^{(1)}$ and matches it to the first equation on the $\mathbf{D}$ matrix to determine $\mathbf{x}_j^{(1)}$, takes the second score index and matches it to the second equation, etc. Some examples will make this perfectly clear.

▷ Example

Here is what a matrix with equation names looks like:

```
. matrix list D
symmetric D[6,6]
                       1:            1:            1:            2:            2:
                    price       foreign        _cons         price       foreign
  1:price      1.240e-08
  1:foreign   -1.401e-06      .593554
  1:_cons     -.00007592   -.13992997     .61347545
  2:price      4.265e-09    -5.366e-07    -.00002693    1.207e-08
  2:foreign   -1.590e-06     .37202357    -.02774147   -3.184e-06     .56833685
  2:_cons      -.0000265    -.0343682      .20468675   -.00007108    -.1027108
                       2:
                    _cons
  2:_cons      .54017838
```

The call to _robust would then be

```
. _robust s1 s2, v(D)
```

where s1 and s2 are the score indexes for equation 1 and equation 2, respectively.

Covariance matrices from models with auxiliary parameters look just like multiple-equation matrices:

```
. matrix list D
symmetric D[5,5]
                        eq1:          eq1:          eq1:          eq1:        sigma:
                     weight    gear_ratio       foreign         _cons         _cons
   eq1:weight     5.978e-07
eq1:gear_ratio     .00069222    2.2471526
  eq1:foreign      .00011344    -.88159935    1.4426905
  eq1:_cons       -.00392566    -8.6029018    1.8864693    37.377729
sigma:_cons       -7.217e-15    -1.663e-10    2.147e-10    -6.464e-09    .07430437
```

The second equation consists of the auxiliary parameter only. The call to _robust would be the same as before:

```
. _robust s1 s2, v(D)
```

◁

▷ Example

We will now give an example using ml and _robust to produce an estimation command that has robust and cluster() options. You can actually accomplish all of this easily using ml without using the _robust command since ml has robust and cluster() options. We will pretend that these two options are unavailable to illustrate the use of _robust.

To keep the example simple, we will do linear regression as a maximum likelihood estimator. In this case, the log likelihood is

$$l_j = -\frac{1}{2}\left\{\left(\frac{y_j - \mathbf{x}_j\boldsymbol{\beta}}{\sigma}\right)^2 + \ln\left(2\pi\sigma^2\right)\right\}$$

There is an auxiliary parameter σ, and we have two score indexes:

$$\frac{\partial l_j}{\partial(\mathbf{x}_j\boldsymbol{\beta})} = \frac{y_j - \mathbf{x}_j\boldsymbol{\beta}}{\sigma^2}$$

$$\frac{\partial l_j}{\partial \sigma} = \frac{1}{\sigma}\left\{\left(\frac{y_j - \mathbf{x}_j\boldsymbol{\beta}}{\sigma}\right)^2 - 1\right\}$$

Here are programs to compute this estimator. We have two ado-files: `mymle.ado` and `likereg.ado`. The first ado-file contains two programs `mymle` and `Scores`. `mymle` is the main program, and `Scores` is a subprogram that computes the score indexes after we compute the maximum likelihood solution. Since `Scores` is only called by `mymle`, we can nest it in the `mymle.ado` file; see [U] **20 Ado-files**.

```
──────────────────────────────────────────── top of mymle.ado ───────────
program mymle, eclass
        version 8.0
        local options "Level(integer 'c(level)')"
        if replay() {
                if "'e(cmd)'"!="mymle" {
                        error 301
                }
                syntax [, 'options']
                ml display, level('level')
                exit
        }
        syntax varlist [if] [in] [, /*
                */ 'options' Robust CLuster(varname) ]
// Determine estimation sample.
        marksample touse
        if "'cluster'"!="" {
                markout 'touse' 'cluster', strok
                local clopt "cluster('cluster')"
        }
// Get starting values.
        tokenize 'varlist'
        local depn "'1'"
        macro shift

        quietly summarize 'depn' if 'touse'
        local cons = r(mean)
        local sigma = r(sd)
// Do ml.
        ml model lf likereg ('depn'='*') /sigma if 'touse', /*
                */ init(/eq1='cons' /sigma='sigma')  max /*
                */ title("MLE linear regression") nooutput 'options'
        if "'robust'"!="" | "'cluster'"!="" {
                tempvar s1 s2
                Scores 'depn' 's1' 's2'
                _robust 's1' 's2' if 'touse', 'clopt'
        }
        ereturn local cmd "mymle"
        ml display, level('level')
end
```

```
program Scores
      version 8.0
      args depn s1 s2
      quietly {
            predict double 's1'
            gen double 's2' = ((('depn' - 's1')/[sigma][_cons])^2 - 1) /*
            */                /[sigma][_cons]
            replace 's1' = ('depn' - 's1')/([sigma][_cons]^2)
      }
end
```
——————————————————————————————————— end of mymle.ado ———————

Our `likereg` program computes the likelihood. Since it is called by Stata's `ml` commands, we cannot nest it in the other file.

———————————————————————————————— top of likereg.ado ———————
```
program likereg
      version 8.0
      args lf xb s
      qui replace 'lf' = -0.5*((($ML_y1 - 'xb')/'s')^2 + log(2*_pi*'s'^2))
end
```
——————————————————————————————————— end of likereg.ado ———————

Note the following:

1. Our command `mymle` will produce robust variance estimates if either the `robust` or the `cluster()` option is specified. Otherwise, it will display the traditional estimates.

2. We used the `lf` method with `ml`; see [R] **ml**. We could have used the `deriv1` or `deriv2` methods. Since you will probably include code to compute the first derivatives analytically for the `robust` option, there is no point in using `deriv0`. (However, one could compute the first derivatives numerically and pass these to _robust.)

3. Our `Scores` program uses `predict` to compute the index $x_j\beta$. Since we had already posted the results using `ml`, `predict` is available to us. Note that, by default, `predict` computes the index for the first equation.

4. Again, since we had already posted the results using `ml`, we can use `[sigma][_cons]` to get the value of σ; see [U] **16.5 Accessing coefficients and standard errors** for the syntax of accessing coefficients from multiple-equation models.

5. `ml` calls `ereturn post`, so when we call _robust, it alters the posted covariance matrix, replacing it with the robust covariance matrix. _robust also sets e(vcetype), and if the `cluster()` option is specified, it sets e(clustvar) as well.

6. We let `ml` produce Z statistics, even when we specified the `cluster()` option. If the number of clusters is small, it would be better to use t statistics. To do this, you could specify the `dof()` option on the `ml` command, but you would have to compute the number of clusters in advance. Alternatively, you could get the number of clusters from _robust's r(N_clust) and then re-post the matrices using `ereturn post`.

If we run our command with the cluster() option, we get

```
. mymle mpg weight gear_ratio foreign, cluster(rep78)
initial:       log likelihood =   -219.4845
rescale:       log likelihood =   -219.4845
rescale eq:    log likelihood =   -219.4845
Iteration 0:   log likelihood =   -219.4845  (not concave)
Iteration 1:   log likelihood = -207.02829  (not concave)
Iteration 2:   log likelihood =   -202.6134
Iteration 3:   log likelihood = -189.81321
Iteration 4:   log likelihood = -181.94707
Iteration 5:   log likelihood = -181.94473
Iteration 6:   log likelihood = -181.94473
```

```
MLE linear regression                          Number of obs    =          69
                                               Wald chi2(3)     =      135.82
Log likelihood = -181.94473                    Prob > chi2      =      0.0000
                            (standard errors adjusted for clustering on rep78)
```

mpg	Coef.	Robust Std. Err.	z	P>|z|	[95% Conf. Interval]	
eq1						
weight	-.005893	.000803	-7.34	0.000	-.0074669	-.0043191
gear_ratio	1.904503	2.134518	0.89	0.372	-2.279075	6.08808
foreign	-2.149017	1.178012	-1.82	0.068	-4.457879	.1598441
_cons	34.09959	4.121243	8.27	0.000	26.02211	42.17708
sigma						
_cons	3.380223	.8840543	3.82	0.000	1.647508	5.112937

These results are similar to the earlier results that we got with our first myreg program and regress, cluster.

Note that our likelihood is not globally concave. Linear regression is not globally concave in β and σ. ml's lf convergence routine encountered a little trouble in the beginning, but had no problem coming to the right solution.

◁

Saved Results

_robust saves in r():

Scalars

r(N)	number of observations
r(N_strata)	number of strata
r(N_clust)	number of clusters (PSUs)
r(sum_w)	sum of weights (if weights are specified)
r(N_subpop)	number of observations for subpopulation (subpop() only)
r(sum_wsub)	sum of weights for subpopulation (subpop() and weights only)

Note that r(N_strata) and r(N_clust) are always set. If the strata() option is not specified, r(N_strata) = 1 (there truly is one stratum). If neither the cluster() nor the psu() option is specified, r(N_clust) equals the number of observations (each observation is a PSU).

When _robust alters the post of ereturn post, it also saves in e():

Macros
    e(vcetype)   "Robust"
    e(clustvar)   name of cluster (PSU) variable

e(vcetype) controls the phrase ereturn display displays above "Std. Err."; e(vcetype) can be set to another phrase (or to empty for no phrase) if you wish. e(clustvar) displays the banner "(standard errors adjusted for clustering on *varname*)", or it can be set to empty (ereturn local clustvar "") if you do not wish this banner to be displayed.

Methods and Formulas

We give the formulas here for complex survey data, this being the most general case.

Our parameter estimates $\widehat{\beta}$ are the solution to the estimating equation

$$\mathbf{G}(\beta) = \sum_{h=1}^{L} \sum_{i=1}^{n_h} \sum_{j=1}^{m_{hi}} w_{hij} \mathbf{S}(\beta; y_{hij}, \mathbf{x}_{hij}) = \mathbf{0}$$

where (h, i, j) index the observations: $h = 1, \ldots, L$ are the strata, $i = 1, \ldots, n_h$ are the sampled PSUs (clusters) in stratum h, and $j = 1, \ldots, m_{hi}$ are the sampled observations in PSU (h, i). The outcome variable is represented by y_{hij}, the explanatory variables are $\mathbf{x}_{hij}$ (a row vector), and w_{hij} are the weights.

If no weights are specified, $w_{hij} = 1$. If the weights are aweights, they are first normalized to sum to the total number of observations in the sample: $n = \sum_{h=1}^{L} \sum_{i=1}^{n_h} m_{hi}$. If the weights are fweights, the formulas below do not apply; fweights are treated in such a way to give the same results as unweighted observations duplicated the appropriate number of times.

For maximum likelihood estimators, $\mathbf{S}(\beta; y_{hij}, \mathbf{x}_{hij}) = \partial l_j / \partial \beta$ is the score vector, where l_j is the log likelihood. Note that for survey data, this is not a true likelihood, but a "pseudo" likelihood; see [SVY] **svy estimators**.

Let

$$\mathbf{D} = -\frac{\partial \mathbf{G}(\beta)}{\partial \beta} \bigg|_{\beta=\widehat{\beta}}^{-1}$$

For maximum likelihood estimators, $\mathbf{D}$ is the traditional covariance estimate—the negative of the inverse of the Hessian. Note that in the following, the sign of $\mathbf{D}$ does not matter.

The robust covariance estimate calculated by _robust is

$$\widehat{V}(\widehat{\beta}) = \mathbf{DMD}$$

where $\mathbf{M}$ is computed as follows. Let $\mathbf{u}_{hij} = \mathbf{S}(\beta; y_{hij}, \mathbf{x}_{hij})$ be a row vector of scores for the (h, i, j) observation. Let

$$\mathbf{u}_{hi\bullet} = \sum_{j=1}^{m_{hi}} w_{hij} \mathbf{u}_{hij} \quad \text{and} \quad \overline{\mathbf{u}}_{h\bullet\bullet} = \frac{1}{n_h} \sum_{i=1}^{n_h} \mathbf{u}_{hi\bullet}$$

$\mathbf{M}$ is given by

$$\mathbf{M} = \frac{n-1}{n-k} \sum_{h=1}^{L} (1 - f_h) \frac{n_h}{n_h - 1} \sum_{i=1}^{n_h} (\mathbf{u}_{hi\bullet} - \overline{\mathbf{u}}_{h\bullet\bullet})'(\mathbf{u}_{hi\bullet} - \overline{\mathbf{u}}_{h\bullet\bullet})$$

where k is the value given in the `minus()` option. By default, $k = 1$, and the term $(n-1)/(n-k)$ vanishes. Stata's `regress, robust` and `regress, robust cluster()` use k equal to the number of explanatory variables in the model including the constant (Fuller et al. 1986). All `svy` commands use $k = 1$.

The specification $k = 0$ is handled differently. If `minus(0)` is specified, $(n-1)/(n-k)$ and $n_h/(n_h - 1)$ are both replaced by 1.

The factor $(1 - f_h)$ is the finite population correction. If the `fpc()` option is not specified, $f_h = 0$ is used. If `fpc()` is specified and the variable is greater than or equal to n_h, it is assumed to contain the values of N_h, and f_h is given by $f_h = n_h/N_h$, where N_h is the total number of PSUs in the population belonging to the hth stratum. If the `fpc()` variable is less than or equal to 1, it is assumed to contain the values of f_h. See [SVY] **svymean** for details and cautionary remarks.

For the `vsrs()` option and the computation of $\widehat{V}_{\text{srswor}}$, the `subpop()` option, and the `srssubpop` option, see [SVY] **svymean**.

References

Binder, D. A. 1983. On the variances of asymptotically normal estimators from complex surveys. *International Statistical Review* 51: 279–292.

Fuller, W. A. 1975. Regression analysis for sample survey. *Sankhyā, Series C* 37: 117–132.

Fuller, W. A., W. Kennedy, D. Schnell, G. Sullivan, H. J. Park. 1986. *PC Carp*. Ames, IA: Statistical Laboratory, Iowa State University.

Gail, M. H., W. Y. Tan, and S. Piantadosi. 1988. Tests for no treatment effect in randomized clinical trials. *Biometrika* 75: 57–64.

Gould, W. W. and W. M. Sribney. 1999. *Maximum likelihood estimation with Stata*. College Station, TX: Stata Press.

Huber, P. J. 1967. The behavior of maximum likelihood estimates under nonstandard conditions. In *Proceedings of the Fifth Berkeley Symposium on Mathematical Statistics and Probability*. Berkeley, CA: University of California Press, vol. 1, 221–233.

Kent, J. T. 1982. Robust properties of likelihood ratio tests. *Biometrika* 69: 19–27.

Kish, L. and M. R. Frankel. 1974. Inference from complex samples. *Journal of the Royal Statistical Society* B 36: 1–37.

Lin, D. Y. and L. J. Wei. 1989. The robust inference for the Cox proportional hazards model. *Journal of the American Statistical Association* 84: 1074–1078.

MacKinnon, J. G. and H. White. 1985. Some heteroskedasticity consistent covariance matrix estimators with improved finite sample properties. *Journal of Econometrics* 29: 305–325.

Rogers, W. H. 1993. sg17: Regression standard errors in clustered samples. *Stata Technical Bulletin* 13: 19–23. Reprinted in *Stata Technical Bulletin Reprints*, vol. 3, pp. 88–94.

Royall, R. M. 1986. Model robust confidence intervals using maximum likelihood estimators. *International Statistical Review* 54: 221–226.

White, H. 1980. A heteroskedasticity-consistent covariance matrix estimator and a direct test for heteroskedasticity. *Econometrica* 48: 817–830.

——. 1982. Maximum likelihood estimation of misspecified models. *Econometrica* 50: 1–25.

Also See

Complementary:	[P] **ereturn**,
	[R] **ml**
Related:	[SVY] **svy estimators**, [SVY] **svymean**,
	[R] **estimation commands**, [R] **regress**
Background:	[U] **21 Programming Stata**,
	[U] **23.14 Obtaining robust variance estimates**,
	[U] **29 Overview of Stata estimation commands**

Title

scalar — Scalar variables

Syntax

scalar [define] *scalar_name* = *exp*

scalar { dir | list } [_all | *scalar_name(s)*]

scalar drop { _all | *scalar_name(s)* }

Description

scalar define defines the contents of the scalar variable *scalar_name*.

scalar dir and list are the same command—both list the contents of currently defined scalars.

scalar drop eliminates defined scalars from memory.

Remarks

Stata scalars are named entities that store numbers which may include missing values. For instance,

```
. scalar a = 2
. display a+2
4
. scalar b = a+3
. display b
5
. scalar root2 = sqrt(2)
. display %18.0g root2
 1.414213562373095
. scalar im = sqrt(-1)
. display im
.
```

scalar list can be used to display the contents of macros (as can display for reasons that will be explained below) and scalar drop can be used to eliminate scalars from memory:

```
. scalar list
       im =            .
    root2 =   1.4142136
        b =           5
        a =           2
. scalar list a b
        a =           2
        b =           5
. scalar drop a b
. scalar list
       im =            .
    root2 =   1.4142136
. scalar drop _all
. scalar list
.  _
```

365

While scalars can be used interactively, their real use is in programs. Stata has macros and Stata has scalars, and deciding when to use which can be confusing.

▷ Example

Let's examine a problem where either macros or scalars could be employed in the solution. There will be occasions in your programs where you need something that we will describe as a mathematical scalar—a single number. For instance, let us assume that you are writing a program and need the mean of some variable for use in a subsequent calculation. You can obtain the mean after summarize from r(mean) (see *Saved Results* in [R] **summarize**), but you must obtain it immediately because the numbers stored in r() are reset almost every time you give a statistical command.

Let us complicate the problem: to make some calculation, you need to calculate the difference in the means of two variables which we will call var1 and var2. One solution to your problem is to use macros:

```
summarize var1, meanonly
local mean1 = r(mean)
summarize var2, meanonly
local mean2 =  r(mean)
local diff = 'mean1' - 'mean2'
```

Subsequently, you use 'diff' in your calculation. Let's understand how this works: You summarize var1, meanonly; inclusion of the meanonly option suppresses the output from the summarize command and the calculation of the variance. You then save the contents of r(mean)—the just-calculated mean—in the local macro mean1. You then summarize var2, again suppressing the output, and store that just-saved result in the local macro mean2. Finally, you create another local macro called diff that contains the difference. In making this calculation, you must put the mean1 and mean2 local macro names in single quotes because you want the contents of the macros. If the mean of var1 is 3 and var2 is 2, you want the numbers 3 and 2 substituted into the formula for diff to produce 1. If you omitted the single quotes, Stata would think you are referring to the difference not of the contents of macros named mean1 and mean2, but of two variables named mean1 and mean2. Those variables probably do not exist, so Stata would then produce an error message. In any case, you put the names in the single quotes.

Now let's consider the solution using Stata scalars:

```
summarize var1, meanonly
scalar m1 = r(mean)
summarize var2, meanonly
scalar m2 = r(mean)
scalar df = m1 - m2
```

The program fragments are quite similar, although note that this time we did not put the names of the scalars used in calculating the difference—which we called df this time—in single quotes. Stata scalars are allowed only in mathematical expressions—they are a kind of variable—and Stata knows you want the contents of those variables.

So, which solution is better? There is certainly nothing to recommend one over the other in terms of program length—both programs have the same number of lines and, in fact, there is a one-to-one correspondence between what each of the lines does. Nevertheless, the scalar-based solution is better, and here is why:

Macros are printable representations of things. When we said local mean1 = r(mean), Stata took the contents of r(mean), converted it into a printable form from its internal (and highly accurate) binary representation, and stored that string of characters in the macro mean1. When we created mean2, Stata did the same thing again. Then, when we said local diff = 'mean1' - 'mean2', Stata first substituted the contents of the macros mean1 and mean2—which are really strings—into the command. If the means of the two variables are 3 and 2, then the printable string representations stored in mean1 and mean2 are "3" and "2". After substitution, Stata was looking at the command local diff = 3 - 2. It then processed that, converting the 3 and 2 back into internal binary representation to take the difference, producing the number 1, which it then converted into the printable representation "1", which it finally stored in the macro diff.

All of this conversion from binary to printable representation and back again is a lot of work for Stata. Moreover, while there are no accuracy issues with numbers like 3 and 2, had the first number been $3.67108239891 \times 10^{-8}$, there would have been. When converting to printable form, Stata produces representations containing up to 17 digits, and, if necessary, uses scientific notation. The first number would have become 3.6710823989e-08 and the last digit would have been lost. In computer scientific notation, 17 printable positions provides you with a minimum of 13 significant digits. This is quite a lot, but not as many as Stata carries internally.

Now let us trace the execution of the solution using scalars. scalar m1 = r(mean) quickly copied the binary representation stored in r(mean) into the scalar m1. Similarly, executing scalar m2 = r(mean) did the same thing, although it saved it in m2. Finally, scalar df = m1 - m2 took the two binary representations, subtracted them, and copied the result to the scalar df. This produces a more accurate result.

◁

Naming scalars

Scalars can have the same names as variables in the data and Stata will not become confused. You, however, may. Consider the following Stata command:

```
. generate newvar = alpha*beta
```

What does it mean? It certainly means to create a new data variable named newvar, but what will be in newvar? There are four possibilities:

1. Take the data variable alpha and the data variable beta and multiply the corresponding observations together.

2. Take the scalar alpha and the data variable beta, multiply each observation of beta by alpha.

3. Take the data variable alpha and the scalar beta, multiply each observation of alpha by beta.

4. Take the scalar alpha and the scalar beta, multiply them together, and store the result repeatedly into newvar.

How Stata decides among these four possibilities is the topic of this section.

Stata's first rule is that if there is only one alpha, be it a data variable or a scalar, and one beta, be it a data variable or a scalar, Stata selects the single feasible solution and does it. If, however, there is more than one alpha or more than one beta, Stata always selects the data-variable interpretation in preference to the scalar.

For instance, assume you have a data variable called alpha and a scalar called beta:

```
. list

         alpha
 1.          1
 2.          3
 3.          5
```

```
. scalar list
      beta =              3
. gen newvar = alpha*beta
. list
          alpha     newvar
  1.          1          3
  2.          3          9
  3.          5         15
```

The result was to take the data variable `alpha` and multiply it by the scalar `beta`. Now let's start again, but this time, assume you have a data variable called `alpha` and both a data variable and a scalar called `beta`:

```
. scalar list
      beta =              3
. list
          alpha       beta
  1.          1          2
  2.          3          3
  3.          5          4
. gen newvar = alpha*beta
. list
          alpha       beta     newvar
  1.          1          2          2
  2.          3          3          9
  3.          5          4         20
```

The result is to multiply the data variables, ignoring the scalar `beta`. In situations like this, you can force Stata to use the scalar by specifying `scalar(beta)` rather than merely `beta`:

```
. gen newvar2 = alpha*scalar(beta)
. list
          alpha       beta     newvar    newvar2
  1.          1          2          2          3
  2.          3          3          9          9
  3.          5          4         20         15
```

The `scalar()` pseudo-function, placed around a name, says that the name is to be interpreted as the name of a scalar even if a data variable by the same name exists. You can use `scalar()` around all your scalar names if you wish; it is not required that there be a name conflict. Obviously, it will be easiest if you give your data and scalars different names.

❑ Technical Note

The advice to name scalars and data variables differently may work interactively, but in programming situations, you cannot know whether the name you have chosen for a scalar conflicts with the data variables because the data are typically provided by the user and could have any names whatsoever.

One solution—and not a very good one—is to place the `scalar()` pseudo-function around the names of all your scalars when you use them. A much better solution is to obtain the names for your scalars from Stata's `tempname` facility; see [P] **macro**. There are other advantages as well. Let us go back to calculating the sum of the means of variables `var1` and `var2`. Our original draft looked like

```
summarize var1, meanonly
scalar m1 = r(mean)
summarize var2, meanonly
scalar m2 = r(mean)
scalar df = m1 - m2
```

A well-written draft would look like

```
tempname m1 m2 df
summarize var1, meanonly
scalar 'm1' = r(mean)
summarize var2, meanonly
scalar 'm2' = r(mean)
scalar 'df' = 'm1' - 'm2'
```

We first declared the names of our temporary scalars. Actually, what tempname does is create three new local macros named m1, m2, and df, and place in those macros names that Stata makes up, names that are guaranteed to be different from the data. (m1, for your information, probably contains something like __000001.) When we use the temporary names, we put single quotes around them—m1 is not the name we want; we want the name that is stored in the local macro named m1.

That is, if we type

```
scalar m1 = r(mean)
```

we create a scalar named m1. After tempname m1 m2 df, if we type

```
scalar 'm1' = r(mean)
```

we create a scalar named with whatever name happens to be stored in m1. It is Stata's responsibility to make sure that name is valid and unique, and Stata did that when we issued the tempname command. As programmers, we never need to know what is really stored in the macro m1: all we need to do is put single quotes around the name whenever we use it.

There is a second advantage to naming scalars with names obtained from tempname. Stata knows that they are temporary—when our program concludes, all temporary scalars will be automatically dropped from memory. And, if our program calls another program, that program will not accidentally use one of our scalars even if the programmer happened to use the same name. Consider

```
program myprog
        ( lines omitted )
        tempname m1
        scalar 'm1' = something
        mysub
        ( lines omitted )
end
program mysub
        ( lines omitted )
        tempname m1
        scalar 'm1' = something else
        ( lines omitted )
end
```

Both myprog and mysub refer to a scalar 'm1'; myprog defines 'm1' and then calls mysub, and mysub then defines 'm1' differently. When myprog regains control, however, 'm1' is just as it was before calling mysub!

It is unchanged because the scalar is not named m1: it is named something as returned by tempname—a guaranteed unique name—and that name is stored in the local macro m1. When mysub is executed, Stata safely hides all local macros, so the local macro m1 in mysub has no relation to the local macro m1 in myprog. mysub now puts a temporary name in its local macro m1—a different name because tempname always returns unique names—and mysub goes forth to use that different name. When mysub completes, Stata discards the temporary scalars and macros, restores the definitions of the old temporary macros, and myprog is off and running again.

Even if `mysub` had been poorly written in the sense of not obtaining its temporary names from `tempname`, `myprog` would have no difficulty. The use of `tempname` by `myprog` is sufficient to guarantee that no other program can harm it. For instance, pretend `mysub` looked like

```
program mysub
        ( lines omitted )
        scalar m1 = something else
        ( lines omitted )
end
```

Note that `mysub` is now directly using a scalar named `m1`. That will not interfere with `myprog`, however, because `myprog` has no scalar named `m1`. Its scalar is named 'm1', a name obtained from `tempname`.

❏

❏ Technical Note

One result of the above is that scalars are not automatically shared between programs. The scalar 'm1' in `myprog` is different from either of the scalars `m1` or 'm1' in `mysub`. What if `mysub` needs `myprog`'s 'm1'?

One solution is not to use `tempname`: write `myprog` to use the scalar `m1` and `mysub` to use the scalar `m1`. Both will be accessing the same scalar. This, however, is not recommended.

A better solution is to pass 'm1' as an argument. For instance,

```
program myprog
        ( lines omitted )
        tempname m1
        scalar 'm1' = something
        mysub 'm1'
        ( lines omitted )
end
program mysub
        args m1
        ( lines omitted )
        commands using 'm1'
        ( lines omitted )
end
```

We passed the name of the scalar given to us by `tempname`— 'm1' —as the first argument to `mysub`. `mysub` picked up its first argument and stored that in its own local macro by the same name—`m1`. Actually, `mysub` could have stored the name in any macro name of its choosing; the line reading `args m1` could read `args m2` as long as we changed the rest of `mysub` to use the name 'm2' wherever it uses the name 'm1'.

❏

Also See

Complementary:	[P] **matrix**
Related:	[P] **macro**
Background:	[U] **21.3 Macros**,
	[U] **21.7.2 Temporary scalars and matrices**

Title

---

serset — Create and manipulate sersets

Syntax

serset <u>cr</u>eate *varlist* [if *exp*] [in *range*] [, <u>omitanymiss</u> <u>omitallmiss</u>

    <u>omitdupmiss</u> <u>omitn</u>othing sort(*varlist*)]

serset create_xmedians svn_y svn_x [svn_w] [, bands(#) xmin(#) xmax(#)

    logx logy]

serset create_cspline svn_y svn_x [, n(#)]

serset [set] $\#_s$

serset sort [*svn* [*svn* [...]]]

serset <u>s</u>ummarize *svn* [, <u>d</u>etail]

serset use [, clear]

serset

serset reset_id $\#_s$

serset drop [*numlist* | _all]

serset clear

serset dir

In addition, the file command is extended to allow

file sersetwrite *handle*

file sersetread *handle*

The following extended macro functions are also available:

Extended function	Returns from the *current serset*
: serset id	id
: serset k	number of variables
: serset N	number of observations
: serset varnum *svn*	*svnum* of *svn*
: serset type *svn*	storage type of *svn*
: serset format *svn*	display format of *svn*
: serset varnames	list of *svns*
: serset min *svn*	minimum of *svn*
: serset max *svn*	maximum of *svn*

Extended macro functions have the syntax
        local *macname* : ...
The *current serset* is the most recently created or the most recently set by
the serset set command.

In the above syntax diagrams,

$\#_s$ refers to a serset number, $0 <= \# <= 99$.

varlist refers to the usual Stata varlist; that is, a list of variables that appear in the current dataset, not the current serset.

svn refers to a variable in a serset. The variable may be referred to either by its name (e.g., mpg or l.gnp) or its number (e.g., 1 or 5), and which is used makes no difference.

svnum refers to a variable number in a serset.

Description

serset creates and manipulates sersets.

file sersetwrite writes and file sersetread reads sersets into files.

The extended macro function :serset reports information about the current serset.

Options

Options for serset create

omitanymiss, omitallmiss, omitdupmiss, and omitnothing specify how observations with missing values are to be treated.

omitanymiss is the default. Observations in which any of the numeric variables contain missing are omitted from the serset being created.

omitallmiss specifies that only observations in which all the numeric variables contain missing are to be omitted.

omitdupmiss specifies that only duplicate observations in which all the numeric variables contain missing are to omitted. Note that the observations omitted will be a function of the sort order of the original data.

omitnothing specifies that no observations are to be omitted (other than those excluded by the if *exp* and in *range*).

sort(*varlist*) specifies that the serset being created is to be sorted by the specified variables. The result is no different from, after serset creation, using the serset sort command, but total execution time is a little faster. The sort order of the data in memory is unaffected by this option.

Options for serset create_xmedians

bands(#) specifies the number of divisions along the x-scale in which cross-medians are to be calculated; the default is bands(200). bands() may be specified to be between 3 and 200.

Let m and M specify the minimum and maximum value of x. If the scale is divided into n bands (i.e., bands(n) is specified), the first band is m to $m + (M - m)/n$, the second $m + (M - m)/n$ to $m + 2*(M - m)/n$, ..., and the nth $m + (n - 1)*(M - m)/n$ to $m + n*(M - m)/n = m + M - m = M$.

xmin(#) and xmax(#) specify the minimum and maximum values of the x variable to be used in the bands calculation—m and M in the formulas above. The actual minimum and maximum are used if these options are not specified. In addition, if xmin() is specified with a number that is greater than the actual minimum, the actual minimum is used, and if xmax() is specified with a number that is less than the actual maximum, the actual maximum is used.

logx and logy specify that cross medians are to be created using a "log" scale. The exponential of the median of the log of the values is calculated in each band.

Options for serset create_cspline

n(#) specifies the number of points to be evaluated between each pair of x values, which are treated as the knots. The default is n(5), and n() may be between 1 and 300.

Options for serset summarize

detail specifies additional statistics including skewness, kurtosis, the four smallest and four largest values, and various percentiles. This option is identical to the detail option of summarize.

Options for serset use

clear permits the serset to be loaded even if there is a dataset already in memory and even if that dataset has changed since it was last saved.

Remarks

Remarks are presented under the headings

> *Introduction*
> *serset create*
> *serset create x_medians*
> *serset create_cspline*
> *serset set*
> *serset sort*
> *serset summarize*
> *serset use*
> *serset*
> *serset reset_id*
> *serset drop*
> *serset clear*
> *serset dir*
> *file sersetwrite and file sersetread*

Introduction

Sersets are used in implementing Stata's graphics capabilities. When you make a graph, the data for the graph are extracted into a serset, and then, at the lowest levels of Stata's graphics implementation, are graphed from there.

Sersets are like datasets: they contain observations on one or more variables. Each serset is assigned a number, and, in your program, you use that number when referring to a serset. Thus, multiple sersets can reside simultaneously in memory. (Sersets are, in fact, stored in a combination of memory and temporary disk files, and so accessing their contents is slower than accessing the data in memory. Sersets, however, are fast enough to keep up with graphics operations.)

serset create

serset create creates a new serset from the data in memory. For instance,

```
. serset create mpg weight
```

creates a new serset containing variables mpg and weight. When using the serset subsequently, you can refer to these variables by their names, mpg and weight, or by their numbers, 1 and 2.

serset create also returns in r():

r(N)	the number of observations placed into the serset
r(k)	the number of variables placed into the serset
r(id)	the number assigned to the serset

r(N) and r(k) are just for your information; by far the most important returned result is r(id). It is this number that you will need to use in subsequent commands to refer to this serset.

In addition, serset create sets the *current serset* to the one just created. Commands that use sersets always use the current serset. If, in subsequent commands, the current serset is not the one desired, you can set the desired one using serset set, described below.

serset create x_medians

serset create x_medians creates a new serset based on the currently set serset. The basic syntax is

serset create_xmedians svn_y svn_x $\left[svn_w \right] \left[, \ \ldots \right]$

The new serset will contain cross medians. Put that aside. On the serset create_xmedians command, you specify two or three variables. Those two or three variables are to be variables recorded in the current serset. The result is to create a new serset containing two variables (svn_y and svn_x) and a different number of observations. As with serset create, the result will also be to save in r():

r(id)	the number assigned to the serset
r(k)	the number of variables in the serset
r(N)	the number of observations in the serset

The newly created serset will become the current serset.

In actual use, you might code

```
serset create 'yvar' 'xvar' 'zvar'
local base = r(id)
...
serset set 'base'
serset create_xmedians 'yvar' 'xvar'
local cross = r(id)
...
```

serset create_xmedians obtains data from the original serset, and calculates the median values of svn_y and the median values of svn_x for bands of svn_x values. The result is a new dataset of n observations (one for each band) containing median y and median x values, where the variables have the same name as the original variables. These results are stored in the newly created serset. If a third variable is specified, svn_w, the calculation of the medians is made in a weighted fashion.

serset create_cspline

serset create_cspline works in the same fashion as serset create_xmedians: it takes one serset and creates another serset from it, leaving the first unchanged. Thus, as with all serset creation commands, returned in r() is

r(id)	the number assigned to the serset
r(k)	the number of variables in the serset
r(N)	the number of observations in the serset

and the newly created serset will become the current serset.

serset create c_spline performs cubic spline interpolation, and, in this case, the new serset will contain the interpolated points. The original serset should contain the knots through which the cubic spline is to pass. serset create c_spline also has option n(#) that specifies how many points are to be interpolated, so the resulting dataset will have $N + (N - 1) * n()$, where N is the number of observations in the original dataset. A typical use of serset create c_spline would be

```
serset create 'yvar' 'xvar'
local base = r(id)
...
serset set 'base'
serset create_xmedians 'yvar' 'xvar'
local cross = r(id)
...
serset set 'cross'
serset create_cspline 'yvar' 'xvar'
...
```

In this example, the spline is placed through not the original data, but through cross-medians of the data.

serset set

serset set is used to make a previously created serset the current serset. You may omit the set. Typing

```
serset 5
```

is equivalent to typing

```
serset set 5
```

You would never actually know ahead of time the number of a serset that you needed to code. Instead, at serset creation time, you would have recorded the identity of the serset created, say, in a local macro, by typing

```
local id = r(id)
```

and then later, you would make that serset the current serset by coding

```
serset set 'id'
```

serset sort

serset sort changes the order of the observations of the current serset. For instance,

```
serset create mpg weight
local id = r(id)
serset sort weight mpg
```

would place the observations of the serset in ascending order of variable `weight` and, within equal values of `weight`, in ascending order of variable `mpg`.

If no variables are specified after `serset sort`, `serset sort` does nothing. That is not considered an error.

serset summarize

serset summarize returns summary statistics about a variable in the current serset. It does not display output or in any way change the current serset.

Returned in `r()` is exactly what the `summarize` command returns in `r()`.

serset use

serset use loads a serset into memory. That is, it copies the current serset into the current data. The serset is left unchanged.

serset

serset typed without arguments produces no output, but returns in `r()` information about the current serset:

r(id)	the number assigned to the current serset
r(k)	the number of variables in the current serset
r(N)	the number of observations in the current serset

If no serset is in use, `r(id)` is set to -1 and `r(k)` and `r(N)` are left undefined; no error message is produced.

serset reset_id

serset reset_id is a rarely used command. Its syntax is

serset reset_id $\#_s$

serset reset_id changes the id of the current serset—its number—to the number specified, if that is possible. If not, it produces the error message "series $\#_s$ in use"; r(111).

Either way, the same serset continues to be the current serset (i.e., the number of the current serset changes if the command is successful).

serset drop

`serset drop` eliminates (erases) the specified sersets from memory. For instance,

```
serset drop 5
```

would eliminate serset 5, and

```
serset drop 5/9
```

would eliminate sersets 5, 6, 7, 8, and 9. Using `serset drop` to drop a serset that does not exist is not an error; it does nothing.

Typing `serset drop _all` would drop all existing sersets.

Be careful not to drop sersets that are not yours: Stata's graphics system creates and holds onto sersets frequently, and, if you drop one of its sersets that are in use, the graph on the screen will eventually "fall apart" and Stata will produce error messages (Stata will not crash). The graphics system will itself drop sersets when it is through with them.

The `discard` command also drops all existing sersets. This, however, is safe because `discard` also closes any open graphs.

serset clear

`serset clear` is a synonym for `serset drop _all`.

serset dir

`serset dir` displays a description of all existing sersets.

file sersetwrite and file sersetread

`file sersetwrite` and `file sersetread` are extensions to the `file` command; see [P] **file**. These extensions write and read sersets into files. The files may be opened `text` or `binary`, but, either way, what is written into the file will be in a binary format.

`file sersetwrite` writes the current serset. A code fragment might read

```
serset create ...
local base = r(id)
...
tempname hdl
file open `hdl' using "`filename'", write ...
...
serset set `base'
file sersetwrite `hdl'
...
file close `hdl'
```

`file sersetread` reads a serset from a file, creating a new serset in memory. `file sersetread` returns in `r(id)` the serset id of the newly created serset. A code fragment might read

```
tempname hdl
file open `hdl' using "`filename'", read ...
...
file sersetread `hdl'
local new = r(id)
...
file close `hdl'
```

See [P] **file** for more information on the `file` command.

Saved Results

serset create, serset create_xmedians, serset create_cspline, serset set, and serset save in r():

Scalars
    r(id)   the serset id
    r(k)   the number of variables in the serset
    r(N)   the number of observations in the serset

serset summarize returns in r() the same results as returned by the summarize command.

serset use returns in macro r(varnames) the names of the variables in the newly created dataset.

file sersetread returns in scalar r(id) the serset id, which is the identification number assigned to the serset.

Also See

Related: [P] **class**, [P] **file**

Title

sleep — Pause for a specified time

Syntax

> `sleep #`

where # is number of milliseconds (1,000 milliseconds = 1 second).

Description

`sleep` tells Stata to pause for # milliseconds before continuing with the next command.

Remarks

Use `sleep` when you want Stata to wait for some amount of time before executing the next command.

> `. sleep 10000`

pauses Stata for 10 seconds.

Title

smcl — Stata Markup and Control Language

Description

SMCL, which stands for Stata Markup and Control Language and is pronounced "smicle", is Stata's output language. SMCL directives, such as "{it:...}" in the following,

    One can output {it:italics} using SMCL

affect how output appears:

    One can output *italics* using SMCL

All Stata output is processed by SMCL: help files, statistical results, and even the output of display in the programs you write.

Remarks

Remarks are presented under the headings

> *Introduction*
> *SMCL modes*
> *Command summary—general syntax*
> *Formatting commands for use in line and paragraph modes*
> *Link commands for use in line and paragraph modes*
> *Formatting commands for use in line mode*
> *Formatting commands for use in paragraph mode*
> *Commands for use in As-Is mode*
> *Commands for use in Stata 6 help mode*
> *The {ccl} directive*
> *The {char} directive*
> *Advice on using display*
> *Advice on formatting help files*

Introduction

The two main uses of SMCL are in the programs you compose and in the help files you write to document them, although SMCL may be used in any context. Everything Stata displays on the screen is processed by SMCL.

Your first encounter with SMCL was probably the Stata session logs created by the log using command. By default, Stata creates logs in SMCL format and even gives them the file suffix .smcl. The file suffix does not matter, that the output is in SMCL format does. Files containing SMCL can be redisplayed in their original rendition, and SMCL output can be translated to other formats using the translate command; see [R] **translate**.

SMCL is mostly just ASCII text. For instance,

    . display "this is SMCL"
    this is SMCL

but throughout that can be SMCL directives. SMCL directives are enclosed in braces. Try the following:

```
. display "{title:this is SMCL, too}"
this is SMCL, too
```

The "{title:...}" directive told SMCL to output what followed the colon in title format. Exactly how title format appears on your screen—or on paper should you print it—will vary, but SMCL will ensure that it always appears as a recognizable title.

Now try this:

```
. display "now we will try {help summarize:clicking}"
now we will try clicking
```

Type the above into Stata. The word *clicking* will appear as clickable text—probably in some shade of blue. Click on the word. This will bring up Stata's Viewer and show you help for the summarize command. The SMCL {help:...} directive is an example of a *link*. The directive {help summarize:clicking} displayed the word *clicking*, and arranged things so that when the user clicked on the highlighted word, help for summarize appeared.

Here is another example of a link:

```
. display "You can also run Stata commands by {stata summarize mpg:clicking}"
You can also run Stata commands by clicking
```

Click on the word and this time the result will be exactly as if you had typed the command "summarize mpg" into Stata. If you have the automobile data loaded, you will see the summary statistics for the variable mpg.

That is how SMCL is used. You can use it to make your output look better and to add clickable links.

SMCL modes

At all times, SMCL is in one of four modes:

        1. SMCL line mode
        2. SMCL paragraph mode
        3. As-Is mode
        4. Stata 6 help mode

Modes 1 and 2 are nearly alike—in these two modes, SMCL directives are understood, and the modes differ only in that blanks and carriage returns are taken seriously in line mode and less seriously in paragraph mode. In paragraph mode—so called because it is useful for formatting text into paragraphs—SMCL will join one line to the next and split lines to form output with lines that are of nearly equal length. In line mode, SMCL shows the line very much as you entered it. For instance, in line mode, the input text

```
    Variable name        mean        standard error
```

(which might appear in a help file) would be spaced in the output exactly as we entered it. In paragraph mode, the above would be output as "Variable name mean standard error", which is to say, all run together. On the other hand, the text

```
    The two main uses of SMCL are in the programs you compose and in the help files
    you write to document them,  although SMCL may be used in any context.
    Everything Stata displays on the screen is processed by SMCL.
```

would be set into a nicely formatted paragraph in paragraph mode.

In mode 3, As-Is mode, SMCL directives are not interpreted. {title:...}, for instance, has no special meaning—it is just the characters open brace, t, i, and so on. If {title:...} appeared in SMCL input text,

```
{title:My Title}
```

it would be displayed exactly as it appears: {title:My Title}. In As-Is mode, text is taken just as it is and SMCL just displays it. As-Is mode is of little use to people other than those wishing to document how SMCL works, because with As-Is mode, they can show examples of what SMCL input looks like.

Mode 4, Stata 6 help mode, you want to avoid; it is included for backwards compatibility. Prior to Stata 7, Stata's help files had an odd and special encoding that would allow some words to be highlighted, and it also allowed the creation of clickable links to other help files. However, it does not have nearly the features of SMCL, and, moreover, it can only be used in .hlp files. In Stata 6 help mode, SMCL recreates this old environment so that old help files continue to display correctly even if they have not been updated.

Those are the four modes, and the most important of them are the first two, the SMCL modes, and the single most important mode is SMCL line mode—mode 1. Line mode is the mother of all modes in that SMCL continually returns to it, and it is only from line mode that you can get to the other modes. For instance, to enter paragraph mode you use the {p} directive, and you use it from line mode, although you typically do not think of that. Paragraphs end when a blank line is encountered, and what *end* means is that SMCL returns to line mode. Consider the following lines appearing in some help file:

```
{p}
The two main uses of SMCL are in the programs you compose and
the
help files you write to document them,
although SMCL may be used in any context.
Everything Stata displays on the screen is processed by SMCL.

{p}
Your first encounter with SMCL was probably the Stata session
...
```

Between the paragraphs above, SMCL returned to line mode. SMCL stayed in paragraph mode as long as the paragraph continued without a blank line, but, once the paragraph ended, SMCL returned to line mode. There are ways of ending paragraphs other than blank lines, but blank lines are the most common. Regardless of how paragraphs end, SMCL returns to line mode.

In another part of our help file, we might have

```
{p}
SMCL, which stands for Stata Markup and Control Language
and is pronounced "smicle", is Stata's output language.
SMCL directives, for example, the {c -(}it:...{c )-} in the following,
        One can output {it:italics} using SMCL
{p} affects how output appears:  ...
```

Between the paragraphs, we entered line mode, so the "One can output..." part will appear as we have spaced it, namely indented. It will appear that way because we are in line mode.

The other two modes are invoked using the {asis} and {s6hlp} directives and do not end with blank lines. They continue until you enter the {smcl} directive, and, in this case {smcl} must be followed by a carriage return. You may put a carriage return at the end of {asis} or the {s6hlp} directives—it will make no difference—but to return to SMCL line mode, you must put a carriage return directly after the {smcl} directive.

To summarize, when dealing with SMCL, begin by assuming you are in line mode; you almost certainly will be. If you wish to enter a paragraph, you will use the {p} directive, but, once the paragraph ends, you will be back in line mode and ready to start another paragraph if you desire. If you want to enter As-Is mode, perhaps because you are including a piece of ASCII text output, use the {asis} directive, and at the end of the piece, use the {smcl}(carriage return) directive to return to line mode. If you want to include a piece of an old Stata 6 help file, use the {s6hlp} directive to enter Stata 6 help mode, and, at its conclusion, use {smcl}(carriage return) to return to line mode.

Command summary—general syntax

Pretend that {xyz} is a SMCL directive, although it is not. {xyz} might have any of the following syntaxes:

Syntax 1: {xyz}

Syntax 2: {xyz:*text*}

Syntax 3: {xyz *args*}

Syntax 4: {xyz *args*:*text*}

Syntax 1 means, "do whatever it is that {xyz} does". Syntax 2 means, "do whatever it is that {xyz} does, do it on the text *text*, and then stop doing it." Syntax 3 means, "do whatever it is that {xyz} does, as modified by *args*." Finally, Syntax 4 means, "do whatever it is that {xyz} does, as modified by *args*, do it on the text *text*, and then stop doing it."

Not every SMCL directive has all four syntaxes, and which syntaxes are allowed is made clear in the descriptions below.

Also note that in Syntaxes 3 and 4, *text* may contain other SMCL directives, so the following is valid:

```
{center:The use of {ul:SMCL} in help files}
```

The *text* of one SMCL directive may itself contain other SMCL directives. There is, however, one important limitation of which you need be aware: Not only must the braces match, but they must match on the same physical (input) line. To wit,

```
{center:The use of {ul:SMCL} in help files}
```

is correct, but

```
{center:The use of {ul:SMCL} in
help files}
```

is an error. When SMCL encounters an error, it simply displays the text in the output it does not understand, so the result of making the error above would be to display

```
{center:The use of SMCL in
help files}
```

The {ul:...} SMCL understood, but the {center:...} it did not because the braces did not match on the input line, so that part is just displayed. If you see SMCL directives in your output, you have made an error.

Formatting commands for use in line and paragraph modes

{sf}, {it}, and {bf} follow Syntaxes 1 and 2.
These directives specify how the font is to appear. {sf} indicates standard face (font), {it} italic face, and {bf} boldface.

Used in Syntax 1, these directives switch to the font face specified, and that rendition will continue to be used until another one of the commands is given.

Used in Syntax 2, they display *text* in the specified way and then switch the font face back to whatever it previously was.

Examples:
```
the value of {it}varlist {sf}may be specified ...
the value of {it:varlist} may be specified ...
```

{input}, {error}, {result}, and {text} follow Syntaxes 1 and 2.
These directives specify how the text should be rendered: in the style that indicates user input, an error, a calculated result, or the text around calculated results.

These styles are often rendered in terms of color. In the results window, on a black background, Stata by default shows input in white, error messages in red, calculated results in yellow, and text in green. As a result, many users think of these four directives as the "color" directives:

$$\{input\} = white$$
$$\{error\} = red$$
$$\{result\} = yellow$$
$$\{text\} = green$$

It is fine to think of them in this way, but do not get carried away with the metaphor. The relationship between the real colors and {input}, {error}, {result}, and {text} may not be the default (the user could reset it), and, in fact, these renditions may not be shown in color at all. The user might have set {result}, for instance, to show in boldface, or in highlight, or in something else. However the styles are rendered, SMCL tries to distinguish among {input}, {error}, {result}, and {text}.

Examples:
```
{text}the variable mpg has mean {result:21.3} in the sample.
{text}mpg     {c |} {result}21.3
{text}mpg     {c |} {result:21.3}
{error:variable not found}
```

{inp}, {err}, {res}, and {txt} follow Syntaxes 1 and 2.
These four commands are synonyms for {input}, {error}, {result}, and {text}.

Examples:
```
{txt}the variable mpg has mean {res:21.3} in the sample.
{txt}mpg     {c |} {res}21.3
{txt}mpg     {c |} {res:21.3}
{err:variable not found}
```

{cmd} follows Syntaxes 1 and 2.

{cmd} is another style not unlike the "color" styles, and it is the recommended way to show Stata commands in help files. Do not confuse {cmd} with {inp}. {inp} is the way commands actually typed are shown, and {cmd} is the recommended way you show commands you might type. We recommend that help files be presented in terms of {txt} and that commands be shown using {cmd}; use any of {sf}, {it}, or {bf} in a help file, but we recommend that you do not use any of the "colors" {inp}, {err}, or {res}, except in places where you are showing actual Stata output.

Example:
When using the {cmd:summarize} command, specify ...

{cmdab:*text1*:*text2*} follows a variation on Syntax 2 (note the double colons).

{cmdab} is the recommended way to show minimal abbreviations for Stata commands and options in help files; *text1* represents the minimum abbreviation and *text2* represents the rest of the text. When the entire command or option name is the minimal abbreviation, *text2* may be omitted along with the extra colon. In that case, {cmdab:*text*} is equivalent to {cmd:*text*}; it makes no difference which you use.

Examples:
{cmdab:su:mmarize} [{it:varlist}] [{it:weight}] [{cmdab:if} {it:exp}]
the option {cmdab:ef:orm}{cmd:({it:varname})} ...

{hilite} and {hi} follow Syntaxes 1 and 2.

{hilite} and {hi} are synonyms. {hilite} is the recommended way to highlight (draw attention to) something in help files. You might highlight, for example, a reference to a manual, the STB, or a book.

Examples:
see {hilite:[R] anova} for more details.
see {hi:[R] anova} for more details.

{ul} follows Syntaxes 2 and 3.

{ul on} starts underlining mode. {ul off} ends it. {ul:*text*} underlines *text*.

Examples:
You can {ul on}underline{ul off} this way or
you can {ul:underline} this way

{*} follows Syntax 2 and 4.

{*} is the comment indicator. What follows it (inside the braces) is ignored.

Examples:
{* this text will be ignored}
{*:as will this}

{hline} follows Syntaxes 1 and 3.

{hline} (Syntax 1) draws a horizontal line the rest of the way across the page.
{hline #} (Syntax 3) draws a horizontal line of # characters.
{hline} (either syntax) is generally used in line mode.

Examples:
{hline}
{hline 20}

{.-} follows Syntax 1.
    {.-} is a synonym for {hline} (Syntax 1).

    Examples:
    {.-}

{dup #:*text*} follows Syntax 4.
    {dup} repeats *text* # times.

    Examples:
    {dup 20:A}
    {dup 20:ABC}

{char *code*} and {c *code*} are synonyms and follow Syntax 3.
    These directives display the specified characters that otherwise might be difficult to type on your keyboard. See the section *The* {char} *directive* below.

    Examples:
    C{c o'}rdoba es una joya arquitect{c o'}nica.
    {c S|}57.20
    The ASCII character 206 in the current font is {c 206}
    The ASCII character 5a (hex) is {c 0x5a}
    {c -(} is open brace and {c)-} is close brace

{reset} follows Syntax 1.
    {reset} is equivalent to coding {result}{sf}.

    Examples:
    {reset}

Link commands for use in line and paragraph modes

All the link commands share the feature that when Syntax 4 is allowed,

    Syntax 4: {xyz *args*:*text*}

then Syntax 3 is also allowed,

    Syntax 3: {xyz *args*}

and, if Syntax 3 is specified, it is treated as if you specified Syntax 4, inserting a colon and then repeating the argument. For instance, {help} is defined below as allowing Syntaxes 3 and 4. Thus, the directive

```
{help summarize}
```

is equivalent to the directive

```
{help summarize:summarize}
```

Coding {help summarize} or {help summarize:summarize} both display the word summarize, and, if the user clicks on that, the action of help summarize is taken. Thus, you might code

```
See help for {help summarize} for more information.
```

This would display "See help for **summarize** for more information" and make the word summarize clickable. If you wanted to make the words describing the action different from the action, use Syntax 4,

> You can also {help summarize:examine the summary statistics} if you wish.

which results in "You can also **examine the summary statistics** if you wish."

The link commands, which may be used in either line mode or paragraph mode, are

{help *args*[:*text*]} follows Syntaxes 3 and 4.

> {help} displays *text* as clickable and, if the user clicks on the text, displays in the Viewer help on *args*; see [R] **help**. *args* can be omitted since the help command is valid without arguments; {help:*text*} presents the same results as {help help:*text*}.

> *Examples:*
> {help summarize}
> {help summarize:the mean}

{help_d:*text*} follows Syntax 2.

> {help_d} displays *text* as clickable, and, if the user clicks the text, displays a help dialog box from which the user may obtain interactive help on any Stata command of his or her choosing.

> *Example:*
> ... using the {help_d:help system} ...

{search *args*[:*text*]} follows Syntaxes 3 and 4.

> {search} displays *text* as clickable and, if the user clicks on the text, displays in the Viewer the results of search on *args*; see [R] **search**.

> *Examples:*
> {search anova:click here} for the latest information on ANOVA
> Various programs are available for {search anova}

{search_d:*text*} follows Syntax 2.

> {search_d} displays *text* as clickable, and, if the user clicks on the text, displays a search dialog box from which the user may obtain interactive help based on keywords of his or her choosing.

> *Example:*
> ... using the {search_d:search system} ...

{dialog *args*[:*text*]} follows Syntaxes 3 and 4.

> {dialog} displays *text* as clickable and, if the user clicks on the text, launches the dialog box for *args*.

> *Example:*
> ... open the {dialog regress:regress dialog box} ...

{browse *args*[:*text*]} follows Syntaxes 3 and 4.

> {browse} displays *text* as clickable and, if the user clicks on the text, launches the user's browser pointing at *args*. Since *args* is typically a URL and so contains a colon, it is usually necessary that *args* be specified in quotes.

> *Example:*
> ... you can {browse "http://www.stata.com":visit the Stata web site} ...

{view *args*[:*text*]} follows Syntaxes 3 and 4.

{view} displays *text* as clickable and, if the user clicks on the text, presents in the Viewer the filename *args*. If *args* is a URL, be sure to specify it in quotes. {view} would seldom be used in a SMCL file (such as a help file), because one would seldom know of a fixed location for the file unless it was a URL. {view} is sometimes used from programs because the program knows the location of the file it created.

Examples:
```
see {view "http://www.stata.com/man/readme.smcl"}

display '"{view "'newfile'":click here} to view the file created"'
```

{view_d:*text*} follows Syntax 2.

{view_d} displays *text* as clickable, and, if the user clicks on the text, displays a view dialog box from which the user may type the name of a file or a URL to be displayed in the viewer.

Example:
```
{view_d:Click here} to view your current log
```

{news:*text*} follows Syntax 2.

{news} displays *text* as clickable and, if the user clicks on the text, displays in the Viewer the latest news from http://www.stata.com.

Example:
```
For the latest NetCourse offerings, see the {news:news}.
```

{net *args*[:*text*]} follows Syntaxes 3 and 4.

{net} displays *text* as clickable, and, if the user clicks on the text, displays in the Viewer the results of net *args*; see [R] **net**. For security reasons, net get and net install cannot be executed in this way. Instead, use {net:describe ...} to show the page, and, from there, the user can click the appropriate spots if he or she wishes to install the materials. Whenever *args* contains a colon, as it does when *args* is a URL, be sure to enclose *args* in quotes.

args can be omitted because the net command is valid without arguments. {net:*text*} performs the equivalent of {net cd .:*text*}; it presents the contents of the current net location.

Examples:
```
programs are available from {net "from http://www.stata.com":Stata}
Nicholas Cox has written a series of matrix commands which you can obtain
by {net "describe http://www.stata.com/stb/stb56/dm79":clicking here}
```

{net_d:*text*} follows Syntax 2.

{net_d} displays *text* as clickable, and, if the user clicks on the text, displays a search dialog box from which the user may search the net for additions to Stata.

Example:
```
To search the net for the latest additions to Stata available,
{net_d:click here}.
```

{netfrom_d:*text*} follows Syntax 2.

{netfrom_d} displays *text* as clickable, and, if the user clicks on the text, displays a dialog box into which the user may enter a URL and then see the contents of the site. This directive is seldom used.

Example:
```
If you already know the URL, {netfrom_d:click here}.
```

{ado *args*[:*text*]} follows Syntaxes 3 and 4.

    {ado} displays *text* as clickable, and, if the user clicks on the text, displays in the Viewer the results of ado *args*; see [R] **net**. For security reasons, ado uninstall cannot be executed in this way. Instead, use {ado:describe ...} to show the package, and, from there, the user can click to uninstall if he or she wishes to delete the material.

    args can be omitted because the ado command is valid without arguments. {ado:*text*} presents a complete directory of installed packages.

    Example:
```
You can see the user-written packages you have installed (and uninstall
any that you wish) by {ado dir:clicking here}
```

{ado_d:*text*} follows Syntax 2.

    {ado_d} displays *text* as clickable, and, if the user clicks on the text, displays a dialog box from which the user may search for user-written routines he or she previously installed (and uninstall them if desired).

    Example:
```
You can search the user-written ado-files you have installed
by {ado_d:clicking here}.
```

{update *args*[:*text*]} follows Syntaxes 3 and 4.

    {update} displays *text* as clickable and, if the user clicks on the text, displays in the Viewer the results of update *args*; see [R] **update**. If *args* contains a URL, be careful to place the *args* in quotes.

    args can be omitted because the update command is valid without arguments. {update:*text*} is really the best way to use the {update} directive because it allows the user to choose whether and from where to update their Stata.

    Examples:
```
Check whether your Stata is {update:up-to-date}.
Check whether your Stata is {update "from http://www.stata.com":up-to-date}.
```

{update_d:*text*} follows Syntax 2.

    {update_d} displays *text* as clickable, and, if the user clicks on the text, displays an update dialog box into which the user may type a source (typically http://www.stata.com, but perhaps a local CD drive) from which he or she can then install official updates to Stata.

    Example:
```
If you are installing from CD or some other source,
{update_d:click here}.
```

{back:*text*} follows Syntax 2.

    {back} displays *text* as clickable, and, if the user clicks on the text, takes an action equivalent to pressing the Viewer's Back button.

    Example:
```
{back:go back to the previous page}
```

{clearmore:*text*} follows Syntax 2.

{clearmore} displays *text* as clickable and, if the user clicks on the text, takes an action equivalent to pressing Stata's clear-more-condition button. {clearmore} is of little use, but remember that all Stata output goes through SMCL. When —more— appears at the bottom of the screen, you can click on it to clear it. You can do that because, to display the —more— at the bottom of the screen, Stata displays

Example:
{clearmore:{hline 2}more{hline 2}}

{stata *args*[:*text*]} follows Syntaxes 3 and 4.

{stata} displays *text* as clickable, and, if the user clicks on the text, executes the Stata command *args* in the Results window. Stata will first ask before executing the command, but most users will turn off the asking for locally installed files (and leave it on for files over the web). If *args* (the Stata command) contains a colon, remember to enclose the command in quotes.

Example:
... {stata summarize mpg:to obtain the mean of mpg}...

Remember, like all SMCL directives, {stata} can be used in programs as well as files. Thus, you could code

display "... {stata summarize mpg:to obtain the mean of mpg}..."

or, if you were in the midst of outputting a table,

di "{stata summarize mpg:mpg}   {c |}" ...

However, it is more likely that, rather than hardcoding the variable name, the variable name would be in a macro, say 'vn',

di "{stata summarize 'vn':'vn'}   {c |}" ...

and you probably would not know how many blanks to put after the variable name, since it could be of any length. Thus, you might code

di "{ralign 12:{stata summ 'vn':'vn'}} {c |}" ...

thus allocating 12 spaces for the variable name, which would be followed by a blank and the vertical bar. Then, you would want to handle the problem that 'vn' might be longer than 12 characters,

local vna = abbrev('vn',12)
di "{ralign 12:{stata summ 'vn':'vna'}} {c |}" ...

and there you have a line that will output a part of a table, with the clickable variable name on the left, and with the action of clicking on the variable name being to summ 'vn', except, of course, you could make the action whatever else you wanted.

Note concerning paragraph mode: In paragraph mode, you can arrange to have either one space or two spaces at the end of sentences, which is to say, following the characters '.', '?', '!', and ':'. In the output, SMCL puts two spaces after each of those characters if you put two or more spaces after them in your input, or if you put a carriage return; SMCL puts one space if you put one space. Thus,

```
{p}
Dr. Smith was near panic.  He could not reproduce the result.
Now he wished he had read about logging output in Stata.
```

will display as

```
Dr. Smith was near panic.  He could not reproduce the result.  Now he wished he
had read about logging output in Stata.
```

Formatting commands for use in line mode

{title:*text*}(carriage return) follows Syntax 2.

    {title:*text*} displays *text* as a title. {title:...} should be followed by a carriage return, and, usually, by one more blank lines so that the title is offset from what follows. (In help files, we precede titles by two blank lines and follow them by one.)

    Example:
```
{title:Command summary -- general syntax}

{p}
Pretend {cmd:{c -({xyz}c )-}} were a SMCL directive, although ...
```

{center:*text*} and {centre:*text*} follow Syntax 2.

{center #:*text*} and {centre #:*text*} follow Syntax 4.

    {center:*text*} and {centre:*text*} are synonyms; they center the text on the line. {center:*text*} should usually be followed by a carriage return; otherwise, any text that follows it will appear on the same line. With Syntax 4, the directives center the text in a field of width #.

    Examples:
```
{center:This text will be centered}
{center:This text will be centered} and this will follow it
{center 60:This text will be centered within a width of 60 columns}
```

{right:*text*} follows Syntax 2.

    {right} displays *text* with its last character aligned on the right margin. {right:*text*} should be followed by a carriage return.

    Examples:
```
{right:this is right aligned}
{right:this is shifted left one character }
```

{lalign #:*text*} and {ralign #:*text*} follow Syntax 4.

    {lalign} left aligns *text* in a field # characters wide, and {ralign} right aligns *text* in a field # characters wide.

    Example:
```
{lalign 12:mpg}{ralign 15:21.2973}
```

{...} follows Syntax 1.

    {...} specifies that the next carriage return is to be treated as if it were a blank.

    Example:
```
Sometimes you need to type a long line and, while {...}
that is fine with SMCL, some word processors balk. {...}
In line mode, the above will appear as one long line to SMCL.
```

{col #} follows Syntax 3.

    {col #} skips forward to column #. If you are already at or beyond that column on the output, {col #} does nothing.

    Example:
```
mpg{col 20}21.3{col 30}5.79
```

{space #} follows Syntax 3.

> *space* is equivalent to typing # blank characters.
>
> *Example:*
> 20.5{space 20}17.5

{tab} follows Syntax 1.

> {tab} has the same effect as typing a tab character. Tab stops are set every 8 spaces.
>
> *Examples:*
> {tab}This begins one tab stop in
> {tab}{tab}This begins two tab stops in
>
> *Note:* SMCL also understands tab characters and treats them the same as the {tab} command, so you may include tabs in your files.

Formatting commands for use in paragraph mode

{p} follows Syntax 3. The full syntax is {p # # #}.

> {p # # #} enters paragraph mode. The first # specifies how much to indent the first line, the second # how much to indent the second and subsequent lines, and the third # how much to bring in the right margin on all lines. Numbers, if not specified, default to zero, so typing {p} without numbers is equivalent to typing {p 0 0 0}, {p #} is equivalent to {p # 0 0}, and so on. {p} (with or without numbers) may be followed by a carriage return or not; it makes no difference.
>
> Paragraph mode ends when a blank line is encountered, the {p_end} directive is encountered, or {smcl}(carriage return) is encountered.
>
> *Examples:*
> {p}
> {p 4}
> {p 0 4}
> {p 8 8 8}

{p_end} follows Syntax 1.

> {p_end} is a way of ending a paragraph without having a blank line between paragraphs. {p_end} may be followed by a carriage return or not; it will make no difference in the output.
>
> *Example:*
> {p_end}

{bind:*text*} follows Syntax 2.

> {bind:...} keeps *text* together on a line even if that makes one line of the paragraph uncommonly short. {bind:...} can also be used to insert one or more real spaces into the paragraph if you specify *text* as one or more spaces.
>
> *Example:*
> Commonly, bind is used {bind:to keep words together} on a line.

{break} follows Syntax 1.

> {break} is used to force a line break without ending the paragraph.
>
> *Example:*
> {p 4 8 4}
> {it:Example:}{break} Commonly, ...

Commands for use in As-Is mode

{asis} follows Syntax 1.

{asis} begins As-Is mode, which continues until {smcl}(carriage return) is encountered. {asis} may be followed by a carriage return or not; it makes no difference, but {smcl} must be immediately followed by a carriage return. {smcl} returns you to SMCL line mode. No other SMCL commands are interpreted in As-Is mode.

Commands for use in Stata 6 help mode

{s6hlp} follows Syntax 1.

{s6hlp} begins Stata 6 help mode, which continues until {smcl}(carriage return) is encountered. {s6hlp} may be followed by a carriage return or not; it makes no difference, but {smcl} must be immediately followed by a carriage return. {smcl} returns you to SMCL line mode. No other SMCL commands are interpreted in Stata 6 help mode. In this mode, text surrounded by ^carets^ is highlighted, and there are some other features, but those are not documented here. The purpose of Stata 6 help mode is to properly display old help files.

The {ccl} directive

The {ccl} directive outputs the value contained in a constant and current-value class (c()) object. For instance, {ccl pi} provides the value of the constant pi (3.14159...) contained in c(pi). See [P] **creturn** for a list of all the available c() objects.

The {char} directive

The {char} directive—synonym {c}—allows the output of any ASCII character. For instance, {c 106} is equivalent to typing the letter j, because ASCII code 106 is defined as the letter j.

One way you can get to all the ASCII characters is by typing {c #}, where # is between 1 and 255. Or, if you prefer, you can type {c 0x#}, where # is a hexadecimal number between 1 and ff. Thus, {c 0x6a} is also j because the hexadecimal number 6a is equal to the decimal number 106.

In addition, so that you do not have to remember the ASCII numbers, {c} provides special codes for characters that are, for one reason or another, difficult to type. These include

{c S|}	$ (dollar sign)
{c 'g}	' (open single quote)
{c -(}	{ (left curly brace)
{c)-}	} (right curly brace)

{c S|} and {c 'g} are included not because they are difficult to type or cause SMCL any problems, but because in Stata display statements, they can be difficult to make display because they are Stata's macro substitution characters and tend to be interpreted by Stata. For instance,

```
. display "shown in $US"
shown in
```

drops the $US part because Stata interpreted $US as a macro and the global macro was undefined. A way around this problem is to code

```
. display "shown in {c S|}US"
shown in $US
```

{c -(} and {c)-} are included because { and } have special meanings to SMCL. { and } are used to enclose SMCL directives. Although { and } have special meaning to SMCL, SMCL usually displays the two characters correctly when they do not have a special meaning. This is because SMCL follows the rule that, when it does not understand when it thinks ought to be a directive, it shows what it did not understand in unmodified form. Thus,

```
. display "among the alternatives {1, 2, 4, 7}"
among the alternatives {1, 2, 4, 7}
```

works, but

```
. display "in the set {result}"
in the set
```

does not, because SMCL interpreted {result} as a SMCL directive to set the output style (color) to that for results. The way to code the above is

```
. display "in the set {c -(}result{c )-}"
in the set {result}
```

In addition, SMCL provides the following line-drawing characters:

{c -}	a wide — (dash) character
{c |}	a tall | character
{c +}	a wide — on top of a tall |
{c TT}	a top T
{c BT}	a bottom T
{c LT}	a left T
{c RT}	a right T
{c TLC}	a top-left corner
{c TRC}	a top-right corner
{c BRC}	a bottom-right corner
{c BLC}	a bottom-left corner

When you use {hline}, it constructs the line using the {c -} character. The above are not really ASCII: they are instructions to SMCL to draw lines. The "characters" are, however, one-character wide and one-character tall, so you can use them as characters in your output. The result is that Stata output that appears on your screen can look like

```
. summarize mpg weight
    Variable │      Obs        Mean   Std. Dev.       Min        Max
─────────────┼──────────────────────────────────────────────────────
         mpg │       74     21.2973    5.785503        12         41
      weight │       74     3019.459    777.1936       1760        4840
```

but, if the result is translated into straight ASCII, it will look like

```
. summarize mpg weight
    Variable |      Obs        Mean   Std. Dev.       Min        Max
-------------+--------------------------------------------------------
         mpg |       74     21.2973    5.785503        12         41
      weight |       74     3019.459    777.1936       1760        4840
```

because SMCL will be forced to restrict itself to the ASCII characters.

Finally, SMCL provides the following West European characters:

{c a'}	á	{c e'}	é	{c i'}	í	{c o'}	ó	{c u'}	ú
{c A'}	Á	{c E'}	É	{c I'}	Í	{c O'}	Ó	{c U'}	Ú
{c a'g}	à	{c e'g}	è	{c i'g}	ì	{c o'g}	ò	{c u'g}	ù
{c A'g}	À	{c E'g}	È	{c I'g}	Ì	{c O'g}	Ò	{c U'g}	Ù
{c a^}	â	{c e^}	ê	{c i^}	î	{c o^}	ô	{c u^}	û
{c A^}	Â	{c E^}	Ê	{c I^}	Î	{c O^}	Ô	{c U^}	Û
{c a~}	ã					{c o~}	õ		
{c A~}	Ã					{c O~}	Õ		
{c a:}	ä	{c e:}	ë	{c i:}	ï	{c o:}	ö	{c u:}	ü
{c A:}	Ä	{c E:}	Ë	{c I:}	Ï	{c O:}	Ö	{c U:}	Ü
{c ae}	æ	{c c,}	ç	{c n~}	ñ	{c o/}	ø	{c y'}	ý
{c AE}	Æ	{c C,}	ç	{c N~}	Ñ	{c O/}	Ø	{c Y'}	Ý
{c y:}	ÿ	{c ss}	ß	{c r?}	¿	{c r!}	¡		
{c L-}	£	{c Y=}	(yen)	{c E=}	€				

SMCL uses ISO-8859-1 (Latin1) to render the above characters. For instance, {c e'} is equivalent to {c 0xe9}, if you care to look it up. {c 0xe9} will display as é if you are using an ISO-8859-1 (Latin1) compatible font. Most are.

In the case of the Macintosh, however, Stata uses the Macintosh encoding in which, for instance, {c e'} is equivalent to {c 8e}. This should work for Macintosh users unless they are using an ISO-8859-1 (Latin1) encoded font. To find out, run the following experiment:

```
. display "{c e'}"
é
```

Do you see é as we do? If not, and you are on a Macintosh, type

```
. set charset latin1
```

and try the experiment again. If that solves the problem, you will want to include that line in your profile.do. You can set the encoding back to Macintosh style by typing set charset mac. set charset typed without an argument will display the current setting. (set charset works on all platforms but is really only useful on the Macintosh.)

Advice on using display

Do not think twice; you can just use SMCL directives in your display statements and they will work. What we are really talking about, however, is programming, and there are two things to know.

First, remember how display lets you display results as text, as result, as input, and as error, with the abbreviations as txt, as res, as inp, and as err. For instance, a program might contain the lines

```
program ...
        ...
        quietly summarize 'varname'
        display as txt "the mean of 'varname' is " as res r(mean)
        ...
end
```

Results would be the same if the display statement were coded

```
        display "{txt}the mean of 'varname' is {res}" r(mean)
```

That is, the display directive as txt just sends {txt} to SMCL, the display directive as res just sends {res} to SMCL, and so on.

However, as err does not just send {err}. In addition, as err tells Stata that what is about to be displayed is an error message so that, if output is being suppressed, Stata knows to display this message anyway. To wit,

```
display as err "varname undefined"
```

is the right way to issue the error message "varname undefined".

```
display "{err}varname undefined"
```

would not work as well because, if the program was having its output suppressed, the error message would not be displayed because Stata would not know to stop suppressing output. You could code

```
display as err "{err}varname undefined"
```

but that is redundant. display's as error directive both tells Stata that this is an error message and sends the {err} directive to SMCL. The last part makes output appear in the form of error messages, probably in red. The first part is what guarantees that the error message appears even if output is being suppressed.

If you think about this, you will now realize that you could code

```
display as err "{txt}varname undefined"
```

to produce an error message that would appear as ordinary text (meaning it would probably be in green) and yet still display in all cases. Please do not do this. By convention, all error messages should be displayed in SMCL's {err} (default red) rendition.

The second thing to know is how Stata sets the state of SMCL the instant before display displays its output. When you use display interactively—when you use it at the keyboard or in a do-file—Stata sets SMCL in line mode, font face {sf}, and style {res}. For instance, if you type

```
. display 2+2
4
```

the 4 will appear in {sf}{res}, meaning in standard font face and in result style, which probably means in yellow. On the other hand, consider the following:

```
. program demonstrate_display
  1. display 2+2
  2. end
. demonstrate_display
4
```

In this case, the 4 will appear in {sf}{inp}, meaning the result is probably shown in white!

When display is executed from inside a program, no settings are made to SMCL. SMCL is just left in the mode it happens to be in, and, in this case, it happened to be in line mode {sf}{inp} because that was the mode it was in after the user typed the command demonstrate_display.

This is an important feature of display because it means that, in your programs, one display can pick up where the last left off. Perhaps you have four or five displays in a row that produce the text to appear in a paragraph. The first display might begin paragraph mode and the rest of the displays finish it off, with the last display displaying a blank line to end paragraph mode. In this case, it is of great importance that SMCL stay in the mode you left it in between displays.

That leaves only the question of what mode SMCL is in when your program begins. You should assume SMCL is in line mode, but make no assumptions about the style (color) {txt}, {res}, {err}, or {inp}. Within a program, all display commands should be coded as

```
        display as ... ...
```

or

```
        display "one of {txt}, {res}, {err}, or {inp} ..." ...
```

with the exception that you may violate this rule if you really intend one `display` to pick up where another left off. For example,

```
        display as text "{p}"
        display "This display violates the rule but that is all right"
        display "because it is setting a paragraph and we want all"
        display "these displays to be treated as a whole.  Note that"
        display "we did follow the rule with the first display in the"
        display "sequence."
        display
        display "Now we are back in line mode, because of the blank line"
```

You could even code

```
program example2
        display as text "{p}"
        display "Below we will call a subroutine to contribute a sentence"
        display "to this paragraph being constructed by example2:"
        example2_subroutine
        display "The text that example2_subroutine contributed became"
        display "part of this single paragraph.  Now we will end the paragraph."
        display
end

program example2_subroutine
        display "This sentence is being displayed by"
        display "example2_subroutine."
end
```

The result of running this would be

```
. example2
Below we will call a subroutine to contribute a sentence to this paragraph
being constructed by example2: This sentence is being displayed by
example2_subroutine.  The text that example2_subroutine contributed became
part of this single paragraph.  Now we will end the paragraph.
```

Advice on formatting help files

Help files are just files named *whatever*.`hlp` that Stata displays when the user types "`help` *whatever*". The first line of a help file should read

```
{smcl}
```

Because of help files that exist in old format, before displaying a help file, Stata issues a {s6hlp} directive to SMCL before displaying the text, thus putting SMCL in Stata 6 help mode. The {smcl} at the top of your help file returns SMCL to line mode. Old help files do not have that, and, since SMCL faithfully reproduces the old Stata 6 help file formatting commands, they display correctly, too.

After that, it is a matter of style. Our style is to put a header at the top of the page along with a manual reference, skip one line, and follow that by a title.

```
{smcl}
{.-}
help for {cmd:whatever} {right:manual:  {hi:[R] whatever}}
{.-}

{title:Title of help entry}
```

For your personal help files, you might want to use

```
{smcl}
{.-}
help for {cmd:whatever}
{.-}

{title:Title of help entry}
```

or

```
{smcl}
{.-}
help for {cmd:whatever} {right:my name or email address}
{.-}

{title:Title of help entry}
```

After the title, we put the syntax diagrams. This is going to surprise you: we format the syntax diagrams as paragraphs, but with the first line not indented as much as the second and subsequent lines. For instance, we might code

```
{p 8 27}
{cmdab:wh:atever}
[{it:varlist}]
[{it:weight}]
[{cmd:if} {it:exp}]
[{cmd:in} {it:range}]
[{cmd:,}
    {cmdab:d:etail}
    {cmdab:mean:only}
    {cmdab:f:ormat}
    {cmdab:gen:erate}{cmd:(}{it:newvar}{cmd:)}
    {cmdab:s:kip}
]
```

which will produce the reasonable looking syntax diagram

> <u>whatever</u> [*varlist*] [*weight*] [**if** *exp*] [**in** *range*] [, **detail** <u>mean</u>**only**
> **format** <u>gen</u>**erate**(*newvar*) <u>**skip**</u>]

That done, it is just a matter of following that with the titles and contents for

> Description
> Options
> Remarks and/or Examples
> Also see

For the titles, we precede them by two blank lines, use {title} to display the title, and follow that by one more blank line.

Text we always set in paragraphs, generally using {p} (meaning no indenting of the first line or the subsequent lines). For the options, we use {p 0 4}, thus using a hanging indent, and, if the option needs more than one paragraph to be described, subsequent paragraphs are set using {p 4 4}. For example,

```
{p 0 4}
{cmd:generate(}{it:newvar}{cmd:)} creates {it:newvar} containing the values
at each of the knots.  If {cmd:skip} is also specified, ...
```

will produce

> **generate**(*newvar*) creates *newvar* containing the values at each of the knots. If
>   **skip** is also specified, ...

For examples, we would also use paragraphs,

```
{p 8 16}
. {cmd:whatever mpg weight displ}
{p_end}
{p 8 16}
. {cmd:whatever mpg weight displ, generate(knots) skip}
{p_end}
```

Note our use of {p_end} to end paragraphs without putting a blank line between paragraphs. The result of the above is

```
. whatever mpg weight displ
. whatever mpg weight displ, generate(knots) skip
```

Note that we set the second and subsequent line indentation to a number greater than the first-line indentation so that, should a line wrap, it would be obvious. Although we tend to use paragraphs for examples, we would not hesitate to use line mode if we found that more convenient.

If we wanted to show actual Stata output, we could. We could fire up Stata, use log using to create a Stata log, use our command on an example dataset, and then copy that log right into the middle of the help file. If we wanted to do that, we would probably do something like the following:

```
{.-}
{* log begins here ---------------------------------------------- }
copy the .smcl log file to here
{* log ends here ---------------------------------------------- }
{sf}{txt}
{.-}
```

There are two things to note in the above: (1) we used {.-} to set off the log, and (2) after the log, we included {sf}{txt} to get SMCL reset. Concerning the second, help files are done in {sf}{txt}, and, when Stata started our help file, it did that for us. After the inclusion of the log, we may no longer be in that mode, so, to be safe, we reset it.

Finally, for the *Also see* section, we would use paragraph mode,

```
{title:Also see}
{p 0 21}
{bind: }Manual:  {hi:[R] whatever}, {hi:[R] summarize}
{p_end}
{p 0 21}
On-line:  help for
    {help centile},
    {help cf},
    {help ci},
    {help codebook},
    {help compare},
    {help egen},
    {help inspect},
    {help lv},
    {help means},
    {help tabsum}
{p_end}
```

which results in

```
Also see
Manual:  [R] whatever, [R] summarize
On-line:  help for centile, cf, ci, codebook, compare, egen, inspect, lv, means,
               tabsum
```

We included {p_end} at the end of the final "paragraph" rather than a blank line so that a blank line would not appear at the end of our help file.

Pay attention to the number of spaces we typed after "Manual:" and "On-line:". We put two spaces following the colon, and thus SMCL did the same in the output. SMCL puts one space after a colon when we put one space, and two spaces when we put two or more spaces, or a carriage return. If we preferred to have one space after the colon, we could do that, but then we would need to change {p 0 21} to be {p 0 20}, since we would then want subsequent lines indented one less space.

Also See

Complementary:	[P] **display**,
	[GS] **3 The Viewer**
Related:	[R] **log**

Title

> **sortpreserve** — Sort within programs

Description

This entry discusses the use of sort (see [R] **sort**) within programs.

Remarks

Properly written programs do one of three things:

1. Report results
2. Add new variables to the dataset
3. Modify the data in memory

A properly written program does only one of those things, but you do not want to get carried away with the idea. A properly written program might, for instance, (1) report results and yet still have an option to (2) add a new variable to the dataset, but a properly written program would not do all three. The user should be able to obtain reports over and over again by simply retyping the command, and if a command both reports results and modifies the data, that will not be possible.

Properly written programs of the first two types should also not change the sort order of the data. If the data are sorted on mpg and foreign before the command is given, and all the command does is report results, then the data should still be sorted on mpg and foreign at the conclusion of the command. Yet, the command might find it necessary to sort the data to obtain the results it calculates.

This entry deals with how to satisfy both needs. It is easy.

sortpreserve

You may include sort commands inside your programs and leave the user's data in the original order when your program concludes by specifying the option sortpreserve on the program definition line:

```
program whatever, sortpreserve
        ...
end
```

That, in a nutshell, is all there is to it. sortpreserve tells Stata when it starts your program to first record the information about how the data are currently sorted, and then later uses that information to restore the order to what it previously was. Stata will do this no matter how your program ends, whether as you expected, or with an error, or because the user pressed the *Break* key.

The cost of sortpreserve

There is a cost to sortpreserve, so you do not want to specify the option when it is not needed, but the cost is not much. sortpreserve will consume a little computer time in restoring the sort order at the conclusion of your program. Rather than talking about this time in seconds or milliseconds, which can vary according to the computer you use, let's define our unit of time as the time to execute:

```
. generate long x = _n
```

Pretend that you added that command to your program, just as we have typed it, without using temporary variables. You could then make careful timings of your program to find out just how much extra time your program would take to execute. It would not be much. Let's call that amount of time one *genlong* unit. Then,

- sortpreserve, if it has to restore the order because your program has changed it, takes 2 *genlong* units.

- sortpreserve, if it does not need to change the order because your program has not changed it yet, takes one-half a *genlong* unit.

The above results are based on empirical timings using 100,000 and 1,000,000 observations.

How sortpreserve works

sortpreserve works by adding a temporary variable to the dataset before your program starts, and, if you are curious about the name of that variable, it is recorded in the macro '_sortindex'. There are times when you will want to know that name. It is important that the variable '_sortindex' still exist at the conclusion of your program. If your program concludes with something like

```
keep 'id' 'varlist'
```

it is of vital importance that you change that line to read

```
keep 'id' 'varlist' '_sortindex'
```

If you fail to do that, Stata will report the error message "could not restore sort order because variables were dropped". Actually, even that little change may be insufficient because the dataset in its original form might have been sorted on something other than 'id' and 'varlist'. What you really need to do is add, early in your program and before you change the sort order,

```
local sortvars : sort
```

and then change the keep statement to read

```
keep 'id' 'varlist' 'sortvars' '_sortindex'
```

Understand, however, that all of this discussion is only about the use of the command keep, and that very few programs would even include a keep statement because we are skirting the edge of what is a properly written program.

sortpreserve is intended for use in programs that report results or add new variables to the dataset, not programs that modify the data in memory. The inclusion of keep at the end of your program really makes it a class-3 program, and in that case, the idea of preserving the sort order makes no sense anyway.

Use of sortpreserve with preserve

sortpreserve may be used with preserve (see [P] **preserve** for a description of preserve). We can imagine a complicated program that re-sorts the data, and then, under certain conditions, discovers it has to do real damage to the data in order to calculate its results, and so then preserves the data to boot:

```
program ..., sortpreserve
        ...
        sort ...
        ...
        if ... {
                preserve
                ...
        }
        ...
end
```

The above will work. When the program ends, Stata will first restore any `preserve`d data and then re-establish the sort of the original dataset.

Use of sortpreserve with subroutines that use sortpreserve

Programs that use `sortpreserve` may call other programs that use `sortpreserve`, and this can be a good way to speed up code. Consider a calculation where you need the data first sorted by 'i' 'j', then by 'j' 'i', and finally by 'i' 'j' again. You might code

```
program ..., sortpreserve
        ...
        sort 'i' 'j'
        ...
        sort 'j' 'i'
        ...
        sort 'i' 'j'
        ...
end
```

but faster to execute will be

```
program ..., sortpreserve
        ...
        sort 'i' 'j'
        mysubcalculation 'i' 'j' ...
        ...
end
program mysubcalculation, sortpreserve
        args i j ...
        sort 'j' 'i'
        ...
end
```

Also See

Complementary: [P] **byable**, [P] **program**

Title

syntax — Parse Stata syntax

Syntax

args *macroname1* [*macroname2* [*macroname3* ...]]

syntax *description_of_syntax*

Description

There are two ways that a Stata program can interpret what the user types:

1. positionally, meaning first argument, second argument, and so on; or

2. according to a grammar such as standard Stata syntax.

args does the first. The first argument is assigned to *macroname1*, the second to *macroname2*, and so on. In the program, you subsequently refer to the contents of the macros by enclosing their names in single quotes: '*macroname1*', '*macroname2*', ...:

```
program myprog
        args varname dof beta
        (the rest of the program would be coded in terms of 'varname', 'dof', and 'beta')
        ...
end
```

syntax does the second. You specify the new command's syntax on the syntax command; for instance, you might code

```
program myprog
        syntax varlist [if] [in] [, DOF(integer 50) Beta(real 1.0)]
        (the rest of the program would be coded in terms of 'varlist', 'if', 'in', 'dof', and 'beta')
        ...
end
```

syntax examines what the user typed and attempts to match it to the syntax diagram. If it does not match, an error message is issued and the program is stopped (a nonzero return code is returned). If it does match, the individual components are stored in particular local macros where you can subsequently access them. In the example above, the result would be to define the local macros 'varlist', 'if', 'in', 'dof', and 'beta'.

For an introduction to Stata programming, see [U] **21 Programming Stata** and especially [U] **21.4 Program arguments**.

Standard Stata synax is

$$cmd \quad \left[\, varlist \,|\, namelist \,|\, anything \,\right]$$
$$\left[\, \texttt{if} \; exp \,\right]$$
$$\left[\, \texttt{in} \; range \,\right]$$
$$\left[\, \underline{\texttt{using}} \; filename \,\right]$$
$$\left[\, \texttt{=} \; exp \,\right]$$
$$\left[\, weight \,\right]$$
$$\left[\, \texttt{,} \; options \,\right]$$

Each of these building blocks, such as *varlist*, *namelist*, `if`, etc. is outlined below.

Syntax, continued

The *description_of_syntax* allowed by `syntax` includes

description_of_varlist:

type	*nothing*
or	
optionally type	`[`
then type one of	`varlist   varname   newvarlist   newvarname`
optionally type	`(`*varlist_specifiers*`)`
type	`]` (if you typed `[` at the start)

         varlist_specifiers are `default=none   min=#   max=#   `<u>`numeric`</u>`   `<u>`string`</u>`   ts`
                                <u>`generate`</u>   (`newvarlist` and `newvarname` only)

Examples:
```
syntax varlist ...
syntax [varlist] ...
syntax varlist(min=2) ...
syntax varlist(max=4) ...
syntax varlist(min=2 max=4 numeric) ...
syntax varlist(default=none) ...

syntax newvarlist(max=1) ...

syntax varname ...
syntax [varname] ...
```

If you type nothing, then the command does not allow a varlist.

Typing `[` and `]` means that the varlist is optional.

`default=` specifies how the varlist is to be filled in when the varlist is optional and the user does not specify it. The default is to fill it in with all the variables. If `default=none` is specified, it is left empty.

`min=` and `max=` specify the minimum and maximum number of variables that may be specified. Typing `varname` is equivalent to typing `varlist(max=1)`.

`numeric` and `string` restrict the specified varlist to consist of entirely numeric or entirely string variables.

`ts` allows the varlist to contain time-series operators.

`generate` specifies, in the case of `newvarlist` or `newvarname`, that the new variables are to be created and filled in with missing values.

After the `syntax` command, the resulting varlist is returned in '`varlist`'. If there are new variables (you coded `newvarname` or `newvarlist`), the macro '`typlist`' is also defined containing the storage type of each of the new variables, listed one after the other.

description_of_namelist:

type	*nothing*	
or		
optionally type	[	
then type one of	namelist name	
optionally type	(*varlist_specifiers*)	
type	]	(if you typed [at the start)

varlist_specifiers are   name=*name*   id="*text*"   local
min=#   (namelist only) max=#   (namelist only)

Examples:
```
syntax namelist ...
syntax [namelist] ...
syntax name(id="equation name") ...
syntax [namelist(id="equation name")] ...
syntax namelist(name=eqlist id="equation list")...
syntax [name(name=eqname id="equation name")] ...
syntax namelist(min=2 max=2) ...
```

namelist is an alternative to varlist; it relaxes the restriction that the names the user specifies be of variables. name is a shorthand for namelist(min=1 max=1).

namelist is for use when you want the command to have the nearly standard syntax of command name followed by a list of names (not necessarily variable names), followed by if, in, *options*, etc. For instance, perhaps the command is to be followed by a list of variable-label names.

If you type nothing, then the command does not allow a namelist. Typing [and] means that the namelist is optional. After the syntax command, the resulting namelist is returned in 'namelist' unless name=*name* is specified, in which case the result is returned in '*name*'.

id= specifies the name of namelist and is used in error messages. The default is id=namelist. If namelist were required and id= was not specified, and the user typed "mycmd if..." (omitting the namelist), the error message would be "namelist required". If you specified id="equation name", the error message would be "equation name required".

name= specifies the name of the local macro to receive the namelist; not specifying the option is equivalent to specifying name=namelist.

local specifies that the names that the user specifies are to satisfy the naming convention for local macronames. If this option is not specified, standard naming convention is used (names may begin with a letter or underscore, may thereafter also include numbers, and must not be longer than 32 characters). If the user specifies an invalid name, an error message will be issued. If local is specified, then specified names are allowed to begin with numbers, but may not be longer than 31 characters.

(Continued on next page)

description_of_anything:

    type   *nothing*

or

    optionally type   [

    type   `anything`

    optionally type   (followed by any specifiers and then followed by)

    type   ]   (if you typed [at the start)

                      where the optional

                      specifiers are   `name=`*name* `id="`*text*`"` `equalok`

                      Examples: `syntax anything ...`

                                            `syntax [anything] ...`

                                            `syntax anything(id="equation name") ...`

                                            `syntax [anything(id="equation name")] ...`

                                            `syntax anything(name=eqlist id="equation list") ...`

                                            `syntax [anything(name=eqlist id="equation list")] ...`

                                            `syntax [anything(name=0 id=clist equalok)] ...`

`varlist`, `varname`, `namelist`, `name`, and `anything` are alternatives; you may specify at most one.

`anything` is for use when you want the command to have the nearly standard syntax of command name followed by something followed by `if`, `in`, *options*, etc. For instance, perhaps the command is to be followed by an expression or expressions, a list of numbers, etc.

If you type nothing, then the command does not allow an "anything". Typing [and] means the "anything" is optional. After the `syntax` command, the resulting "anything list" is returned in 'anything' unless `name=`*name* is specified, in which case the result is returned in 'name'.

`id=` specifies the name of "anything" and is used only in error messages. For instance, if `anything` were required and `id=` was not specified, and the user typed "`mycmd if...`" (omitting the "anything"), the error message would be "something required". If you specified `id="expression list"`, the error message would be "expression list required".

`name=` specifies the name of the local macro to receive the "anything"; not specifying the option is equivalent to specifying `name=anything`.

`equalok` specifies that `=` is not to be treated as part of `=`*exp* in subsequent standard syntax, but instead as part of the `anything`.

description_of_if:

    type   *nothing*

or

    optionally type   [

    type   `if`

    optionally type   /

    type   ]   (if you typed [at the start)

                      Examples: `syntax ... if ...`

                                            `syntax ... [if] ...`

                                            `syntax ... [if/] ...`

                                          `syntax ... if/ ...`

If you type nothing, then the command does not allow an `if` *exp*.

Typing [and] means that the `if` *exp* varlist is optional.

After the `syntax` command, the resulting `if` *exp* is returned in 'if'. The macro contains `if` followed by the expression unless you specified /, in which case the macro contains just the expression.

(Continued on next page)

description_of_in:

type	*nothing*
or	
optionally type	[
type	in
optionally type	/
type	]

(if you typed [at the start)

Examples: syntax ... in ...
syntax ... [in] ...
syntax ... [in/] ...
syntax ... in/ ...

If you type nothing, then the command does not allow an in *range*.

Typing [and] means that the in *range* is optional.

After the syntax command, the resulting in *range* is returned in 'in'. The macro contains in followed by the range unless you specified /, in which case the macro contains just the range.

description_of_using:

type	*nothing*
or	
optionally type	[
type	using
optionally type	/
type	]

(if you typed [at the start)

Examples: syntax ... using ...
syntax ... [using] ...
syntax ... [using/] ...
syntax ... using/ ...

If you type nothing, then the command does not allow using *filename*.

Typing [and] means that the using *filename* is optional.

After the syntax command, the resulting filename is returned in 'using'. The macro contains using followed by the filename in quotes unless you specified /, in which case the macro contains just the filename and without quotes.

description_of_=exp:

type	*nothing*
or	
optionally type	[
type	=
optionally type	/
type	exp
type	]

(if you typed [at the start)

Examples: syntax ... =exp ...
syntax ... [=exp] ...
syntax ... [=/exp] ...
syntax ... =/exp ...

If you type nothing, then the command does not allow an *=exp*.

Typing [and] means that the *=exp* is optional.

After the syntax command, the resulting expression is returned in 'exp'. The macro contains =, a space, and the expression unless you specified /, in which case the macro contains just the expression.

description_of_weights:

type	*nothing*
or	
type	[
type any of	f̲weight a̲weight p̲weight i̲weight
optionally type	/
type	]

Examples: syntax ... [fweight] ...
                syntax ... [fweight pweight] ...
                syntax ... [pweight fweight] ...
                syntax ... [fweight pweight iweight/] ...

If you type nothing, then the command does not allow weights. A command may not allow both a weight and =*exp*.

You must type [and]; they are not optional. Weights are always optional.

The first weight specified is the default weight type.

After the syntax command, the resulting weight and expression are returned in 'weight' and 'exp'. 'weight' contains the weight type or nothing if no weights were specified. 'exp' contains =, a space, and the expression unless you specified /, in which case the macro contains just the expression.

description_of_options:

type	*nothing*	
or		
type	[,	
type	*option_descriptors*	(these options will be optional)
optionally type	*	
type	]	
or		
type	,	
type	*option_descriptors*	(these options will be required)
optionally type	[	
optionally type	*option_descriptors*	(these options will be optional)
optionally type	*	
optionally type	]	

Examples: syntax ... [, MYopt Thisopt]
                syntax ..., MYopt Thisopt
                syntax ..., MYopt [Thisopt]
                syntax ... [, MYopt Thisopt *]

If you type nothing, then the command does not allow options.

The brackets distinguish optional from required options. All options can be optional, all options can be required, or some can be optional and others be required.

After the syntax command, options are returned to you in local macros based on the first 31 letters of each option's name. If you also specify *, any remaining options are collected and placed, one after the other, in 'options'. If you do not specify *, then if the user specifies any options that you do not list, an error is returned.

option_descriptors are documented below.

(Continued on next page)

option_descriptor optionally_on:

type   OPname   (capitalization indicates minimal abbreviation)

                  Examples: `syntax ..., ... replace ...`
                                          `syntax ..., ... REPLACE ...`
                                          `syntax ..., ... detail ...`
                                          `syntax ..., ... Detail ...`
                                          `syntax ..., ... CONStant ...`

The result of the option is returned in a macro name formed by the first 31 letters of the option's name. Thus, option `replace` is returned in local macro 'replace' and option `detail` in local macro 'detail'.

The macro contains nothing if not specified or else it contains the macro's name, fully spelled out.

Warning: be careful if the first two letters of the option's name are `no`, such as the option called `notice`. You must capitalize at least the `N` in such cases.

option_descriptor optionally_off:

type   no

type   OPname   (capitalization indicates minimal abbreviation)

                  Examples: `syntax ..., ... noreplace ...`
                                          `syntax ..., ... noREPLACE ...`
                                          `syntax ..., ... nodetail ...`
                                          `syntax ..., ... noDetail ...`
                                          `syntax ..., ... noCONStant ...`

The result of the option is returned in a macro name formed by the first 31 letters of the option's name excluding the `no`. Thus, option `noreplace` is returned in local macro 'replace', option `nodetail` in local macro 'detail', and option `noconstant` in local macro 'constant'.

The macro contains nothing if not specified or else it contains the macro's name, fully spelled out, with a `no` prefixed. That is, in the `noREPLACE` example above, macro 'replace' contains nothing or it contains `noreplace`.

option_descriptor optional_integer_value:

type   OPname   (capitalization indicates minimal abbreviation)

type   (integer

type   # (unless the option is required)   (the default integer value)

type   )

                  Examples: `syntax ..., ... Count(integer 3) ...`
                                          `syntax ..., ... SEQuence(integer 1) ...`
                                          `syntax ..., ... dof(integer -1) ...`

The result of the option is returned in a macro name formed by the first 31 letters of the option's name.

The macro contains the integer specified by the user or else it contains the default value.

option_descriptor optional_real_value:

type   OPname   (capitalization indicates minimal abbreviation)

type   (real

type   # (unless the option is required)   (the default value)

type   )

                  Examples: `syntax ..., ... Mean(real 2.5) ...`
                                          `syntax ..., ... SD(real -1) ...`

The result of the option is returned in a macro name formed by the first 31 letters of the option's name.

The macro contains the real number specified by the user or else it contains the default value.

option_descriptor optional_numlist:

type	*OPname*	(capitalization indicates minimal abbreviation)
type	(numlist	
type	<u>asc</u>ending or <u>desc</u>ending or *nothing*	
optionally type	<u>int</u>eger	
optionally type	<u>miss</u>ingokay	
optionally type	min=#	
optionally type	max=#	
optionally type	># or >=# or *nothing*	
optionally type	<# or <=# or *nothing*	
optionally type	sort	
type	)	

Examples:
```
syntax ..., ... VALues(numlist) ...
syntax ..., ... VALues(numlist max=10 sort) ...
syntax ..., ... TIME(numlist >0) ...
syntax ..., ... FREQuency(numlist >0 integer) ...
syntax ..., ... OCCur(numlist missingokay >=0 <1e+9) ...
```

The result of the option is returned in a macro name formed by the first 31 letters of the option's name.

The macro contains the values specified by the user, but listed out, one after the other. For instance, the user might specify time(1(1)4,10) so that the local macro 'time' would contain "1 2 3 4 10".

min and max specify the minimum and maximum number of elements that may be in the list.

<, <=, >, and >= specify the range of elements allowed in the list.

integer indicates the user may specify integer values only.

missingokay indicates the user may specify missing (a single period) as a list element.

ascending specifies the user must give the list in ascending order without repeated values. descending specifies the user must give the list in descending order and without repeated values.

sort specifies that the list be sorted before being returned. Distinguish this from modifier ascending. ascending states the user must type the list in ascending order. sort says the user may type the list in any order, but it is to be returned in ascending order. ascending states the list may have no repeated elements. sort places no such restriction on the list.

(Continued on next page)

option_descriptor optional_varlist:

type	OP*name*	(capitalization indicates minimal abbreviation)
type	(<u>var</u>list or (<u>var</u>name	
optionally type	<u>numeric</u> or <u>string</u>	
optionally type	min=#	
optionally type	max=#	
optionally type	ts	
type	)	

Examples: syntax ..., ... ROW(varname) ...
                 syntax ..., ... BY(varlist) ...
                 syntax ..., ... Counts(varname numeric) ...
                 syntax ..., ... TItlevar(varname string) ...
                 syntax ..., ... Sizes(varlist numeric min=2 max=10) ...

The result of the option is returned in a macro name formed by the first 31 letters of the option's name.

The macro contains the names specified by the user, listed one after the other.

min indicates the minimum number of variables to be specified if the option is given. min=1 is the default.

max indicates the maximum number of variables that may be specified if the option is given. max=800 is the default for varlist (you may set it to be larger) and max=1 is the default for varname.

numeric specifies that the variable list must be comprised entirely of numeric variables; string specifies string variables.

ts indicates the variable list may contain time-series operators.

---

option_descriptor optional_namelist:

type	OP*name*	(capitalization indicates minimal abbreviation)
type	(<u>name</u>list or (name	
optionally type	min=#	
optionally type	max=#	
optionally type	local	
type	)	

Examples: syntax ..., ... GENerate(name) ...
                 syntax ..., ... MATrix(name) ...
                 syntax ..., ... REsults(namelist min=2 max=10) ...

The result of the option is returned in a macro name formed by the first 31 letters of the option's name.

The macro contains the variables specified by the user listed one after the other.

Do not confuse namelist with varlist. varlist is the appropriate way to specify an option that is to receive the names of existing variables. namelist is the appropriate way to collect name of other things—such as matrices—and namelist is sometimes used to obtain the name of a new variable to be created. In that case, it is your responsibility to verify that the name specified does not already exist as a Stata variable.

min indicates the minimum number of names to be specified if the option is given. min=1 is the default.

max indicates the maximum number of names that may be specified if the option is given. The default is max=1 for name. For namelist, the default is the maximum number of variables allowed in Stata *(sic)*.

local specifies that the names the user specifies are to satisfy the naming convention for local macronames.

(Continued on next page)

option_descriptor optional_string:

type	*OPname*	(capitalization indicates minimal abbreviation)
type	(<u>string</u>	
optionally type	asis	
type	)	

	Examples:	syntax ..., ... <u>Title</u>(string) ...
		syntax ..., ... <u>XTRA</u>vars(string) ...
		syntax ..., ... <u>SAV</u>ing(string asis) ...

The result of the option is returned in a macro name formed by the first 31 letters of the option's name.

The macro contains the string specified by the user or else it contains nothing.

asis is rarely specified; if specified, the option's arguments are returned just as the user typed them, without quotes stripped and with leading and trailing blanks. If you specify this modifier, be sure to use compound double quotes when referring to the macro.

---

option_descriptor optional_passthru:

type	*OPname*	(capitalization indicates minimal abbreviation)
type	(passthru)	

	Examples:	syntax ..., ... <u>Title</u>(passthru) ...
		syntax ..., ... <u>SAV</u>ing(passthru) ...

The result of the option is returned in a macro name formed by the first 31 letters of the option's name.

The macro contains the full option—unabbreviated option name, parentheses, and argument—as specified by the user or else it contains nothing. For instance, were the user to type ti("My Title"), the macro would contain title("My Title").

Remarks

Stata is programmable, and that makes it possible to implement new commands. This is done with the program definition statement:

```
program newcmd
        ...
end
```

The first duty of the program is to parse the arguments it receives.

Programmers use positional argument passing for subroutines and for some new commands with exceedingly simple syntax. They do this because it is so easy to program. If program myprog is to receive a variable name (call it varname) and two numeric arguments (call them dof and beta), all they need code is

```
program myprog
        args varname dof beta
        (the rest of the program would be coded in terms of 'varname', 'dof', and 'beta')
        ...
end
```

The disadvantage of this is from the caller's side: Heaven forbid the caller get the arguments in the wrong order, not spell out the variable name, etc.

The alternative is to use standard Stata syntax. syntax makes it easy to make new command myprog have syntax

myprog *varname* $\left[\,, \underline{d}of(\#)\ \underline{b}eta(\#)\,\right]$

and even to have defaults for dof() and beta():

```
program myprog
        syntax varlist(max=1) [, Dof(integer 50) Beta(real 1.0)]
        (the rest of the program would be coded in terms of 'varlist', 'dof', and 'beta')
        ...
end
```

The args command

args splits what the user typed into words and places the first word in the first macro specified, the second in the second macro specified, and so on:

```
program myprog
        args arg1 arg2 arg3 ...
        do computations using local macros 'arg1', 'arg2', 'arg3', ...
end
```

args never produces an error. If the user specified more arguments than macros specified, the extra arguments are ignored. If the user specified fewer arguments than macros specified, the extra macros are set to contain "".

A better version of this program would read

```
program myprog
        version 8.0                              ← new
        args arg1 arg2 arg3 ...
        do computations using local macros 'arg1', 'arg2', 'arg3', ...
end
```

Placing version 8.0 as the first line of the program ensures that the command will continue to work even with future versions of Stata; see [U] **19.1.1 Version** and [P] **version**. We will include the version line from now on.

▷ Example

The following command displays the three arguments it receives:

```
. program argdisp
  1.          version 8.0
  2.          args first second third
  3.          display "1st argument = 'first'"
  4.          display "2nd argument = 'second'"
  5.          display "3rd argument = 'third'"
  6. end
. argdisp cat dog mouse
1st argument = cat
2nd argument = dog
3rd argument = mouse
. argdisp 3.456 2+5-12 X*3+cat
1st argument = 3.456
2nd argument = 2+5-12
3rd argument = X*3+cat
```

Note that arguments are defined by the spaces that separate them. "X*3+cat" is one argument, but, had we typed "X*3 + cat", that would have been three arguments.

If the user specifies fewer arguments than expected by args, the additional local macros are set as empty. By the same token, if the user specifies too many, they are ignored:

```
. argdisp cat dog
1st argument = cat
2nd argument = dog
3rd argument =
. argdisp cat dog mouse cow
1st argument = cat
2nd argument = dog
3rd argument = mouse
```

◁

❑ Technical Note

When a program is invoked, exactly what the user typed is stored in the macro '0'. In addition, the first word of that is also stored in '1', the second in '2', and so on. args merely copies the '1', '2', ... macros. Coding

```
args arg1 arg2 arg3
```

is no different from coding

```
local arg1 '"'1'"'
local arg2 '"'2'"'
local arg3 '"'3'"'
```

❑

The syntax command

syntax is easy to use. syntax parses standard Stata syntax, which is

command varlist if *exp* in *range* [*weight*] using *filename, options*

Actually, standard syntax is a little more complicated than that because you can substitute other things for *varlist*. In any case, the basic idea is that you code a syntax command describing which parts of standard Stata syntax you expect to see. For instance, you might code

```
syntax varlist if in, title(string) adjust(real 1)
```

or

```
syntax [varlist] [if] [in] [, title(string) adjust(real 1)]
```

In the first example, you are saying that everything is required. In the second, everything is optional. You can make some elements required and others optional:

```
syntax varlist [if] [in], adjust(real) [title(string)]
```

or

```
syntax varlist [if] [in] [, adjust(real 1) title(string)]
```

or lots of other possibilities. Square brackets denote optional. Put them around what you wish.

Anyway, you code what you expect the user to type. syntax then compares that with what the user actually did type, and, if there is a mismatch, syntax issues an error message. Otherwise, syntax processes what the user typed and stores the pieces, broken out into categories, in macros. These macros are named the same as the syntactical piece:

The varlist specified	will go into 'varlist'
The if *exp*	will go into 'if'
The in *range*	will go into 'in'
The adjust() option's contents	will go into 'adjust'
The title() option's contents	will go into 'title'

Go back to the section *Syntax, continued*. Where each element is stored is explicitly stated. When a piece is not specified by the user, the corresponding macro is cleared.

▷ Example

The following program simply displays the pieces:

```
. program myprog
  1. version 8.0
  2. syntax varlist [if] [in] [, adjust(real 1) title(string)]
  3. display "varlist contains |'varlist'|"
  4. display "     if contains |'if'|"
  5. display "     in contains |'in'|"
  6. display " adjust contains |'adjust'|"
  7. display "  title contains |'title'|"
  8. end
. myprog
varlist required
r(100);
```

Well, that should not surprise us; we said the varlist was required in the syntax command, so when we tried myprog without explicitly specifying a varlist, Stata complained.

```
. myprog mpg weight
varlist contains |mpg weight|
     if contains ||
     in contains ||
 adjust contains |1|
  title contains ||

. myprog mpg weight if foreign
varlist contains |mpg weight|
     if contains |if foreign|
     in contains ||
 adjust contains |1|
  title contains ||

. myprog mpg weight in 1/20
varlist contains |mpg weight|
     if contains ||
     in contains |in 1/20|
 adjust contains |1|
  title contains ||

. myprog mpg weight in 1/20 if foreign
varlist contains |mpg weight|
     if contains |if foreign|
     in contains |in 1/20|
 adjust contains |1|
  title contains ||

. myprog mpg weight in 1/20 if foreign, title("My Results")
varlist contains |mpg weight|
     if contains |if foreign|
     in contains |in 1/20|
 adjust contains |1|
  title contains |My Results|

. myprog mpg weight in 1/20 if foreign, title("My Results") adjust(2.5)
varlist contains |mpg weight|
     if contains |if foreign|
     in contains |in 1/20|
 adjust contains |2.5|
  title contains |My Results|
```

That is all there is to it.

◁

▷ Example

With this in hand, it would not be difficult to actually make myprog do something. For want of a better example, we will change myprog to display the mean of each variable, with said mean multiplied by adjust():

```
program myprog
        version 8.0
        syntax varlist [if] [in] [, adjust(real 1) title(string)]
        display
        if "'title'" != "" {
                display "'title':"
        }
        foreach var of local varlist {
                quietly summarize 'var' 'if' 'in'
                display %9s "'var'" "  " %9.0g r(mean)*'adjust'
        }
end

. myprog mpg weight
       mpg    21.2973
    weight   3019.459
. myprog mpg weight if foreign==1
       mpg   24.77273
    weight   2315.909
. myprog mpg weight if foreign==1, title("My title")
My title:
       mpg   24.77273
    weight   2315.909
. myprog mpg weight if foreign==1, title("My title") adjust(2)
My title:
       mpg   49.54545
    weight   4631.818
```

◁

❏ Technical Note

myprog is hardly deserving of any further work given what little it does, but let's illustrate two things using it.

First, learn about the marksample command; see [P] **mark**. A common mistake is to use one sample in one part of the program and a different sample in another part. The solution is to create a variable at the outset that contains 1 if the observation is to be used and 0 otherwise. marksample will do this and do it correctly because marksample knows what syntax has just parsed:

(Continued on next page)

```
program myprog
        version 8.0
        syntax varlist [if] [in] [, adjust(real 1) title(string)]
        marksample touse                                    ← new
        display
        if "`title'" != "" {
                display "`title':"
        }
        foreach var of local varlist {
                quietly summarize `var' if `touse'          ← changed
                display %9s "`var'" "  " %9.0g r(mean)*`adjust'
        }
end
```

The second thing we will do is modify our program so that what is done with each variable is done by a subroutine. Pretend, in this, that we are doing something more involved than calculating and displaying a mean.

We want to make this modification to show you the right and proper use of the `args` command. Passing arguments by position to subroutines is convenient and there is no chance of error due to arguments being out of order, or at least there is no chance assuming that we wrote our program properly:

```
program myprog
        version 8.0
        syntax varlist [if] [in] [, adjust(real 1) title(string)]
        marksample touse
        display
        if "`title'" != "" {
                display "`title':"
        }
        foreach var of local varlist {
                doavar `touse' `var' `adjust'
        }
end

program doavar
        version 8.0
        args touse name value
        qui summarize `name' if `touse'
        display %9s "`name'" "  " %9.0g r(mean)*`value'
end
```

❏

Also See

Complementary: [P] **mark**, [P] **numlist**, [P] **program**

Related: [P] **gettoken**, [P] **tokenize**, [P] **unab**,

[TS] **tsrevar**

Background: [U] **14 Language syntax**,

[U] **19.1.1 Version**,

[U] **21 Programming Stata**,

[U] **21.3.1 Local macros**,

[U] **21.3.5 Double quotes**

Title

> **sysdir** — Query and set system directories

Syntax

sysdir [list]

sysdir set *codeword* ["]*path*["]

adopath

adopath + *path_or_codeword*

adopath ++ *path_or_codeword*

adopath − {*path_or_codeword* | #}

set adosize # [, permanently] $10 \leq \# \leq 1000$

where *codeword* is { STATA | UPDATES | BASE | SITE | PLUS | PERSONAL | OLDPLACE }

Description

sysdir lists and resets the identities of Stata's system directories.

adopath provides a convenient way to examine and manipulate the ado-file path stored in the global macro S_ADO.

set adosize sets the maximum amount of memory in kilobytes that automatically loaded do-files may consume. The default is set adosize 400. To view the current setting, type display c(adosize).

These commands have to do with technical aspects of Stata's implementation. With the exception of sysdir list, you should never have to use them.

Remarks

In various part of the Stata documentation, you will read that "Stata searches along the adopath" for such-and-such. Here we describe exactly what that phrase means.

When we say "Stata searches along the adopath", what we really mean is "Stata searches along the path stored in the global macro $S_ADO". Equivalently, we could say "search along the path stored in c(adopath)" because c(adopath) = $S_ADO. These are just two different ways of saying the same thing. If you wanted to change the path, however, you would change the $S_ADO because there is no way to change c(adopath).

Do not, however, directly change $S_ADO. Even if you have good reason to change it, you will find it easier to change via the adopath command.

If you were to look inside $S_ADO (and we will), you would discover that it does not actually contain directory names—although it could—it contains codewords that stand for directory names. The command sysdir will show you the meaning of the codewords and allow you to change them.

419

sysdir

Stata expects to find various parts of itself in various directories (folders). Rather than describe these directories as C:\stata\ado\base or /usr/local/stata/ado, these places are referenced by codewords. Here are the definitions of the codewords on a particular Windows computer:

```
. sysdir
    STATA:  C:\STATA\
  UPDATES:  C:\STATA\ado\updates\
     BASE:  C:\STATA\ado\base\
     SITE:  C:\STATA\ado\site\
     PLUS:  C:\ado\plus\
 PERSONAL:  C:\ado\personal\
 OLDPLACE:  C:\ado\
```

Even if you use Stata for Windows, when you type sysdir, you might see different directories listed.

The sysdir command allows you to obtain the correspondence between codeword and actual directory and it allows you to change the mapping. Each of the directories serves a particular purpose:

STATA refers to the directory where the Stata executable is to be found.

UPDATES is where the updates to the official ado-files that were shipped with Stata are installed. The update command places files in this directory; see [R] **update**.

BASE is where the original official ado-files that were shipped with Stata are installed. This directory was written when Stata was installed, and thereafter the contents are never changed.

SITE is relevant only on networked computers. It is where administrators may place ado-files for sitewide use on networked computers. No Stata command writes in this directory, but administrators may move files into the directory or obtain ado-files using net and choose to install them into this directory; see [R] **net**.

PLUS is relevant on all systems. It is where ado-files written by other people that you obtain using the net command are installed; by default, net installs files to this directory; see [R] **net**.

PERSONAL is where you are to copy ado-files that you write and that you wish to use regardless of your current directory when you use Stata. (The alternative is to put ado-files in your current directory, and then they will only be available when you are in that directory.)

OLDPLACE is included for backwards compatibility. Stata 5 users used to put ado-files here, both the personal ones and the ones written by others. Nowadays they are supposed to put their personal files in PERSONAL and the ones written by others in PLUS.

Do not change the definitions of UPDATES or BASE, You may want to change the definitions of SITE, PERSONAL, PLUS, or especially OLDPLACE. For instance, if you wanted to change the definition of OLDPLACE to d:\ado, type

```
. sysdir set OLDPLACE "d:\ado"
```

Resetting a system directory affects only the current session; the next time you enter Stata, the system directories will be set back to being as they originally were. If you want to reset a system directory permanently, place the sysdir set command in your profile.do; see [GSW] **A.7 Executing commands every time Stata is started**, [GSM] **A.6 Executing commands every time Stata is started**, or [GSU] **A.7 Executing commands every time Stata is started**.

adopath

adopath displays and resets the contents of the global macro $S_ADO, the path over which Stata searches for ado-files. The default search path is

```
. adopath
  [1]  (UPDATES)    "C:\STATA\ado\updates"
  [2]  (BASE)       "C:\STATA\ado\base"
  [3]  (SITE)       "C:\STATA\ado\site"
  [4]               "."
  [5]  (PERSONAL)   "C:\ado\personal"
  [6]  (PLUS)       "C:\ado\plus"
  [7]  (OLDPLACE)   "C:\ado"
```

In reading the above, you want to focus on the codewords on the left. adopath mentions the actual directories, but, were you to change the meaning of a codeword using sysdir, that change would affect adopath.

The above states that, when Stata looks for an ado-file, first it looks in UPDATES. If the ado-file is found, that copy is used. If it is not found, Stata next looks in BASE, and, if it is found there, that copy is used. And so the process continues. Note that at the fourth step, Stata looks in the current directory (for which there is no codeword).

adopath merely presents the information in $S_ADO in a more readable form:

```
. display "$S_ADO"
UPDATES;BASE;SITE;.;PERSONAL;PLUS;OLDPLACE
```

adopath can also change the contents of the path. In general, you should not do this unless you are sure of what you are doing, because many features of Stata will stop working if you change the path incorrectly. At worst, however, you might have to exit and re-enter Stata, so you cannot do any permanent damage. Moreover, it is safe to add to the end of the path.

The path may include actual directory names, such as c:\myprogs, or codewords, such as PERSONAL, PLUS, and OLDPLACE. To add c:\myprogs to the end of the path, type

```
. adopath + c:\myprogs
  [1]  (UPDATES)    "C:\STATA\ado\updates"
  [2]  (BASE)       "C:\STATA\ado\base"
  [3]  (SITE)       "C:\STATA\ado\site"
  [4]               "."
  [5]  (PERSONAL)   "C:\ado\personal"
  [6]  (PLUS)       "C:\ado\plus"
  [7]  (OLDPLACE)   "C:\ado"
  [8]               "c:\myprogs"
```

If later you want to remove c:\myprogs from the adopath, you could type adopath - c:\myprogs, but easier is

```
. adopath - 8
  [1]  (UPDATES)    "C:\STATA\ado\updates"
  [2]  (BASE)       "C:\STATA\ado\base"
  [3]  (SITE)       "C:\STATA\ado\site"
  [4]               "."
  [5]  (PERSONAL)   "C:\ado\personal"
  [6]  (PLUS)       "C:\ado\plus"
  [7]  (OLDPLACE)   "C:\ado"
```

When followed by a number, 'adopath -' removes that element from the path. If you cannot remember what the numbers are, you can first type adopath without arguments.

❑ Technical Note

adopath ++ *path* works like adopath + *path* except that it adds to the beginning rather than to the end of the path. Our recommendation is that you not do this. When looking for *name*.ado, Stata loads the first file it encounters as it searches along the path. If you did not like our implementation of the command ci, for instance, even if you wrote your own and stored it in ci.ado, Stata would continue to use the one in the Stata directory because that is the directory listed earlier in the path. To force Stata to use yours rather than ours, you would have to put at the front of the path the name of the directory where your ado-file resides.

You should not, however, name any of your ado-files the same as we have named ours. If you add to the front of the path, you assume exclusive responsibility for the Stata commands working as documented in this manual.

❑

❑ Technical Note

This note is of interest only to users of Stata 7 or earlier releases who installed STB, *Stata Journal*, or other user-written commands using Stata's net command.

Older versions of Stata used the codeword STBPLUS and directory C:\ado\stbplus\ (e.g., in the case of Windows) for ado-files installed via the net command rather than PLUS. When Stata starts, it checks for the existence of this directory, and, if it exists, uses it for the value of the PLUS directory. If this directory does not exist, C:\ado\plus\ (e.g., in the case of Windows) will be used.

❑

set adosize

Stata keeps track of the ado-commands you use and discards from memory commands that have not been used recently. Stata discards old commands to keep the amount of memory consumed by such commands below adosize. The default value of 400 means the total amount of memory consumed by ado-commands is not to exceed 400K. When an ado-command has been discarded, Stata will have to reload the command the next time you use it.

You can increase adosize. Typing set adosize 450 would allow up to 450K to be allocated to ado-commands. This would improve performance slightly if you happened to use one of the not-recently-used commands, but at the cost of some memory no longer being available for your dataset. In practice, there is little reason to increase adosize.

adosize must be between 10 and 1,000.

Methods and Formulas

adopath is implemented as an ado-file.

Also See

Complementary:	[R] **net**, [R] **query**, [R] **update**
Background:	[U] **20.5 Where does Stata look for ado-files?**

Title

tabdisp — Display tables

Syntax

tabdisp *rowvar* [*colvar* [*supercolvar*]] [if *exp*] [in *range*], <u>c</u>ellvar(*varname(s)*)

  [by(*superrowvar(s)*)) <u>f</u>ormat(%*fmt*) <u>cen</u>ter <u>l</u>eft <u>con</u>cise <u>m</u>issing <u>t</u>otals

  dotz <u>cell</u>width(*#*) csepwidth(*#*) scsepwidth(*#*) <u>stub</u>width(*#*)]

by ... : may be used with tabdisp; see [R] **by**.

Rows, columns, supercolumns, and superrows are thus defined as

Description

tabdisp displays data in a table. tabdisp calculates no statistics and is intended for use by programmers.

For the corresponding command that calculates statistics and displays them in a table, see [R] **table**.

Although tabdisp is intended for programming applications, it can be used interactively for listing data.

Options

cellvar(*varname(s)*) is not optional; it specifies the numeric or string variables containing the values to be displayed in the table's cells. Up to five variable names may be specified.

423

by(*superrowvar(s)*) specifies numeric or string variables to be treated as superrows. Up to four variables may be specified in *varlist*.

format(*%fmt*) specifies the display format for presenting numbers in the table's cells. format(%9.0g) is the default; format(%9.2f) is a popular alternative. The width of the format you specify does not matter, except that *%fmt* must be valid. The width of the cells is chosen by tabdisp to be what it thinks looks best. Option cellwidth() allows you to override tabdisp's choice.

center specifies that results are to be centered in the table's cells. The default is to right-align results. For centering to work well, you typically need to specify a display format as well. center format(%9.2f) is popular.

left specifies that column labels are to be left-aligned. The default is to right-align column labels to distinguish them from supercolumn labels, which are left-aligned. If you specify left, both column and supercolumn labels are left-aligned.

concise specifies that rows with all missing entries are not to be displayed.

missing specifies that, in cells containing missing values, the missing value (., .a, .b, ..., or .z) is to be displayed. The default is that cells with missing values are left blank.

totals specifies that observations where *rowvar*, *colvar*, *supercolvar*, and/or *superrowvar(s)* contain the system missing value (.) are to be interpreted as containing the corresponding totals of cellvar(), and that the table should be labeled accordingly. If option dotz is also specified, it will be observations where the stub variables contain .z that will be so interpreted.

dotz specifies that the roles of missing values . and .z are to be interchanged in labeling the stubs of the table. By default, if any of *rowvar*, *colvar*, *supercolvar*, and *superrowvar(s)* contain missing (., .a, .b, ..., or .z), then "." is placed last in the ordering. dotz specifies that .z should be placed last. In addition, if option totals is specified, then .z values rather than "." values will be labeled "Total".

cellwidth(*#*) specifies the width of the cell in units of digit widths; 10 means the space occupied by 10 digits, which is 1234567890. The default cellwidth() is not a fixed number, but a number chosen by tabdisp to spread the table out while presenting a reasonable number of columns across the page.

csepwidth(*#*) specifies the separation between columns in units of digit widths. The default is not a fixed number, but a number chosen by tabdisp according to what it thinks looks best.

scsepwidth(*#*) specifies the separation between supercolumns in units of digit widths. The default is not a fixed number, but a number chosen by tabdisp according to what it thinks looks best.

stubwidth(*#*) specifies the width, in units of digit widths, to be allocated to the left stub of the table. The default is not a fixed number, but a number chosen by tabdisp according to what it thinks looks best.

Remarks

Remarks are presented under the headings

Limits
Introduction
Treatment of string variables
Treatment of missing values

Limits

Up to 4 variables may be specified in the by(), so with the three row, column, and supercolumn variables, seven-way tables may be displayed.

Up to 5 variables may be displayed in each cell of the table.

The sum of the number of rows, columns, supercolumns, and superrows is called the number of margins. A table may contain up to 3,000 margins. Thus, a one-way table may contain 3,000 rows. A two-way table could contain 2,998 rows and 2 columns, 2,997 rows and 3 columns, . . . , 1,500 rows and 1,500 columns, . . . , 2 rows and 2,998 columns. A three-way table is similarly limited by the sum of the number of rows, columns, and supercolumns. A $r \times c \times d$ table is feasible if $r + c + d \leq 3{,}000$. Note that the limit is set in terms of the sum of the rows, columns, supercolumns, and superrows, and not, as you might expect, their product.

Introduction

If you have not read [R] **table**, please do so. Then understand that tabdisp is what table uses to display the tables.

tabdisp calculates nothing. tabdisp instead displays the data in memory. In this, think of tabdisp as an alternative to list. Consider the following little dataset:

```
. list
```

	a	b	c
1.	0	1	15
2.	0	2	26
3.	0	3	11
4.	1	1	14
5.	1	2	12
6.	1	3	7

We can use tabdisp to list it:

```
. tabdisp a b, cell(c)
```

	b		
a	1	2	3
0	15	26	11
1	14	12	7

tabdisp is merely an alternative way to list the data. It is when the data in memory are statistics by category that tabdisp becomes really useful. table provides one prepackaging of that idea.

Unlike list, tabdisp is unaffected by the order of the data. Here are the same data in a different order,

(Continued on next page)

```
. list
```

	a	b	c
1.	1	3	7
2.	0	3	11
3.	1	2	12
4.	1	1	14
5.	0	1	15
6.	0	2	26

and yet the output of tabdisp is unaffected.

```
. tabdisp a b, cell(c)
```

		b	
a	1	2	3
0	15	26	11
1	14	12	7

Nor does tabdisp care if one of the cells is missing in the data.

```
. drop in 6
(1 observation deleted)
. tabdisp a b, cell(c)
```

		b	
a	1	2	3
0	15		11
1	14	12	7

On the other hand, tabdisp assumes that each value combination of the row, column, superrow, and supercolumn variables occurs only once. If that is not so, tabdisp displays the earliest occurring value:

```
. input
            a           b           c
6. 0 1 99
7. end
. list
```

	a	b	c
1.	1	3	7
2.	0	3	11
3.	1	2	12
4.	1	1	14
5.	0	1	15
6.	0	1	99

```
. tabdisp a b, cell(c)
```

a	b 1	2	3
0	15		11
1	14	12	7

Thus, our previous claim that `tabdisp` was unaffected by sort order has this one exception.

Finally, `tabdisp` uses variable and value labels when they are defined:

```
. label var a "Sex"
. label define sex 0 male 1 female
. label values a sex
. label var b "Treatment Group"
. label def tg 1 "controls" 2 "low dose" 3 "high dose"
. label values b tg
. tabdisp a b, cell(c)
```

Sex	Treatment Group controls	low dose	high dose
male	15		11
female	14	12	7

There are two things you can do with `tabdisp`.

You can use it to list data, but be certain you have a unique identifier. In the automobile dataset, the variable `make` is unique:

```
. use http://www.stata-press.com/data/r8/auto
(1978 Automobile Data)
. list make mpg weight displ rep78
```

	make	mpg	weight	displa~t	rep78
1.	AMC Concord	22	2,930	121	3
2.	AMC Pacer	17	3,350	258	3
3.	AMC Spirit	22	2,640	121	.
	(output omitted)				
74.	Volvo 260	17	3,170	163	5

```
. tabdisp make, cell(mpg weight displ rep78)
```

Make and Model	Mileage (mpg)	Weight (lbs.)	displacement	rep78
AMC Concord	22	2,930	121	3
AMC Pacer	17	3,350	258	3
AMC Spirit	22	2,640	121	
(output omitted)				
Volvo 260	17	3,170	163	5

Mostly, however, `tabdisp` is intended for use when you have a dataset of statistics that you want to display:

```
. collapse (mean) mpg, by(foreign rep78)
. list
```

	rep78	foreign	mpg
1.	1	Domestic	21
2.	2	Domestic	19.125
3.	3	Domestic	19
4.	4	Domestic	18.4444
5.	5	Domestic	32
6.	.	Domestic	23.25
7.	3	Foreign	23.3333
8.	4	Foreign	24.8889
9.	5	Foreign	26.3333
10.	.	Foreign	14

```
. tabdisp foreign rep78, cell(mpg)
```

Car type	1	2	Repair Record 1978 3	4	5	.
Domestic	21	19.125	19	18.4444	32	23.25
Foreign			23.3333	24.8889	26.3333	14

```
. drop if rep78>=.
(2 observations deleted)
. label define repair 1 Poor 2 Fair 3 Average 4 Good 5 Excellent
. label values rep78 repair
. tabdisp foreign rep78, cell(mpg) format(%9.2f) center
```

Car type	Poor	Fair	Repair Record 1978 Average	Good	Excellent
Domestic	21.00	19.12	19.00	18.44	32.00
Foreign			23.33	24.89	26.33

Treatment of string variables

The variables specifying the rows, columns, supercolumns, and superrows may be numeric or string. In addition, the variables specified for inclusion in the table may be numeric or string. In the example below, all variables are strings, including `reaction`:

```
. tabdisp agecat sex party, c(reaction) center
```

Age category	Female (Democrat)	Male (Democrat)	Female (Republican)	Male (Republican)
Old	Disfavor	Indifferent	Favor	Strongly Favor
Young	Disfavor	Disfavor	Indifferent	Favor

Treatment of missing values

The cellvar() variable(s) specified for inclusion in the table may contain missing values, and whether the variable contains a missing value or the observation is missing altogether makes no difference:

```
. list
```

	sex	response	pop
1.	0	0	12
2.	0	1	20
3.	0	2	.a
4.	1	0	15
5.	1	1	11

```
. tabdisp sex response, cell(pop)
```

	Response		
Sex	0	1	2
0	12	20	
1	15	11	

In the above output, the $(1, 3)$ cell is empty because the observation for $sex = 0$ and $response = 2$ has a missing value for pop. The $(2, 3)$ is empty because there is no observation for $sex = 1$ and $response = 2$.

If you specify the option missing, rather than cells being left blank, the missing value will be displayed:

```
. tabdisp sex response, cell(pop) missing
```

	Response		
Sex	0	1	2
0	12	20	.a
1	15	11	.

Missing values of the row, column, superrow, and supercolumn variables are allowed, and, by default, missing values are given no special meaning. The output below is from a different dataset.

```
. list
```

	sex	response	pop
1.	0	0	15
2.	0	1	11
3.	0	.	26
4.	1	0	20
5.	1	1	24
6.	1	.	44
7.	.	.	70
8.	.	0	35
9.	.	1	35

```
. tabdisp sex response, cell(pop)
```

		response	
sex	0	1	.
0	15	11	26
1	20	24	44
.	35	35	70

If you specify the option `total`, however, the system missing values are labeled as reflecting totals:

```
. tabdisp sex response, cell(pop) total
```

		response	
sex	0	1	Total
0	15	11	26
1	20	24	44
Total	35	35	70

It is important to understand that `tabdisp` did not calculate the totals; it merely labeled the results as being totals. The number 70 appears in the lower right because there happens to be an observation in the dataset where both `sex` and `response` contain a system missing value and `pop` = 70.

In this example, the row and column variables were numeric. Had they been strings, the option `total` would have given the special interpretation to `sex` = "" and `response` = "".

Also See

Related: [R] **table**, [R] **tabstat**, [R] **tabulate**

Title

tokenize — Divide strings into tokens

Syntax

<u>token</u>ize $\left[\left[\,`\,\right]\,"\right]\left[string\right]\left["\right]\left[\,'\,\right]$ $\left[\,,\ \underline{\text{p}}\text{arse}(\,"pchars"\,)\right]$

Description

tokenize divides *string* into tokens, storing the result in '1', '2', ... (the positional local macros). Tokens are determined based on the parsing characters *pchars*, which default to a space if not specified.

Options

parse("*pchars*") specifies the parsing characters. If parse() is not specified, parse(" ") is assumed and *string* is split into words.

Remarks

tokenize may be used as an alternative or supplement to the syntax command for parsing command line arguments. Generally, it is used to further process the local macros created by syntax as shown below.

```
program myprog
        version 8.0
        syntax [varlist] [if] [in]
        marksample touse

        tokenize 'varlist'
        local first '1'
        macro shift
        local rest '*'

        ...
end
```

▷ Example

We interactively apply tokenize, and then display several of the numbered macros to illustrate how the command works.

```
. tokenize some words
. di "1=|'1'|, 2=|'2'|, 3=|'3'|"
1=|some|, 2=|words|, 3=||

. tokenize "some more words"
. di "1=|'1'|, 2=|'2'|, 3=|'3'|, 4=|'4'|"
1=|some|, 2=|more|, 3=|words|, 4=||
```

```
tokenize '""Marcello Pagano""Rino Bellocco""'
. di "1=|'1'|, 2=|'2'|, 3=|'3'|"
1=|Marcello Pagano|, 2=|Rino Bellocco|, 3=||
. local str "A strange++string"
. tokenize 'str'
. di "1=|'1'|, 2=|'2'|, 3=|'3'|"
1=|A|, 2=|strange++string|, 3=||
. tokenize 'str', parse(" +")
. di "1=|'1'|, 2=|'2'|, 3=|'3'|, 4=|'4'|, 5=|'5'|, 6=|'6'|"
1=|A|, 2=|strange|, 3=|+|, 4=|+|, 5=|string|, 6=||
. tokenize 'str', parse("+")
. di "1=|'1'|, 2=|'2'|, 3=|'3'|, 4=|'4'|, 5=|'5'|, 6=|'6'|"
1=|A strange|, 2=|+|, 3=|+|, 4=|string|, 5=||, 6=||
. tokenize
. di "1=|'1'|, 2=|'2'|, 3=|'3'|"
1=||, 2=||, 3=||
```

These examples illustrate that the quotes surrounding the string are optional; the space parsing character is not saved in the numbered macros; non-space parsing characters are saved in the numbered macros together with the tokens being parsed; and more than one parsing character may be specified. Also, when called with no string argument, tokenize resets the local numbered macros to empty.

◁

Also See

Complementary:	[P] **syntax**
Related:	[P] **foreach**, [P] **gettoken**, [P] **macro**
Background:	[U] **21 Programming Stata**

Title

> **trace** — Debug Stata programs

Syntax

<u>set</u> <u>trace</u> { on | off }

<u>set</u> <u>trace</u>depth #

<u>set</u> <u>trace</u>expand { on | off } [, <u>perma</u>nently]

<u>set</u> <u>trace</u>sep { on | off } [, <u>perma</u>nently]

<u>set</u> <u>trace</u>indent { on | off } [, <u>perma</u>nently]

<u>set</u> <u>trace</u>number { on | off } [, <u>perma</u>nently]

Description

set trace on traces the execution of programs for debugging. set trace off turns off tracing after it has been set on.

set tracedepth # specifies how many levels to descend in tracing nested programs. The default is 32000, which is equivalent to ∞.

set traceexpand { on | off } indicates whether the lines before and after macro expansion are to be shown. The default is on.

set tracesep { on | off } indicates whether to display a horizontal separator line that displays the name of the subroutine whenever a subroutine is entered or exited. The default is on.

set traceindent { on | off } indicates whether displayed lines of code should be indented according to the nesting level. The default is on.

set tradenumber { on | off } indicates whether the nesting level should be displayed at the beginning of the line. Lines in the main program are preceded with 01, lines in subroutines called by the main program with 02, etc. The default is off.

Options

permanently, specifies that, in addition to making the change right now, the setting is to become the default setting for when you invoke Stata.

Remarks

The set trace commands are extremely useful for debugging your programs.

▷ Example

Stata does not normally display the lines of your program as it executes them. With `set trace` on, however, it does:

```
. program list simple
simple:
  1. args msg
  2. if '"'msg'"'=="hello" {
  3.         display "you said hello"
  4. }
  5. else display "you did not say hello"
  6. display "good-bye"
. set trace on
. simple
────────────────────────────────────────────────── begin simple ──
  - args msg
  - if '"'msg'"'=="hello" {
  = if '""'=="hello" {
    display "you said hello"
    }
  - else display "you did not say hello"
you did not say hello
  - display "good-bye"
good-bye
──────────────────────────────────────────────────── end simple ──
. set trace off
```

Lines that are executed are preceded by a dash. The line is shown before macro expansion, just as it was coded. If the line has any macros, it is shown again; this time preceded by an equal sign, and this time with the macro expanded, showing the line exactly as Stata sees it.

In our simple example, Stata substituted nothing for 'msg', as we can see by looking at the macro-expanded line. Since nothing is not equal to "hello", Stata skipped the display of "you said hello", so a dash did not precede this line.

Stata then executed lines 5 and 6. (They are not reshown preceded by an equal sign because they did not contain any macros.)

To suppress the printing of the macro-expanded lines, `set traceexpand off`.

The output from our program is interspersed with the lines that caused the output. This can be greatly useful when our program has an error. For instance, we have written a more useful program called `myprog`. Here is what happens when we run it:

```
. myprog mpg, prefix("new")
invalid syntax
r(198);
```

We did not expect this and, look as we will at our program code, we cannot spot the error. Our program contains many lines of code, however, so we have no idea even where to look. By setting `trace` on, we can quickly find the error:

(Continued on next page)

```
. set trace on
. myprog mpg, prefix("new")
                                                   ─── begin myprog ───
  - version 8.0
  - syntax varname , [Prefix(string)]
  - local newname "'prefix''varname'
  = local newname "new
invalid syntax
                                                   ─── end myprog ───
  r(198);
```

The error was close to the top—we omitted the closing quote in the definition of the local `newname` macro.

◁

Also See

Complementary:	[P] **program**,
	[R] **query**, [R] **set**
Background:	[U] **21 Programming Stata**

Title

unab — Unabbreviate variable list

Syntax

Standard variable lists

> unab *lmacname* : $\left[\textit{varlist}\right]$ $\left[$, min(#) max(#) name(*string*) $\right]$

Variable lists that may contain time-series operators

> tsunab *lmacname* : $\left[\textit{varlist}\right]$ $\left[$, min(#) max(#) name(*string*) $\right]$

Description

unab expands and unabbreviates a *varlist* (see [U] **14.4 varlists**) of existing variables, placing the result in the local macro *lmacname*. unab is a low-level parsing command. The syntax command is a high-level parsing command that, among other things, also unabbreviates variable lists; see [P] **syntax**.

The difference between unab and tsunab is that tsunab will allow time-series operators to modify the variables in *varlist*; see [U] **14.4.3 Time-series varlists**.

Options

min(#) specifies the minimum number of variables allowed. The default is min(1).

max(#) specifies the maximum number of variables allowed. The default is max(32000).

name(*string*) provides a label that is used when printing error messages.

Remarks

In most cases, the syntax command will automatically handle the unabbreviating of variable lists; see [P] **syntax**. In a few cases, unab will be needed to obtain unabbreviated variable lists.

▷ Example

The separate command (see [R] **separate**) provides an example of the use of unab. Required option by(*byvar* | *exp*) takes either a variable name or an expression. This is not handled automatically by the syntax command.

In this case, the syntax command for separate takes the form

```
syntax varname [if] [in], BY(string) [ other options]
```

After syntax performs the command line parsing, the local variable by contains what the user entered for the option. We now need to determine if it is an existing variable name or an expression. If it is a variable name, we may need to expand it.

```
      capture confirm var 'by'
      if _rc == 0 {
              unab by: 'by', max(1) name(by())
      }
      else {
              ( parse 'by' as an expression)
      }
```
◁

▷ Example

We interactively demonstrate the unab command with the auto dataset.

```
. unab x : mpg wei for, name(myopt())
. display "'x'"
mpg weight foreign
. unab x : junk
variable junk not found
r(111);
. unab x : mpg wei, max(1) name(myopt())
myopt():  too many variables specified
          1 variable required
r(103);
. unab x : mpg wei, max(1) name(myopt()) min(0)
myopt():  too many variables specified
          0 or 1 variables required
r(103);
. unab x : mpg wei, min(3) name(myopt())
myopt():  too few variables specified
          3 or more variables required
r(102);
. unab x : mpg wei, min(3) name(myopt()) max(10)
myopt():  too few variables specified
          3 - 10 variables required
r(102);
. unab x : mpg wei, min(3) max(10)
mpg weight:
too few variables specified
r(102);
```
◁

▷ Example

If we created a time variable and used tsset to declare the dataset as time series, we can also expand time-series variable lists.

```
. gen time = _n
. tsset time
. tsunab mylist : l(1/3).mpg
. display "'mylist'"
L.mpg L2.mpg L3.mpg
. tsunab mylist : l(1/3).(price turn displ)
. di "'mylist'"
L.price L2.price L3.price L.turn L2.turn L3.turn L.displ L2.displ L3.displ
```
◁

Also See

Related: [P] **syntax**

Background: [U] **14 Language syntax,**
                [U] **21 Programming Stata**

Title

> **unabcmd** — Unabbreviate command name

Syntax

unabcmd *commandname_or_abbreviation*

Description

unabcmd verifies that *commandname_or_abbreviation* is a Stata command name or an abbreviation of a Stata command name. unabcmd makes this determination by looking at both built-in commands and ado-files. If *commandname_or_abbreviation* is a valid command, unabcmd returns in local r(cmd) the unabbreviated name. If it is not a valid command, unabcmd displays an appropriate error message.

Remarks

Stata's built-in commands can be abbreviated. For instance, the user can type gen for generate or reg for regress. Commands implemented as ado-files cannot be abbreviated.

Given a command name *c*, unabcmd applies the same look-up rules Stata applies internally. If it is found, the full command name is returned in r(cmd).

▷ Example

```
. unabcmd reg
. return list

macros:
              r(cmd) : "regress"

. unabcmd kappa         // kappa is an ado-file
. return list

macros:
              r(cmd) : "kappa"

. unabcmd ka
command ka not found as either built-in or ado-file
r(111);
```

◁

unabcmd is included just in case you, as a programmer, want the command name spelled out. There is no reason why you should.

Methods and Formulas

unabcmd is implemented as an ado-file.

439

Also See

Complementary: [P] **findfile**,

[R] **which**

Title

> **version** — Version control

Syntax

version

version _#_ [, <u>mis</u>sing]

version _#_ [, <u>mis</u>sing] : _command_

Description

In the first syntax, version shows the current internal version number to which the command interpreter is set. When appropriate, a message is also presented indicating that the modern treatment of missing values is in force, even though the version number is less than 8.

In the second syntax, version sets the command interpreter to internal version number _#_. version _#_ is used to allow old programs to run correctly under more recent versions of Stata and to ensure that new programs run correctly under future versions of Stata.

In the third syntax, version executes _command_ under version _#_, and then resets the version back to what it was before the version _#:..._ command was given.

For information on external version control, see [R] **which**.

Options

missing requests the modern treatment of missing values. missing is allowed only when _#_ is less than 8 (because otherwise, modern treatment of missing values is implied).

Before version 8, there was only one missing value (.). To keep old programs working, when version is set less than 8, Stata acts as if . = .a = .b = ... = .z. Thus, old lines such as "... if x!=." continue to exclude all missing observations.

Specifying missing will cause old programs to break. The only reason to specify missing is because you want to update the old program to distinguish between missing value codes and you do not want to update it to be modern in other ways. Few, if any, programs need this.

Remarks

version ensures that programs written under an older release of Stata will continue to work under newer releases of Stata. If you do not write programs and if you use only the programs distributed by us, you can ignore version. If you do write programs, see [U] **21.11.1 Version** for guidelines to follow to ensure compatibility of your programs across future releases of Stata.

❑ Technical Note

The details of how `version` works are as follows. When Stata is invoked, it sets its internal version number to the current version of Stata, which is 8.0 at the time this was written. Typing `version` without arguments shows the current value of the internal version number:

```
. version
version 8.0
```

One way to make old programs work is to set the internal version number interactively to that of a previous release:

```
. version 7.0
. version
version 7.0
```

Now Stata's default interpretation of a program is the same as it was for Stata 7.0.

You cannot set the version to a number higher than the current version. Since we are using Stata 8.0, we cannot set the version number to 8.7, for instance.

```
. version 8.7
version 8.7 not supported
r(9);
```

❑

❑ Technical Note

We strongly recommend that all ado- and do-files begin with a `version` command. In the case of programs (ado-files), the `version` command should appear immediately following the `program` command:

```
program myprog
        version 8.0
        ( etc.)
end
```

❑

For an up-to-date summary of version changes, see `help version`.

Also See

Related:	[P] **display**,
	[R] **which**
Background:	[U] **21.11.1 Version**

Title

> **while** — Looping

Syntax

```
while exp {
        stata_commands
}
```

Braces must be specified with `while` and

1. the open brace must appear on the same line as the `while`;

2. nothing may follow the open brace except, of course, comments; the first command to be executed must appear on a new line;

3. the close brace must appear on a line by itself.

(In versions prior to Stata 8, putting the open brace, command, and close brace on the same line as the `while` was allowed. Old behavior is restored under version control; see [P] **version**.)

Description

`while` evaluates *exp*, and, if it is true (nonzero), executes the commands enclosed in the braces. It then repeats the process until *exp* evaluates to false (zero). `while`s may be nested within `while`s. If the *exp* refers to any variables, their values in the first observation are used unless explicit subscripts are specified; see [U] **16.7 Explicit subscripting**.

Also see [P] **foreach** and [P] **forvalues** for alternatives to `while`.

Remarks

`while` may be used interactively, but it is most frequently used in programs. See [U] **21 Programming Stata** for a complete description of programs.

The *stata_commands* enclosed in the braces may be executed once, many times, or not at all. For instance,

```
program demo
        local i = '1'
        while 'i'>0 {
                display "i is now 'i'"
                local i = 'i' - 1
        }
        display "done"
end

. demo 2
i is now 2
i is now 1
done

. demo 0
done
```

443

The above example is a bit contrived in that the best way to count down to one would be

```
program demo
        forvalues i = '1'(-1)1 {
                display "i is now 'i'"
        }
        display "done"
end
```

`while` is mostly used in parsing contexts

```
program ...
        ...
        gettoken tok 0 : 0
        while "'tok'" != "" {
                ...
                gettoken tok 0 : 0
        }
        ...
end
```

or in mathematical contexts where we are iterating

```
program ...
        ...
        scalar 'curval'  = .
        scalar 'lastval' = .
        while abs('lastval' - 'curval') > 'epsilon' {
                scalar 'lastval' = 'curval'
                scalar 'curval'  = ...
        }
        ...
end
```

or in any other context in which loop termination is based on calculation (whether it be numeric or string).

You can also create endless loops using `while`,

```
program ...
        ...
        while 1 {
                ...
        }
end
```

which is not really an endless loop if the code reads

```
program ...
        ...
        while 1 {
                if (...) exit
                ...
        }
        // this line is never reached
end
```

Should you make a mistake and really create an endless loop, you can stop program execution by pressing the *Break* key.

Also See

Related:	[P] **continue**, [P] **foreach**, [P] **forvalues**, [P] **if**
Background:	[U] **16 Functions and expressions**, [U] **21 Programming Stata**

Title

window fopen — Display open/save dialog box

Syntax

<u>win</u>dow {<u>fo</u>pen | <u>fs</u>ave} *macroname* "*title*" "*filter*" [*extension*]

Description

`window fopen` and `window fsave` allow Stata programmers to use standard **File–Open** and **File–Save** dialog boxes in their programs.

Remarks

`window fopen` and `window fsave` call forth the operating system's standard **File–Open** and **File–Save** dialog boxes. The commands do not themselves open or save any files; they merely obtain from the user the name of the file to be opened or saved and return it to you. The filename returned is guaranteed to be valid and includes the full path.

The filename is returned in the global macro *macroname*. In addition, if *macroname* is defined at the outset, its contents will be used to fill in the default filename selection.

title is displayed as the title of the dialog.

filter must be specified. One possible specification is "", meaning no filter. Alternatively, *filter* consists of pairs of descriptions and wildcard file selection strings separated by '|', such as

    "Stata Graphs|*.gph|All Files|*.*"

Stata uses the filter to restrict the files the user sees. The above example allows the user either to see Stata graph files or to see all files. The dialog will display a drop-down list from which the user can select a file type (extension). The first item of each pair (`Stata Graphs` and `All Files`) will be listed as the choices in the drop-down list. The second item of each pair restricts the files displayed in the dialog box to those that match the wildcard description. For instance, if the user selects `Stata Graphs` from the list box, only files with extension `.gph` will be displayed in the file dialog box.

Finally, *extension* is optional. It may contain a string of characters to be added to the end of filenames by default. For example, if the *extension* were specified as `xyz`, and the user typed a filename of `abc` in the file dialog box, `abc.xyz` would be returned in *macroname*.

In Windows, the default *extension* is ignored if a *filter* other than `*.*` is in effect. For example, if the user's current filter is `*.gph`, the default extension will be `.gph`, regardless of what *extension* was specified.

❑ Technical Note

Since Windows allows long filenames, *extension* can lead to unexpected results. For example, if *extension* were specified as `xyz` and the user typed a filename of `abc.def`, Windows would append `.xyz` before returning the filename to Stata, so the resulting filename is `abc.def.xyz`. Windows users should be aware that if they want to specify an extension different from the default, then they must enter a filename in the file dialog box enclosed in double quotes: `"abc.def"`. This applies to all programs, not just Stata.   ❑

If the user presses the **Cancel** button on the file dialog, `window fopen` and `window fsave` set *macroname* to be empty and exit with a return code of 601. Programmers should use the `capture` command to prevent the 601 return code from appearing to the user.

▷ Example

```
──────────────────────────────────────────────── top of dtaview.ado ──────────
program dtaview
        version 8.0
        capture window fopen D_dta "Select a dataset to use:" /*
                */ "Stata Data (*.dta)|*.dta|All Files (*.*)|*.*" dta
        if _rc==0 {
                display "User chose $D_dta as the filename."
                use "$D_dta"
        }
end
──────────────────────────────────────────────── end of dtaview.ado ──────────
```

```
. gphview
```

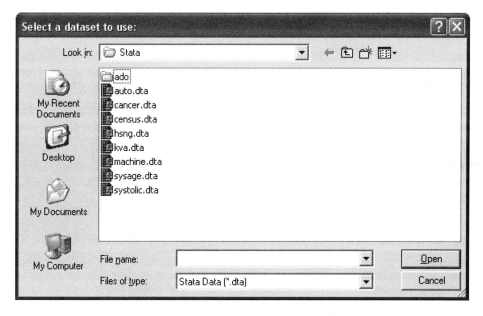

◁

Also See

Complementary: [P] **window stopbox**

Title

> **window manage** — Manage window characteristics

Syntax

<u>win</u><u>man</u>age minimize   (*Windows and Macintosh only*)

<u>win</u><u>man</u>age restore

<u>win</u><u>man</u>age prefs {load | save | default}

<u>win</u><u>man</u>age update variable

<u>win</u><u>man</u>age print {graph | viewer}

<u>win</u><u>man</u>age associate   (*Windows only*)

<u>win</u><u>man</u>age forward *window-name*

where *window-name* can be command, doeditor, graph, help, results, review, variables, or viewer.

Description

window manage gives Stata programs the ability to invoke features from Stata's main menu.

Remarks

window manage accesses various parts of Stata's windowed interface that would otherwise be available only interactively. For instance, say a programmer wanted to ensure that the Graph window was brought to the front. An interactive user would do that by selecting **Graph** from the **Window** menu. A Stata program could be made to do the same thing by coding 'window manage forward graph'.

Remarks are presented under the headings

> *Minimizing the main Stata window (Windows and Macintosh only)*
> *Restoring the main Stata window (Windows only)*
> *Windowing preferences*
> *Refreshing the Variables window*
> *Printing graphs and logs*
> *Restoring file associations (Windows only)*
> *Bringing windows forward*

Minimizing the main Stata window (Windows and Macintosh only)

window manage minimize minimizes (hides) the Stata window. With Stata for Windows, this has the same effect as clicking on the minimize button on Stata's title bar. With Stata for Macintosh, this has the same effect as selecting **Hide Stata** from the **Stata** menu.

For example,

```
window manage minimize
```

minimizes the overall Stata window if you are using Stata for Windows and hides Stata's windows if you are using Stata for Macintosh.

Restoring the main Stata window (Windows and Macintosh only)

`window manage restore` restores the Stata window if necessary. This command is allowed only with Stata for Windows and Stata for Macintosh.

With Stata for Windows, this command has the same effect as clicking the Stata button on the taskbar. With Stata for Macintosh, this command has the same effect as clicking on the Stata icon on the Dock.

For example,

```
window manage restore
```

restores Stata's overall window to its normal, nonminimized state.

Windowing preferences

`window manage prefs { load | save | default }` loads, saves, and restores windowing preferences.

Stata for Macintosh and Stata for Unix allow only `window manage prefs default`, which is equivalent to **Prefs–Restore Defaults**.

Stata for Windows allows `load`, `save`, or `default`. `window manage prefs save` is equivalent to pulling down **Prefs–Save Windowing Preferences**. `window manage prefs load` is equivalent to pulling down **Prefs–Load Windowing Preferences**. `window manage prefs default` is equivalent to pulling down **Prefs–Default Windowing**.

For example,

```
window manage prefs default
```

restores Stata's windows to their "factory" appearance.

Refreshing the Variables window

`window manage update variable` forces an update of Stata's Variables window, the window that displays the currently loaded variable names and their labels. Stata normally updates this window between interactive commands only. If you run a long do- or ado-file that changes the data in a way which would affect the Variables window, the change will not be visible until the do- or ado-file completes.

`window manage update variable` allows a do- or ado-file to force an early update of the Variables window to reflect any changes.

For example,

```
───────────────────────────────────────────────── top of vars.do ───────────
    use auto
    drop make
    window manage update variable
    drop price
    window manage update variable
    drop mpg
    window manage update variable
    label variable weight "Weight of car"
    window manage update variable
───────────────────────────────────────────────── end of vars.do ───────────
```

If you were to run the above do-file and there were no `window manage update variable` commands in it, you would not see the changes made to the variables until after the do-file completed.

Printing graphs and logs

`window manage print { graph | viewer }` invokes the actions of the **File–Print Graph** and **File–Print Viewer** menu items. If there is no current graph or Viewer window, `window manage print` does nothing; it does not return an error.

For example,

```
    window manage print graph
```

displays the print dialog box just as if you pulled down **File–Print Graph**.

Restoring file associations (Windows only)

In Stata for Windows, `window manage associate` restores the default actions for Stata file types. For example, another application could take over the `.dta` extension so that double-clicking on a Stata dataset would no longer launch Stata. `window manage associate` restores the association between all Stata file extensions (such as `.dta`) and Stata. This is equivalent to selecting **Restore File Associations** from the **Prefs** menu.

Bringing windows forward

`window manage forward` *window-name* brings the specified window to the top of all other Stata windows. This command is equivalent to selecting one of the available windows from the **Window** menu. The following table lists the *window-name*s that `window manage forward` understands:

window-name	Stata window
command	Command window
doeditor	Do-file editor window
graph	Graph window
help	Help/search window
results	Results window
review	Review window
variables	Variables window
viewer	Viewer window

If a window had not been available on Stata's **Window** menu (if it had been grayed out), specifying that *window-name* after `window manage forward` would do nothing. For example, if there is no current graph, `window manage forward graph` will do nothing; it is not an error.

For example,

```
window manage forward results
```

brings the Results window to the top of the other Stata windows.

Under Stata for Unix, specifying the Command, Results, Review, or Variables windows will bring the main Stata window forward since these windows are all contained within one window.

Title

window menu — Create menus

Syntax

<u>win</u>dow <u>menu</u> clear

<u>win</u>dow <u>menu</u> append submenu *"defined_menuname"* *"appending_menuname"*

<u>win</u>dow <u>menu</u> append item *"defined_menuname"* *"entry_text"* *"command_to_execute"*

<u>win</u>dow <u>menu</u> append separator *"defined_menuname"*

<u>win</u>dow <u>menu</u> refresh

Note: the quotation marks above are required.

"defined_menuname" is the name of a previously defined menu or one of the user-accessible menus
"stUser", "stUserData", "stUserGraphics", or "stUserStatistics".

Description

window menu allows you to add new menu hierarchies.

Remarks

Remarks are presented under the headings

> *Overview*
> *Clearing previously defined menu additions*
> *Defining submenus*
> *Defining menu items*
> *Defining separator bars*
> *Activating menu changes*
> *Keyboard shortcuts (Windows only)*
> *Examples*
> *Advanced features: dialogs and built-in actions*
> *Advanced features: Creating checked menu items*
> *Putting it all together*

Overview

A menu is a list of choices. Each choice may be another menu (known as a submenu) or an item. When you click on an item, something happens, such as a dialog box appearing or a command being executed. Menus may also contain separators, which are horizontal bars that help divide the menu into groups of related choices.

Stata provides the top-level menu **User** and three submenus of it—**Data**, **Graphics**, and **Statistics**—to which you may attach your own submenus, items, or separators.

You can see in the screenshot above that a submenu **Regression** has been appended to the built-in **User–Statistics** menu.

A menu hierarchy is the collection of menus and how they relate.

`window menu` allows you to create menu hierarchies, set the text that appears in each menu, set the actions associated with each menu item, and add separators to menus.

New menu hierarchies are defined from the top down, not the bottom up. Here is how you create a new menu hierarchy:

1. You append to some existing Stata menu a new submenu using `window menu append submenu`. That the new submenu is empty is of no consequence.

2. You append to the new submenu other submenus, items, or separators, all done with `window menu append`. In this way, you fill in the new submenu you already appended in step 1.

3. If, in step 2, you appended submenus to the menu you defined in step 1, you append to each of them so that they are fully defined. This requires even more `window menu append` commands.

4. You keep going like this until the full hierarchy is defined. Then, you tell Stata's menu manager that you are done using `window menu refresh`.

Everything you do up to step 4 is merely definitional. It is at step 4 that what you have done takes effect.

You can add menus to Stata. Then, you can add more menus. Later, you can add even more menus. What you cannot do, however, is ever delete a little bit of what you have added. You can add some menus and `window menu refresh`, then add some more and `window menu refresh`, but you cannot go back and remove part of what you added earlier. What you can do is remove all the menus you have added, restoring Stata to its original configuration. `window menu clear` does this.

So, in our opening example, how did the **Regression** submenu ever get defined? By typing

```
. window menu append submenu "stUserStatistics" "Regression"
. window menu append item "Regression" "Simple" ...
. window menu append item "Regression" "Multiple" ...
. window menu append item "Regression" "Multivariate" ...
. window menu refresh
```

`stUserStatistics` is the special name for Stata's **User–Statistics** built-in menu. The first command appended a submenu to `stUserStatistics` named **Regression**. At this point, **Regression** is an empty submenu.

The next three commands filled in **Regression** by appending to it. All three are items, meaning that when chosen, they invoke some Stata command or program. (We have not shown you what the Stata commands are; we just put '...'.)

Finally, `window menu refresh` told Stata we were done and to make our new additions available.

Clearing previously defined menu additions

```
window menu clear
```

clears any additions that have been made to Stata's menu system.

Defining submenus

```
window menu append submenu "defined_menuname" "appending_menuname"
```

defines a submenu. This command creates a submenu with the text *appending_menuname* (the double-quote characters do not appear in the submenu when displayed) attached to the "*defined_menuname*". It also declares that the "*appending_menuname*" can later have further submenus, items, and separators appended to it. Submenus may be appended to Stata's built-in **User** menu using the command

```
window menu append submenu "stUser" "appending_menuname"
```

For example,

```
window menu append submenu "stUser" "New Menu"
```

appends **New Menu** to Stata's **User** menu. Likewise, submenus may be appended to the built-in submenus of **User**—**Data**, **Graphics**, and **Statistics**—by using stUserData, stUserGraphics, or stUserStatistics as the *defined_menuname*.

Defining menu items

```
window menu append item "defined_menuname" "entry_text" "command_to_execute"
```

defines menu items. This command creates a menu item with the text "*entry_text*", which is attached to the "*defined_menuname*". When the item is selected by the user, "*command_to_execute*" is invoked.

For example,

```
window menu append item "New Menu" "Describe" "describe"
```

appends the menu item **Describe** to the **New Menu** submenu defined previously, and specifies that if the user selects **Describe** the describe command is to be executed.

Defining separator bars

```
window menu append separator "defined_menuname"
```

defines a separator bar. The separator bar will appear in the position in which it is declared and is attached to an existing submenu.

For example,

```
window menu append separator "New Menu"
```

adds a separator bar to **New Menu**.

Activating menu changes

> <u>win</u>dow <u>m</u>enu refresh

activates the changes made to Stata's menu system.

Keyboard shortcuts (Windows only)

When you define a menu item, you may assign a keyboard shortcut. A shortcut (or keyboard accelerator) is a key that allows a menu item to be selected via the keyboard in addition to the usual point-and-click method.

By placing an ampersand (&) immediately preceding a character, you define that character to be the shortcut. The ampersand will not appear in the menu item. Rather the character following the ampersand will be underlined to alert the user of the shortcut. The user may then choose the menu item by either clicking with the mouse or holding down *Alt* and pressing the shortcut key. Actually, you only have to hold down *Alt* for the top-level menu. For the submenus, once they are pulled down, holding down *Alt* is optional.

If you need to include an ampersand as part of the "*entry_text*", place two ampersands in a row.

It is your responsibility to avoid creating conflicting keyboard shortcuts. When the user types in a keyboard shortcut, Stata finds the first item with the defined shortcut.

Example:

> window menu append submenu "stUserStatistics" "&Regression"

defines a new submenu named **Regression** that will appear in the **User–Statistics** menu and that users may access by pressing *Alt-U* (to open the **User** menu), then *S* (to open the **Statistics** menu), and finally *R*, the shortcut defined for **Regression**.

Examples

▷ Example

Below we use the window menu commands to add to Stata's existing top-level menu. The following may be typed interactively:

```
window menu clear
window menu append submenu "stUser" "&MyData"
window menu append item "My Data" "&Describe data" "describe"
window menu refresh
```

window menu clear
    Clears any user-defined menu items and restores the menu system to the default.

window menu append submenu "stUser" "&My Data"
    Appends to the **User** a new submenu called My Data. Note that you may name this new menu anything you like. You can capitalize its name or not. You may include spaces in it. The new menu appears as the last item on the **User** menu.

window menu append item "My Data" "&Describe data" "describe"
    Defines a menu item (including a keyboard shortcut) named **Describe data** to appear within the **My Data** submenu. This name is what the user will actually see. It also specifies the command to execute when the user selects the menu item. In this case, we will run the describe command.

`window menu refresh`
  Causes all the menu items that have been defined and appended to the default system menus to become active and to be displayed.

◁

Advanced features: dialogs and built-in actions

Recall that menu items can have associated actions:

<u>win</u>dow <u>m</u>enu append item "*defined_menuname*" "*entry_text*" "*command_to_execute*"

Actions other than Stata commands and programs can be added to menus. In the course of designing a menu system, you may include menu items that will invoke dialogs, open a Stata dataset, save a Stata graph, or perform some other common Stata menu command.

You can specify "*command_to_execute*" as one of the following

"DB *dialog_to_invoke*"
  invokes the dialog box defined by the file *dialog_to_invoke*.dlg. For example, specifying "DB regress" as the "*command_to_execute*" results in the dialog box for Stata's regress command being invoked when the item is selected.

"XEQ about"
  displays Stata's About dialog box. The About dialog box is accessible from the default system menu by selecting **About** from the **File** menu.

"XEQ save"
  displays Stata's File Save dialog box in order to save the dataset in memory. This dialog box is accessed from the default system menu by selecting **Save** from the **File** menu.

"XEQ saveas"
  displays Stata's File Save As dialog box in order to save the dataset in memory. This dialog box is accessible from the default system menu by selecting **Save As...** from the **File** menu.

"XEQ savegr"
  displays the Save Stata Graph File dialog box that saves the currently displayed graph. This dialog box is accessible from the default system by selecting **Save Graph** from the **File** menu.

"XEQ printgr"
  prints the graph displayed in the graph window. This is available in the default menu system by selecting **Print Graph** from the **File** menu. Also see [P] **window manage**.

"XEQ use"
  displays Stata's File Open dialog box that loads a Stata dataset. This is available in the default menu system by selecting **Open...** from the **File** menu.

"XEQ exit"
  exits Stata. This is available from the default menu system by selecting **Exit** from the **File** menu (or selecting **Quit** from the **Stata** menu on Macintosh).

"XEQ conhelp"
  opens the Stata help system to the default welcome topic. This is available by clicking on the **Help!** button in the help system.

Advanced features: Creating checked menu items

command_to_execute in

    window menu append item "*defined_menuname*" "*entry_text*" "*command_to_execute*"

may also be specified as CHECK *macroname*.

Another detail that menu designers may want is the ability to create checked menu items. A checked menu item is one that appears in the menu system as either checked (includes a small check mark to the right) or not.

"CHECK *macroname*" specifies that the global macro *macroname* should contain the value as to whether or not the item is checked. If the global macro is not defined at the time that the menu item is created, Stata defines the macro to contain zero and the item is not checked. If the user selects the menu item in order to toggle the status of the item, Stata will place a check mark next to the item on the menu system and redefine the global macro to contain one. In this way, you may write programs that access information that you gather via the menu system.

Note that you should treat the contents of the global macro associated with the checked menu item as "read only". Changing the contents of the macro will not be reflected in the menu system.

Putting it all together

In the following example, we create a larger menu system. Note that each submenu defined using window menu append submenu contains other submenus and/or items defined with window menu append item that invoke commands.

(Continued on next page)

```
                                                              ── top of lgmenu.do ──
capture program drop mylgmenu
program mylgmenu
    version 8.0
    win m clear
    win m append submenu "stUserStatistics" "&Regression"
    win m append submenu "stUserStatistics" "&Tests"

    win m append item "Regression" "&OLS" "DB regress"
    win m append item "Regression" "Multi&variate" "choose multivariate"

    win m append item "stUserGraphics" "&Scatterplot" "choose scatterplot"
    win m append item "stUserGraphics" "&Histogram" "myprog1"
    win m append item "stUserGraphics" "Scatterplot &Matrix" "choose matrix"
    win m append item "stUserGraphics" "&Pie chart" "choose pie"

    win m append submenu "Tests" "Test of &mean"
    win m append item "Tests" "Test of &variance" "choose variance"

    win m append item "Test of mean" "&Unequal variances" "CHECK DB_uv"
    win m append separator "Test of mean"
    win m append item "Test of mean" "t-test &by variable" "choose by"
    win m append item "Test of mean" "t-test two &variables" "choose 2var"

    win m refresh
end
capture program drop choose
program choose
    version 8.0
    if "'1'" == "by" | "'1'" == "2var" {
            display as result "'1'" as text " from the menu system"
            if $DB_uv {
                    display as text "  use unequal variances"
            }
            else {
                    display as text "  use equal variances"
            }
    }
    else {
            display as result "'1'" as text " from the menu system"
    }
end
capture program drop myprog1
program myprog1
    version 8.0
    display as result "myprog1" as text " from the menu system"
end
                                                              ── end of lgmenu.do ──
```

Running this do-file will define a program `mylgmenu` that we may use to set the menus. Note that, other than the **OLS** item which launches the `regress` dialog box, the menu items will not run any interesting commands as the focus of the example is in the design of the menu interface only. To see the results, type `mylgmenu` in the Command window after you run the do-file. Below is an explanation of the example.

The command

```
        win m append submenu "stUserStatistics" "&Regression"
```

adds a submenu named **Regression** to the built-in menu **Statistics** under the **User** menu. If the user clicks on **Regression**, we will display another menu with items defined by

```
        win m append item "Regression" "&OLS" "DB regress"
        win m append item "Regression" "Multi&variate" "choose multivariate"
```

Since none of these entries open further menus, they use the `item` version instead of the `submenu` version of the `window menu append` command. This part of the menu system appears as

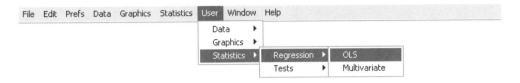

Similarly, the built-in **User–Graphics** menu is populated using `window menu item` commands.

```
win m append item "stUserGraphics" "&Scatterplot" "choose scatterplot"
win m append item "stUserGraphics" "&Histogram" "myprog1"
win m append item "stUserGraphics" "Scatterplot &Matrix" "choose matrix"
win m append item "stUserGraphics" "&Pie chart" "choose pie"
```

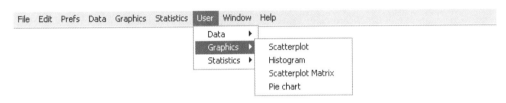

For the **Tests** submenu, we decided to have one of the entries be another submenu for illustration. First, we declared the **Tests** menu to be a submenu of **User–Statistics** using

```
win m append submenu "stUserStatistics" "&Tests"
```

We then defined the entries that were to appear below the **Tests** menu. There are two entries: one of them is another submenu and the other is an item. For the submenu, we then defined the entries that are below it.

Finally, note how the commands that are run when the user makes a selection from the menu system are defined. For most cases, we simply call the same program and pass an argument that identifies the menu item that was selected. Each menu item may call a different program if you prefer. Also note how the global macro that was associated with the checked menu item is accessed in the programs that are run. When the item is checked, the global macro will contain a 1. Otherwise, it contains zero. Our program merely has to check the contents of the global macro to see if the item is checked or not.

Also See

Complementary: [P] **dialogs**, [P] **window manage**

Title

> **window push** — Copy command into Review window

Syntax

<u>win</u>dow push *command-line*

Description

`window push` copies the specified *command-line* onto the end of the command history. *command-line* will appear as the most recent command in the `#review` list, and will appear as the last command in the Review window.

Remarks

`window push` is useful when one Stata command creates another Stata command and executes it. Normally, commands inside ado-files are not added to the command history, but an ado-file such as a dialog interface to a Stata command might exist solely to create and execute another Stata command.

`window push` allows the interface to add the created command to the command history (and therefore to the Review window) after executing the command.

▷ Example

```
──────────────────────────────────────────────── top of example.ado ───────────
program example
        version 8.0
        display "This display command is not added to the command history"
        display "This display command is added to the command history"
        window push display "This display command is added to the command history"
end
──────────────────────────────────────────────── end of example.ado ───────────
. example
This display command is not added to the command history
This display command is added to the command history

. #review
3
2 example
1 display "This display command is added to the command history"

.
```

◁

Also See

Complementary: [R] **#review**

Title

> **window stopbox** — Display message box

Syntax

window <u>stopbox</u> { stop | note | rusure } ["*line 1*" ["*line 2*" ["*line 3*" ["*line 4*"]]]]

Description

window stopbox allows Stata programs to display message boxes. Up to four lines of text may be displayed on a message box.

Remarks

There are three types of message boxes available to Stata programmers. The first is the stop message box. window stopbox stop displays a message box intended for error messages. This type of message box always exits with a return code of 1.

▷ Example

```
. window stopbox stop "You must type a variable name."  "Please try again."
```

```
--Break--
r(1);
```

◁

The second message box is the note box. window stopbox note displays a message box intended for information messages or notes. This type of message box always exits with a return code of 0.

(Continued on next page)

▷ Example

      . window stopbox note "You answered 3 of 4 questions correctly." "Press OK to continue."

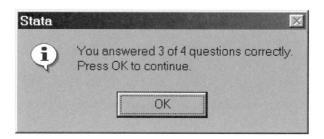

◁

The only way to close the first two types of message boxes is to click the **OK** button displayed at the bottom of the box.

The third message box is the rusure (say, "Are you sure?") box. This message box lets a Stata program ask the user a question. The user can close the box by clicking either **OK** or **Cancel**. The message box exits with a return code of 0 if the user clicks **OK** or exits with a return code of 1 if the user clicks **Cancel**.

A Stata program should use the capture command to determine whether the user clicked **OK** or **Cancel**.

▷ Example

      . capture window stopbox rusure "Do you want to clear the current dataset from memory?"
        "Press OK to clear or Cancel to abort."

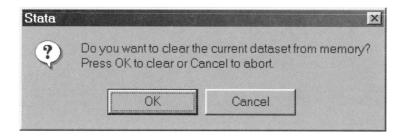

      . if _rc == 0 clear

◁

Also See

Complementary: [P] **capture**

Subject and author index

This is the subject and author index for the *Stata Programming Reference Manual*. Readers interested in topics other than programming and graphics should see the combined subject index at the end of Volume 4 of the *Stata Base Reference Manual*, which indexes the *Stata Base Reference Manual*, the *Stata User's Guide*, the *Stata Cluster Analysis Reference Manual*, the *Stata Cross-Sectional Time-Series Reference Manual*, the *Stata Survey Data Reference Manual*, the *Stata Survival Analysis & Epidemiological Tables Reference Manual*, the *Stata Time-Series Reference Manual*, and this manual. Readers interested in graphics topics should see the index at the end of the *Stata Graphics Reference Manual*.

Semicolons set off the most important entries from the rest. Sometimes no entry will be set off with semicolons; this means all entries are equally important.

* comment indicator, [P] **comments**
/* */ comment delimiter, [P] **comments**
// comment indicator, [P] **comments**
/// comment indicator, [P] **comments**
., class, [P] **class**
; delimiter, [P] **#delimit**

A

abbreviations,
    unabbreviating command names, [P] **unabcmd**
    unabbreviating variable list, [P] **unab**; [P] **syntax**
accum, matrix subcommand, [P] **matrix accum**
add, return subcommand, [P] **return**
ado-files, [P] **sysdir**, [P] **version**
    adding comments to, [P] **comments**
    debugging, [P] **trace**
    long lines, [P] **#delimit**
adopath command, [P] **sysdir**
adosize, [P] **sysdir**; [P] **creturn**, [P] **macro**
    set adosize, [P] **sysdir**
algebraic expressions, functions, and operators,
    [P] **matrix define**
alphanumeric variables, *see* string variables
Anderson, E., [P] **matrix eigenvalues**
appending rows and columns to matrix, [P] **matrix define**
args command, [P] **syntax**
arithmetic operators, [P] **matrix define**
arrays, class, [P] **class**
.Arrdropel built-in class modifier, [P] **class**
.arrindexof built-in class function, [P] **class**
.arrnels built-in class function, [P] **class**
.Arrpop built-in class modifier, [P] **class**
.Arrpush built-in class modifier, [P] **class**
ASCII text files, reading and writing, [P] **file**
assignment, class, [P] **class**

B

_b[], [P] **matrix get**
Bai, Z., [P] **matrix eigenvalues**
BASE directory, [P] **sysdir**
basis, orthonormal, [P] **matrix svd**
Becketti, S., [P] **pause**
binary files, reading and writing, [P] **file**
Binder, D. A., [P] **_robust**
Bischof, C., [P] **matrix eigenvalues**
Blackford, S., [P] **matrix eigenvalues**
bootstrap sampling and estimation, [P] **postfile**
break command, [P] **break**
Break key,
    interception, [P] **break**, [P] **capture**
built-in, class, [P] **class**
by *varlist*: prefix, [P] **byable**
byable(), [P] **byable**
by-groups, [P] **byable**

C

c(adopath) c-class value, [P] **creturn**; [P] **sysdir**
c(adosize) c-class value, [P] **creturn**; [P] **sysdir**
c(born_date) c-class value, [P] **creturn**
c(byteorder) c-class value, [P] **creturn**
c(changed) c-class value, [P] **creturn**
c(checksum) c-class value, [P] **creturn**
c(cmdlen) c-class value, [P] **creturn**
c(console) c-class value, [P] **creturn**
c(current_date) c-class value, [P] **creturn**
c(current_time) c-class value, [P] **creturn**
c(dirsep) c-class value, [P] **creturn**
c(dp) c-class value, [P] **creturn**
c(epsdouble) c-class value, [P] **creturn**
c(epsfloat) c-class value, [P] **creturn**
c(filedate) c-class value, [P] **creturn**
c(filename) c-class value, [P] **creturn**
c(flavor) c-class value, [P] **creturn**
c(graphics) c-class value, [P] **creturn**
c(httpproxy) c-class value, [P] **creturn**
c(httpproxyauth) c-class value, [P] **creturn**
c(httpproxyhost) c-class value, [P] **creturn**
c(httpproxyport) c-class value, [P] **creturn**
c(httpproxypw) c-class value, [P] **creturn**
c(httpproxyuser) c-class value, [P] **creturn**
c(k) c-class value, [P] **creturn**
c(level) c-class value, [P] **creturn**
c(linegap) c-class value, [P] **creturn**
c(linesize) c-class value, [P] **creturn**
c(logtype) c-class value, [P] **creturn**
c(machine_type) c-class value, [P] **creturn**
c(macrolen) c-class value, [P] **creturn**
c(matsize) c-class value, [P] **creturn**

c(max_cmdlen) c-class value, [P] **creturn**
c(max_k_current) c-class value, [P] **creturn**
c(max_k_theory) c-class value, [P] **creturn**
c(max_macrolen) c-class value, [P] **creturn**
c(max_matsize) c-class value, [P] **creturn**
c(max_N_current) c-class value, [P] **creturn**
c(max_N_theory) c-class value, [P] **creturn**
c(max_width_current) c-class value, [P] **creturn**
c(max_width_theory) c-class value, [P] **creturn**
c(maxbyte) c-class value, [P] **creturn**
c(maxdb) c-class value, [P] **creturn**
c(maxdouble) c-class value, [P] **creturn**
c(maxfloat) c-class value, [P] **creturn**
c(maxint) c-class value, [P] **creturn**
c(maxlong) c-class value, [P] **creturn**
c(maxstrvarlen) c-class value, [P] **creturn**
c(maxvar) c-class value, [P] **creturn**
c(memory) c-class value, [P] **creturn**
c(min_matsize) c-class value, [P] **creturn**
c(minbyte) c-class value, [P] **creturn**
c(mindouble) c-class value, [P] **creturn**
c(minfloat) c-class value, [P] **creturn**
c(minint) c-class value, [P] **creturn**
c(minlong) c-class value, [P] **creturn**
c(mode) c-class value, [P] **creturn**
c(more) c-class value, [P] **creturn**; [P] **more**
c(N) c-class value, [P] **creturn**
c(namelen) c-class value, [P] **creturn**
c(os) c-class value, [P] **creturn**
c(osdtl) c-class value, [P] **creturn**
c(pagesize) c-class value, [P] **creturn**
c(pi) c-class value, [P] **creturn**
c(printcolor) c-class value, [P] **creturn**
c(pwd) c-class value, [P] **creturn**
c(rc) c-class value, [P] **creturn**; [P] **capture**
c(reventries) c-class value, [P] **creturn**
c(rmsg) c-class value, [P] **creturn**; [P] **rmsg**
c(rmsg_time) c-class value, [P] **creturn**
c(scheme) c-class value, [P] **creturn**
c(scrollbufsize) c-class value, [P] **creturn**
c(SE) c-class value, [P] **creturn**
c(searchdefault) c-class value, [P] **creturn**
c(seed) c-class value, [P] **creturn**
c(stata_version) c-class value, [P] **creturn**
c(sysdir_base) c-class value, [P] **creturn**; [P] **sysdir**
c(sysdir_oldplace) c-class value, [P] **creturn**;
        [P] **sysdir**
c(sysdir_personal) c-class value, [P] **creturn**;
        [P] **sysdir**
c(sysdir_plus) c-class value, [P] **creturn**; [P] **sysdir**
c(sysdir_site) c-class value, [P] **creturn**; [P] **sysdir**
c(sysdir_stata) c-class value, [P] **creturn**;
        [P] **sysdir**
c(sysdir_updates) c-class value, [P] **creturn**;
        [P] **sysdir**
c(timeout1) c-class value, [P] **creturn**
c(timeout2) c-class value, [P] **creturn**

c(trace) c-class value, [P] **creturn**; [P] **trace**
c(tracedepth) c-class value, [P] **creturn**; [P] **trace**
c(traceexpand) c-class value, [P] **creturn**; [P] **trace**
c(traceindent) c-class value, [P] **creturn**; [P] **trace**
c(tracenumber) c-class value, [P] **creturn**; [P] **trace**
c(tracesep) c-class value, [P] **creturn**; [P] **trace**
c(type) c-class value, [P] **creturn**
c(varlabelpos) c-class value, [P] **creturn**
c(version) c-class value, [P] **creturn**; [P] **version**
c(virtual) c-class value, [P] **creturn**
c(width) c-class value, [P] **creturn**
capture command, [P] **capture**
casewise deletion, [P] **mark**
c-class, [P] **creturn**
cdir, classutil subcommand, [P] **classutil**
char command, [P] **char**
characteristics, [P] **char**
charset, [P] **smcl**
Cholesky decomposition, [P] **matrix define**
cholesky() matrix function, [P] **matrix define**
class command, [P] **class**
        class cdir, [P] **classutil**
        class describe, [P] **classutil**
        class dir, [P] **classutil**
        class drop, [P] **classutil**
        class exit, [P] **class exit**
        class which, [P] **classutil**
class definition, [P] **class**
class instance, [P] **class**
class programming, [P] **class**
class programming utilities, [P] **classutil**
.classmv built-in class function, [P] **class**
.classname built-in class function, [P] **class**
classutil command, [P] **classutil**
classwide, class, [P] **class**
clear, ereturn subcommand, [P] **ereturn**; [P] **return**
clear, _estimates subcommand, [P] **_estimates**
clear, postutil subcommand, [P] **postfile**
clear, return subcommand, [P] **return**
clear, serset subcommand, [P] **serset**
clear, sreturn subcommand, [P] **return**;
        [P] **program**
clearing estimation results, [P] **ereturn**, [P] **_estimates**
close, file subcommand, [P] **file**
cluster analysis, programming, *see Cluster Analysis Reference Manual*
_coef[], [P] **matrix get**
coefficients (from estimation),
        accessing, [P] **ereturn**, [P] **matrix get**
coleq, matrix subcommand, [P] **matrix rowname**
collinear variables, removing, [P] **_rmcoll**
colnames, matrix subcommand, [P] **matrix rowname**
colnumb() matrix function, [P] **matrix define**
color, *also see Graphics Reference Manual*
        specifying in programs, [P] **display**
colsof() matrix function, [P] **matrix define**

columns of matrix,
    appending to, [P] **matrix define**
    names, [P] **ereturn**, [P] **matrix define**, [P] **matrix rowname**
    operators, [P] **matrix define**
command arguments, [P] **gettoken**, [P] **syntax**, [P] **tokenize**
command parsing, [P] **gettoken**, [P] **syntax**, [P] **tokenize**
commands,
    aborting, [P] **continue**
    repeating automatically, [P] **byable**, [P] **continue**, [P] **foreach**, [P] **forvalues**, [P] **while**
    unabbreviating names of, [P] **unabcmd**
comments, adding to programs, [P] **comments**
compatibility of Stata programs across releases, [P] **version**
compound double quotes, [P] **macro**
condition statement, [P] **if**
confirm command, [P] **confirm**
console,
    controlling scrolling of output, [P] **more**
    obtaining input from, [P] **display**
constrained estimation,
    programming, [P] **matrix constraint**
constraint command, [P] **matrix constraint**
context, class, [P] **class**
continue command, [P] **continue**
Cook, R. D., [P] **_predict**
.copy built-in class function, [P] **class**
corr() matrix function, [P] **matrix define**
correlation matrices, [P] **matrix define**
covariance matrix of estimators, [P] **ereturn**, [P] **matrix get**
Cox, N. J., [P] **matrix define**
create_cspline, serset subcommand, [P] **serset**
create, serset subcommand, [P] **serset**
create_xmedians, serset subcommand, [P] **serset**
creturn list, [P] **creturn**
cross-product matrices, [P] **matrix accum**

D

data,
    characteristics of, see characteristics
    current, [P] **creturn**
    preserving, [P] **preserve**
date and time, [P] **creturn**
debugging, [P] **trace**; [P] **discard**, [P] **pause**
.Declare built-in class modifier, [P] **class**
declare, class, [P] **class**
define, matrix subcommand, [P] **matrix define**

define, program subcommand, [P] **program**
#delimit command, [P] **#delimit**
delimiter,
    for comments, [P] **comments**
    for lines, [P] **#delimit**
Demmel, J., [P] **matrix eigenvalues**
describe, class, [P] **classutil**
describe, classutil subcommand, [P] **classutil**
destructors, class, [P] **class**
det() matrix function, [P] **matrix define**
determinant of matrix, [P] **matrix define**
diag() matrix function, [P] **matrix define**
diag0cnt() matrix function, [P] **matrix define**
diagonals of matrices, [P] **matrix define**
dialog box, [P] **dialogs**, [P] **window fopen**, [P] **window stopbox**
dialog programming, [P] **dialogs**; [P] **window menu**
dir, classutil subcommand, [P] **classutil**
dir, _estimates subcommand, [P] **_estimates**
dir, macro subcommand, [P] **macro**
dir, matrix subcommand, [P] **matrix utility**
dir, postutil subcommand, [P] **postfile**
dir, program subcommand, [P] **program**
dir, _return subcommand, [P] **_return**
dir, serset subcommand, [P] **serset**
directories and paths, [P] **creturn**
directory, class, [P] **classutil**
discard command, [P] **discard**
dispCns, matrix subcommand, [P] **matrix constraint**
display command, [P] **display**; [P] **macro**
display, ereturn subcommand, [P] **ereturn**
display formats, [P] **macro**
displaying,
    macros, [P] **macro**
    matrix, [P] **matrix utility**
    output, [P] **display**, [P] **quietly**, [P] **smcl**, [P] **tabdisp**
    scalar expressions, [P] **display**, [P] **scalar**
do-files, [P] **version**,
    adding comments to, [P] **comments**
    long lines, [P] **#delimit**
Dongarra, J., [P] **matrix eigenvalues**
double quotes, [P] **macro**
drop, class, [P] **classutil**
drop, classutil subcommand, [P] **classutil**
drop, _estimates subcommand, [P] **_estimates**
drop, macro subcommand, [P] **macro**
drop, matrix subcommand, [P] **matrix utility**
drop, program subcommand, [P] **program**
drop, _return subcommand, [P] **_return**
drop, serset subcommand, [P] **serset**
dropping programs, [P] **discard**
.dta file suffix,
    technical description, [P] **file formats .dta**
Du Croz, J., [P] **matrix eigenvalues**
.dynamicmv built-in class function, [P] **class**

E

e() scalars, macros, matrices, functions, [P] **ereturn**,
   [P] **_estimates**, [P] **return**
e(sample) function, [P] **ereturn**, [P] **return**, *also see
   Base Reference Manual*
e-class command, [P] **program**, [P] **return**
eigenvalues, [P] **matrix eigenvalues**, [P] **matrix
   symeigen**
eigenvalues and eigenvectors, [P] **matrix symeigen**;
   [P] **matrix svd**
eigenvalues, matrix subcommand, [P] **matrix
   eigenvalues**
el() matrix function, [P] **matrix define**
else command, [P] **if**
environment variables (Unix), [P] **macro**
equation names of matrix, [P] **matrix rowname**;
   [P] **ereturn**, [P] **matrix define**
ereturn command, [P] **ereturn**
   ereturn clear, [P] **ereturn**; [P] **return**
   ereturn display, [P] **ereturn**
   ereturn list, [P] **ereturn**
   ereturn local, [P] **ereturn**; [P] **return**
   ereturn matrix, [P] **ereturn**; [P] **return**
   ereturn post, [P] **ereturn**; [P] **matrix constraint**,
      [P] **return**
   ereturn repost, [P] **ereturn**; [P] **return**
   ereturn scalar, [P] **ereturn**, [P] **return**
error command, [P] **error**
error handling, [P] **capture**, [P] **confirm**, [P] **error**
error messages and return codes, [P] **error**, [P] **rmsg**;
   also see error handling
_estimates command, [P] **_estimates**
   _estimates clear, [P] **_estimates**
   _estimates dir, [P] **_estimates**
   _estimates drop, [P] **_estimates**
   _estimates hold, [P] **_estimates**
   _estimates unhold, [P] **_estimates**
estimation commands, [P] **ereturn**, [P] **_estimates**
   accessing stored information from, [P] **matrix get**
   allowing constraints in, [P] **matrix constraint**
   eliminating stored information from, [P] **discard**
   obtaining predictions after, [P] **_predict**
   obtaining robust estimates, [P] **_robust**
   saving results from, [P] **_estimates**
estimation results,
   clearing, [P] **ereturn**, [P] **_estimates**
   listing, [P] **ereturn**, [P] **_estimates**
   saving, [P] **ereturn**, [P] **_estimates**
estimators,
   covariance matrix of, [P] **ereturn**, [P] **matrix get**
exit class program, [P] **class exit**
exit, class subcommand, [P] **class exit**
exit command, [P] **capture**, [P] **exit**
exiting Stata, *see* exit command
expressions, [P] **matrix define**
extended macro functions, [P] **char**, [P] **display**,
   [P] **macro**, [P] **macro lists**, [P] **serset**

F

file command, [P] **file**
   file close, [P] **file**
   file open, [P] **file**
   file query, [P] **file**
   file read, [P] **file**
   file seek, [P] **file**
   file sersetread, [P] **serset**
   file sersetwrite, [P] **serset**
   file set, [P] **file**
   file write, [P] **file**
file, find in path, [P] **findfile**
file format, Stata, [P] **file formats .dta**
files,
   opening, [P] **window fopen**
   reading ASCII text or binary, [P] **files**
   saving, [P] **window fopen**
   temporary, [P] **macro**, [P] **preserve**, [P] **scalar**
   writing ASCII text or binary, [P] **files**
findfile command, [P] **findfile**
finding file in path, [P] **findfile**
Flannery, B. P., [P] **matrix symeigen**
foreach command, [P] **foreach**
formatting contents of macros, [P] **macro**
forvalues command, [P] **forvalues**
Frankel, M. R., [P] **_robust**
Fuller, W. A., [P] **_robust**
functions, *also see Base Reference Manual*
   extended macro, [P] **char**, [P] **display**, [P] **macro**
      [P] **macro lists**, [P] **serset**
   matrix, [P] **matrix define**

G

g2 inverse of matrix, [P] **matrix define**, [P] **matrix svd**
Gail, M. H., [P] **_robust**
generalized inverse of matrix, [P] **matrix define**;
   [P] **matrix svd**
get() matrix function, [P] **matrix get**; [P] **matrix
   define**
gettoken command, [P] **gettoken**
Global class prefix operator, [P] **class**
global command, [P] **macro**
glsaccum, matrix subcommand, [P] **matrix accum**
Gould, W. W., [P] **matrix mkmat**, [P] **postfile**,
   [P] **_robust**
graphical user interface, [P] **dialogs**
Greenbaum, A., [P] **matrix eigenvalues**
Greene, W. H., [P] **matrix accum**
GUI programming, [P] **dialogs**

H

hadamard() matrix function, [P] **matrix define**
Hamilton, J. D., [P] **matrix eigenvalues**
Hammarling, S., [P] **matrix eigenvalues**

Heinecke, K., [P] **matrix mkmat**
heteroskedasticity,
    robust variances, *see* robust
hexadecimal report, [P] **hexdump**
hexdump command, [P] **hexdump**
hold, _estimates subcommand, [P] **_estimates**
hold, _return subcommand, [P] **_return**
Huber, P. J., [P] **_robust**
Huber/White/sandwich estimator of variance,
    [P] **_robust**

I

I() matrix function, [P] **matrix define**
identifier, class, [P] **class**
identity matrix, [P] **matrix define**
if *exp*, [P] **syntax**
if programming command, [P] **if**
immediate commands, [P] **display**
implied context, class, [P] **class**
in *range* modifier, [P] **syntax**
information matrix, [P] **matrix get**
inheritance, [P] **class**
initialization, class, [P] **class**
input, matrix subcommand, [P] **matrix define**
input, obtaining from console in programs, *see* console
instance, class, [P] **class**
instance-specific, class, [P] **class**
.instancemv built-in class function, [P] **class**
inv() matrix function, [P] **matrix define**
inverse of matrix, [P] **matrix define**, [P] **matrix svd**
.isa built-in class function, [P] **class**
.isofclass built-in class function, [P] **class**
issym() matrix function, [P] **matrix define**

J

J() matrix function, [P] **matrix define**

K

Kennedy, W., [P] **_robust**
Kent, J. T., [P] **_robust**
Kish, L., [P] **_robust**
Kronecker product, [P] **matrix define**

L

label values, [P] **macro**
language syntax, [P] **syntax**
level command and value, [P] **macro**
limits,
    numerical and string, [P] **creturn**
    system, [P] **creturn**

Lin, D. Y., [P] **_robust**
linear combinations, forming, [P] **matrix score**
lines, long, in do-files and ado-files, [P] **#delimit**
list, creturn subcommand, [P] **creturn**
list, ereturn subcommand, [P] **ereturn**
list manipulation, [P] **macro lists**
list, macro subcommand, [P] **macro**
list, matrix subcommand, [P] **matrix utility**
list, program subcommand, [P] **program**
list, sysdir subcommand, [P] **sysdir**
listing,
    estimation results, [P] **ereturn**, [P] **_estimates**
    macro expanded functions, [P] **macro lists**
local ++ command, [P] **macro**
local -- command, [P] **macro**
Local class prefix operator, [P] **class**
local command, [P] **macro**
local, ereturn subcommand, [P] **ereturn**
local, return subcommand, [P] **return**
local, sreturn subcommand, [P] **return**
long lines in ado-files and do-files,
    [P] **#delimit**
looping, [P] **continue**, [P] **foreach**, [P] **forvalues**,
    [P] **while**
lvalue, class, [P] **class**

M

MacKinnon, J. G., [P] **_robust**
macro command, [P] **macro**
    macro dir, [P] **macro**
    macro drop, [P] **macro**
    macro list, [P] **macro**
    macro shift, [P] **macro**
macro substitution, [P] **macro**
    class, [P] **class**
macros, [P] **macro**; [P] **creturn**, [P] **scalar**, [P] **syntax**,
    also see e()
macval() macro expansion function, [P] **macro**
makeCns, matrix subcommand, [P] **matrix constraint**
mark command, [P] **mark**
markin command, [P] **mark**
marking observations, [P] **mark**
markout command, [P] **mark**
marksample command, [P] **mark**
matcproc command, [P] **matrix constraint**
mathematical functions and expressions, [P] **matrix**
    define, *also see Base Reference Manual*
matmissing() matrix function, [P] **matrix define**
matname command, [P] **matrix mkmat**
matrices, [P] **matrix**
    accessing internal, [P] **matrix get**
    accumulating, [P] **matrix accum**
    appending rows and columns, [P] **matrix define**
    Cholesky decomposition, [P] **matrix define**
    coefficient matrices, [P] **ereturn**
    column names, *see* matrices, row and column names

matrices, *continued*
  constrained estimation, [P] **matrix constraint**
  copying, [P] **matrix define**, [P] **matrix get**,
      [P] **matrix mkmat**
  correlation, [P] **matrix define**
  covariance matrix of estimators, [P] **ereturn**,
      [P] **matrix get**
  cross-product, [P] **matrix accum**
  determinant, [P] **matrix define**
  diagonals, [P] **matrix define**
  displaying, [P] **matrix utility**
  dropping, [P] **matrix utility**
  eigenvalues, [P] **matrix eigenvalues**, [P] **matrix
      symeigen**
  eigenvectors, [P] **matrix symeigen**
  elements, [P] **matrix define**
  equation names, *see* matrices, row and column
      names
  estimation results, [P] **ereturn**, [P] **_estimates**
  functions, [P] **matrix define**
  identity, [P] **matrix define**
  input, [P] **matrix define**
  inversion, [P] **matrix define**, [P] **matrix svd**
  Kronecker product, [P] **matrix define**
  labeling rows and columns, *see* matrices, row and
      column names
  linear combinations with data, [P] **matrix score**
  listing, [P] **matrix utility**
  name space and conflicts, [P] **matrix**, [P] **matrix
      define**
  number of rows and columns, [P] **matrix define**
  operators such as addition, [P] **matrix define**
  orthonormal basis, [P] **matrix svd**
  partitioned, [P] **matrix define**
  posting estimation results, [P] **ereturn**,
      [P] **_estimates**
  renaming, [P] **matrix utility**
  row and column names, [P] **ereturn**, [P] **matrix
      define**, [P] **matrix mkmat**, [P] **matrix rowname**
  rows and columns, [P] **matrix define**
  saving matrix, [P] **matrix mkmat**
  scoring, [P] **matrix score**
  store variables as matrix, [P] **matrix mkmat**
  submatrix extraction, [P] **matrix define**
  submatrix substitution, [P] **matrix define**
  subscripting, [P] **matrix define**
  sweep operator, [P] **matrix define**
  temporary names, [P] **matrix**
  trace, [P] **matrix define**
  transposing, [P] **matrix define**
  variables, make into matrix, [P] **matrix mkmat**
  zero, [P] **matrix define**
matrix command, [P] **matrix**
  matrix accum, [P] **matrix accum**
  matrix coleq, [P] **matrix rowname**
  matrix colnames, [P] **matrix rowname**
  matrix define, [P] **matrix define**
  matrix dir, [P] **matrix utility**
  matrix dispCns, [P] **matrix constraint**
  matrix drop, [P] **matrix utility**
  matrix eigenvalues, [P] **matrix eigenvalues**
  matrix glsaccum, [P] **matrix accum**

matrix command, *continued*
  matrix input, [P] **matrix define**
  matrix list, [P] **matrix utility**
  matrix makeCns, [P] **matrix constraint**
  matrix opaccum, [P] **matrix accum**
  matrix rename, [P] **matrix utility**
  matrix roweq, [P] **matrix rowname**
  matrix rownames, [P] **matrix rowname**
  matrix score, [P] **matrix score**
  matrix svd, [P] **matrix svd**
  matrix symeigen, [P] **matrix symeigen**
  matrix vecaccum, [P] **matrix accum**
matrix, ereturn subcommand, [P] **ereturn**
matrix() pseudo-function, [P] **matrix define**
matrix, return subcommand, [P] **return**
matsize, [P] **creturn**, [P] **macro**
matuniform() matrix function, [P] **matrix define**
McKenney, A., [P] **matrix eigenvalues**
member programs, [P] **class**
member variables, [P] **class**
memory, reducing utilization, [P] **discard**
memory settings, [P] **creturn**
menus, programming, [P] **window menu**; [P] **dialogs**
messages and return codes, *see* error messages and
      return codes
mkmat command, [P] **matrix mkmat**
Monte Carlo simulations, [P] **postfile**
more command and parameter, [P] **macro**, [P] **more**
mreldif() matrix function, [P] **matrix define**

N

n-class command, [P] **program**, [P] **return**
name space and conflicts, matrices and scalars,
      [P] **matrix**, [P] **matrix define**
names,
  conflicts, [P] **matrix**, [P] **matrix define**, [P] **scalar**
  matrix row and columns, [P] **ereturn**, [P] **matrix**,
      [P] **matrix define**, [P] **matrix rowname**
.new built-in class function, [P] **class**
nobreak command, [P] **break**
noisily prefix, [P] **quietly**
nullmat() matrix function, [P] **matrix define**
numeric list, [P] **numlist**, [P] **syntax**
numlist command, [P] **numlist**

O

object, [P] **class**
object-oriented programming, [P] **class**
.objkey built-in class function, [P] **class**
.objtype built-in class function, [P] **class**
observations, marking, [P] **mark**
OLDPLACE directory, [P] **sysdir**
opaccum, matrix subcommand, [P] **matrix accum**
open, file subcommand, [P] **file**
operators, [P] **matrix define**

options, in a programming context, [P] **syntax**, [P] **unab**
orthonormal basis, [P] **matrix svd**
output,
    displaying, [P] **display**, [P] **smcl**
    suppressing, [P] **quietly**
output, set subcommand, [P] **quietly**
output settings, [P] **creturn**
overloading, class program names, [P] **class**

P

paging of screen output, controlling, [P] **more**
parameters, system, [P] **creturn**
Park, H. J., [P] **_robust**
parsing, [P] **syntax**; [P] **gettoken**, [P] **numlist**, [P] **tokenize**
partitioned matrices, [P] **matrix define**
paths and directories, [P] **creturn**
pause command, [P] **pause**
pausing until key is pressed, [P] **more**
PERSONAL directory, [P] **sysdir**
Piantadosi, S., [P] **_robust**
PLUS directory, [P] **sysdir**
polymorphism, [P] **class**
post command, [P] **postfile**
post, ereturn subcommand, [P] **ereturn**, [P] **matrix constraint**
postclose command, [P] **postfile**
postfile command, [P] **postfile**
postutil command, [P] **postfile**
    postutil clear, [P] **postfile**
    postutil dir, [P] **postfile**
_predict command, [P] **_predict**
predict command, [P] **ereturn**, [P] **_estimates**
predictions, obtaining after estimation, [P] **_predict**
preserve command, [P] **preserve**
preserving user's data, [P] **preserve**
Press, W. H., [P] **matrix symeigen**
program command, [P] **program**
    program define, [P] **program**
    program dir, [P] **program**
    program drop, [P] **program**
    program list, [P] **program**
programming functions, *see Base Reference Manual*
programs,
    adding comments to, [P] **comments**
    debugging, [P] **trace**
    dropping, [P] **discard**

Q

query, file subcommand, [P] **file**
quietly prefix, [P] **quietly**
quitting Stata, *see* exit command
quotes to expand macros, [P] **macro**

R

r() function, [P] **discard**, [P] **return**
r-class command, [P] **program**, [P] **return**
_rc built-in variable, [P] **capture**
rc (return codes), *see* error messages and return codes
read, file subcommand, [P] **file**
reading and writing ASCII text and binary files, [P] **file**
reading console input in programs, *see* console
.ref built-in class function, [P] **class**
.ref_n built-in class function, [P] **class**
references, class, [P] **class**
regression (generic sense), *also see* estimation commands
    accessing coefficients and std. errors, [P] **matrix get**
Reinsch, C., [P] **matrix symeigen**
release marker, [P] **version**
rename, matrix subcommand, [P] **matrix utility**
repeating commands, [P] **continue**, [P] **foreach**, [P] **forvalues**
replay() function, [P] **ereturn**, [P] **_estimates**
repost, ereturn subcommand, [P] **return**
reset_id, serset subcommand, [P] **serset**
restore command, [P] **preserve**
restore, _return subcommand, [P] **_return**
results,
    clearing, [P] **ereturn**, [P] **_estimates**, [P] **_return**
    listing, [P] **ereturn**, [P] **_estimates**, [P] **_return**
    returning, [P] **_return**, [P] **return**
    saving, [P] **ereturn**, [P] **_estimates**, [P] **postfile**, [P] **_return**, [P] **return**
return codes, *see* error messages and return codes
_return command, [P] **_return**
    _return dir, [P] **_return**
    _return drop, [P] **_return**
    _return hold, [P] **_return**
    _return restore, [P] **_return**
return command, [P] **return**
    return add, [P] **return**
    return clear, [P] **return**
    return local, [P] **return**
    return matrix, [P] **return**
    return scalar, [P] **return**
returning results, [P] **return**
    class programs, [P] **class**
_rmcoll command, [P] **_rmcoll**
_rmdcoll command, [P] **_rmcoll**
rmsg, [P] **rmsg**; [P] **creturn**, [P] **error**
    set rmsg, [P] **rmsg**
_robust command, [P] **_robust**
robust, Huber/White/sandwich estimator of variance, [P] **_robust**
Rogers, W. H., [P] **_robust**
roweq, matrix subcommand, [P] **matrix rowname**
rownames, matrix subcommand, [P] **matrix rowname**
rownumb() matrix function, [P] **matrix define**

rows of matrix,
  appending to, [P] **matrix define**
  names, [P] **ereturn**, [P] **matrix define**, [P] **matrix rowname**
  operators, [P] **matrix define**
rowsof() matrix function, [P] **matrix define**
Royall, R. M., [P] **_robust**
rvalue, class, [P] **class**

S

s() saved results, [P] **return**
s-class command, [P] **program**, [P] **return**
S_ macros, [P] **creturn**, [P] **macro**
sandwich/Huber/White estimator of variance, *see* robust, Huber/White/sandwich estimator of variance
save estimation results, [P] **ereturn**, [P] **_estimates**
saved results, [P] **_return**, [P] **return**
saving results, [P] **ereturn**, [P] **_estimates**, [P] **postfile**, [P] **_return**, [P] **return**
scalar command and scalar() pseudo-function, [P] **scalar**
scalar, ereturn subcommand, [P] **ereturn**
scalar, return subcommand, [P] **return**
scalars, [P] **scalar**
  name space and conflicts, [P] **matrix**, [P] **matrix define**
Schnell, D., [P] **_robust**
scope, class, [P] **class**
score, matrix subcommand, [P] **matrix score**
scoring, [P] **matrix score**
scrolling of output, controlling, [P] **more**
_se[], [P] **matrix get**
seek, file subcommand, [P] **file**
serset command, [P] **serset**
  serset clear, [P] **serset**
  serset create, [P] **serset**
  serset create_cspline, [P] **serset**
  serset create_xmedians, [P] **serset**
  serset dir, [P] **serset**
  serset drop, [P] **serset**
  serset reset_id, [P] **serset**
  serset set, [P] **serset**
  serset sort, [P] **serset**
  serset summarize, [P] **serset**
  serset use, [P] **serset**
sersetread, file subcommand, [P] **serset**
sersetwrite, file subcommand, [P] **serset**
set command, *also see Base Reference Manual*
  set adosize, [P] **sysdir**
  set output, [P] **quietly**
  set rmsg, [P] **rmsg**
  set trace, [P] **trace**
  set tracedepth, [P] **trace**
  set traceexpand, [P] **trace**
  set traceindent, [P] **trace**
  set tracenumber, [P] **trace**
  set traceset, [P] **trace**

set, file subcommand, [P] **file**
set, serset subcommand, [P] **serset**
set, sysdir subcommand, [P] **sysdir**
settings,
  efficiency, [P] **creturn**
  graphics, [P] **creturn**
  memory, [P] **creturn**
  network, [P] **creturn**
  output, [P] **creturn**
  program debugging, [P] **creturn**
  trace, [P] **creturn**
shared object, [P] **class**
shift, macro subcommand, [P] **macro**
simulations, Monte Carlo, [P] **postfile**
singular value decomposition, [P] **matrix svd**
SITE directory, [P] **sysdir**
sleep command, [P] **sleep**
Smith, B. T., [P] **matrix symeigen**
SMCL, [P] **smcl**
Sorensen, D., [P] **matrix eigenvalues**
sort order, [P] **byable**, [P] **macro**, [P] **sortpreserve**
sort, serset subcommand, [P] **serset**
sortpreserve option, [P] **sortpreserve**
sreturn command, [P] **return**
  sreturn clear, [P] **return**
  sreturn local, [P] **return**
Sribney, W. M., [P] **matrix mkmat**, [P] **_robust**
standard errors,
  accessing, [P] **matrix get**
  robust, *see* robust
Stata,
  data file format, technical description, [P] **file formats .dta**
  exiting, *see* exit command
  Markup and Control Language, [P] **smcl**
STATA directory, [P] **sysdir**
string functions, *see Base Reference Manual*
string variables, parsing, [P] **gettoken**, [P] **tokenize**
subscripting matrices, [P] **matrix define**
Sullivan, G., [P] **_robust**
summarize, serset subcommand, [P] **serset**
Super, class prefix operator, [P] **class**
.superclass built-in class function, [P] **class**
suppressing terminal output, [P] **quietly**
survey sampling, [P] **_robust**
survival analysis programming, *see Survival Analysis Reference Manual*
svd, matrix subcommand, [P] **matrix svd**
svmat command, [P] **matrix mkmat**
sweep() matrix function, [P] **matrix define**
symeigen, matrix subcommand, [P] **matrix symeigen**
syminv() matrix function, [P] **matrix define**
syntax command, [P] **syntax**
syntax of Stata's language, [P] **syntax**
sysdir command, [P] **sysdir**
  sysdir list, [P] **sysdir**
  sysdir set, [P] **sysdir**

system limits, [P] **creturn**
system parameters, [P] **creturn**
system values, [P] **creturn**

T

tabdisp command, [P] **tabdisp**
tables,
     N-way, [P] **tabdisp**
     of statistics, [P] **tabdisp**
Tan, W. Y., [P] **_robust**
tempfile command, [P] **macro**
tempname, class, [P] **class**
tempname command, [P] **macro**, [P] **matrix**, [P] **scalar**
temporary files, [P] **macro**, [P] **preserve**, [P] **scalar**
temporary names, [P] **macro**, [P] **matrix**, [P] **scalar**
temporary variables, [P] **macro**
tempvar command, [P] **macro**
terminal,
     obtaining input from, [P] **display**
     suppressing output, [P] **quietly**
Teukolsky, S. A., [P] **matrix symeigen**
time of day, [P] **creturn**
time-series, *also see Time-Series Reference Manual*
     analysis, [P] **matrix accum**
     unabbreviating varlists, [P] **unab**
TMPDIR Unix environment variable, [P] **macro**
tokenize command, [P] **tokenize**
trace() matrix function, [P] **matrix define**
trace of matrix, [P] **matrix define**
trace, set subcommand, [P] **trace**; [P] **creturn**
tracedepth, set subcommand, [P] **trace**; [P] **creturn**
traceexpand, set subcommand, [P] **trace**;
     [P] **creturn**
traceindent, set subcommand, [P] **trace**;
     [P] **creturn**
tracenumber, set subcommand, [P] **trace**;
     [P] **creturn**
tracesep, set subcommand, [P] **trace**; [P] **creturn**
transposing matrices, [P] **matrix define**
tsunab command, [P] **unab**
Tukey, J. W., [P] **if**
type parameter, [P] **macro**

U

unab command, [P] **unab**
unabbreviate,
     command names, [P] **unabcmd**
     variable list, [P] **unab**; [P] **syntax**
unabcmd command, [P] **unabcmd**
.uname built-in class function, [P] **class**
unhold, _estimates subcommand, [P] **_estimates**
UPDATES directory, [P] **sysdir**
use, serset subcommand, [P] **serset**
user interface, [P] **dialogs**
using data, [P] **syntax**

V

value labels, [P] **macro**
variable labels, [P] **macro**
variable types, [P] **macro**
     class, [P] **class**
variables,
     characteristics of, [P] **char**, [P] **macro**
     temporary, [P] **macro**
     unabbreviating, [P] **unab**; [P] **syntax**
variance–covariance matrix of estimators, [P] **ereturn**,
     [P] **matrix get**
variance, Huber/White/sandwich estimator, *see* robust
variance, nonconstant, *see* robust
varlist, [P] **syntax**
vec() matrix function, [P] **matrix define**
vecaccum, matrix subcommand, [P] **matrix accum**
vecdiag() matrix function, [P] **matrix define**
vectors, *see* matrices
version command, [P] **version**
     class programming, [P] **class**
version control, *see* version command
Vetterling, W. T., [P] **matrix symeigen**

W

Weesie, J., [P] **matrix define**
Wei, L. J., [P] **_robust**
which, class, [P] **classutil**
which, classutil subcommand, [P] **classutil**
while command, [P] **while**
White, H., [P] **_robust**
White/Huber/sandwich estimator of variance, *see* robust
Wilkinson, J. H., [P] **matrix symeigen**
window fopen command, [P] **window fopen**
window manage command, [P] **window manage**
window menu command, [P] **window menu**
window push command, [P] **window push**
window stopbox command, [P] **window stopbox**
write, file subcommand, [P] **file**
writing and reading ASCII text and binary files, [P] **file**

Z

zero matrix, [P] **matrix define**